This book takes up some central themes of Aristotle's metaphysical theory and the various transformations they undergo before their full expression in the *Metaphysics*. Aristotle's metaphysics is bedeviled by classic puzzles involving such notions as form, predication, universal, and substance, which result from his attempt to adapt the various requirements on primary substance developed in his earlier works to the very different metaphysical picture in his later work. Professor Lewis argues that Aristotle is himself aware of most, if not all, of these difficulties and in the *Metaphysics* works hard to ensure the coherence of his theory. He presents Aristotle's views as a formal theory complete with axioms, definitions, and theorems.

This is a major contribution to the understanding of one of the most difficult works of the great philosopher.

Substance and Predication
in Aristotle

Substance and Predication in Aristotle

FRANK A. LEWIS

University of Southern California

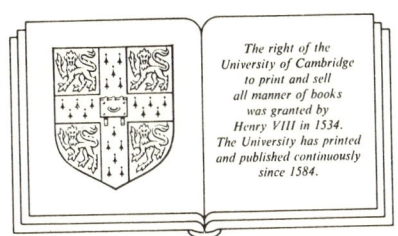

The right of the
University of Cambridge
to print and sell
all manner of books
was granted by
Henry VIII in 1534.
The University has printed
and published continuously
since 1584.

CAMBRIDGE UNIVERSITY PRESS

Cambridge

New York   *Port Chester*   *Melbourne*   *Sydney*

Published by the Press Syndicate of the University of Cambridge
The Pitt Building, Trumpington Street, Cambridge CB2 1RP
40 West 20th Street, New York, NY 10011, USA
10 Stamford Road, Oakleigh, Melbourne 3166, Australia

© Cambridge University Press 1991

First published 1991

Printed in the United States of America

Library of Congress Cataloging-in-Publication Data
Lewis, Frank A.
Substance and predication in Aristotle / Frank A. Lewis
p.   cm.
Includes bibliographical references.
ISBN 0-521-39159-8
1. Aristotle – Metaphysics.   II. Title.
B491.M4L48   1991
110 – dc20   91-9108
                                                        CIP

A catalog record of this book is available from the British Library.

ISBN 0-521-39159-8 hardback

Contents

PART IV
SUBSTANCE AND PREDICATION IN
ARISTOTLE'S *METAPHYSICS*

Preface

This book takes up some central themes in Aristotle's metaphysical theory and the various transformations they undergo, from their first appearance, in some cases at least, as a response to ideas in Plato's metaphysics to their full expression principally in books *Zeta* and *Eta* of the *Metaphysics*. Work on the book began, inconveniently, in the middle, with the topic of accidental compounds – such entities as Socrates seated and the masked one – which I take to be an accompaniment of Aristotle's earlier theorizing in the *Categories*, although the theory survives without real change in the *Metaphysics* as well. A major purpose of the book is to work out the details of how – having started with an idea about the way individual substances, Socrates and the like, can be compounded with accidents, being seated and the rest, to make accidental compounds – Aristotle can go on to extend this idea to the analysis of individual substances themselves, which he comes to see in the *Physics* – but not right off in the *Categories* – as compounds of matter and form.

The two ideas of accidental compounds and form–matter compounds provided the original core of the book. But central ideas have a way of collecting peripheries, and the periphery in this case perhaps covers more ground than usual. I have found it impossible to begin the discussion of accidental compounds without first sketching the larger background in Aristotle's early metaphysics against which the theory of accidental compounds takes shape. And Aristotle's early metaphysics, in turn, occasions some remarks on the relation between his earlier views and their antecedents – by contrast as well as by similarity – in Plato. All of this introductory material is balanced at the end of the book by an account of some of the leading ideas in Aristotle's later metaphysics in books *Zeta* and *Eta* of the *Metaphysics*. Here I shall argue in part for an essential continuity with many of the themes set out first in the *Categories*. But I shall also be concerned with the many differences between the earlier and the later theories, to which the injection of the notions of form and matter inevitably gives rise.

The book is organized into four parts, corresponding to what I take to be the different stages in Aristotle's metaphysical thinking. Part I offers a sketch of perhaps the earliest phase of Aristotle's thinking in the *Categories* and his reaction to the background in Plato's metaphysical theory. Part II examines Aristotle's notions of substance, accident, accidental compounds, and the two sameness relations '*x* is accidentally the same as *y*' and '*x* is the same in being as *y*'. Part III extends the treatment of accidental compounds in Part II to form–matter compounds and to the notions of form and matter, which do not appear in Aristotle's earlier works but are central to the theories of the *Metaphysics*. Part IV, finally, addresses the special problems that Aristotle's new metaphysical theory brings. I set out some of the classic puzzles that bedevil Aristotle's later metaphysics – for example, the puzzle of how in the *Metaphysics* an Aristotelian form is apparently both a primary substance and a universal, while Aristotle also insists that "no universal is a substance," or again, the puzzle of how form is a primary substance and a universal, and hence predicated of many, while "primary substance is not predicated of any subject" – and argue that they result from Aristotle's attempt to adapt the various requirements on primary substance developed in his earlier works (the *Categories* and *Topics* especially) to the very different metaphysical picture – including a different choice of what to count as primary substance! – in the *Metaphysics*. I also show how the solutions I suggest to these puzzles fit within the overall theory, large parts of which have already been laid out in earlier chapters.

In setting out even this cursory sketch of the topics of the book, with its talk of earlier and later phases in Aristotle's thought, I adopt at least the language of the *developmental* view that has been a feature of Aristotelian scholarship since Jaeger (1923 [1948]). Jaeger detects in the Aristotelian corpus a steady move away from an early adherence to Platonism; this idea is pressed further with particular application to the psychology in Nuyens (1948), but it is called into question in Owen (1960 [1979], 1965), who argues that Aristotle's anti-Platonism is at its height at the beginning and that Aristotle reverts to a more nearly Platonic position later in the *Metaphysics*. For all their differences, these are all *unabashed* forms of developmentalism. As such, they stand in contrast to the view in Furth (1988), which I also hold, that the best form of developmentalism is "as if" developmentalism, in which what matters is the *conceptual* relationships between theories underlying different parts of the corpus, and the developmental story is icing on the cake, evidentially posterior to the conceptual relations it serves to dramatize. Disagreement also exists over the nature and

extent of the differences between the "earlier" and "later" theories
(although reference to "earlier" and "later" should not be taken to
suggest that Aristotle's views sort themselves tidily into just two
phases). Furth's view of the *Categories* as a "primer" for Aristotle's
full-blown metaphysical theories is more or less at one end of the
spectrum: this account downplays differences among the different
parts of Aristotle's work, supposing that even in the *Categories* (an early
work on most accounts) Aristotle has available, but for strategic or
expository reasons suppresses, the theory of matter and form that
ordinarily is taken as typifying the later works. At the opposite end of
the spectrum, in a defence of a radical form of developmentalism,
Graham (1987) argues that the gulf between the different strata in
Aristotle's thought is so great that they fall into two "systems" that are
incompatible, even incommensurable, Aristotle himself either being
unaware of the difficulties or falsely thinking they can be reconciled.
(There are remarks on Graham's view in the Introduction to Part IV
and throughout Part IV itself.) The account I shall argue for lies
midway between these options: deep and important differences
with the views of the *Categories* emerge in particular in the *Metaphysics*,
but Aristotle himself is aware of the differences and works hard in
the *Metaphysics* to save as much as he can of his earlier views within the
new theory.

I have suggested that my interest in this book is in the conceptual
relationships underlying the different parts of Aristotle's text, rather
than in the chronology of his works. A distinctive feature of the treatment that follows is again directed at getting clear on the conceptual
issues at stake in the text. Thus, some – although by no means all – of
the treatment is "formal": at many points, I proceed by *reconstructing*
Aristotle's theories by means of definitions, axioms, and theorems. (In
adopting this style of interpreting Aristotle, I have been much influenced by unpublished work on Aristotle by Kit Fine.) By 'reconstruct'
here, I mean not just 'paraphrase' or 'interpret': the aim is to find
precise formulations of Aristotle's ideas that bring out to the full the
different logical relationships, not only within a given phase of his
thought among views that scholars so far may have supposed were
logically independent, but also between the propositions proprietary
to one stage of his thinking and those proprietary to another.

The object of the formalism is, in part, simply to indicate the power
and elegance of Aristotle's metaphysical theory as well as the deductive relationships among his various views. At the same time, however,
I argue that there is also a specific payoff in terms of solutions to some
of the classic puzzles involving such notions as substance, form, and
universal, noted three paragraphs earlier, that threaten the coherence
of Aristotle's later metaphysical theory.

Despite the quest for rigour, I hope that large parts of the book will still be intelligible and useful to readers who have no taste for formalism. It must be admitted that in the places where I have resorted to a formal approach, the formalism does not directly reproduce anything present in Aristotle's own text. I suspect, however, that this reflects only a difference in presentation, and not any fundamental departure from Aristotelian methods or sympathies. While my project in many places is admittedly a reconstruction of Aristotle's arguments, rather than a simple paraphrase, I would argue that Aristotle's metaphysical thinking does in fact rest on a deductive framework of the kind I have attempted to provide. There is most assuredly room for disagreement over the details, but I do not believe that the project itself is misguided from the start.

Still other parts of the book discuss Aristotle's ideas in technical terms that are the product of contemporary philosophical writing, although here, as often as not, these contemporary notions have already been injected into the discussion of Aristotle by other writers. Perhaps everyone would agree that there is nothing to be gained from straitjacketing Aristotle's philosophical concepts so that they appear to line up directly with the familiar concepts of contemporary philosophy, or from simply assimilating Aristotle's views to suit contemporary fashion. Exercises of this sort will most likely be unenlightening for what they reveal about contemporary concerns and will be bad history of philosophy besides. The fact remains, however, that there is no "neutral" perspective from which to do the history of philosophy. Historians of philosophy are bound to come to their task with the methods and preconceptions of their own time, and the interest of the history of philosophy lies not in pretending to suppress these various contemporary concerns, but in making them explicit and asking about the exact nature of the relation of Aristotle's conceptual apparatus to our own – with the expectation that, in most cases at least, the relation will be anything but simple.

Finally, a word about some omissions. Others have not been idle during the years this book has been gestating; the resulting wave of recent books on Aristotle's *Metaphysics* includes Graham (1987), Frede and Patzig (1988), Furth (1988), Gill (1989), and Witt (1989). These came into my hands well after the body of the book was finished; where time has permitted, I have drawn attention to points of agreement or disagreement in the notes, but I am conscious that I have not been able to give these works the full attention they deserve.

The book has four parts, each with its own introduction. The introductions are meant partly to give a preliminary sketch of the major themes under discussion in each part, but they are also intended as a guide to the overall geography of the book. They are probably the portions of the book to read first. Still more guidance is to be had from the table of contents, and a still more detailed prospectus is given in the opening paragraphs of each chapter.

Acknowledgements

This book has been some years in the making, and it is a pleasure to recall the many exchanges with friends and colleagues, written as well as in conversation, that have influenced me. I owe a special debt to Kit Fine, whose unpublished paper, "Aristotle on Substance," first showed me the power that a formal approach to Aristotle's theories can have. I have not produced the thoroughgoing account that his manuscript begins, but I hope that the occasional forays into formalism do not fall too far short of the promise that, applied to the right subject matter, such an approach holds out. I am grateful also to Fine for continued discussion since this project began. A special debt is owed as well to Alan Code. I have been influenced by both the content and the methods of the steady stream of papers on Aristotle that have flowed from his pen. I have learned more than I can now record in conversations with him over the years, and parts of Chapter 1 were first written and delivered as a response to a paper of his at the Predication Conference at Pitzer College in the spring of 1981. Code read the entire penultimate draft and devoted a week of his time to discussing the manuscript with me, sometimes page by page. Whatever the merits of the finished product, it is vastly better than anything I could have produced without his generous help. Russell Dancy also read the entire penultimate draft; his guidance too has materially improved the finished version. Others who have read and commented on various parts of the book at different stages in its development include Patricia Blanchette, James Bogen, Tyler Burge, David Charles, John Driscoll, Montgomery Furth, Wolfgang Gombocz, Herbert Granger, Joan Kung, Michael Loux, Edwin McCann, Henry Mendell, Ronald Milo, Julius Moravcsik, Henry Newell, Lynne Spellman, Michael White, and Charles Young. I am grateful also to John Malcolm and Michael Wedin, who devoted two valuable days to translating and discussing with me recent German scholarship bearing on the subject matter of Part IV, and to Sandra Peterson for help of a similar nature. My gratitude to these individuals, and to others whose contributions the length of time I have spent on the book has now obscured, is tempered only by the sense of the inadequacy of the acknowledgement. I should also say that none of those whose help I acknowledge here should be accused of agreeing with the views I put forward.

I am grateful to Harry Brighouse for compiling the indexes to the book. I wish also to record my debt to the American Council of Learned Societies for a Fellowship in 1981–2 that allowed work on the book to get under way in earnest. Finally, I express my admiration and appreciation to my family, Ildiko and Steven, for their agility in keeping clear of the more tiresome excesses of the author while this book was being completed.

Chapter 1 is a revision and expansion of ideas already presented in "Plato's Third Man Argument and the 'Platonism' of Aristotle," in *How Things Are: Essays in Predication,* ed. James Bogen and J. E. McGuire, Dordrecht: Reidel, 1985, pp. 133–74. An earlier version of my account of accidental compound theory appears in "Accidental Sameness in Aristotle," *Philosophical Studies* 37 (1982), pp. 1–41. Some of the ideas in Chapters 6, 7, and 11 have already been given an airing in the essay "Form and Predication in Aristotle's Metaphysics," in the volume edited by Bogen and McGuire just cited (pp. 59–83). Both chapters in this volume were originally presented at the Conference on Predication at Pitzer College in the spring of 1981. Different portions of Part IV were also read at the University of Texas at Austin in the spring of 1982, at the Claremont Colleges in the spring of 1983, and at the University of Southern California in the spring of 1984. An earlier version of some of the material in the Postscript to Part III was included in a paper presented at the Oriel Conference on Aristotle's Metaphysics in the summer of 1989; an abridged version of Chapter 2 was read in the spring of 1990 at the Claremont Colleges and at the twentieth anniversary meeting of the West Coast Aristotelian Society at Half Moon Bay, California, in the spring of the same year.

Abbreviations of Sources

Works of Aristotle

An. Pr.	*Analytica Priora*
An. Po.	*Analytica Posteriora*
De Int.	*De Interpretatione*
GA	*De Generatione Animalium*
GC	*De Generatione et Corruptione*
PA	*De Partibus Animalium*
SE	*De Sophisticis Elenchis*

The Greek Commentators on Aristotle

Simplicius *In Catg.*	Simplicius, *In Categorias*
Simplicius *In Phys.*	Simplicius, *In Physica*
Alexander *In Met.*	Alexander, *In Metaphysica*

Full references to the Greek commentators are given in the Bibliography.

PART I

Aristotle's Earlier Metaphysical Theory

Metaphysical Predication:
A Preliminary Survey

The notions of substance and predication that are the subject of this book occupy virtually the center of Aristotle's metaphysical theory, from the very beginning in the *Categories,* all the way through to his latest metaphysical writings in the central books of the *Metaphysics.*[1] The question 'What is substance?' is one that in a less exact form, according to Aristotle, has occupied all philosophers from the beginning:

Indeed, what has been sought after of old, and now, and always, and is always puzzled over, namely, What is being? is this: What is substance? (*Metaphysics* Z1, 1028b2–4)

On this account, the question 'What is being?' is as old as philosophy itself. Aristotle's reworking of this traditional question in terms of substance (*ousia*) is based on the notion of *focal meaning* developed in *Metaphysics* Γ and E.[2] There are irreducibly different kinds of being. Yet among these, one, substance, is primary, and by studying different modes of dependency on primary being or substance, according to Aristotle, we are able to study being in general.[3] What, then, is sub-

---

1 Here I engage in the fiction that we know that the *Categories* is early, and that *Zeta, Eta,* and *Theta* of the *Metaphysics* are late. But as explained in the Preface, talk of this kind is based solely on interpretative hypotheses about how the philosophical strands in the different works tie together: I shall not suppose that we have any other handle on the relative dating of Aristotle's works, independent of how in our judgement the various conceptual issues in his writings work themselves out.

2 *Metaphysics* Γ2, E1; see the references in note 3. The term 'focal meaning' is due to Owen (1960).

3 In the catch phrase, theology or first philosophy is "universal in this way, because it is first" (*katholou houtōs hoti prōtē; Metaphysics* E1, 1026a30–1): by studying what is *primary* (the immoveable substances of theology) first philosophy is itself not only prior but also, for that very reason, universal. Aristotle's account of how the primacy of substance makes possible a general study of being thanks to the device of focal meaning is set out in *Metaphysics* Γ2, 1003b11–19, 1004a22–31, and E1, 1026a23–32. Focal meaning is then put to work in the first chapter of *Zeta;* compare also the retrospective summary at the beginning of *Theta:* Θ1, 1045b27–32.

stance? What are the *basic* entities – those entities that, as Aristotle tells it, are prior to everything else in definition and in knowledge and in time (*Metaphysics* Z1, 1028a31–b2)? The tradition offers various candidates for substance and various explanations of why these are fittingly substances. Aristotle himself has his own favoured cases; and he is also at work both early and late in the corpus on the parallel task of developing the appropriate *criteria* for substancehood. He is also liable to produce further refinements of the question: for example, what among the substances are the *primary* substances? Other subtleties include the *relational* notion of substance developed in the *Metaphysics* – the substance *of* a thing – and the idea in the discussion of sensible substances in the *Metaphysics* that the substances that are primary are also the substance *of* something.

The theory of substance and our second topic, predication, are never far apart in Aristotle. One in particular among the many complexities in Aristotle's various notions of predication requires immediate mention here. Our dominant notion of predication today is exclusively linguistic, so that both the subject and what is predicated of it are invariably linguistic items – a grammatical subject and a predicate. For Aristotle, by contrast, the subject is an item in the ontology and not a linguistic item, and more often than not what is predicated is not linguistic either: it is not a predicate, but a predicable. Let us say that a predicate (a linguistic item) is *linguistically predicated of* its subject, but that a predicable (a metaphysical item) is *metaphysically predicated of* its subject.[4] Tidying Aristotle's usage somewhat, by 'predication' in what follows I ordinarily mean metaphysical predication and occasionally say so, parenthetically, as a reminder.

Our subject in the two chapters of this part will be some of the main themes of Aristotle's earlier metaphysical theory. I shall begin with the theory of (metaphysical) predication, in particular the contrast between the Platonic theory of (metaphysical) predication, as Aristotle sees it, and Aristotle's own rival theory in the *Categories*.[5] (Aristotle's views in the *Categories* are by no means his last words on the topics at hand, but we will defer until Parts III and IV details of the modifications his theory later undergoes.) Plato and Aristotle agree in finding

4 To accommodate our usage as well as Aristotle's, it will be convenient to allow that the subject of a linguistic predication can be either a linguistic item or an entity in the ontology. But the subject of a metaphysical predication will invariably be an ontological item, and not linguistic.

5 Nehamas (1979), p. 103, argues that a theory of predication, properly so-called, emerges in Plato only in the *Sophist* (his remarks apply equally to metaphysical and to linguistic predication); at the same time, many of the other details of Plato's position under discussion here come from the earlier dialogues. The composite, even stereotypical, picture of Plato that results is unavoidable if we are to operate from Aristotle's perspective in the controversy with Plato; see the discussion two paragraphs below in the main text and note 12.

in the regress argument Plato introduces in the *Parmenides* a touchstone of the first importance for any acceptable theory of (metaphysical) predication. In Chapter 1, we discuss not only the use Plato himself makes of the argument in its original form, as the Third Largeness Argument, but also the reworking of the argument implied by Aristotle's title for it as the Third *Man* Argument.[6] Discussion of the different regress arguments brings to light a variety of assumptions regarding (metaphysical) predication that Plato and Aristotle variously affirm or deny. They agree, for example, in distinguishing different *levels* of entities – for example, in Plato's theory, sensibles (which are of level zero) and forms (of level 1 and up) – but, notoriously, they differ over the nature of the entities that exist at each level. As we shall see, there is dispute over other significant components in the theory as well.

In Chapter 2, we leave the discussion of Plato's regress argument and its various ramifications to consider the larger metaphysical theory Aristotle constructs in the *Categories* around his notion of (metaphysical) predication. In this chapter, we also take up the topic of substance, which in Aristotle's theory has its proper place side by side with the account of (metaphysical) predication. In the *Categories*, Aristotle divides the "things that are" into substances and nonsubstances, and substances in turn into primary substances (the individual substances) and those that are secondary. His arguments for the primacy of individual substances, which will be our main concern, come directly from his theory of (metaphysical) predication.

By way of introduction to these various issues, the rest of this introduction is devoted to greatly oversimplified sketches of the theory of (metaphysical) predication that Aristotle finds in Plato, and of the rival theory with which he means to oppose Plato's in the *Categories*. The sketches are oversimplified, since our purpose is to find a common ground from which to study Plato's and Aristotle's theories together: the versions of the two theories in the next few pages, then, are stereotypical ones designed to exhibit to maximum effect the differences between the competing points of view. In particular, since our main interest is in Aristotle's perspective on the issues at hand, a good many subtleties in the Platonic dialogues will not be reflected here. Similarly, when Aristotle himself debates the issues over which he and Plato are at odds, the version of Platonism he discusses is again a stereotypical one: not necessarily a straw man – a version especially vulnerable to his own hostile scrutiny – but a form of Plato's theory

---

6 For convenience in what follows, I shall refer to the argument in this new version as *Aristotle's* reworking of Plato's original argument. But while the title helps dramatize the battle of ideas, it is strictly a fiction; we cannot be sure that the reworking is not due to someone other than Aristotle – for all we know, even to Plato himself.

that allows Aristotle to dramatize best the differences that separate him from Plato.[7]

In Aristotle's view, then, all Platonic forms are related in just a single way to their sensible subjects. Socrates (say) *participates in* each of his forms – in pallor, for example, in man, and the like.[8] In the Platonic picture, as Aristotle sees it, there is no sense that some forms are more important than others to Socrates' continued existence. The ultimate consequence of this view is the "bare substrate" ontology of the *Timaeus*. Sensibles are, to borrow Sellars's phrase, "leaky bundles of abstract particulars," made up of "copies" of forms, collected together in different regions of (otherwise featureless) space.[9] Each bundle is leaky, because Plato supplies no principle to hold it together: he makes no room for the idea that some items in the bundle are essential for its existence, while others are merely accidental to it. On this conception, Plato's theory is what Code and Grice have called a theory of Having, in which sensibles Have all their properties, and Having is understood to be an *accidental* relation between a predicable and its subject.[10]

It is likely, however, that Plato has a *different* account for how *forms* are related to their predicables. Forms are eternal and unchanging: they are not apt to alter their properties. For forms, then, Plato has a theory of Being ("Izzing," in the jargon of Code and Grice), according to which forms Are what they are.[11] There are hints of this idea in the *Sophist,* where Plato says:

May we now be bold to say that that which is not unquestionably *is* a thing that has a nature of its own: just as the tall *was* tall and the beautiful *was* beautiful, so too with the not-tall and the not-beautiful – and in that sense that which is not also, on the same principle, both *was* and *is* what is not, a single form to be reckoned among the many things that are? (258b9–14; after Cornford's translation)

---

7 A less sympathetic appraisal of Aristotle's approach to his polemic with Plato can be found in Cherniss (1944).

8 There is dispute in the secondary literature over whether there is a separable form of man in Plato (sceptics include Irwin [1977], p. 6, n. 9), but it is sufficient for my purposes that Aristotle should take Plato to hold such a view – that the view Aristotle attacks does include a commitment to such forms.

9 Sellars (1967), p. 77.

10 The Code–Grice terminology of Having (also sometimes rendered "Hazzing") first appeared in print in Code (1986). It is also used in Grice (1988). The dual of Having is Izzing, introduced in the next paragraph in the main text. The "Having"–"Izzing" jargon gives us a useful way of talking about notions that are common to both Plato's and Aristotle's theories; another, incidental advantage, since Izzing is the converse of the SAID OF relation and Having the converse of the IN relation, is that the new jargon avoids what can be for us the awkwardness of Aristotle's terminology – 'Man is SAID OF Socrates', 'Pallor is IN Socrates', and the like – in the *Categories,* which reverses the natural order of English and Greek alike.

11 See the helpful remarks on the "restrictive" use of 'is' appropriate for forms in Nehamas (1979), pp. 95–103.

In the two halves of the theory just sketched, it is worth noting that sensibles Have all their predicables and Are nothing at all, while forms Are what they are and Have none of their predicables.[12] Having is the lot of sensibles, and of them alone, while it is the sole prerogative of forms that they Are their various predicables. Plato, then, gives what I shall call a *uniform* account of predication at the level of sensibles, and similarly at the level of forms, but – true to the "two-world" ontology he defends – they are two *different* notions of predication at the two different levels.

A dichotomy of this sort is a plausible backdrop to the Third Largeness Argument Plato offers in the *Parmenides*. Arguably, Plato can use a distinction between the way in which sensibles take their properties and forms take theirs to fashion a way out of the regress that the argument threatens. The regress itself can be constructed roughly as follows: Suppose that the term 'large' applies both to every member of a plurality, Π, of sensibles that are large and to the form, largeness, that (by the One-over-Many Assumption) is "over" all the members of Π.[13] Suppose, next, that we can form a new plurality of things that are large, Π *with* largeness, whose members are just the members of Π together with the form largeness.[14] Suppose, finally, that given this new plurality, Π *with* largeness, we must also (by the One-over-Many Assumption again) introduce a new form, largeness-1, which is "over" all the members of Π *with* largeness.[15] If these further steps go through, then we are well on the way to an infinite regress of forms of largeness.

One means of blocking formation of the plurality Π *with* largeness and the subsequent introduction of largeness-1 is ready to hand. Plato can maintain that there is an essential difference between Π *with* largeness and the original plurality Π. Π satisfies what later we will call a *homogeneity* condition: when we say that each of the members of Π *is*

12 The theory under discussion ignores developments in the notion of participation presented in the *Sophist*, where Plato allows cases of form–form participation that cannot be identified with Having. (It is consistent with this, however, that sensible–form participation *is* always Having.) It is perhaps best to say that Aristotle is criticizing a stereotypical or composite "Platonic" position, built mainly around the middle period theory of forms and, in most respects, stopping well short of developments in the *Sophist* (but for a possible exception, see note 5). Similar remarks apply to developments in the theory of forms in the *Philebus;* cf. Frede ([1978] 1987), p. 57.

13 The second clause is a version of the Self-Predication Assumption familiar in contemporary reconstructions of the argument: the assumption is discussed further in Chapter 1, Section 5.

14 To show that the plurality is truly new, we must assume a version of the Nonidentity Assumption, so that largeness itself is not identical with any of the members of Π; a comparable assumption will also hold for each of the further pluralities generated by the argument. Some version of the Nonidentity Assumption is a standard feature of Aristotle's as well as contemporary reconstructions of the argument; see Chapter 1, Sections 1 and 5.

15 For the claim that largeness-1 is genuinely a new form, see note 14.

large, the 'is' is being used in the same sense in every case. There is no reason to suppose otherwise, for all the members of Π are of the same level – they are all *sensibles*. The case will be quite different, however, with the advent of higher-level pluralities, whose members include forms as well as sensibles. If any higher-level pluralities exist, Plato may argue, they will *fail* the homogeneity condition. In particular, all the sensibles that are members of Π *with* largeness *Have* largeness, but largeness itself (also a member of that same plurality) *Is* large. Accordingly, it is illegitimate to form such higher-level pluralities in the first place. But since the One-over-Many Assumption applies only to bona fide pluralities, the familiar move to the existence of a single form, largeness-1 (say), in virtue of which all the members of Π *with* largeness alike are large, is no longer available.

In a word, Plato can overcome the Third Largeness Argument of the *Parmenides* by claiming that, in general, if both a form and a sensible are *F*, they are not *F* in the same sense of 'is'.[16] In the jargon of Code and Grice, while the sensible is *F* (the ordinary-language version) because it Has *F*-ness, the form is *F* (again, the ordinary-language version) because it Is *F*.

A major feature of Aristotle's strategy against Plato in the *Categories* is to collapse this dichotomy that Plato's theory of (metaphysical) predication attempts to make out between forms and sensibles. In Aristotle's theory, Socrates Is some of his predicables, but Has others. He Is what is essential to him, and he Has the rest. For example, Socrates Is (a) man, but Has largeness and the rest.[17] Alternatively, in Aristotle's own jargon, man is SAID OF Socrates, while largeness is IN him.[18] These different relations between Socrates and his various predicables form a large part of the motivation for the further ontological distinctions Aristotle draws in the *Categories*. Socrates is a *primary* substance: he is a lowest member of the category of substance, and he takes some

16 For earlier examples of this strategy in the secondary literature, see Cherniss (1957) and Allen ([1960] 1965). (But the assumption both make, that where a form and a sensible are both *F*, the *is* in the case of the form is the *is* of identity, does not seem promising; cf. Nehamas [1979], p. 96, n. 14.)

17 "(a) man": in contrast to English, there is no indefinite article in Greek. The point is important, since it has a consequence for the distinction Aristotle is concerned to make between the assertion 'Socrates is (a) man', for example, and 'Socrates is pale'. The job we tend to think of as done by the indefinite article, which marks assertions of the first kind ('Socrates is a man'), for Aristotle is done by other means, namely, the change in inflection that converts the noun 'pallor' into the properly adjectival form 'pale' in assertions of the second kind. But Aristotle is aware that such transformations, to which he gives the name *paronymy*, are typically but not invariably needed for assertions of this kind. On the topic of paronymy, see Chapter 2.

18 The uppercase letters are meant to mark the generic relation; its different subrelations will be indicated by lowercase 'in' and 'said of'. The account of these different relations is worked out in detail in Chapter 2.

of his predicables – those, in the jargon of Izzing and Having, that he Is – from higher up in that same category.[19] Thus, nothing else Is Socrates, but Socrates Is (a) man, Is (an) animal, and the rest. These last, meanwhile, man, animal, and so on, are the *secondary* substances: they are not "one in number" (*hen arithmōi*) or "indivisible" (*atomon*) but divide into their lower kinds (e.g., as animal divides into the various species of animals) or into individuals (as man divides into Socrates, Callias, and the others).[20]

There are also the nonsubstances, which stand in a very different relation to Socrates. In Aristotle's terms, these are IN him rather than SAID OF him; in the jargon of Code and Grice, they are predicables that Socrates Has and not what he Is; hence, they are accidental to him. (At the same time, we can also distinguish among the items in a given nonsubstance category those that are lowest in that category – these are the items that nothing else Is – and higher items, which other items in the category Are.)

The cornerstone of this new, anti-Platonic theory of (metaphysical) predication is the way in which the two kinds of predication can combine in the single person of Socrates. Aristotle responds to Plato's theory of the *accidental* relation between sensibles and their predicables by arguing that Socrates, for example, Is some of his predicables, which are his kinds, and that he must first (*logically* first) Be those things before he can be a fit subject for the accidents that he Has.[21]

Aristotle's reworking of the Third Largeness Argument into the Third *Man* Argument[22] is typical of this new interest in kinds. The problem of a thing's kinds is a distinctively Aristotelian one. For Plato, a sensible has all its properties accidentally; for Plato, then, there is no special pleading involved in the choice of example if we claim on his behalf that any regress argument can be blocked by the plea that sensibles Have largeness but that the form largeness itself Is large. But if Aristotle's view prevails, that Socrates Is some of his properties, for

---

19 I repeat here the received wisdom that Aristotle's theory in the *Categories* includes a category of being called *substance*. Doubts about this view have been expressed in Frede ([1981] 1987).

20 In the *Categories*, "indivisible" and "one in number" appear to amount to the same thing (see 1b6, 3b12), and the two notions are explicitly identified by Minio-Paluello (1949) in the Index to the Oxford Classical Text of the *Categories* and *De Interpretatione*. Both notions *fail* for things said of a subject (1b6–7), in particular for secondary substances: man and animal are "not one but ‹apply› to many (*kata pollōn*)," 3b16–18; cf. 3a33–b2, b7, secondary substances (the *genos* and the *eidos*) are not *atoma*. The theory of *division* that underlies these notions is mentioned briefly at *Categories* 10a19 and at greater length at 14b34–15a3. The topic is taken up elsewhere in the *Organon* at *An. Pr.* A30 and *An. Po.* B5 and B13, 96b25–97b6, and also at *PA* A2–4 and *Metaphysics* Z12.

21 The point has been stressed recently by Code (1985), pp. 103, 112. Similar points are made, e.g., by Owen (1965), p. 138, and Woods (1974–5), p. 178.

22 "Aristotle's reworking": see note 6.

example, that he Is a man, then the regress argument takes on new life. For in Aristotle's view, sensible men and man alike Are men, so that any plurality that has them all as members satisfies the homogeneity condition mentioned earlier: all of its members, regardless of level, *are* men in the same sense of 'is'. On this line of thought, the new theory of Izzing and Having fits nicely within the dialectic of the regress arguments – first the Third Largeness Argument, later the Third Man Argument – that Plato and Aristotle in turn bring to bear on the Platonic theory of forms.

Aristotle suggests, as we have seen, that an individual like Socrates both Has certain of his predicables, which are his accidents, and Is others, which are essential to him. Aristotle also holds that the universal, man, too Is certain of its predicables – it Is, say, (an) animal[23] – but at the same time Has other properties: for example, man Has pallor, if some individual man is pale. Both ideas challenge the Platonic view that *uniform* accounts of (metaphysical) predication prevail both at the level of sensibles and at the level of forms. Meanwhile, together with the denial of uniformity *at* a level, there goes a principle of homogeneity *across* levels in certain cases. Like man, for example, Socrates too Is an animal. Thus, a sensible and a universal can stand in the *same* relation to the *same* predicable in certain cases. In holding that a particular Is certain of its predicables, Aristotle attributes to sensibles at least some measure of the invariance that for Plato was a prerogative exclusively of forms. Conversely, the idea that a universal can Have certain of its properties challenges Plato's view that forms eternally and abidingly Are what they are. In this way, Aristotle's theory obviously suggests some revision in Plato's view of the significance of the difference in levels. In fact, the revision is virtually total, for Aristotle also reverses Plato's choice of the level of entity that is to count as primary substance. According to Plato, clearly, the primary realities are the forms. In Aristotle's theory, however, higher items even in the category of substance are counted as *secondary* substances, and the primary substances are instead the sensible individual substances, Socrates, Callias, and the like.

Aristotle promotes sensible individuals to the rank of primary substance, mainly under the influence of his theory of (metaphysical) predication. In the *Categories,* Aristotle's chief reason for counting a thing as a primary substance is its role as a subject:

Further, it is *because the primary substances are subjects for everything else* that they are called substances most strictly. (*Categories* 5, 2b37–3a1, Ackrill's translation; my emphasis; cf. 5, 2a34 ff., b15–17)

23 "(an) animal": see note 17.

This view gives Aristotle what we may call a *monolithic* view of the subject of (metaphysical) predication. In the final analysis, according to this view, the only real subjects of predication are primary substances. In some cases, it is obvious that a (metaphysical) predication has a primary substance as its subject: Socrates, for example, is a primary substance, and he is a subject to both his kinds and his accidents. In other cases, however, an item is (metaphysically) predicated of something other than a primary substance – for example, animal is predicated of man, or pallor is predicated of animal. These further kinds of (metaphysical) predication, which do not have individual substances as their subjects, are possible *only because* they are founded in other (metaphysical) predications whose subject is after all a primary substance. For example, pallor is predicated of animal only because some primary substance is both an animal and pale (strictly, it Is [an] animal and Has pallor). In general, then, as we shall see, every (metaphysical) predication can be analysed ultimately in terms of the existence of some primary substance that is the subject for predicables.

It will be useful to end by recapitulating some of the major features that, on the account given, separate the Platonic theory of (metaphysical) predication, as Aristotle construes it, and Aristotle's own rival theory in the *Categories*. True to his "two-world" ontology, Plato's theory is sensitive to the *level* of the subject of a given predication, and a *different* notion of predication prevails according to whether the subject is of level zero (a sensible) or higher level (a form). Accordingly, for Plato, for any plurality that has both sensibles and forms as members, no version of *homogeneity* is ever true: no predicable applies in virtue of the same predication relation both to sensibles and to forms. *Within* each level, however, Plato's account of predication is absolutely *uniform*. The theory contains a uniform account of how sensibles are related to forms: invariably, sensibles Have or participate in their respective forms. Again, the theory gives a completely uniform account of how forms stand in relation to their various properties: invariably, forms Are what they are.

Aristotle takes over Plato's difference in levels, but with considerable modifications. *At* each level, in the case of items in the category of substance, he replaces Plato's uniform theory with a *dual* account of how a subject is related to its various properties. The predicates 'man' and 'large' typify the difference in logical behaviour Aristotle has in mind: Socrates, for example, Is (a) man but Has largeness. If we accept this modification of the Platonic theory of Having in the case of Socrates and the predicable man, but agree with Plato that man Is (a) man and Is (an) animal, then the denial of uniformity *at* a level can also lead to a principle of homogeneity that holds *across* levels in the case of certain predicables. For example, in Aristotle's theory, Socrates (a particular) Is (a) man and Is (an) animal, while at the same time, the species, man, too Is (a) man and Is (an) animal. The same relation, then, holds between a sensible and certain of its predicables, and between a universal and those same predicables.

Finally, Aristotle and Plato disagree over the subjects of (metaphysical) predication. For Plato, there are two irreducibly different subjects of predication, sensibles and forms, and no (metaphysical) predication involving the one kind of subject can be replaced by a (metaphysical) predication involving the other. In the *Categories*, however, Aristotle appears to argue in favour of ultimately a *monolithic* conception of the subject of (metaphysical) predication, according to which every predication either itself has a primary substance as its subject or is analysed in terms of predications each of which has a primary substance as its subject.

In the two chapters that follow, I fill out the details of these various issues that separate the rival Platonic and Aristotelian theories and also set out the positive metaphysical theory that Aristotle constructs in the *Categories*.

1

Aristotle on Plato's Third Man Argument and the Anti-Platonism of the *Categories*

Aristotle's *Categories* is at heart a contentious work.[1] Ironically, it shares its main target with Plato's own critique of the Platonic theory of forms in the *Parmenides,* most notably in the regress argument at *Parmenides* 131e8–132b2. No proper exposition of Plato's regress argument appears in the surviving text of Aristotle. But there are scattered references in the text to an argument Aristotle calls the "Third *Man* Argument" (TMA); I shall suppose that this is a reworking of Plato's original regress argument, offering a regress of things that are *men,* in contrast to the Platonic original, which is a regress of things that are *large.* And (although again we have no way of telling for sure) I shall also talk as though we know that the reformulation is the work of Aristotle himself. The assumption that Aristotle initiated the reworking, or at least seized on it when it became current, is a fruitful source of hypotheses about Aristotle's *Categories* – not just about the features of Platonic metaphysics that Aristotle means to challenge there, but also about the shape of the positive theory he wishes to put in place of Plato's. In particular, I shall suppose that there is a way out of the celebrated regress argument in the original form in which it appears in the *Parmenides* (for dramatic purposes again, I shall call this *Plato's* way out) and that the theory of the *Categories* is devised at least in part in order to sustain a reformulation of the argument (the TMA properly so-called) that Plato will not so easily evade.

We have seen that in the surviving text, Aristotle nowhere enters into the details of Plato's regress argument. In the brief references he makes to the argument (if we are right that it is the same argument), even its title has changed – it is now the "Third *Man* Argument," in contrast to Plato's regress of things that are large. Aristotle often

---

1 In this chapter, I borrow freely from the account in F. Lewis (1985b), which in turn is heavily indebted to that in Code (1985).

seems to suggest that the TMA pinpoints exactly the differences that separate a sound Aristotelian metaphysics from the heresies of Platonism: the Platonic theory has the fault of making its universals thises, rather than suches. Or again, Plato's theory makes the mistake of separating its universals. But it is hard not to feel that these remarks by themselves are too sketchy to be of any real help.[2]

There is indirect evidence, however, for the details of Aristotle's views in the commentary by Alexander on Aristotle's criticism of the Platonic theory of forms in *Metaphysics* A9, put together by Alexander around the turn of the second century A.D., evidently with knowledge of Aristotle's now-lost treatise *On the Ideas*. My account of Aristotle's treatment of the TMA relies heavily on the discussion in Alexander.[3] Once the main outlines of Alexander's version of the TMA are in place in Section 1, I turn in the next three sections to the various philosophical disagreements with Plato that (I am supposing) Aristotle dramatizes with the aid of the argument. In the last section of the chapter, I consider briefly the rather different treatment of the anti-Platonism of Aristotle's *Categories* by Owen.

2 'This' is my translation of Aristotle's technical term, *tode ti;* 'such' translates his *toionde* (*Metaphysics* Z8, 1033b23) or *poion ti* (*Categories* 5, 3b15; cf. *peri ousian to poion*, b20). In what follows, I shall suppose that separation is materially equivalent to the thisness condition; on this assumption, I shall discuss the latter condition, but not the former. At *Metaphysics* Z13, 1038b34–1039a3, Aristotle remarks that taking universals as thises is sufficient to give the TMA, while in *Metaphysics* M9 he says that separation is responsible for all the problems of Plato's theory. Although the point is hardly decisive, the two passages together offer some support for the equivalence of separation and the thisness condition. For a similar speculation about thisness and separation, see White (1971a), p. 167, and for a fuller discussion of separation, see the exchanges between G. Fine (1984, 1985) and Morrison (1985a, b). The distinction between thises and suches is the subject of Kung (1981).

3 The TMA exists in many forms. In its original version as the Third Largeness Argument, it appears in Plato's *Parmenides* at 131e8–132b2. Plato also gives a related regress argument at *Parmenides* 132c12–133a4. In his commentary on Aristotle, *Metaphysics* A9, Alexander gives a batch of unrelated arguments that pass under the name 'Third Man Argument' (84.7–21); he also offers three separate accounts of the version of the argument to be attributed to Aristotle: one at 83.34–84.7 (said at 85.10–11 to be Eudemus's form of the argument), a second at 84.21–85.3 (this argument is directly attributed to Aristotle at 85.11–12, and at 85.3–5 is said to be the same as the first at 83.34–84.7), and a third at 93.1–7, identified at 93.7 with the argument at 84.21–85.3. On the various cross-references between these three accounts of the argument, see Cherniss (1944), n. 210 and App. 4, pp. 500–1. Alexander apparently regards himself as describing the same argument at all three places, yet there are significant differences between the three accounts. This laxity about what counts as the same argument makes him perhaps an uncertain authority for the version of the TMA that Aristotle has in mind. Yet another reason for caution in looking for a single Aristotelian version of the TMA in Alexander is that (as the current literature attests) people's views about the TMA change. It is not inconceivable, then, that even Aristotle may have had more than one version of the argument in mind at different stages in his career.

1   The TMA According to Alexander

Two assumptions, both supported in Alexander's text, allow us to describe the general strategy of the TMA:

Alex-OM. If each member of a plurality, Π, of objects is a man, then there is an X such that

(1) X is a man,

and

(2) X is (metaphysically) predicable of each member of Π.

Alex-NI. If an entity is (metaphysically) predicable of each member of a plurality Π then it is distinct from each member of Π.[4]

The argument begins by assuming that there exists a plurality, Π, of objects, all of them sensibles and all of them men.[5] This permits the first application of Alex-OM, which generates the existence of the universal X, which is itself a man and is predicated of each member of Π. Next, we go to Alex-NI to show that X is not identical with any member of Π. This done, we must assume that there exists a new plurality, Π *with X*,[6] to clear the way for a second application of Alex-

---

4 Code (1985), notes 13 and 14, cites the authority of Alexander for a variant on these two assumptions. Accounts that rely on Alexander in this way share an important assumption with Owen (see Section 5): they are literalists in their view of Aristotle's version of the TMA, in the sense that they require that we can attribute an interest in one or another assumption of the TMA to Aristotle only if the assumption is attested in the version of the argument Alexander describes as Aristotle's. Obviously, any *non*literalist hypotheses about Aristotle's version of the TMA will lack the virtue of direct evidence, which literalism claims to provide. But there are difficulties, both textual and philosophical, with literalism too. To take the textual arguments first: there are, as we have seen (note 3), no less than three separate descriptions of the TMA in Alexander. (In this connection, notice that the first and second accounts at 83.34–84.7 and 84.21–85.3 are *not* parts of a discontinuous but *single* account.) There are significant differences among the three accounts; yet Alexander apparently regards them all as accounts of the *same* argument. Can we be sure that Alexander is sufficiently strict about what counts as the same argument to rely on his authority for the version of the TMA that Aristotle has in mind? A philosophical doubt about literalism concerns the assumption that Aristotle had just one version of the TMA consistently in mind throughout his philosophical career. As suggested in note 3, the frequent changes of heart undergone by modern exponents of the argument indicate the need for caution with regard to this hypothesis.

5 Here 'Π' occurs as an individual constant, referring to a given plurality, while in Alex-OM and Alex-PM, the same letter occurs as a variable ranging over pluralities. I shall allow symbols to double as variables and as constants in this way, where there is no danger of misunderstanding.

6 Π *with X* has as members all the members of Π together with X. The 'Π *with X*' terminology is adapted from a device of Geach's. I avoid the devices of modern set theory in order to avoid the suggestion that pluralities can be identified in a straightforward way with sets. In fact, not all sets are pluralities, as we shall see later in this section. Like sets, however, pluralities have members.

OM, which will generate the existence of an entity, Y. Then we go again to Alex-NI to show that Y is not identical with any member of Π *with* X, in particular that it is not identical with X. And so on to infinity.

One feature of the assumptions that help generate this argument requires immediate comment. The stipulation in Alex-OM that the universal that is (metaphysically) predicable of each member of a plurality of men, *itself is a man,* introduces a version of a "self-predication" assumption that in one form or another has been a part of modern reconstructions of Plato's regress since the classic paper by Vlastos.[7] It is worth emphasizing from the start that the version of the assumption that appears in Alex-OM (2) is the *weakest* version of anything that can plausibly pass under the name 'self-predication'. It is an instance of what I shall call *syntactic self-predication,* for while it requires that there be true sentences of the form 'Man is (a) man', nothing has yet been said about the *interpretation* such sentences are to receive. Alex-OM (2) by itself does not require, for example, that the form man *be* a man in precisely the sense of 'is' in which Socrates is a man, that is, on Plato's account, that man *participates in* or Has itself. How such sentences are to be interpreted in the present context will be settled by other assumptions to be discussed later in this section.

If we are to develop the TMA in the way just suggested, we must assume that Π is a plurality, that Π *with* X is a plurality, that (Π *with* X) *with* Y is a plurality, and so on. The assumption that such pluralities exist appears in Alexander as the assumption that there exist many things that are *alike* (*homoia*). In particular, both the (sensible) men and the forms generated by the regress are alike.[8] And at 93.1–2, Alexander notes explicitly the assumption that there is the same kind (*eidos*) and the same account (*logos*) both for the participants and for the form; in accordance with this,

just as, in the case of the participants, which are of the same kind (*homoeidesin*), there is something common, so too in the case of these and the form from which these ‹depend›, there will be something common predicated: for it too [sc., the form] is of the same kind (*homoeides*) as they. (Alexander *In Met.* 93.2–5)

Alexander goes on to identify the argument under discussion here with what is often taken to be his canonical version of the TMA at 84.21–85.3.

These texts allow us to add a principle governing the formation of pluralities to the assumptions that Alexander assigns to the TMA. The

---

7 Vlastos (1954).

8 *esti de ho logos houtos tōi prōtōi ho autos epei ethento ta homoia tou autou tinos metousiai homoia einai. homoioi gar hoi te anthrōpoi kai hai ideai* (85.4–5); the reference back is to 83.34–84.7, especially 84.1–2, *eti ta homoia allēlois tou autou tinos metousiai homoia allēlois einai, ho kuriōs esti touto kai touto einai tēn idēan.*

first two clauses together will generate all the pluralities we will need; the third, extremal clause rules out any other cases:

Alex-PL
(1) Any collection of sensibles, all of which are alike (in the same respect), is a plurality.[9]
(2) If an object is predicable of each member of a plurality Π and it and each member of Π are alike (in the same respect), then the result of adding that object to Π is itself a plurality.
(3) Nothing else is a plurality.

In general, the *level* of a plurality is equal to the level of its highest-level member, where sensibles are of level zero, a form (immediately) "over" a plurality of sensibles is of level 1, and so on. Alex-PL, then, countenances two kinds of pluralities: pluralities of level zero, whose members are all sensibles, and higher-level pluralities of level 1 or above, with a mixed membership of sensibles and forms combined.[10]

Alex-PL requires that pluralities of any level have members that are *alike* in a given respect. What does this requirement amount to? The simple answer, that (e.g.) they should all be men, papers over a number of rather different possibilities. One obvious possibility concerns the different occurrences of the predicate 'man' in the argument. Say that

> a predicate *has the same sense* used of a given set of items if and only if it picks out the same predicable in each of those different occurrences.

The notion of sameness of sense suggests this condition on any plurality that is to have a place in the TMA:

Univocity
(1) If all the members of a plurality of sensibles are men, then there is a sense of the predicate 'man' such that 'man' has that same sense used of each member of that plurality.
(2) If all the members of a plurality Π are men and there is a sense of the predicate 'man' such that 'man' has that same sense used of each

---

9 The conventional assumption that our initial plurality has at least two sensibles as members begins with Plato, *Parmenides* 132a2, *poll' atta megala*, cf. Alexander, *tinōn pleionōn*, 84.22, and *pleionōn ontōn*, 84.26, although this seems a consequence of how Plato typically states the One-over-Many Assumption than a feature necessary to the theory or to the TMA. There seems no reason why there should not be a form corresponding to a *unique* sensible (exactly this hypothesis is made with respect to the visible world, created after the pattern of *to panteles on*, in the *Timaeus*), and also no reason why there should not be a one-member plurality from which we can generate a regress of forms along the lines of the TMA. Alex-PL itself, then, does not rule out the possibility that there exist one-member pluralities.

10 So the theory of pluralities at work in this version of the TMA has something akin to a *cumulative* type structure: a plurality of level n includes not only some entity of level n (as in simple type theory), but also for every m, $0 \leq m < n$, at least one entity of level m (for these different kinds of type theory, see Drake [1974], pp. 1–2).

member of Π, then where the universal, X, that is "over" Π is itself a man, there is a sense of the predicate 'man' such that 'man' has that same sense used of all the members of Π and of X as well.[11]

The Univocity condition concerns the interpretation of the *predicate* in various contexts and requires that it be univocal in each case. Notice, however, that the principle has no bearing on the kind of *predication* at work in each case: it says nothing about how the copula is to be interpreted in a given context. The principle Univocity deals expressly with the predicate 'man', but a similar condition applies straightforwardly to the predicate 'large' in the Third Largeness Argument in Plato's *Parmenides*. Clause (1) of Univocity captures a minimal sense in which a number of sensibles must be alike, if they are to form a genuine plurality open to the use of Alex-OM in order to generate the existence of a universal that is "over" that plurality.[12] Clause (2) then extends this idea to the ensuing pluralities that the regress argument generates.

There are signs in Alexander, however, that more than Univocity by itself may be required. Suppose that there is a collection of sensibles, all of which are men. Then we can use Alex-PL to form a plurality, Π, of level zero, all of whose members are men, according to Alexander, only if there is a single form in which they all participate.[13] The condition Univocity already takes care of the requirement that all the members of Π be related to *the same form*. But Alexander's mention

11 It does *not* follow from Univocity (1) that 'man' has one and only one sense (names exactly one predicable) asserted of each member of a plurality of sensibles, for we do not disallow the possibility that 'man' has more than one meaning or that in some meanings it is true of some but not other members of the plurality. We require only that there is at least one meaning of the predicate such that the predicate is true of every member of the plurality in that meaning. Compare, e.g., the predicate 'alien': in one sense, it is true of Dr. Spock but false of Prince Charles that he is an alien, but there is a different sense, one having to do with the immigration laws of the United States, such that both Spock and Charles are aliens. The point takes on real importance in the case of Univocity (2): 'man' used of all members of a plurality, Π, of sensibles names the universal man; but by Alex-NI, when used of all the members of the higher-level plurality Π *with* man, it names the *different* universal man-1. In the latter case, there is a single sense of 'man' such that 'man' has that sense used of each member of Π *with* man; that is, it names the same predicable, man-1. But it hardly follows that 'man' has one and only one sense, or names exactly one predicable; for when used of *some* of the members of Π *with* man, namely, the members of the original plurality Π, it also names the *different* predicable, man.

12 Universals correspond to some natural division between things, in contrast to the general run of properties, which on some modern accounts, at any rate, exist as correlates to *any* set one may care to construct. Cf. D. Lewis (1983).

13 *tou autou tinos metousiai;* see note 8. I assume that in using this language, Alexander means to require that a *single* notion of metaphysical predication should be at work in all the relevant cases; but I take him to be neutral on the question of *which* variety of metaphysical predication is involved, Izzing or Having. On this account, *'metousia'* cannot be restricted to Plato's technical notion of participation (which is a variety of Having).

of participation suggests the further requirement that they all stand *in the same relation* to that form. Plausibly, Alexander would say that a similar requirement also holds for higher-level pluralities. For example, let X be the form in which every member of Π participates. Then we can form a new, higher-level plurality, Π *with X*, by Alex-PL, only if X and every member of Π all *participate in* the same form.[14]

Alexander's discussion suggests a way in which all the members of a plurality may be alike in a given respect, which goes beyond mere Univocity. In the case relevant to the TMA, two things are alike with respect to the predicable man only if when we say that each is a man, the 'is' is to be understood in exactly the same way in the two cases. In contrast to the notion of univocity, then, which specifies that the same *predicable* be picked out by different occurrences of the same *predicate,* our new notion will be defined by whether *the same relation of (metaphysical) predication* is at work in different cases.[15] I shall say that any plurality all of whose members are alike in this way is *homogeneous:*

> A plurality, Π, of entities that are of levels $m, \ldots, n$ ($m \geq 0$) is *homogeneous* with respect to the predicate 'man' if and only if there is a single relation of metaphysical predication (a single sense of 'is') such that each member of Π *is* a man in virtue of that same relation (each *is* a man in exactly the same sense of 'is' in each case).

Homogeneity as I have defined it is a *cross-level* notion – it can hold for pluralities that have entities of *different* levels as members; but we shall allow that it can also apply in the limiting case to a plurality all of whose members are sensibles, and hence of level zero. For the TMA to work, we must assume that homogeneous pluralities in the sense defined are in fact available at each stage in the argument:

Homogeneity
(1) For any plurality, Π, of sensibles that are men, Π is homogeneous with respect to the predicate 'man'.
(2) For any plurality, Π, of men (of any level) and universal X, where X is "over" Π and is itself a man, the plurality Π *with X* is homogeneous with respect to 'man'.

According to Homogeneity, the *same* predicative link connects each member of a plurality of men, however high the level of that plurality,

14 See notes 8 and 13.
15 I emphasize that accepting Univocity, governing an occurrence of the *predicate,* has no consequences for or against any given view about the kind of *predication* involved. In particular, agreeing to Univocity will not force a philosopher into accepting the Homogeneity condition set out immediately ahead in the main text. For a similar distinction in the interpretation of Plato, see Nehamas (1979), p. 97 and n. 20; cf. note 17, this chapter.

with the relevant predicable. That is, as Alexander tells us, they all participate in the predicable in question.[16] (But we will need a separate application of Univocity to tell us that the predicate 'man' is univocal in all these different uses, so that it names the same predicable in each case, namely, the universal that is "over" the plurality in question.)

The principle Homogeneity is stated in terms of the predicate 'man' featured in Aristotle's version of Plato's regress argument. The principle is controversial, as we shall see. In the first place, the principle is by no means obviously generalizable to *all* predicates. Aristotle himself, for example, must concede that there is no counterpart to Homogeneity (2) for the predicate 'large', for in his own theory in the *Categories*, ordinary large things Have largeness, while at best largeness itself *Is* large. If no counterpart to Homogeneity governs the relation of metaphysical predication applied to the predicate 'large', then, arguably, a crucial condition for any regress argument involving things that are large is lacking, and Plato has an easy way out of the Third Largeness Argument given in the *Parmenides*. Perhaps the chief motive for Aristotle's shift to a Third *Man* Argument is that a homogeneity principle for the predicate 'man' is not so easily denied. In Aristotle's own theory in the *Categories*, for example, Socrates and man alike Are men – that is, arguably, the predicative link is the *same* in both cases. If Plato can be forced to accept the same assumption, then

---

16 See note 13. It is important to distinguish the notion of homogeneity just introduced from that of *uniformity* discussed in the Introduction to this part. Like homogeneity, uniformity is defined in terms of the predication relation, but it cannot hold across levels. Uniformity has to do with all the members of a given plurality, all of which are *of the same level*, and specifies a single relation of metaphysical predication for *all* the predicables that belong to those entities. For example, the world of sensibles for Plato makes up a uniform plurality: *all* sensibles have *all* their predicables by virtue of a single relation, namely, Having. (But in the theory of the *Categories*, primary substances – Socrates, Callias, and the rest – do not make up a uniform plurality, for Socrates Has some of his predicables, but Is others.) The Homogeneity condition, by contrast, is set out in terms of the single predicable man (counterparts of the notion exist for other predicables). In the usual case, it holds for pluralities that have entities of *different* levels as members, and it specifies that all those entities, of whatever level, are related to man in virtue of a single relation of metaphysical predication. (This, however, leaves open the possibility that those same entities may stand in quite different relations of [metaphysical] predication to predicables *other than* man.) Thus, for Aristotle, the plurality whose members are Socrates, Callias, and the secondary substance man (say) is homogeneous: all three alike Are men. (But, of course, Socrates and Callias Have pallor and their other accidents.) Both uniformity and homogeneity should be distinguished from the notion of *univocity*, which is defined not in terms of the predication relation, but in terms of predicates and predicables.

A number of modern characterizations of "self-predication" in Plato are in effect committed to Homogeneity for higher-level pluralities containing sensibles as well as forms: for example, the view that the form man is "logically on a par with *other members of the class*" (Owen [1968], p. 117, my emphasis) and the similar appeal to class membership in Vlastos (1973), p. 258, n. 97; cf. also point (iv) of his p. 348, n. 28.

the TMA is threatening to him in a way that the original Third Largeness Argument was not.

A second difficulty with Homogeneity is that Plato will want to deny
that the principle holds for any predicate whatever. The trouble again
lies with the second half of Homogeneity. The principle may seem
trivial in clause (1), where the men that are members of the plurality
are all entities of the same level: that is, they are all *sensibles*. Clause (2)
of Homogeneity, however, is far from trivial, for it places a condition
on all the later pluralities of men that Alex-PL injects into the argument, which are higher level and count forms as well as sensibles
among their members. Aristotle can argue that the TMA has special
bite against the Platonic theory only if he can first show that Plato must
in fact accept the homogeneity of higher-level pluralities of men.
Prima facie at least, however, Plato will certainly want to resist this
application of Homogeneity.[17] Further details of this controversy are
given in Section 3.

Two further ways of fleshing out the "likeness" condition on the
members of a plurality also require notice. The first involves Aristotle's idea in the *Categories* that the species man, for example, is
predicated *synonymously* of its subjects. To understand this new condition, we should begin with Aristotle's explanation of (plain) synonymy
by itself at the beginning of the *Categories:*

When things have the term (*onoma*) in common and the definition of being
which corresponds to the term is the same, they are called synonymous.[18]
Thus, for example, both a man and an ox are animals. Each of these is called
‹an› animal in virtue of a common term, and the definition of being is also the
same; for if one is to give the definition of each – what being an animal is for
each of them – one will give the same definition. (*Categories* 1, 1a6–12; following Ackrill's translation)

Two things are synonyms, then, just in case the same term applies to
both, and they also have the definition that goes with that term in

17 Cf. Nehamas (1979), pp. 95–7, who argues that, for Plato, the predicate 'just' has the
    same meaning applied to the form justice and to sensibles; but properly, only justice
    is just (this is the "restricted" use of *is*, which is the same as our Izzing; see note 11
    of the Introduction to this part), and quite differently, the sensibles participate in,
    or are named after, the form. That is, in this example, according to Plato, Univocity
    is true, but the appropriate counterpart of Homogeneity is false. On the account I
    shall offer, denying Homogeneity constitutes Plato's primary move against the
    TMA. It is a *consequence* of this (but *not* Plato's first line of defence against the TMA,
    as some have seen it: Vlastos [1954], pp. 233 ff., Geach [1956], pp. 274–5, Cohen
    [1971], p. 473, n. 42) that pluralities not of level zero (i.e., pluralities whose member-
    ship includes forms as well as sensibles) are no longer admissible in the TMA.
18 *sunōnuma, Categories* 1, 1a6. Edgehill, in the (unrevised) Oxford translation, trans-
    lates 'univocal', but I reserve this term for a different notion, to be discussed in the
    main text.

common. More precisely, they are synonyms *with respect to* the term in question. Schematically,

> *x* and *y* are *synonyms with respect to* the term '*F*' if and only if
>
> (i) '*F*' applies to both *x* and *y*,
>
> and
>
> (ii) there is a single definition associated with '*F*' that applies to both *x* and *y*.

For example, if a man and an ox are synonyms with respect to the term 'animal', then the term 'animal' applies to both, and the appropriate definition is the same in both cases – that is, they are both animate objects (say) endowed with sensation.[19]

Given this account of synonymy, Aristotle goes on to develop a notion of *synonymous predication:*

> *x* is *predicated synonymously of y* (*y* is *called synonymously after x, Categories* 5, 3a33–4, b8–9) if and only if there is a predicate '*F*' "from" *x* (*hai apo toutōn katēgoriai,* 3a34–5), such that *x* and *y* are synonyms with respect to '*F*'.[20]

For example, man is predicated synonymously of an individual man: from the universal man comes the term 'man'; 'man' applies both to man and to the individual man (both are men); and finally, the definition that goes with 'man' applies to both as well (both are rational animals).

With this notion of synonymous predication at hand, Aristotle can stipulate that the pluralities of the TMA are also subject to this third condition:

> **Synonymy.** The universal man that is "over" a plurality, Π, of men (of any level) is predicated synonymously of each member of Π.

According to Synonymy, all the members of Π and man are alike in this further respect, that man and each member of Π share the same name (they all are men) and, further, the definition associated with

---

19 In definition, according to Aristotle, a name (*onoma*) or shorter phrase is replaced by a longer phrase. But what is defined is an item from the ontology – what is named by the *onoma* or phrase in the definiendum in the linguistic definition. Aristotle will often say that *x* is the definition of *y*, where strictly what is meant is that *x* is signified by the definiens (the longer phrase) in a linguistic definition of *y*.

20 There is an extensive discussion of the meaning of '*katēgoria*' in the *Categories* and *Topics* in Frede ([1981] 1987), pp. 32–5; Frede favours the translation 'predication' over 'predicate', but he does not mention the passage under discussion in the text. The definitions of *synonymy* and *synonymous predication* given here should be contrasted with the definitions of *strong* synonymy and *strong* synonymous predication given in Section 3.

'man' applies equally to them all. We will say more about this condition in Section 3.[21]

The three conditions, Univocity, Homogeneity, and Synonymy, given in the preceding paragraphs, all fill out in different ways the requirement that, broadly, the predicate 'man' should apply "on equal terms" to every member of a plurality of men, of whatever level. In particular, it should apply on equal terms both to a Platonic form of man, whether of level 1 or higher, and to all the particular men, Socrates, Callias, and the rest. One more condition, however, may be needed before the logic with which we treat the universal man is squarely on all fours with that suitable for particular men. The higher-level pluralities required by the TMA combine the form man, which is of level 1, with the sensibles that are men, each of which is of level zero, and these in turn with the higher-level forms man-1 (of level 2), man-2 (level 3), and so on. Can we be sure that these "mixed" pluralities containing entities of different levels along the lines the TMA requires really do exist? In the account Aristotle will give in the *Categories*, Socrates is a *this* while man is a *such,* and Aristotle is apparently committed to principles governing thises and suches that will stop the TMA after one step with the introduction of the first form, man, "over" the plurality of sensibles that are men. At the same time, according to Aristotle, Plato holds that, like Socrates, man too is a this. Plausibly, then, Aristotle thinks that the *this–such* distinction gives himself a means of blocking the TMA that must be denied to Plato. If this is Aristotle's thinking, he must assume that the pluralities that figure in the TMA are governed by this further requirement:

Thisness
(1) Each member of a plurality, Π, of sensibles that are men is a this.
(2) For any plurality, Π, of men (of any level), each member of Π and the universal, man, that is "over" Π are all alike thises.[22]

---

21 In particular, in contrast to the notion of *strong* synonymous predication defined in Section 3, where man is synonymously predicated of Socrates in the sense stipulated in Synonymy, we do not yet know if Socrates and man Are men and Are rational animals.

It is also worth noting that the two conditions Univocity (2) and Synonymy are materially equivalent. It can be shown that man is predicated synonymously of a given subject, *a*, just in case the predicate 'man', taken "from" man, has the same sense applied both to man and to *a*. (Thus, by definition, [i] man is predicated synonymously of *a* just in case the predicate 'man' is taken "from" man, and 'man' and the associated definition apply both to man and to *a*. But [ii] by the principle that a predicate *has the same definition* in a given set of uses if and only if it *names the same predicable* in each of those uses, 'man' and the associated definition apply to man and to *a* just in case 'man' names the same predicable in both occurrences. Finally, by definition again, [iii] 'man' names the same predicable in both occurrences just in case 'man' has the same sense in both occurrences.) It follows that a plurality Π and the universal, *X*, that is "over" Π satisfy Univocity (2) just in case they satisfy Synonymy.

22 On this condition, see the discussion in Kung (1981) and in Section 4.

Aristotle will find Thisness (1) unexceptionable. Thisness (2) is quite a different story. Thisness (2) is not satisfied within Aristotle's theory; the fact that it *is* satisfied in Plato's ontology, however, in Aristotle's view is what exposes Plato fatally to the TMA. Given the assumption that both Socrates and man are thises (and similarly for any higher-order forms of man as well), then despite any remaining differences between forms and sensibles – for example, the "categorial" differences that, unlike sensibles, forms are immutable, eternal, objects of thought rather than sense perception, and the rest – still they can all be combined into pluralities of the kind the TMA requires. Thisness is the last of four conditions – Univocity, Homogeneity, Synonymy, and finally Thisness itself – individually necessary and jointly sufficient for the "similarity" requirement in Alex-PL. If Plato's theory satisfies each of these four conditions, and if the three conditions from Alexander – Alex-OM, Alex-NI, and Alex-PL – are satisfied as well, there seems no avoiding the infinite sequence of forms that the TMA predicts.

2   A Dispute over the Predication Relation: The Predicates 'Man' and 'Large'

Perhaps the most distinctive feature of Aristotle's treatment of the regress argument from Plato's *Parmenides,* as we have seen, is the transformation from a Third *Largeness* Argument to an argument concerning pluralities of things that are *men*. This transformation is not idle. On the reconstruction I am envisioning, Aristotle will try to use the regress argument to decide the issue between his own and Plato's theory of predication. There are important respects, however, in which the two theories *agree* on how they treat the predicate 'large'. In particular, as we have seen, Aristotle's own treatment of 'large' in the *Categories* suggests a way out of the Third Largeness Argument that Aristotle can hardly deny to Plato too. The two theories diverge, however, over their treatment of the predicate 'man'. In this instance, perhaps, Aristotle will be able to show that Plato's theory, but not his own, is liable to some version of Plato's original regress argument, now reworked as the TMA, and possibly to other difficulties as well.

We can begin with some points of agreement between the two rival theories. Suppose that Socrates is large. In both theories, the predicate 'large' applies to every particular large thing in virtue of the fact that it Has largeness. For Aristotle, 'large' is true of Socrates by virtue of what may be called a cross-categorial relation: Socrates Has largeness (the details of Aristotle's theory are given in Chapter 2). Again, in Plato's theory, the relation between sensibles and forms is invariably a relation of participation or Having. The predicate 'large' too, then, applies to the various sensibles that are large in virtue of the fact that they all Have the universal largeness in common.

At the same time, Plato apparently holds that forms do not Have their various properties. In particular, then, 'large' applies to the form largeness not in virtue of something that it Has, but in virtue of what it Is. Equally, Aristotle will argue that if nothing can belong in two categories at once, and if Having is a *cross*-categorial relation, then largeness cannot Have itself.

Both theories, then, agree that Socrates and Callias Have largeness, but that largeness itself Is large, Is (a) size, and so on. Consequently, the two theories agree that there is no counterpart to the principle Homogeneity with respect to the predicable largeness. In particular, if each member of a plurality of sensibles is large and the universal largeness that is "over" that plurality is also large, still there is no single relation of (metaphysical) predication at work in the two sets of cases.

Agreement between Plato and Aristotle's theory in the *Categories* goes only so far, however. A fundamental point of disagreement emerges when we turn to the predicate 'man'. In line with his overall theory of the relation between sensibles and forms, Plato will say that Socrates participates in or Has the form man. And in general, the predicate 'man' applies to the various sensibles that are men, in virtue of the fact that they all *Have* a universal, man, in common. At the same time, however, there is reason to think that, for Plato, forms do not Have their properties: in particular, then, 'man' applies to the universal man, *not* in virtue of something that it Has, but in virtue of what it *Is*. The two ideas that sensibles Have all their forms, whereas forms Are their various properties, together suggest that Plato will want to deny Aristotle's homogeneity principle for the predicate 'man'. Homogeneity (2) maintains that 'man' applies to each member of a plurality of men and to the universal man, which is predicated of each member of that plurality, in virtue of one and the same relation of (metaphysical) predication: in Plato's theory, such a claim is clearly false.

In resisting Homogeneity, Plato's treatment of 'man' exactly mirrors his treatment of 'large'. Sensibles Have largeness and Have man; the form largeness Is large, and the form man Is (a) man; so (finally) a principle of homogeneity is never true. Here, Plato makes room for two kinds of predication relation; but he gives a single, uniform account of the relation of (metaphysical) predication for all predicates alike at each level.

Despite the identity of treatment that Plato gives to the predication relation in the case of both 'man' and 'large', Aristotle's theory in the *Categories* brings to light one difference between the two predicates that, speculatively, he may hope Plato will be willing to concede. In the

Categories, as we have seen, Aristotle argues that Socrates and his species, man, are synonyms with respect to the predicate 'man'. That is, first, the predicate 'man' is taken "from" the species man, and the term applies both to Socrates and to his species. Further, the definition that goes with the predicate applies both to Socrates and to the species: both Socrates and man are (rational) animals. But, Aristotle supposes, largeness and a particular large thing are not synonyms with respect to 'large'; for, "Socrates is large, but he is not what largeness is."[23] So, Aristotle will say, largeness is not predicated synonymously of Socrates. Both the term 'large' and the associated definition apply to largeness itself. But at most the term (and strictly not even that in the usual case, where paronymy is involved; see Chapter 2), and *not* the definition, applies to Socrates.[24]

Accordingly, where Π is a plurality of men and man is "over" Π, the relation between man and the members of Π is governed by the principle Synonymy from Section 1. But again, according to Aristotle, the analogous principle *fails* where Π is a plurality of things that are large and largeness is the universal that is "over" Π: largeness is not predicated synonymously of the members of Π. The principle Synonymy, then, apparently signals a real difference in the logical behaviour of 'large' and 'man'. And for all we have seen so far, it may also be a difference that Plato too can accept without difficulty.[25]

On this point, then, Plato and Aristotle can perhaps agree that the predicates 'man' and 'large' diverge. Beyond the possibility of agreement over Synonymy, however, Plato and Aristotle continue to differ radically over the nature of the predication relation in the case of the predicate 'man'. Aristotle insists that Plato's theory of participation or Having is false applied to the relation between Socrates and the predicable man picked out by 'man'. Participation is an accidental relation, and so, appropriately, Socrates Has his various accidents. But being a man is not an accident of Socrates: Socrates, then, Is (a) man.

Given this disagreement over participation, disagreement over Homogeneity (2) is also inevitable. Aristotle thinks that Socrates Is (a) man; since he also holds that the species man Is (a) man, he will argue in favour of Homogeneity (2). Plato agrees that the universal Is various of its properties: man, for example, Is (a) man and Is (an) animal. He must, then, surely *resist* Homogeneity (2) if he is to preserve what he sees as an essential feature peculiar to sensibles, that invariably a sensible Has or participates in all its predicables. At the same time, by resisting Homogeneity, Plato will also be able to fend off the TMA.

23 *An. Po.* A22, 83a24–30; *Metaphysics* Γ4, 1007a32–3.
24 *Categories* 5, 2a27–34, 3a15–17; see also Chapter 2, Section 2.
25 For an argument that despite what is said in this paragraph, Plato will not accept Aristotle's conclusions about Synonymy, see Section 3.

Plato concedes that every sensible that is a man is a man in the same sense of 'is': in his theory, each Has man. So there is no impediment to forming pluralities of sensibles that are men or to supposing that by Alex-OM, there exists a universal, man, that is "over" lowest-level pluralities of this sort. But it is not the case that the universal man *is* a man in exactly the same sense of 'is' as when we say that each sensible man *is* a man. Plausibly, then, we cannot use Alex-PL to form any higher-level pluralities of men, whose members include forms as well as sensibles. Accordingly, we are denied the use of Alex-OM to generate universals at a level beyond that of man itself at level 1, "over" the plurality of sensibles that are men.

3   Some Arguments That Plato Must Accept Homogeneity

Denying Homogeneity (2) is a key element in the defence we are constructing on Plato's behalf against the TMA. Conversely, Aristotle will try to revitalize the TMA by showing that Plato must after all *accept* this principle. What will it take for Aristotle to succeed in forcing Homogeneity (2) on Plato? One place to begin might be to find a way of controverting Plato's claim that sensibles invariably participate in or Have their forms. If Plato can be made to agree that Socrates (say) Is (a) man, then given his view that the form man Is (a) man, the truth of Homogeneity (2) follows immediately. But the attempt to weaken Plato's resistance to Homogeneity (2) by attacking his theory of participation tackles things in precisely the wrong order. The argument starts with the falsity of Plato's theory of participation, in particular his view that Socrates Has man; but participation is not a peripheral feature of Plato's theory, and hence not a likely point of entry for Aristotle's argument against him. It is, rather, a fundamental tenet of Platonism, and hence more plausibly Aristotle's ultimate target. Accordingly, Aristotle will want to use the truth of Homogeneity (2) (together with the fact that man Is [a] man) in order to establish the falsity of the Platonic theory of participation, rather than the other way around.

Possibly, however, Aristotle has available a different and more satisfactory means of forcing Plato to accept Homogeneity (2). For help, he can turn to the notion of synonymy set out in the *Categories*. As Aristotle understands it, synonymy apparently indicates one way in which the logical behaviours of the two predicates, 'man' and 'large', do after all differ. Suppose now that Plato has no good reason to object to the notion of synonymy or to deny the principle Synonymy governing the predicate 'man'. Possibly Aristotle can show that Synonymy entails Homogeneity (2). If so, then unless Plato can find independent reasons for rejecting Synonymy, Aristotle will be able to use Synonymy as a lever to force Plato into accepting Homogeneity (2), and Homogeneity (2) in turn as a means for overturning Plato's use of participation or Having to explain the relation between Socrates (say) and the form man.

In fact, I think, Plato will be by no means as compliant over synonymy as the argument just sketched demands. There is a crucial vagueness in Aristotle's concept of synonymy as it stands. Interpreted one way, Synonymy does entail Homogeneity – but it is manifestly false for Plato. But as we shall see, Synonymy in any form Plato will find acceptable does not entail Homogeneity.

Undoubtedly, as we have seen, Aristotle holds that Synonymy and Homogeneity (2) are both true within his own theory of predication in the *Categories*. The mere fact that Aristotle holds both does not by itself tend to show that the one *entails* the other. Arguably, in Aristotle's own theory, the entailment does hold. We can construct two arguments on his behalf. Suppose, first, that Synonymy is true, that is, that man is predicated synonymously of each particular man. It follows virtually immediately that man is also predicated synonymously of itself.[26] But if man is predicated synonymously of itself and of each particular man, then presumably it is predicated of both *by means of one and the same predication relation*.

Again, Aristotle can argue, if Synonymy is true, so that man is predicated synonymously of Socrates (say), it follows by formal principles governing Code and Grice's *Is* that man is essentially predicable of Socrates, and hence that Socrates Is (a) man.[27] This gives Homogeneity (2), since we already agree that man Is (a) man. More important, it refutes outright Plato's claim that Socrates participates in or Has all his properties, in particular that he participates in or Has man.

Both arguments are undermined by the same point. They beg the question, since they presuppose that where Synonymy holds, Homogeneity holds too – that where the name and the definition apply both to Socrates and to man, so that the *predicable* is the same in both sets of cases, the *relation of (metaphysical) predication* will also be the same. Thus, Plato can respond to the two arguments with the protest that if man is predicated synonymously of Socrates, it follows by definition

26 By (D1) in Chapter 2 (and assuming for the sake of argument that one thing is predicated synonymously of another only if the first is said of* the second), man is predicated synonymously of man if and only if (i) for any primary substance *x*, necessarily man is predicated synonymously of *x* only if man is predicated synonymously of *x*, and in fact (ii) there is some primary substance such that man is predicated synonymously of *y*. Clause (i) is trivially true. And (ii) is true by hypothesis. For we have assumed that man is predicated synonymously of Socrates, and Socrates is a primary substance.

27 This argument is put forward in Code (1985), pp. 103–4.

that the predicate 'man' applies to Socrates, but not that Socrates Is (a) man. And in general, Plato will say, it is false that x is predicated synonymously of y only if y Is x.

In more detail, suppose we grant that man is predicated synonymously of Socrates. By definition, then, Socrates and man are synonyms with respect to 'man', that is, 'man' applies to Socrates and to man, and the relevant definition applies to them both as well. Plato need not have difficulty with any of this. He holds that the form, man, Is (a) man and that it Is (a) rational animal (if this is the definition of man). So he can cheerfully concede that both the predicate 'man' and the definition that goes with it can apply to the form man. Disagreement with Aristotle comes with the next step. Aristotle urges that the predicate 'man' and the accompanying definition also apply to Socrates, so that Socrates too Is (a) man and Is (a) rational animal. Plato may well jib at this last inference. He can accept Aristotle's premiss that both 'man' and the associated definition apply to Socrates, as they also apply to man itself. But he will contest the sense of "applies to" here. In denying Homogeneity (2), Plato is defending the view that a *different* predicative link grounds the fact that Socrates (say) is a man and that man is a man. He is not likely to concede, then, that the *same* predicative link is in effect – that the sense of 'is' is the same – both in the claim that Socrates is a man or a rational animal and in the claim that man is a man or a rational animal. Accordingly, Plato can accept Synonymy and agree that the form man, for example, Is (a) man and Is (a) rational animal, while at the same time insisting that Socrates Has all his properties.

Underlying this debate is a crucial vagueness in the notions of synonymy and synonymous predication as already formulated. Synonymous predication as defined in Section 1 is a variety of *linguistic* predication. But the truth of a given linguistic predication does not settle exactly which metaphysical relation the sentence is being used to assert. Compare, for example, the linguistic notions of synonymy and synonymous predication as defined earlier with *strong* synonymy and *strong* synonymous predication:

Strong synonymy. x and y are strongly synonymous with respect to 'F' if and only if

(i) both x and y Are (an) F,

and

(ii) there is a single (linguistic) definition associated with 'F' such that both x and y Are the entity signified by that definition.

For example, according to Aristotle, Socrates and Coriscus are strongly synonymous with respect to 'man': both Are men, and both Are rational animals.

Strong synonymous predication. x is *predicated strongly synonymously of y* (*y is called strongly synonymously after x*) if and only if

(i)   x is (metaphysically) predicated of y,

and

(ii) there is a predicate 'F' "from" x such that x and y are strong synonyms with respect to 'F'.[28]

For example, man is predicated strongly synonymously of Socrates, for (again), in Aristotle's book, both Socrates and man Are men, and both Are rational animals.

Although his official accounts of synonymy and synonymous predication seem to require nothing more than the *weak* or *linguistic* version of synonymous predication, when Aristotle puts the two notions to work, he apparently has *strong* synonymy and *strong* synonymous predication in mind.[29] Accordingly, if man is (strongly) synonymously predicated of Socrates, then Socrates and man are men in virtue of the same (metaphysical) predication relation: both Are men. At the same time, largeness is *not* predicated strongly synonymously of Socrates: largeness Is large, but Socrates Has largeness. In contrast to this, Plato can argue that *no* predicable is ever predicated strongly synonymously of any sensible subject. Socrates, for example, Has largeness (while largeness Is large), and he Has man (but man Is [a] man).

At the same time, Plato can also argue that the relation between *every* predicable x and its subject satisfies the definition of (weak) synonymous predication. The relation between the stock example, man,

---

28 In this definition, strictly speaking, (i) is idle since it can be obtained from the definition of strong synonymy and the principle that x Is y only if y is (metaphysically) predicated of x. But it is more perspicuous if the clause is explicitly present in the definition.

29 As far as I can tell, the formulation of synonymous predication at *Categories* 5, 3a33–b8, like the definition of synonymy in the opening chapter of the *Categories*, runs almost exclusively in terms of *linguistic* predication (there is a short-lived exception at b4–5), and so suggests only the weak or linguistic version of synonymous predication. It may seem that there is a hint of *strong* synonymy in the formulation in *Categories* 1: synonyms are those things that have the name and *the definition of being* that goes with the name (*ho kata tounoma logos tēs ousias*) in common; for example, man and ox are both animals (1a6–7). Possibly, Aristotle means to suggest that the definition that goes with the term 'animal' is also *the definition of the being both of man and of ox* – it answers the question of what man and ox both *Are*. But Aristotle may have in mind only that what man and ox have in common is the entity that answers the question of what *animal* Is: animal Is (a) living creature, endowed with sensation (say), so 'living creature, endowed with sensation' applies both to man and to ox (cf. a10–12), and whether the relation is to be Izzing or Having is left unspecified. Again, at 5, 2a19–27, Aristotle discusses the phenomenon he later labels "synonymous predication" in terms of an example involving the SAID OF relation and at a27 denies that the same phenomenon applies in the case of accidents, which are IN their subject. Clearly, what he has in mind in this case amounts to *strong* synonymy, but this is more a feature of his example than of his official definition.

and its subject satisfies the definition, as we have already seen. But the relation between largeness and its subject also satisfies it, for the predicate 'large' applies to Socrates, and largeness Is (a) size – but at the same time, 'size' also applies to Socrates, for Socrates Has size. Again, Socrates Has pallor, while pallor Is (a) colour; but Socrates Has (a) colour – he is a coloured thing if he is a pale thing. The weaker notion of synonymous predication, then, makes for no distinction at all among predicables: all predicables alike are weakly synonymously predicated of their subjects. But for Plato, no predicable is ever strongly synonymously predicated of any sensible subject.

Aristotle would have to agree that the weak linguistic notion of synonymous predication holds for every predicable. Contrary to Plato, however, he will argue that some predicables (e.g., man) are strongly synonymously predicated of their subjects, but others (large, say) are not. His grounds, however, for thinking that some predicables are strongly synonymously predicated of their subject are not grounds that Plato is likely to accept; for they are (simply) that man Is (a) man and (an) animal, while contrary to the Platonic theory of participation, Socrates too Is (a) man and Is (an) animal.

To summarize our results so far: if man is strongly synonymously predicated of the members of a plurality, Π, of entities that are men, then the plurality Π *with* man satisfies Homogeneity – but Plato is not likely to agree that man is strongly synonymously predicated of any *sensible* that is a man. Meanwhile, the notion of synonymy and synonymous predication that Aristotle can expect Plato to find uncontroversial is not strong synonymy but the weaker linguistic version; but if man is weakly synonymously predicated of the members of Π, it does *not* follow that Π *with* man satisfies Homogeneity (2). On the contrary, Plato can cheerfully accept a notion of weak synonymous predication for all predicables of sensibles whatever.

According to Aristotle, the predicate 'man' applies in virtue of the same relation of (metaphysical) predication both to each particular man and to the universal man (this is just Homogeneity (2)). Meanwhile, the predicate 'large' applies in different ways to Socrates and to largeness itself: Socrates Has largeness, but largeness itself Is large. For Plato, however, there can be *no* case in which a predicate applies in virtue of the same relation of predication both to each member of a plurality of sensibles and to the universal "over" that plurality. In this respect, 'man' and 'large' behave exactly alike, and a cross-level principle of homogeneity is *never* true.

To this point, Aristotle has not succeeded in overturning Plato's position. In particular, he can show that the predicates 'man' and 'large' differ with respect to his notion of synonymy, only if he adopts a notion of *strong* synonymy that begs the question against Plato and against Plato's denial of Homogeneity.[30]

The fact that there is apparently no knock-down argument in support of Homogeneity that Plato too would find conclusive suggests a broader moral. Behind the dispute over Homogeneity, there lies a deeper divergence over ontology and (metaphysical) predication that is still less easily resolved. If Plato is to succumb to the version of the TMA sketched here, he must first accept Homogeneity. But his opposition to Homogeneity is not based merely on the desire to evade the TMA. His resistance is embedded in the details of his own ontology and theory of predication, in particular the twin ideas that sensibles invariably Have their properties, while forms Are what they are. If Plato sticks resolutely to these two ideas, he can resist Homogeneity and remain immune to the TMA. At the same time, if he were after all to concede the truth of Homogeneity, the consequences for the theory of forms would be enormous, even without the TMA. If a principle of homogeneity is imposed *across* levels – for example, if the universal man Is (a) man and Socrates Is (a) man, with the same relation of (metaphysical) predication in both cases – then a key component in the contrast between forms and sensibles is lost. At the same time, a

---

30 Perhaps, however, there are other means of separating the two classes of predicate. For example, one further way in which the predicates 'man' and 'large' differ, according to Alexander, is that 'man' is predicated *kuriōs* both of the universal man and of each of the particular men. But 'large' is predicated *kuriōs* only of the universal largeness and not of any sensible large thing. Owen (1957) argues that this difference in logical behaviour between the two kinds of predicate forms the basis of the argument at Alexander *In Met.* 82.9–83.17; cf. Aristotle, *Metaphysics* A9, 990b15–17. The same difference also underlies the contrast between the argument concerning relatives Alexander is dealing with at 82.9–83.17 and the TMA, to which he turns next. Code (1985), pp. 109–10, suggests that Aristotle uses *this* difference, which (again) Plato must accept, to explain why Plato must also accept Homogeneity (2), even while he rejects the analogous principle for 'large'. According to Code, Aristotle's strategy falls into two parts: (i) Aristotle uses Synonymy to support the idea that 'man' is predicated *kuriōs* both of man and of particular men; he then argues (ii) that this use of *kuriōs* predication in turn establishes the truth of Homogeneity (2). These suggestions depend for their force on how we interpret the key expression '*x* is predicated *kuriōs* of *y*'. One account on the market is that it singles out complete as opposed to incomplete predicates (Owen [1957]; see also Code [1985], Sec. 3). Suppose that this is right, and that we can in fact use Synonymy to establish that 'man' is predicated *kuriōs* alike of the universal man and of each of the particular men. Even so, this by itself does not seem to be enough to force Plato to accept Homogeneity. By contrast, Aristotle/Alexander's appeal to the notion of *kuriōs* predication may mean to invoke some stronger doctrine: the only obvious candidate is Synonymy and the various notions of synonymous predication that have already been discussed. On the present showing, then, either the notion of *kuriōs* predication is too weak to force acceptance of Homogeneity or it is simply equivalent to Synonymy and the different notions of synonymous predication so that (i) and (ii) in the argument Code sketches collapse into one, and the old difficulties of supporting Homogeneity directly by reference to Synonymy return in full force.

principle of homogeneity also goes along with the abandonment of uniformity *at* a level if, with Aristotle, we stick with Plato's theory for how Socrates is large (he Has largeness) but, contrary to Plato, hold that 'man' applies to Socrates and to man in virtue of exactly the same relation of (metaphysical) predication – both alike Are men. These different changes by themselves would constitute a massive disturbance in the theory of forms – no less a disturbance, perhaps, than the success of the TMA by itself would bring about.

4 Thises and Suches

To this point, apparently, the debate over the TMA is at a stalemate. Plato can accept the principle, Homogeneity, needed for the TMA, only if he is first willing to accept changes in the theory of forms no less far-reaching than those the success of the TMA itself would require. Plato may reasonably argue, then, that the TMA shows only that he is right to resist Homogeneity and that he can with impunity retain his theory unaltered, so long as Homogeneity remains safely at bay. So the TMA does not provide the decisive test in the dispute between Aristotelian and Platonic metaphysics for which Aristotle must have hoped.

Suppose, however, that we were to give Aristotle the benefit of the argument over Homogeneity, so that Plato after all drops the view that sensible particulars Have man and agrees that Socrates and man alike Are men. Granting this, and even supposing that Plato already concedes Univocity and Synonymy, we will still not have sufficient materials to let the TMA go through. Aristotle would concede this point, as we can see from the fact that, in the *Categories,* he himself accepts all three principles for certain classes of predicates. Presumably, he thinks that, even together, the three by themselves can be harmless.

What must be added to obtain a set of principles that are jointly sufficient for the TMA? A tempting candidate, as we have seen, is a principle that is satisfied if sensible particulars and forms alike are *thises:*

Thisness
(1) Each member of a plurality, Π, of sensibles that are men is a this.
(2) For any plurality, Π, of men (of any level), each member of Π and the universal, man, that is "over" Π are all alike thises.

But being a this and being a such are notions proprietary to Aristotle, not Plato; how, then, can Aristotle plausibly attribute Thisness to Plato? Plato is committed to Thisness in Aristotle's eyes, not so much because he has independent grounds of his own for accepting the principle, but because he does not distinguish thises and suches, as

Aristotle does. Aristotle sees a way of using the distinction to block the TMA, so he can plausibly add a principle tantamount to the *rejection* of that distinction to the assumptions needed to get the TMA going. But granted that Plato does not accept the *this–such* distinction, why saddle him with the view that all things are thises, rather than all suches or perhaps even neither? Plato is taken to assume without question Aristotle's own view that sensibles are thises; as in Aristotle's theory, then, Thisness (1) is satisfied. But he rejects the distinction between thises and suches, and in any case, notoriously, as Aristotle sees it, Plato fashions forms after sensibles;[31] it follows that, for Plato, forms too are thises. Unlike Aristotle, then, Plato will also think that Thisness (2) will be satisfied.

Plato's commitment to Thisness, I have argued, is based on his failure to accept Aristotle's distinction between thises and suches. Aristotle sets out his distinction in a passage in *Categories* 5 that fairly reeks of controversy with Plato, even if Plato's name is never directly mentioned.[32] Aristotle's explanations run in terms of his prevailing theory of predication. At 3b10–18, he suggests that primary substances are thises, because they are indivisible and one in number (*atoma kai hen arithmōi*, 3b12). (Items that are indivisible and one in number are the *lowest* members of their respective categories and may be IN a subject, but not SAID OF a subject; *Categories* 2, 1b6–9.) But he corrects the received view (*dokei*, 3b10) that *secondary* substances are also thises. Secondary substances are not one, as primary substances are, but are said of many (*kata pollōn . . . legetai*, 3b17); hence, they are not thises but suches.[33] Later in the chapter, it becomes clear that thises are items that are indivisible and one in number *in the category of substance* (3b17–19).[34] That is, they are the primary substances, and they are not (metaphysically) predicable of a subject at all. Accordingly,

(1) *x* is a this if and only if *x* is indivisible and one in number in the category of substance.

At the same time,

(2) *x* is a such if and only if *x* is not a this.

Socrates and Callias are both indivisible and one in number, hence, both thises; in general, then, Aristotle need have no problem with Thisness (1). Man, however, is said of many – in particular, it is said of

---

31 This is the familiar complaint by Aristotle that Platonic forms just reduplicate sensibles and are introduced simply by adding the prefix '*auto*' to the name of a class of sensibles: *auto*-man, 'man-itself'; *auto*-horse; and the like (*Metaphysics* Z16, 1040b32–4; cf. A9, 990a34–b8).
32 But for a very different reading of the passage, see Furth (1988), pp. 30–3.
33 Contra Furth (1988), pp. 31–2.
34 For the restriction to substance, see *Metaphysics* Z4, 1030a5–6.

Socrates and Callias – hence, it is a such. Now Socrates and Callias make up a plurality ripe for the application of Alex-OM to generate the appropriate universal, man – for short, let us say that they *OM-generate* man, while man is OM-generated from them. It is tempting to think that the distribution of thises and suches in effect in this example holds generally, so that we have the *polarity* principle:

(3) x OM-generates y (and y is OM-generated from x) only if x is a this and y is a such.[35]

Principle (3) runs directly counter to Thisness (2). Its immediate motive comes from a desire to avoid the TMA. Suppose that Socrates and Callias together OM-generate man. By (3), then, Socrates and Callias are both thises, and man is a such. By (3) again, then, these three together cannot themselves OM-generate some further entity, man*.[36]

Plato, however, as Aristotle pictures him, is innocent of the distinction between thises and suches. So he cannot use Aristotle's polarity principle (3) to fend off the TMA. According to Aristotle's Plato, man is OM-generated from Socrates and Callias (say), and all three alike are thises. On this story, Thisness (2) is satisfied, and nothing stands in the way of combining the form man with Socrates and the other sensibles that are men in order to put together the higher-order plurality from which to generate the new form man*.

It is interesting to speculate on the deeper reasons, over and above the immediate exigencies of the TMA, that lead Aristotle to restrict what can OM-generate what in the way the polarity principle (3) demands. I suggest that he may be thinking along the following lines: OM-generators "generate" entities only in the highly attenuated sense that they permit the inference to the existence of some entity. But (i) in Aristotle's own theory, the direction of OM-generation *also reflects the direction of ontological dependence:* where a sensible particular OM-generates something, what is OM-generated is ontologically

---

35 Is (3) a type distinction? To attribute a view of this kind to Aristotle, we would need to know that he was committed not to (3), but to (3*):

(3*) ⌜x OM-generates y⌝ is significant, only if x is a this and y is a such (x and y are of different types).

A theory of types of the kind relevant here has two components: a difference in levels and a *significance assumption* of the kind just set out (see Russell [1903], pp. 517–23, and Copi [1971], pp. 22–4). In the absence of evidence that Aristotle would hold the stronger (3*), it is best not to attribute a doctrine of types to him. (Here I part company with F. Lewis [1985b] and with the provocative views of Penner and Kung recorded in Kung [1981].)

36 It is worth pointing out that to stop the TMA in this way, *any* binary distinction will do, if it can be used to constrain the relation of OM-generation as in (3). For this reason, I will not say anything more about the *content* of the *this–such* distinction itself. The relevance of (3) to the TMA is discussed further in Chapter 2, Section 1.

dependent on what OM-generates it. Socrates, for example, is a *primary* substance in Aristotle's theory, and man and animal, which Socrates helps OM-generate, are both *secondary* substances. So the existence of Socrates and the other sensible particulars that are men underwrites the existence of man in a far more substantial sense than flows from the notion of OM-generation by itself. At the same time (ii) Aristotle also holds that the ontological primacy of the sensible particular in the strong sense in which he intends this demands that the relevant ontological dependencies are all *in one step*. That is, x is ontologically dependent on y only if there is no z such that x is ontologically dependent on z and z is ontologically dependent on y. For example, we cannot mediate the dependence of animal on Socrates and the other particular men by supposing that animal is dependent on man and then pointing to the further dependence of man on Socrates and his fellow men. Both animal and man alike are *directly* dependent on Socrates and the rest, *in one step*. In this way, the doctrine of one-step dependency insists on the absolute dependency of everything other than sensible particulars on the existence of sensible particulars.[37]

Finally, it follows from (i) and (ii) that: (iii) what is OM-generated from something cannot itself be involved in OM-generating something else. In particular, to take the case relevant to the TMA, we cannot first use Socrates and Callias to OM-generate man and then think that Socrates, Callias, and man together are a suitable OM-basis for generating some further entity, man*. For in this case, man* is OM-generated in *two* steps from the sensible particulars that are men, and hence is dependent on them in *two* steps for its own existence. Aristotle's own doctrine of thises and suches prevents the generation of man*; in so doing, it also preserves the principle of one-step ontological dependency central to the metaphysical theory of the *Categories*.[38]

I end this section with a cautionary note about the relation between Aristotle's correction of the received view that man is this and the target of the TMA. On the account I have been suggesting, the TMA can be read as a *reductio* of the assumption that the members of each successive plurality in the argument, of level zero or higher, are all thises. Its target is often stated more narrowly. The difficulty the argument dramatizes is taken to be one exclusively about Platonic forms, which are only a *proper part* of the membership of the pluralities

---

37 Plausibly, one-step ontological dependency is also a precursor of Aristotle's later notion of focal meaning. We shall return to the theme of one-step ontological dependencies in the discussion of the theory of metaphysical predication in the *Categories* in Chapter 2.
38 See the argument in Chapter 2, Section 1.

in the TMA, to the effect that *Platonic forms are thises*.[39] The view that forms are thises is problematic, however, only in the context of one further assumption, that sensibles too are thises. So the objection is not a point about Platonic forms in isolation, but rather about forms and sensibles together and their relation to one another. Plato's mistake is to think that *everything – forms and sensibles alike – is a this*. And strictly, for his argument against Plato to be watertight, Aristotle must be able to show that Plato does not, or better, cannot, adopt *any* binary distinction that will suitably constrain the relation of OM-generation, and so block the TMA.

In this light, the complaint that man is not a this, but a such, suggests that Plato's theory violates the rule, not that

No universal is a this,

but rather that

Nothing is both itself a this and universal *to other thises*.

In the *Categories*, as we shall see, no universal is a this, so that a fortiori, no this is universal to other thises, and the difference between the two principles is no difference at all in that context. The difference between them becomes important, however, when the possibility opens up of an entity that is both a universal and a this, but universal to things that are not themselves thises. In the interpretation I offer in Chapter 11, Aristotle's theory of forms in the *Metaphysics* countenances universals of this sort, which obey the second rule, but not the first. In Aristotle's later theory, then, the difference between the two rules may well be crucial.

5 Self-predication and Nonidentity in the *Categories* and the TMA

In this section, I conclude the account of Aristotle's reactions to the TMA with a look at the very different treatment of the same topics in Owen (1965). Owen attempts to trace some key theses from Aristotle's *Categories* and *Metaphysics* back to what he argues are their origins in Aristotle's reflections on the TMA and its original, the

39 This idea is perhaps encouraged by *Metaphysics* Z13, 1038b34–1039a3: "Nothing predicated universally signifies a this, but a such; otherwise, many absurdities result, in particular, the Third Man"; cf. B6, 1003a7–12. Against this, however, see the fuller statement of the view Aristotle finds objectionable at *SE* 22, 178b36 ff.: "It is not isolation (*ekthesis*) which creates the Third Man, but the admission that it is essentially a this (*to hoper tode ti einai sunchōrein*). For what man is cannot be a this, *as Callias is*" (179a3–5, my emphasis).

Third Largeness Argument, in Plato's *Parmenides*. Following Alexander,[40] he attributes to Aristotle a version of the TMA built around these key premisses:

Self-predication (SP). What is predicated is itself a subject of that same predicate.[41]

Nonidentity (NI). What is predicated . . . is always something different from the subjects of which it is predicated.

According to Owen, these premisses (or their denial) figure prominently both towards the beginning of Aristotle's career in his theorizing about predication in the *Categories* and in his later theory of essence, especially the thesis that each thing is (essentially) the same as its essence in *Metaphysics* Z6. In order to avoid the regress generated by the TMA, Owen argues, Aristotle is careful not to assert both NI and SP jointly. But on Owen's view, Aristotle held that there is no *general* answer to the question Which of NI and SP is false? Instead, there are *two* kinds of predication to be distinguished, based on a division between two kinds of predicate, and each variety of predication takes a different stand on which of the two premisses from the TMA to assert and which to deny.

Aristotle's chief weapon in making the distinction in kinds of predicate with which his theory of predication begins is the notion of synonymy set out in the *Categories*. On the one side, there are predicates like 'man', which "is used in the same sense whether we use it to describe Socrates or to speak of the kind or species under which Socrates falls."[42] In support of this, Owen points to Aristotle's view that the definition of man applies equally well to the particular man Socrates.[43] On the other side, we find the predicate 'white', for example, whose logical behaviour is quite different. If Socrates is white, then he is coloured in a certain way. But white is not white in this same sense. White is not coloured in any way; rather, it is a colour of a certain sort.[44]

The difference between the predicates 'white' and 'man', according to Owen, leads Aristotle to posit a corresponding difference in kinds

40 See notes 3 and 4.
41 The context shows that by 'predicate' here, Owen (1965), p. 134, means 'predicable'. The formulations of SP and NI given here are taken from Owen (1965). Owen does not systematically separate linguistic from metaphysical predication in the way I try to do; since there is no serious danger of confusion, in discussing his views in this section it will be simpler to let the word 'predication' serve for either notion as needed.
42 Ibid., p. 135.
43 Ibid., pp. 135–6. These are the related principles of Univocity and Synonymy from Section 1; see esp. note 21. For univocity, see also Owen (1957), pp. 297–8.
44 Owen (1965), p. 136; cf. Aristotle *Topics* B2, 109a34–b12. Here it seems that Owen's discussion strays from Univocity and Synonymy (see note 43) into Homogeneity.

of predication. In one form of predication, illustrated by 'Socrates is white', SP is not implied, for "white is not white in the sense in which Socrates is white."[45] For the remaining kind of predication, however, 'Socrates is (a) man,' for example, SP does hold: Socrates and man presumably are both men "in the same sense."[46] Ultimately, then, Aristotle will recognize one variety of predication for which SP holds, but not NI (Owen's "strong," or essential, predication), and a second variety for which, conversely, NI holds but SP fails ("weak," or accidental, predication).

The notion of self-predication at work in this account requires some comment. Owen seems to suggest that SP holds for the kind of predication illustrated by 'Socrates is a man' (but not that illustrated by 'Socrates is white'), because (in contrast to the other case) Socrates is a man "in the same sense in which" man is a man. His other comments seem to suggest that "sameness of sense" here must be understood in terms of principles of univocity and synonymy. If this reading of Owen is even approximately correct, then he has moved a good distance away from his official definition of "self-predication" set out in SP.[47]

The *Categories* represents an intermediate stage in the development of Aristotle's theory of predication, according to Owen. Accidental predication is already in place in the *Categories* and is governed by NI and the denial of SP. The theory of essential predication, by contrast, is only partly formed; for although Aristotle is already committed to asserting SP for this kind of predication, he has not yet seen his way to denying NI. Instead, he holds that although man is a man, or an animal, in the same sense in which Socrates is (hence, according to Owen, SP is satisfied),[48] still man is nonidentical with Socrates, but (by way of mitigating the impact of SP) "what is predicated of an individual is not another individual" (p. 135), that is, " 'man' does not stand for any individual thing" (p. 136).

45 Owen (1965), p. 136.
46 What is it for a kind of predication, or for a true sentence exemplifying a given kind of predication, to imply self-predication in the sense relevant here? In the true sentence, 'Socrates is a man', we can replace the subject term 'Socrates' by a second occurrence of the general term 'man' occurring in the predicate to produce another true sentence: 'Man is a man'. Loosely speaking, the context ' . . . is a man' is to be understood in the same way in both sentences: the exact force of "understood in the same way" will be spelled out later in this section. Suppose now that we use the same method to obtain from the true sentence 'Socrates is white' the new sentence 'White is white'. If this second sentence is true, we will not understand the context ' . . . is white' here in the same way as in the original sentence. That is, self-predication is *not* implied.
47 For the appeal to univocity and synonymy here, see note 43, and on further shifts in Owen's notion of self-predication, see the upcoming discussion in the main text.
48 But this is manifestly not the official notion set out previously in Owen's SP, given the nonidentity between Socrates and man.

By the time that *Metaphysics Zeta* was written, however, Aristotle has dropped his earlier doubts about the status of man in favour of the view that the subject of an essential predication and the essence that is asserted of it are the same: that is, according to Owen, he has now come to deny NI for this variety of predication. This move in turn forces a revision in his view of what can be a subject of an essential predication of this canonical sort – not an individual, Socrates or Callias (say), for these apparently share their essence, and two things that are the same as the same essence must be themselves the same. Instead, the appropriate subject within the new theory of essential predication, in Owen's view, will be the species, for example, man, which has its essence uniquely. In this way, according to Owen, the species threatens to supplant the individual substance of the *Categories* as the primary subject of discourse.[49]

Owen's hypotheses regarding the influence of the TMA on Aristotle's own theories of predication are subject to an immediate difficulty if we are to take Owen's NI and SP *au pied de la lettre* as transcriptions of what Aristotle took to be the premises of the TMA. In the reconstruction Owen has in mind, the regress is thought to follow from the assumption that the predication relation is nonempty, that is, that something is predicated of something – call this assumption "P" – together with the two principles, SP and NI, that govern the predication relation. It is easily shown that the premiss-set {P, SP, NI} is inconsistent,[50] and hence capable of generating any conclusion whatever. This result trivializes the inference to an infinite sequence of forms for which the TMA argues. Clearly, NI, SP, and P cannot jointly be true – not, however, because they permit the inference to an infinite sequence of forms, but because they form an inconsistent set, and so supply an inference to any conclusion whatever.

In fact, however, Aristotle does seem to regard the Third Man regress as a significant result. Arguably, Aristotle himself was unaware of, or if aware of it, indifferent to, the objection that {P, SP, NI} is an inconsistent set. Alternatively, and I think preferably, he had in mind a premiss-set for the argument that is different from the one Owen proposes.[51]

49 But I would not agree that the species, as opposed to the species-form, is a candidate for primary substance in the *Metaphysics;* see Chapters 6 and 7.
50 Owen (1965), p. 134, says that NI and SP are incompatible; he does not notice that we must also add P to obtain an inconsistent set. He also fails to see that if the premiss-set for the TMA is inconsistent in this way, then both the TMA itself and the programme of building an account of Aristotle's philosophical development upon it become pointless, in the sense explained in the main text.
51 In his account of Plato's original argument, Vlastos (1954) gives a version of the self-predication and nonidentity assumptions that also forms an inconsistent set, and claims that these are *required* for the argument; this idea is effectively criticized in Cohen (1971), pp. 451–2; see also Geach (1956). An early attempt to supply a

Along the same lines, there is also a difficulty for the version of "strong" or essential predication that Owen finds in the interim theory in the *Categories*. For according to Owen, Aristotle sees that SP and NI (strictly, with the addition of P) form an inconsistent set, yet on Owen's account, Aristotle asserts SP for this variety of predication, but he has not yet seen his way to denying NI. Perhaps, however, the right conclusion is that Owen does not have exactly the same notion of "self-predication" in mind in his discussion of the TMA and in his account of Aristotle's own theory in the *Categories*.[52] In the remainder of this section, I look in more detail at Owen's SP and NI in turn and ask whether they are suited to play the role Owen sees for them in the debate between Plato and Aristotle over the philosophical consequences of the TMA.

Self-predication

What evidence is there that Owen's SP genuinely belongs in the version of the TMA derived from Alexander? If we check the account of Alexander's argument given in Section 1, it may seem that SP appears in clause (1) in the consequent of Alex-OM and that it will also appear by detachment as a line in the main body of the argument. As Code correctly argues, SP is not present in the argument in even this way.[53] Suppose there exists a plurality, Π, of objects that are men. Then, by Alex-OM, there is an X that is a man and that is predicable of each member of Π. All we know from Alex-OM is that there is a true sentence of the form 'Man is (a) man' – but Alex-OM tells us nothing about how such sentences are to be *interpreted*. As it turns out, some constraints on how we are to understand a syntactic self-predication will yield a logically vicious result; others, however, would make the result wholly benign. For example, if man Is (a) man, as Aristotle himself holds, it is not clear that this is logically vicious. (I argue in Chapter 2 that instances of metaphysical self-predication of this kind are in fact harmless.)[54] There is the additional difficulty already noted

consistent premiss-set for Plato's argument appears in Sellars (1955) (reprinted in Sellars [1967]) (other early attempts are in Geach [1956] and Strang ([1963] 1971)), with replies from Vlastos (1955, 1969) (the latter appears in revised form in Vlastos [1973]): while Vlastos's formulation of the argument has changed in these different places, his conviction that the argument has an inconsistent premiss-set apparently has not.

52 Code (1985) also points out that Owen's account portrays Aristotle in the *Categories* as committed simultaneously to both SP and NI for "strong," or intracategorial, predication. See also G. Fine (1982), p. 20. For the possible shifts in Owen's notion of "self-predication," see the discussion later in the main text.

53 Code (1985), p. 106.

54 For a benign interpretation of syntactic self-predications, compare the notion of *Pauline* Predications due to Peterson (1973).

that Owen's SP conflicts with the nonidentity assumption. SP, then, cannot be the same as Alex-OM (1), which requires only that where Socrates and man are men, both are men in virtue of one and the same form, man* – leaving it open whether or not man* is identical with man.

Finally, Owen says that SP constitutes a logically vicious notion of self-predication, and also that Aristotle himself accepts SP for strong predication in the *Categories*. But what is logically pernicious for Plato must also be so for Aristotle; unless, then, Aristotle and Plato are to be tarred with the same brush, Owen must have *different* notions of self-predication in mind in the two cases. Once these different treatments are in place, any story that sees the TMA and the theory of the *Categories* as successive stages in a debate over SP is in severe danger of unravelling.

In fact, however, it is questionable whether Aristotle need attribute to Plato anything approaching a notion of vicious self-predication in pressing the TMA against him. Vicious self-predication is, presumably, the view that, for example, man Has itself: vicious self-predication is self-*participation*.[55] But it is unlikely that Plato can be held to such a view, for two reasons. First, as we have reconstructed the controversy between Plato and Aristotle, a crucial step in the TMA is for Plato to accept Homogeneity and to accede to Aristotle's view that Socrates and man alike *Are* men. Far from attributing self-participation to him, Aristotle is inviting Plato to *give up* the theory of participation or Having altogether as an account of how either Socrates or man can *be* (a) man. Second, as we have seen, by the nonidentity assumption, no account of how man is a man can be constructed in terms of a relation between man *and itself*.

On the present account, the version of the TMA in Alexander shows no trace of the narrow notion of self-predication captured by Owen's SP. Yet Owen also uses the term 'self-predication' for various notions that are quite different from what is spelled out in his SP. Perhaps, then, there is some other notion of self-predication that is after all present in the version of the TMA in Alexander and that also falls under Aristotle's scrutiny in the *Categories*.

Looking beyond Owen's SP, then, we should try to find some alternative characterization of self-predication often attributed to Plato and thought to figure in the TMA. Informally, self-predication commits the fault of assimilating the logic appropriate to the universal man to that suitable for particular men: it treats the form man as just "one more for the census-takers to count."[56] The starting point for such a view is undoubtedly something like Alexander's requirement in

55 Cf. Code (1986), pp. 419 ff.   56 White (1971a), p. 167; cf. Owen (1968), p. 117.

Alex-PL, that the members of the pluralities the TMA requires must all be *alike* in some suitable way. Thus, if Socrates and man are members of a plurality because both are men, the predicate 'man' must have the same sense in both occurrences (Univocity) and the same definition (Synonymy); again, the two subjects, Socrates and man, must both *be* men in the same sense of 'is' (Homogeneity), and must both be thises (Thisness). Owen's own notion of self-predication often wanders beyond the official notion in SP to take in one or more of these conditions. In some places, his notion of self-predication is apparently based on Univocity and Synonymy alone.[57] Sometimes he adds Homogeneity; for example, he describes a "paradeigmatic" form as "logically on a par with *other members of the class.*"[58] That is, the same predicative link, in this case, class membership, explains both how Socrates is a man and how man itself is a man.[59] Still elsewhere, Owen takes Plato's notion of self-predication to include Thisness as well.[60]

I suspect that it is more misleading than helpful to use the term 'self-predication' for different combinations of these various notions. If we set aside the issue of self-predication, we can think of the debate between Plato and Aristotle over the TMA in terms of two focal points, Homogeneity and Thisness. Aristotle and Plato agree that man Is (a) man. But Aristotle accepts Homogeneity and argues that Socrates too Is (a) man. Meanwhile, notably, Plato holds that Socrates Has man and is resistant to Homogeneity. If Aristotle is to use the TMA successfully against Plato, he must suppose that Plato changes his mind on both points: that he gives up his view that Socrates Has man, thus clearing the way to also dropping his resistance to Homogeneity. Once these concessions are in place, Aristotle is in a position to portray the disagreement with Plato as one over the remaining principle, Thisness.

On the account I have given, SP itself has no role in Aristotle/ Alexander's version of the TMA. As far as wider conceptions of "self-predication" are concerned, a *syntactic* or *linguistic* notion of self-predication enters the argument by way of Alex-OM (1). Beyond this, self-predication in any substantive sense has no place in the argument. Various other principles, however – Univocity, Synonymy, Homogeneity, Thisness – do in one way or another contribute to fleshing out Alexander's *similarity* condition on sensible particulars and universals in Alex-PL. These principles form the common ground Owen was looking for between the TMA and Aristotle's own theorizing in the *Categories*.

57 See note 43.   58 Owen (1968), p. 117; my emphasis.
59 For other places where Owen endorses this view, see the references in G. Fine (1982), n. 13.
60 E.g., Owen (1968), p. 109, n. 1.

Nonidentity

I have been sceptical whether Owen's SP represents any common ground between the version of the TMA reported by Alexander and Aristotle's own views in the *Categories*. A connection between the nonidentity assumption that Owen finds at work in the TMA and the thesis of *Metaphysics* Z6 is equally unlikely. According to Owen, Aristotle sees that SP and NI cannot be true together. Ultimately, he concludes that there is one kind of predication for which NI is true and SP false, and another for which SP is true and NI false. The rejection of NI for this second kind of predication, according to Owen, leads to the thesis in *Metaphysics* Z6 that each thing is the same as its essence.

An immediate objection concerns the relevance of SP to the repudiation of NI. As we have seen, the notion of self-predication that, according to Owen, Aristotle accepts in the *Categories* and elsewhere is apparently quite different from the notion that, on Owen's account, Aristotle finds at work in the TMA. If the thesis of self-predication changes its meaning in this way, then Aristotle himself cannot have the same motivation for denying NI in his own theory that a philosopher would have who accepted SP as the correct formulation of the notion of self-predication at work in the TMA and who reasoned that self-predication so understood and NI could not both be true.

Other objections have to do with the move from rejecting NI to embracing the sameness thesis of Z6. Owen perhaps reasons as follows. Given the thought that (i) the essence of a thing is (metaphysically) predicated of that very same thing, and supposing too that (ii) where one thing is predicated of another they must be identical, contrary to NI, it follows that (iii) a thing and its essence will be identical. An initial criticism is due to Code. Step (ii) in this argument makes a mistake over the form the denial of NI will take. If NI is false, then it is *not* the case that what is predicated is *always* something different from the subject of which it is predicated. But for the argument I am imagining Owen has in mind, we need rather the assumption that for the variety of predication in question, what is predicated is *never* something different from the subject of which it is predicated. The negation of NI is simply too weak to express this, and to suppose that Aristotle thought otherwise is to have him confuse 'not . . . always' and 'never'.[61]

---

61 A similar objection holds against Owen's claim that Plato himself held NI to avoid the result that if Socrates and Plato are both men, and each is the same as man, then each is the same as the other, which is absurd. To keep clear of this result, Plato needs only something much weaker than NI, namely, the assumption that for any sensible x and form y, y is predicated of x only if x is not identical with y. Cf. G. Fine (1982), p. 16.

There is in any case no support for the other premiss, (i), in the argument I attribute to Owen. The sameness thesis in *Metaphysics* Z6 is surrounded by chapters that contain a notion of (metaphysical) predication radically different from the notion in the *Categories,* where according to Owen NI is first formulated. In the *Metaphysics,* exactly two cases of (metaphysical) predication are primitive in Aristotle's theory: either an accident is (metaphysically) predicated of a substance, or a form is (metaphysically) predicated of (a portion of) matter.[62] If these are the only two cases of (metaphysical) predication there are, then in contrast to (i), an essence *is not (metaphysically) predicated of that of which it is the essence:*

x is (metaphysically) predicated of y only if x is not the essence of y.

For, an accident is not the essence of a substance of which it is (metaphysically) predicated, and a form is not the essence of the matter of which it is (metaphysically) predicated. It follows that the mature notion of (metaphysical) predication at work in the *Metaphysics* is simply *irrelevant* to the relation between a primary substance and its essence. In the absence of (i), considerations about whether what is predicated is or is not identical with its subject have no implications for the Z6 thesis of the identity of a thing with its essence.

Why should anyone think that, contrary to what is argued here, an essence is after all (metaphysically) predicated of that of which it is the essence? Part of the difficulty may be a confusion between metaphysical and linguistic predication. From the fact that an essence can be linguistically predicated of that of which it is the essence, it does not follow that there exists a relation of metaphysical predication between an essence and that of which it is the essence. There is no need to introduce this additional variety of (metaphysical) predication on Aristotle's behalf in order to explain the relevant linguistic predications: the relation in question is simply the familiar essence-of relation.[63] Suppose, however, that Aristotle had been willing to recognize some broader notion of metaphysical predication, such that an essence can after all be (metaphysically) predicated of a primary substance. The claim that an essence is not predicated of that of which it is the essence was formulated in terms of the *primary* notion of (metaphysical) predication; such claims are neither contradicted nor confirmed by properties that hold of some *other,* secondary notion of (metaphysical) predication.[64] By the same token, the controversy over NI and the

---

62 This account of Aristotle's theory of predication in the *Metaphysics* is defended at length in Chapter 7.

63 Here I part company with Code (1985). The properties of the essence-of and various associated relations are discussed in detail in F. Lewis (1984).

64 The admissible varieties of predication, primary and secondary, relevant here are discussed in Chapter 7.

various claims and counterclaims about whether what is predicated is or is not identical with its subject were formulated in terms of the primary notion of (metaphysical) predication. So the introduction of a fresh variety of predication has no bearing on that controversy, and does nothing to connect any change of heart over NI with the alleged conclusion of the sameness of a thing with its essence.

I turn next to some more general difficulties with Owen's view of the relation between the rejection of NI and the sameness thesis in *Metaphysics* Z6. Far from having its roots in the debate with Plato under way in the *Categories*, as Owen suggests, the Z6 thesis is in an important sense quite distant from the anti-Platonism of the *Categories*. By way of underlining this, I argue that the sameness conclusion from Z6 suggests a new criticism of Plato, unconnected with the TMA, that is inimical not only to the Platonic theory of forms, but also to Aristotle's own theory in the *Categories*.

The actual argument Aristotle offers for the Z6 thesis at *Metaphysics* Z6, 1031b28–1032a2, does not invoke the threat of the TMA, but rests instead on a network of principles governing essence, definition, and substance that takes us well beyond the conceptual resources of the *Categories*. While the thesis itself is very close in content to a principle governing definition stated already in the *Topics* (but not the *Categories*), the argument in Z6 takes a surprisingly circuitous route to its conclusion, taking in not only the notion of a thing's essence, but notions of the substance and the definition of a thing as well.[65] Notably, the *Categories* shows no sign of the notion of the substance *of* a thing.[66] Similarly, the notion of essence does not appear in the

65 Code has argued convincingly that the sameness thesis of *Metaphysics* Z6 follows from materials already present in the *Topics* (Code [1985, Section (IV)(A)]). But the thesis cannot be formulated within the conceptual apparatus expressly given in the *Categories*. On this point, then, as on others (examples are given immediately ahead in the main text and in note 66), the *Topics* lines up more with the *Metaphysics* than with the *Categories*, despite the fact that in other ways the *Categories* and the *Topics* are closer to one another than they are to the *Metaphysics*. Aristotle's actual argument in Z6 is discussed at length in Code (1985), pp. 119 ff., and in F. Lewis (1985a), pp. 17 ff.

66 The notion of the substance *of* a thing is fundamental to the theory in the central books of the *Metaphysics*, where Aristotle adds to the question 'What is substance?' the further question 'What is the *substance of* a thing?' and sees in the notion of the substance of a thing the proper clue to his earlier questions about *primary* substance. This is not to deny that a comparable notion appears elsewhere in the *Organon*, outside the *Categories*: see, e.g., *Topics* Z8, 146b3–4; *An. Po.* A3, 73a35, A33, 89a19–20, B4, 91b7–9, B6, 92a6, 34–5, B7, 92b12–14, B9, 93b26, B13, 96a34–5, b6, and 97a12–14. Like most scholars, however, I suppose that the notions of matter and form of a thing do not appear in the *Organon*, so that the notions of the substance or essence of a thing at work in these passages are quite different from their counterparts later in the *Metaphysics*.

Categories – although it does appear elsewhere in the *Organon*, for example, in the definition at *Topics* H3, 153a15–22 – which knows only to ask the question, *ti estin*, What is it?, of a thing.

Aristotle's notion of the substance *of* a thing, conspicuously absent from the *Categories*, brings out the real anti-Platonic thrust of the Z6 thesis. At the same time, the criticism of Plato that the thesis implies will work with equal effect against Aristotle's own views in the *Categories*.

Aristotle's thesis that each thing is (essentially) the same as its essence takes its start from the fundamental question 'What is substance?' or 'What are the substances?' He and Plato disagree over Plato's answer: Platonic forms. Given Plato's answer, however, if Platonic forms are the substances, we must be able to say what they are the substances *of* (here, quite clearly Aristotle is speaking the language of his own, post-*Categories* theory of substance). The answer he gives on Plato's behalf is that Platonic forms are the substances of their participants. This answer, even more than the question, is dubiously faithful to Platonic theory. Participation, construed as a relation of Having, is a relation that holds only *accidentally* between a sensible and a form, when it holds at all.[67] But a predicable cannot be both accidental to and also the substance of the subject on which it supervenes. Aristotle in places removes this difficulty by supposing that, in certain cases, participation holds *non*accidentally between a subject and a form,[68] so that a form can after all be the substance of a sensible. This now leaves Plato open to attack by means of the sameness thesis from Z6. If a thing and its essence or substance are (essentially) the same, and a form is the substance of the thing, it follows that form and thing are identical. But of course, no form is identical with any sensible.

It may seem that this objection can be deflected by a move Aristotle is perfectly ready to permit within his own theory. In Z6, Aristotle expressly notes that, if his sameness thesis is true, a Platonic form and its essence will be essentially the same (1031a28–b3): that is, I take it,

---

67 The accidental character of the relation is even more evident when it is reinterpreted in the *Timaeus* as a relation between a given region of space and the likeness of a form that supervenes on it. *Metaphysics* Z4, 1030a13–14, seems to agree that participation is an accidental relation. See also Cohen (1978), p. 82.

68 *Metaphysics* M5, 1080a1 (*hai ideai ousiai tōn pragmatōn ousai*); cf. A6, 988a8–11 (*ta gar eidē tou ti estin aitiai tois allois*, a10–11), A7, 988b4–5 (*alla to ti ēn einai hekastōi tōn allōn ta eidē parechontai*). Possibly the same point is involved in the controversial passage at A9, 990b27–34; see Alexander's comment and the parallel passage at M4, 1079a24–33. At M5, 1079b15–17, Aristotle argues that the claim that forms are the substances of sensibles cannot be sustained. And some of the arguments in Z14 take Plato to task on the related idea that certain forms are the substance of other forms ("the form man is not *accidentally* composed of animal," 1039b7–9, 9–10, 12–13, 15–16); Aristotle remarks at the end of the chapter that similar arguments apply to the relation between forms and sensibles.

the form has *itself* as its substance. Given this result, however, Plato can argue in a way Aristotle himself is quite willing to do in similar circumstances within his own theory, that the form is the substance of the sensibles that participate in it in only a reduced sense of 'substance of', for which the sameness result does not hold.

Arguably, Plato's theory does not leave room for this response. If the Platonic form, man (say), is the substance of Socrates, then not only is it the case, as always, that man Is a man, but also Socrates Is a man. It seems to follow that man is the substance of Socrates and the substance of itself *in the same sense of 'substance of'*. So Aristotle's sameness result should hold in both cases, if it holds at all.

If this reasoning is good against Plato, however, it will be good against *any* view that holds both that man is the substance of Socrates and that Socrates and man alike Are men. On any such view, man will be the substance of Socrates and of itself in the same sense of 'substance of', so that, by the sameness result in Z6, man and Socrates are identical. In the *Categories*, strikingly, Aristotle argues that, in fact, Socrates and man alike both Are; this by itself, then, gives him a motive for excluding as he does the notion of the substance *of* a thing from the theory of the *Categories*. If this is right, however, it is hard to think that the Z6 thesis, which Aristotle argues for by reference to notions of the substance or essence or definition of a thing, can have its origins in a strategy for evading the TMA that began life in the philosophical environment of the *Categories*.

A final point can be mentioned only briefly here. Despite its central role in the debate over the Platonic theory of forms, I shall argue later that the TMA is flatly irrelevant to the theory of Aristotelian form in the *Metaphysics*. To the extent that Plato has an interest in fending off the TMA in the *Metaphysics*, it is in order to protect a theory of kinds. But on the account I shall offer, Aristotelian forms are not kinds, and unlike kinds, they are not (metaphysically) predicated of individual substances. The details of this story are given in Chapter 11, Section 6.

2

Primacy and Dependence in
Aristotle's *Categories*

In this chapter, I focus less on Aristotle's dispute with Plato, which was the subject of Chapter 1, and concentrate more on the details of Aristotle's own account of metaphysical predication in the *Categories*. I shall suppose that the *Categories* presents in a more or less informal, even unsystematic, way what is in reality a *theory* of (metaphysical) predication, which can be reconstructed relatively formally. The advantages of a formal presentation of Aristotle's views are partly those of clarity: once his views are set out formally as a theory, we can see more perspicuously how different components of his views are related logically to one another. But the formalism will also strengthen the account I shall offer for the *motivation* for Aristotle's views. In the *Categories*, Aristotle argues for the central place of *individual substances* in his metaphysical scheme – the idea that individual substances are the *primary* substances, while (as I understand him) everything else in his categorial scheme exists thanks to relations of *one-step ontological dependency* on primary substances. The notion of one-step ontological dependencies gives a quite strict sense to Aristotle's conclusions about the primacy of primary substances. His arguments for primacy in this strong form draw on the theory of (metaphysical) predication. In particular, I argue, the real work in his arguments is done by two core notions of (metaphysical) predication that are at the same time relations of one-step ontological dependency. But to establish that the relevant one-step dependencies in fact exist and can perform as promised, we must be able to define those cases of (metaphysical) predication that do *not* obviously involve a primary substance as subject, in terms of (metaphysical) predications that *do* have a primary substance as their subject. Nothing short of producing the actual definitions will carry conviction here, and this (relatively formal) task is undertaken in Section 4 towards the end of the chapter.

The argument in the main body of the chapter, however, will be largely informal. I begin in Section 1 with one-step ontological dependence and argue that the concept has application outside the *Categories* in the context of the TMA, which as we have seen for Aristotle plays a starring role in the dispute between a Platonic and an Aristotelian metaphysics. In Section 2, I give a quick sketch of the general outline of Aristotle's theory in the *Categories*. This clears the way for the main business of the chapter in Section 3, which takes up Aristotle's dictum "Primary substances are subjects for everything else." This *monolithic* view of the subject of (metaphysical) predication forms the backbone of the argument for two theses about the primacy of individual substances in Aristotle's scheme. First, individual substances are subjects to everything else, because they are subjects to two core notions of metaphysical predication: *without individual substances as subjects for the core relations of (metaphysical) predication, (metaphysical) predication would not be possible at all.* Second, the core relations of (metaphysical) predication are also relations of one-step ontological dependency. Accordingly, without individual substances as subjects for the core relations of (metaphysical) predication, nothing else would exist: *things other than individual substances exist only because they stand in relations of ontological dependency on individual substances, in one step.* These two theses require a quite specific view of (metaphysical) predication; the formal theory that underlies this view is presented in Section 4. In the Appendix, I contrast my reconstruction of Aristotle's theory with the quite different accounts in Ackrill and Furth.

1   One-Step Ontological Dependency and the TMA

A well-known pair of arguments in Plato's *Parmenides* suggests an attack against Plato's theory of forms along the following lines. Suppose that on the Platonic account,

(1) Socrates is large *because R* (Socrates, largeness) and largeness is large.

The relation R is some relation or other of *ontological dependence* and is brought to life most vividly perhaps in the Copy Theory first set out in the middle dialogues; the Ingredience or Inherence Theory offers a different account of R but, again, one consistent with the idea that largeness is ontologically prior to Socrates.[1] Given (1), parity of reasoning suggests that

(2) Largeness is large *because R* (largeness, largeness*) (largeness ≠ largeness*) and largeness* is large,

---

1 The priority is less obvious in the Ingredience Theory. But on this theory, the form largeness that is in Socrates will be prior to him insofar as, in general, Platonic forms are *causes* and presumably (not just equal to but) *greater than* their effect. For the causal principles at stake here, see Lloyd (1976).

and so on ad infinitum. Plato has an easy response to the argument in this form. Sensibles stand in a very different relation to their predicables from the relation that joins a form with its predicables; in the jargon of Grice and Code, sensibles Have their various predicables, while invariably forms Are what they are. Accordingly, Socrates Has largeness, but largeness Is large, and the account of how Socrates is large in (1) cannot be appropriated to explain how largeness is large, as (2) attempts to do.

This is not where things rest. One of the innovations of Aristotle's *Categories* is to invite us to think that Socrates Is (a) man, rather than Has man, as Plato would have it. So if we grant the basic apparatus of the *Categories* and choose the right example, the regress threatens once more:

(3) Socrates Is a man *because* R (Socrates, man) and man Is a man,
(4) Man Is a man *because* R (man, man*) (man ≠ man*) and man* Is a man,

and so on ad infinitum.

This revamped argument is made possible by the new environment of Aristotelian metaphysics. If the argument is effective, there is the danger that if Aristotle is not careful, he will find himself standing together with Plato in the same line of fire. There is no comfort to be had here from the thought that Aristotle's and Plato's metaphysics are after all so different from the start that an argument that works against Plato could not possibly have any purchase against Aristotle. Suppose, minimally, that R is the relation of what I shall call "OM-generation" ("O" for "one," "M" for "many"). This is the relation that holds when we infer from the existence of members of a given many to that of the relevant one "over" that many. If both Socrates and Callias are large, for example, they each OM-generate the one, largeness; if both are men, they OM-generate the one, man. OM-generation by itself carries no particular implications about the metaphysical *status* of the one – man, largeness, and the rest – hence, OM-generation is a notion Aristotle himself need not find problematic.[2] But if this is so, how will Aristotle protect himself against the following moves?

(5) If Socrates and Callias alike Are men, they OM-generate man, which Is a man,
(6) If Socrates, Callias, and man alike Are men, then they OM-generate man* (man ≠ man*), which Is a man,

and so on ad infinitum.

Remarks in the *Categories* and elsewhere suggest that Aristotle sees a way out of this argument that he thinks Plato denies himself. The

2 On this point, compare the remarks about the "logically hygienic" use of *para* in White (1971a).

key move is to require that one of the two terms on either side of the relation of OM-generation be a *this,* the other, a *such.* Whatever this proposal means in detail, it follows immediately that we cannot set up "chains" of OM-generation with more than two members. If x OM-generates y, and y in turn OM-generates z, then y will be *both* a this *and* a such, which Aristotle assumes is impossible.[3] The point here is purely formal and does not require any particular account of the *content* of being a this or being a such. *Any* binary distinction like that between thises and suches is capable of stopping the TMA and its congeners dead in their tracks, after just one step.

Aristotle concedes, I think, that much the same way out could have been available to Plato, even with a different reading of the relation R, if only Plato had gone along with the *this–such* distinction. For a good Platonic reading of R, let R be the relation of ontological dependency. Suppose further that the relation is subject to the following condition:

(*) x is ontologically dependent on y, only if y is a this and x is a such.

It follows immediately by the same reasoning as before that there are no chains of ontological dependency with more than two members: it cannot be the case that x is ontologically dependent on y and y is ontologically dependent on z. So even if Socrates is ontologically dependent on man, there cannot be a further form, man*, such that man in turn is ontologically dependent on man*.[4]

Without protection of this kind from the *this–such* distinction, according to Aristotle, the TMA goes through against the Platonic theory of forms along the lines begun in (3) and (4). On this showing, Socrates is ontologically dependent on man, and man in turn is onto-logically dependent on man*, and so on ad infinitum. The extension to infinity gives the argument its drama, but the first two steps of the argument by themselves do sufficient damage to Plato's theory. If x is ontologically dependent on y and y is dependent on z, then by transi-tivity, presumably, x will be ontologically dependent on z. The depen-dency of x on z will be *in two steps:* the dependency by x on z is mediated by the fact that x is dependent on y, and y in turn dependent on z. This contradicts what one might reasonably expect from Plato's theory of

3 For the argument here, see Chapter 1, Section 4.
4 I have suggested that *any* binary distinction will do in order to save Plato from the TMA; for this reason, if there are doubts about which of forms and sensibles are thises according to Plato, and which are suches, we can without penalty substitute this variant for the principle (*) in the main text:

(**) x is ontologically dependent on y, only if exactly one of x and y is a this and exactly one a such;

or more noncommittally still, if the *this–such* distinction is not exhaustive as well as mutually exclusive,

(***) x is ontologically dependent on y, only if *either* one of x and y is a this and the other is not, *or* one is a such and the other is not.

forms, that where a sensible is ontologically dependent on a given form, the priority of the form relative to the sensible should be *absolute:* its priority should not be diluted by the existence of some second, intermediate form, such that the sensible is dependent on the second form and it in turn is dependent on the form with which we began.

The strictures of the preceding paragraph revolve around a notion of one-step ontological dependency:

> **One-step ontological dependency.** x is ontologically dependent on y in one step, only if there is no z such that x is ontologically dependent on z and z is ontologically dependent on y.

What is troubling about the TMA at bottom is the violation of one-step ontological dependency. Plato's theory requires that Socrates be ontologically dependent on man; but Plato cannot allow that man in turn is ontologically dependent on man*, so that Socrates is ontologically dependent at two removes on man*. If the argument gets this far, it can be reiterated ad infinitum, so that Socrates is ontologically dependent on infinitely many entities at infinitely many removes. But even the first violation of one-step ontological dependency fundamentally weakens Plato's theory.

Finally, it is worth emphasizing the argument of three paragraphs back that if Aristotle accepts a tie between ontological dependency and the *this–such* distinction along the lines of the principle (*), this by itself will commit him to the view that all ontological dependencies must be in one step.[5]

In this section, I have argued that the result of the TMA is objectionable because it violates a principle of one-step ontological dependency. If this is right, it is not out of the question that in setting out his own views in the *Categories,* Aristotle should want to devise a theory that *observes* one-step dependency. Before we move to the issue of one-step dependency in the *Categories,* however, it will be useful first to make some remarks about the general shape of Aristotle's metaphysical theory there. This is the subject of the next section.

2 Some Generalities about the Metaphysical Theory of the *Categories*

One of Aristotle's major tools in the *Categories* is the distinction between the relations 'x is SAID OF y' and 'x is IN y'. The two relations are

---

5 Again, for this point see also the argument in Chapter 1, Section 4. Notice that even if Aristotle is committed to the principle (*), he cannot think that it is the *definition* of a this that it is the basis entity in relations of ontological dependence. In *Metaphysics* Z3, Aristotle argues that the end product of *aphairesis*, namely, prime matter, cannot be (primary) substance on the grounds that it is not *chōriston* or a this (see Chapter 10); if priority were built into the definition of being a this, this argument would simply beg the question.

introduced abruptly in *Categories* 2, where they are used to distinguish among four different kinds of "things that are" (*tōn ontōn,* 1a20). Where *x* is a thing that is, Aristotle tells us, either

(i) *x* is SAID OF something, but not IN anything,

or

(ii) *x* is IN something, but not SAID OF anything,

or

(iii) *x* is SAID OF something and also IN something

(here, as it turns out, invariably *x* is IN and SAID OF *different* things), or finally,

(iv) *x* is neither IN nor SAID OF anything.

In the course of drawing up these four classes, Aristotle gives a brief and largely negative explanation of the relation '*x* is IN *y*' ("By what is in a subject, I mean what is in something not as a part, and cannot exist separately from what it is in," a24–5). At the beginning of the next chapter and in chapter 5, he discusses the SAID-OF relation in somewhat greater detail,[6] and at 5, 3a33–b9, he connects it with the notion of synonymy defined in *Categories* 1. Following this, and after introducing the theory of categories in chapter 4, in chapter 5 he finally connects the fourth of the four classes distinguished in chapter 2 with the primary members of the category of substance:[7] primary substances are those entities that are neither SAID OF nor IN any subject. Secondary substances are introduced in terms of the primary ones: secondary substances are the species or genera of the primary substances. Alternatively, secondary substances belong to the first class specified in *Categories,* chapter 2: each is SAID OF, but not IN, a subject. All else, finally, is IN some subject and belongs to one of the nonsubstance categories (classes (ii) and (iii)).

It quickly becomes clear that the IN and SAID OF relations are varieties of what I have been calling *metaphysical predication.* As before, metaphysical predication is a relation between items in the ontology:

---

6   *Categories* 3, 1b10–15, 5, 2a19–27, 3a17–20, a25–8 (on differentiae), and especially 3a33–b9; see also *Topics* Δ3, 123a28–9, Δ5, 127b6–7, H4, 154a16–18. This may be the point to notice that with the exception of *Topics* Δ5, 127b1–4, the distinction between the IN and SAID-OF relations does not reappear outside the *Categories;* cf. Owen (1965), p. 97. Arguably, however, Aristotle's distinction between *kath' hauto* and *kata sumbebēkos* predication does the same work; cf. Code (1985), n. 8, and (1986), p. 414. On the issues involved here, see the further references in Benson (1988), nn. 13 and 14.

7   Here I follow the traditional view and set aside Frede's ([1981] 1987) doubts about whether Aristotle's account in the *Categories* recognizes a category of substance.

between a metaphysical subject, Socrates (say), and – not a predicate (a linguistic item), but – a predicable, man (say) or pallor, without quotation marks. This is in contrast to *linguistic* predication, where what is predicated is a linguistic item – a grammatical predicate.[8] By "predication" here, I continue to mean *metaphysical* predication, unless I expressly say otherwise.[9]

Aristotle himself does not explicitly draw the distinction between metaphysical and linguistic predication. He is also silent, therefore, on how the two kinds of predication are related. In fact, it is easy to suppose that the theory of metaphysical predication is intended to supply the metaphysical underpinnings for various forms of linguistic predication. In particular, as we shall see, his theory of metaphysical predication is concerned primarily to give the metaphysical configurations that underlie sentences of these two kinds:

(7) Socrates is pale,
(8) Socrates is (a) man.

If (7) is true, then pallor is IN Socrates or, as I shall also say (borrowing again the convenient terminology of Code and Grice), Socrates Has pallor. If (8) is true, then man is SAID OF Socrates, equivalently in the Code–Grice jargon, Socrates Is (a) man.

Once the connection is made between (7) and (8) and the corresponding metaphysical predications, the analysis of various other linguistic predications also falls into place, for example, 'Man is (an) animal', 'Man is pale', and 'Pallor is (a) colour'; I will return to the details of this story later. But one complication should be noted now. As we shall see, there are different cases of the IN relation, and among these, one is primitive and the others are defined in terms of it. The IN relation, with uppercase letters, is the *generic* relation and is defined in terms of its various subrelations. If (7) is true, for example, then

8 For metaphysical predication and the distinction between it and linguistic predication, see the Introduction to this part. As we saw there (note 4), the subject of a linguistic predication can be either a linguistic item or an item in the ontology; but the subject of a metaphysical predication will always be an ontological, and never a linguistic, item.

9 The moves back and forth between a linguistic and a metaphysical notion of predication in the *Categories* raise time-honoured questions about the extent to which in the *Categories* Aristotle is dealing with matters of language and the extent to which he is doing ontology ("time-honoured": for a sampling, with some discussion of earlier views, see Simplicius *In Cat.* 9.4–12.3 [I am indebted for the reference to Long (1990)]). On the view offered here, the ways in which his two notions of predication interact show that he is doing both. The old view that the *Categories* is entirely a *linguistic* investigation, so that what goes into the various categories, for example, are *linguistic* items (as both the [unrevised] Oxford and the Loeb translations suggest) is properly put to rest in Ackrill's translation and commentary; cf. Moravscik (1967b), pp. 83, 85, and n. 12, where the distinction between metaphysical and linguistic predication is also particularly clearly drawn.

pallor is IN (uppercase) Socrates. At the same time, where as here the subject is an individual substance, the subrelation that fits most exactly is the *core* relation, which is undefined: in this case, we can drop the uppercase notation and say simply that pallor is in (lowercase) Socrates.

Similar remarks apply to the SAID-OF relation. The SAID-OF relation too is the union of different subrelations; of these, as we shall see, one is the core relation, which holds between an individual substance and a kind. To express this core relation, we will again drop the use of uppercase letters; for example, if (8) is true, then man is said of (lowercase) Socrates.

For all its ties with linguistic predication, Aristotle's notion of metaphysical predication is squarely ontological in character. But we need to take some care in spelling out the nature of the connection Aristotle sees between (metaphysical) predication and the other parts of his ontological theory, in particular the divisions into primary and secondary substances and the different varieties of nonsubstances. At the beginning of *Categories* 5, recalling the fourth of the four classes distinguished in the second half of chapter 2, Aristotle introduces the notion of a primary substance by way of the theory of (metaphysical) predication:

A *substance* – that which is called a substance most strictly, primarily, and most of all – is that which is neither said of a subject nor in a subject, e.g., the individual man or the individual horse. (*Categories* 5, 2a11–14; Ackrill's translation and emphasis)

Later in the same chapter, he uses notions of (metaphysical) predication to get a fix on the notions of substance and secondary substance:

It is a characteristic common to every substance (*koinon pasēs ousias*) not to be in a subject

(the secondary substances, meanwhile, are SAID OF but not IN a subject).[10] The dominant criterion for primary substance in *Categories* 5 also draws on the theory of (metaphysical) predication:

It is *because the primary substances are subjects for everything else* that they are called substances most strictly. (*Categories* 5, 2b37–3a1; Ackrill's translation; my emphasis; cf. 5, 2a34 ff. b15–17)

10 *Categories* 5, 3a7–15. With the idea that things SAID OF something but not IN something are the secondary substances, as Aristotle admits at 3a21–8, notoriously, we run into the problem of differentiae, which turn out to be secondary substances on this account. The fact that, according to Aristotle, differentiae are SAID OF their subjects (3a22–4) aligns them with substances; otherwise, however, Aristotle seems clear that they are not substances (see, e.g., 5, 2b36–7, 3a21). For further discussion of the problem of differentiae, see Ackrill (1963), pp. 82, 85–7; Granger (1984).

Much of the *Categories* is concerned with working out the consequences of this condition on primary substance.[11] But despite these
moves *from* considerations having to do with (metaphysical) predication *to* his various ontological classifications, it is hazardous to assume
that Aristotle means to use the different kinds of (metaphysical) predication in order to *define* the notions of substance, nonsubstance, and
the rest. The subject criterion for primary substance, for example,
appeals to the notion of (metaphysical) predication, but, it turns out,
our grip on (metaphysical) predication itself is only as good as our
understanding of the distinctions between substances and nonsubstances and the like. Aristotle expressly draws attention to the latter
dependency in the *Analytics*. He insists that if a sentence expresses a
genuine (metaphysical) predication, the subject entity itself must be a
genuine subject, that is, a lowest member of the category of substance,
and not a combination of a substance with an accident: it must not be
an accidental compound. For example, the sentence 'The musical is
pale', where 'the musical' names a compound of an individual substance with an accident, must be recast as 'There is a substance, *a*,
which happens to be musical and is pale'.[12] Recasting the sentence in
this form makes clear the role of the substance *a* as the subject for both
pallor and musicality.

I have suggested that, for Aristotle, a thing's ontological status as a
substance or a nonsubstance, or as a higher or lower member of its
category, can be determined by the niche it occupies in the *Categories'*
scheme of (metaphysical) predication. At the same time, he seems also
to say that our explanations can as well run in the opposite direction,
so that the appropriate notions of (metaphysical) predication can be
properly specified only in terms of the distinctions between substances
and nonsubstances and the rest. In these circumstances, Aristotle cannot mean *both* sets of explanations to be taken as definitions. In fact, I
shall suppose, his explanations in *neither* direction constitute a definition, so that both groups of notions alike include notions that are
primitive in Aristotle's theory. On the side of the various ontological
classifications, I suspect that the notion of substance, like that of a
category itself, is undefined. And in the theory of (metaphysical)
predication, the core relations '*x* is in *y*' and '*x* is said of *y*' (lowercase
in both instances) both go undefined.

The conclusion that Aristotle does not define the (lowercase) in or
said-of relations in the *Categories* is not uncontested. For example,
Ackrill thinks that Aristotle means to *define* the notion of being in a
subject at 1a24–5: "By what is in a subject, I mean what is in some-

<hr>

11 The subject criterion for primary substance is discussed further in Section 3.
12 Cf. *An. Po.* A4, 73b6, 7, A22, 83a2, 10–12; *An. Pr.* A27, 43a35. Aristotle's point in
   these passages is discussed further in Chapter 3.

thing not as a part, and cannot exist separately from what it is in."[13] One difficulty, as Ackrill acknowledges, is that the alleged definition appears to be circular;[14] to counter this, Ackrill suggests that in the definiens, 'in' has a nontechnical sense that can be understood independently of the technical sense being defined. Alternatively, the supposed definition might be rewritten in such a way that the circularity disappears.[15] But there is the further difficulty that what Aristotle says here does not obviously separate the IN relation from the SAID-OF relation. When he says that what is IN a subject "cannot exist separately from what it is in," does he mean that it cannot exist apart from some container or other, or apart from the very thing that it is IN? Only the second gives a genuine difference from the SAID-OF relation, but the reading is a contentious one, as we shall see. Finally, the inseparability condition just noted is a highly charged piece of anti-Platonic polemic, so Aristotle cannot reasonably support it by saying simply that it is true by definition. On the contrary, the claim needs *arguing*, as Dancy emphasizes.[16] The inseparability requirement for nonsubstances surely comes down to this, that nonsubstances are in some sense ontologically dependent on individual substances. So the wanted arguments for the inseparability condition governing nonsubstances are just the arguments in connection with ontological dependence advanced in *Categories* 5 and discussed in Section 3.

I shall suppose, then, that the core relation 'x is in y' goes undefined in Aristotle's theory. At the same time, Aristotle insists that the relation also resists assimilation to other, more familiar notions that lie outside his theory. Contra Ackrill, the disclaimer that an accident is "in something, not as a part" (*Categories* 2, 1a24–5; cf. 5, 3a31–2), is a warning *not* to look for any ordinary sense of being in, for example, being (literally) a (spatiotemporally determined) part of,[17] to illumine

---

13 Ackrill (1963), p. 74.
14 On this point, as also on the two objections that follow, I follow Dancy (1975), pp. 344–7.
15 Ackrill supposes that what is to be defined is the locution 'in X', where the definiens is 'in X, not as a part of X, and incapable of existing separately from what it is in'. In the text, however, the phrase allegedly being defined is 'x is *in a subject*', and the alleged definiens is 'for some y, x is in y, and x is not a part of y, and x cannot exist separately from what it is in'. Had the definiendum not expressed a relational property, but been explicitly two place from the start, the circularity could have been avoided:

x is in y $=_{df}$ x is not a part of y, and y cannot exist separately from y.

But we can think that Aristotle means to offer this as a definition of the in relation only if we accept Ackrill's favoured reading of the "no separate existence" clause, contrary to what I argue below.
16 Dancy (1975), pp. 346–7.
17 In Aristotle's Greek, one can say both that a finger is "in" the hand and that its contents are "in" the containing vessel (see *Physics* Δ3, 210a15–16, 24). Only the second example suggests the correct model for the relation Aristotle has in

the special use intended here.[18] This is part of a wider policy by which Aristotle frequently and emphatically decries the use of metaphors, which appeal to familiar, nontechnical notions, in order to explain the primitive notions of his metaphysics.[19]

The core relation '*x* is in *y*' (lowercase) is very close to the notion of compounding, to be discussed in Part II. As we shall see, an accidental compound is the result of compounding the accident φ with the individual substance *a*. For example, Socrates seated is the accidental compound of the substance Socrates and the accident sitting. The relation '*x* is in *y*' and the notion of compounding are connected in the natural way:

> φ is in *a* if and only if there exists the accidental compound of *a* with the accident φ.

I take it that these two notions, inherence and compounding, are both primitive in Aristotle's theory. The biconditional given, then, uses the relation '*x* is in *y*' in order to say exactly when the relevant accidental compound exists, but the biconditional is not meant as a *definition* of the inherence relation.

I also suppose that the core relation '*x* is said of *y*' is primitive in Aristotle's theory: this assumption too may be controversial. For example, Frede thinks that all cases of the SAID-OF relation can be defined in terms of Aristotle's notion of synonymy, set out in the very first chapter of the *Categories*.[20] The SAID-OF relation and synonymy are apparently connected by this principle:

mind. The finger and the hand are not totally discrete items, and if the finger is in the hand, the result is just the hand itself, not some entity over and above the hand. But a vessel and its contents are totally discrete from one another, and the result of putting the contents in the vessel is some third entity: the vessel with its contents or, equivalently, a *compound* of the two. This said, however, it should be emphasized that Aristotle means not to select the most appropriate of the ordinary uses of 'in' to illustrate the technical use he has in mind, but to dissociate his technical use of 'in' from *any* of the ordinary uses. I take it that it is a straightforward *physical* notion of a part that Aristotle wishes to distance from his IN relation: this is the point of the disclaimer later at *Categories* 5, 3a29–32, that by denying that what is IN a substance is itself a substance, he is *not* denying that the ordinary physical parts of a substance are also substances (for this latter view, see *Categories* 7, 8a13–21, b15–21; *Metaphysics* Δ8, 1017b10–13, Z2, 1028b9–10, Z16, 1040b6–8).

For the point made in the text, see also Dancy (1975), p. 348, and for a very different account of "not as a part" at 1a24–5 and the remarks at 5, 3a29–32, see Frede ([1978] 1987), pp. 61–2.

18 Consistent with this, in the list of uses of 'in' in *Physics* Δ3, 210a14–24, the similar use of 'in' for the relation between form and matter has a separate entry and is not assimilated to any more familiar use. A similar point applies to the discussion of the senses of 'have', which go pari passu with those of 'in', in *Metaphysics* Δ23 (cf. *Categories* 15).

19 See Chapter 6, Section 3, esp. note 36.

20 Frede ([1978] 1987), p. 53; cf. Code (1985), pp. 103–4, cited in Chapter 1, Section 3. But Frede does not say that Aristotle actually offers the definition Frede sets

x is SAID OF *y* if and only if *x* is predicated synonymously of *y*, that is, if and only if there is a predicate '*F*', "from" *x*, such that *x* and *y* are synonyms with respect to '*F*'.[21]

For example, man is predicated synonymously of Socrates: the term 'man', which is taken "from" the species man, applies to Socrates and to man, and the relevant definition, 'rational animal' (say), also applies to both.[22]

This explanation is less helpful than at first appears. Aristotle's biconditional connects the SAID-OF relation with the truth of various *linguistic* predications; for example, if man is SAID OF Socrates, then the terms 'man' and 'rational animal' apply both to Socrates and to man. Setting out these various connections with linguistic predication, however, cannot count as *defining* the SAID-OF relation if Aristotle's purpose in introducing the different varieties of metaphysical predication in the first place is to uncover the metaphysical underpinnings for different kinds of linguistic predication. If the various metaphysical relations are meant to underlie and explain different portions of language in this way, they cannot themselves in turn be defined in terms of the truth of different linguistic idioms.

A more serious defect is that the account of the SAID-OF relation in terms of synonymy is outright false as it stands. Notoriously, there is room for disagreement over *which* variety of metaphysical predication underlies the linguistic predication 'Socrates is a man', for example, or

out. Also, Frede does not distinguish between the generic SAID-OF relation, which I agree is defined, and the core said-of relation, which I argue is not; but his strategy for defining the SAID-OF relation, unlike mine, also implies a definition for the lowercase said-of relation.

21 An example involving the relation '*x* is predicated synonymously of *y*' for the case where *x* is a genus is given at *Topics* B2, 109a34–b12. For the explication of "predicated synonymously of," see Chapter 1, Section 1.

In *Categories* 5, Aristotle argues that both substances and differentiae are predicated synonymously of their subjects: "It is a feature of (*huparchei*) substances and differentiae that all things ‹that are called from them› are called from them synonymously." By "substances" here, Aristotle makes it clear that he means *secondary* substances: of the different kinds of substances, only these "yield a predicate" in the appropriate way (there is a predicate "*apo*" them; *Categories* 5, 3a36–7). The species man, for example, is predicated synonymously of Socrates. It may seem puzzling that Aristotle here mentions only substances and differentiae and has nothing to say about cases where *x* is SAID OF *y* and *x* and *y* are items in some nonsubstance category. Again, in contrast to the biconditional given in the main text, Aristotle's statement here supports only a conditional claim in one direction. But the language "it is a feature of" (*huparchei*) does not imply that *only* predications involving substances or differentiae as predicables will count as synonymous predications. If we provide for the further cases where what is SAID OF a subject is from some nonsubstance category, then what Aristotle says here can be strengthened to the biconditional in the main text.

22 Here I suppose that by "definition," Aristotle means "*linguistic* definition." As we shall see in succeeding paragraphs, it makes no real difference to the points at issue here if he has in mind instead the metaphysical entity, (rational) animal, that is *named* by the linguistic definition.

'Socrates is an animal'. For Plato, the sentences are true if and only if Socrates Has man or Has animal; for Aristotle, on the contrary, they are true just in case Socrates Is (a) man or Is (an) animal. Both philosophers can agree, however, that the terms 'man' and 'animal' *apply to* Socrates (a notion of *linguistic* predication). Now the account of ordinary, garden-variety synonymy stipulates only that a given predicate should *apply to* its appropriate subject (again, a linguistic notion); hence, it does not select between the different (metaphysical) options of Izzing and Having. Moreover, it is of no use to suppose instead that the entity *named* by 'man' or 'animal' is *metaphysically* predicated of Socrates; for we still do not know whether the relation between Socrates and these predicables is that of Izzing (as Aristotle would claim) or Having (the Platonic option).

It follows that the notion of synonymy thus appealed to is useless for sorting between those predicables that are SAID OF their subject and those that are merely IN a subject.[23] Thus, suppose that Socrates Has pallor and that pallor Is (a) penetrative colour. Then surely Socrates Has (a) penetrative colour. That is, the term 'pallor' applies both to Socrates and to pallor (in the first case, with a switch from the noun to the adjective, for we say that Socrates is *pale*),[24] and the associated definition, 'penetrative colour', also applies to both (again with the switch from noun to adjective as needed).[25] Alternatively, the universals pallor and penetrative colour are metaphysically predicated of Socrates. By the biconditional given, then, and contrary to Aristotle's theory, pallor is SAID OF Socrates.

We can avoid this undesirable result by replacing the notion of straight synonymy and straight synonymous predication in the biconditional given with those of *strong* synonymy and *strong* synonymous predication defined in Chapter 1:

> *x* is SAID OF *y* if and only if *x* is predicated *strongly* synonymously of *y*, that is, if and only if there is a predicate '*F*', "from" *x*, such that *x* and *y* are *strong* synonyms with respect to '*F*'.[26]

23 Here, I part company again with Frede ([1978] 1987), p. 53; see note 20.
24 This is the phenomenon of *paronymy*, discussed later in this section.
25 Cases in which terms derived paronymously from both the species and the genus apply to a single subject are discussed at *Topics* B4, 111a33–b11. For example, "if someone has knowledge or is spoken of paronymously from knowledge, he will also have grammatical ‹knowledge› (*grammatikēn*) or musical ‹knowledge› (*mousikēn*) or one of the other knowledges, or will be called paronymously from one of them, for example, grammatical (*grammatikos*) or musical (*mousikos*)" (111a38–b4). Examples of this kind have been used as counterexamples to Aristotle's theory from virtually the beginning of Aristotelian scholarship; see the criticisms attributed to Andronicus and others in Simplicius *In Cat.* 54.8–21. (The examples are particularly intriguing: "If Socrates is a philosopher, and a philosopher is a knower, then Socrates too will be a knower. And if body is white and white is colour, body will be colour.") I owe my knowledge of the passage in Simplicius to Long (1990).
26 For the explication of strong synonymous predication and strong synonymy, see Chapter 1, Section 3.

For example, man is predicated strongly synonymously of Socrates: the term 'man' is taken from the species man, and Socrates and man are strongly synonymous with respect to 'man' – both Are men, and both Are rational animals. But Socrates and pallor are *not* strongly synonymous with respect to 'pale', and pallor is *not* predicated strongly synonymously of Socrates. We now have the means, then, to distinguish the relation between Socrates and pallor from that between Socrates and man, in the way that Aristotle wants. But again, we will not be able to use strong synonymy in order to define the SAID-OF relation; for strong synonymy is itself defined in terms of Izzing or the SAID-OF relation, and our definition will be blatantly circular. So Aristotle's discussion of the SAID-OF relation in terms of synonymy may informally offer light on that relation, but there is no hope of *defining* the relation by way of synonymy. By the same token, synonymy is interestingly related to the core said-of relation, but again we will not be able to define the second in terms of the first.

Aristotle notes several times in *Categories* 5 that the relation 'x is IN y' *fails* the synonymy condition (interpreted as *strong* synonymy, as Aristotle intends) given earlier. If x is predicated (strongly) synonymously of y, as we have seen, one and the same term, 'F', "from" x, must apply to both x and y in such a way that both Are (an) F and the definition associated with 'F' must apply to both x and y; that is, here, both Are what that definition signifies. Invariably, in cross-categorial predication, the second part of this condition fails: the definition of the predicable will not also apply to its subject in the requisite way (*Categories* 5, 2a29–34, 3a15–21). For example, suppose that pallor, *to leukon*, is IN Socrates. Socrates and pale are not (strong) synonyms with respect to the term 'pale': pallor is an accident of Socrates, for Socrates Has pallor, but he Is not what pallor is (cf. *Metaphysics* Γ4, 1007a32–3). That is, the definition of pallor does not apply to Socrates in the way required, for it is not the case that Socrates Is a colour.

More often than not in cross-categorial predication, Aristotle observes, the first part of the synonymy condition fails as well. That is, where x is IN y, the very same term will not apply to both x and y, at least not without a telltale "difference in ending."[27] For example, we call Socrates 'pale', but we do not apply the term 'pallor' to him.

Here Aristotle appeals to a syntactic criterion, which he calls "paronymy," to indicate when a predication is not a synonymous predication. Like synonymy, the notion of paronymy is drawn from the first chapter of the *Categories*:

27 *Categories* 1, 1a12–13. Examples of paronymy, where the "difference in ending" occurs ("*neither the name* nor the definition [of a given predicable] applies to the subject"), appear in *Categories* 5, *passim;* see also *Categories* 7, 6b12–14, 8, 10a27–32; *Topics* B2, 109a34–b12, B4, 111a34–b4.

When things are called after something in accordance with ‹its› name, but differing in ending, they are said to be *paronyms*. Thus, for example, the grammarian gets his name from grammar, the brave ‹one› gets his from bravery. (1, 1a12–15)[28]

For example, Socrates is called 'pale' after pallor, and the accidental compound that results can be called 'the pale one' or 'pale Socrates'.[29] The occurrence of the adjective 'pale' gets the same gloss in all these cases alike: it comes by a difference in ending or inflection from the abstract noun 'pallor'. And in general, when we say that a thing is pale, the difference in ending is enough to show that pallor is not SAID OF the subject, but rather is IN it.

This test is not reliable, however, for language does not always succeed in mirroring the underlying metaphysical relationships, and the "difference in ending" does not always exist.[30] Where Greek forms an abstract noun directly from the neuter adjective – 'the pale', *to leukon,* directly from the adjective 'pale', *leukon* – there is no significant difference between noun and adjective, and paronymy does not occur. In some cases, however, there exists an abstract noun that is formed independently of the neuter adjective – 'pallor' or 'whiteness', for example, *leukotēs,* as opposed to the adjective 'pale' or 'white', *leukon.* Here, paronymy will take place – we say that Socrates is pale, not that he is pallor – and *both* parts of the condition for (strong) synonymy fail to be satisfied.

I conclude that the notion of strong synonymy does correctly sort cases of the SAID-OF and IN relations. Where *x* is SAID OF *y*, one and the same term '*F*', "from" *x*, must apply to both *x* and *y* in such a way that both Are (an) *F*, and the definition associated with '*F*' will also apply to both in such a way that both Are what that definition signifies. But where one item is IN another, one or both of these conditions will fail. Strong synonymy, however, *presupposes* the distinction between the IN and SAID-OF relations; Aristotle's notion of synonymy does not offer any noncircular way of defining the core *in* and *said-of* relations.

3 Aristotle's Dictum, "Primary Substances Are Subjects for Everything Else"

I turn now to the main subject of the chapter: the principal arguments Aristotle uses to establish the primacy of primary substances. I begin with a key passage from *Categories* 5:

28 The passage quoted is discussed further in Chapter 3.
29 The interpretation of referring expressions of this form is discussed in Chapter 3, Section 1.
30 See Chapter 3, Section 1.

All the other things are either said of the primary substances as subjects or in them as subjects. This is clear from an examination of cases. For example, animal is predicated of man and therefore also of the individual man; for were it predicated of none of the individual men it would not be predicated of man at all. Again, colour is in body and therefore also in an individual body; for were it not in some individual body it would not be in body at all. Thus all the other things are either said of the primary substances as subjects or in them as subjects. So if the primary substances did not exist it would be impossible for any of the other things to exist. (2a34–b6c; Ackrill's translation)

In previous sections, we have seen that Aristotle's theory of (metaphysical) predication in the *Categories* leaves room for two different ways in which a predicable may be related to its subject, Izzing and Having. Side by side with this pluralism with regard to the kinds of predication, however, Aristotle appears to hold a *monolithic* view concerning the subject of predication: as he says, primary substances are subjects for everything else, and everything else is either in or said of some primary substance. This monolithic view supplies a prominent condition on primary substance in *Categories* 5:

It is *because the primary substances are subjects for everything else* that they are called substances most strictly. (2b37–3a1; Ackrill's translation; my emphasis; cf. 5, 2a34 ff., b15–17)

This condition sets apart the individual substances, which Aristotle counts as primary, from the remaining substances, which are of lesser grade, and from everything in the various nonsubstance categories. The contrast between primary and secondary substances is especially instructive. Socrates, for example, is both a member of various kinds, which are secondary substances, and a subject to different nonsubstances, which are his accidents. But secondary substances are subjects to the same accidents that the primary substances are subjects to: *because* you can call the individual man grammatical and so forth, *for that reason* you can call man and animal too grammatical.[31] Since the accidents of the individual men accrue to man as well, man itself is a subject in a sufficiently robust sense to be a substance of a sort (5, 2b29–3a6). But man is also a kind relative to the various individual men, Socrates and the rest, and it is predicated of them, so it is a substance to only a lesser degree.[32] Socrates himself, meanwhile, is *not* a kind relative to anything: Socrates is a this, and both one in number and *atomon*, or "indivisible" (5, 3b10–13; cf.2, 1b6–7), and he is a primary substance.

---

31 *Categories* 5, 3a3–6. Notably, then, at least as far as its accidents go, what holds of man – the secondary substance – is *grounded in* what holds of the individual man, Socrates (say). This will be important later in the section; see also (D3) in Section 4.
32 *Categories* 5, 2b15–22.

These points establish an obvious sense in which a primary substance is a subject for everything else. It can be the subject both for predicables from within its own category and for accidents from the other, nonsubstance categories. At the same time, it is not itself predicated of anything else, within its category or without. But Aristotle has an even stronger point in mind. In fact, an individual substance is involved, either overtly or covertly, as a subject in *every* case of (metaphysical) predication. In the obvious cases, the subject is overtly a primary substance: man is SAID OF Socrates (say), while pallor, or colour, is IN Socrates. In other instances, however, the subject is not obviously an individual substance. For example, animal is predicated of man (for man Is [an] animal), and grammar is predicated of man (for man Has grammar); finally, colour is predicated of pallor (for pallor Is [a] colour). Aristotle says that every predicable is predicated of an individual substance: at the very least, then, each of the three predicables in our three examples is also predicated of some individual substance. But he also means something more. Consider the first case: man is an animal. In the passage quoted at the beginning of this section, Aristotle remarks, defending his claim that individual substances are "subjects for everything,"

... animal is predicated of man and therefore also of the individual man; for were it predicated of none of the individual men it would not be predicated of man at all. (*Categories* 5, 2a36–2b1; Ackrill's translation)

We can assume that an individual man is an individual substance of which man is predicated. With this assumption, at a minimum Aristotle means to assert that animal is predicated of man (or man Is [an] animal), *only if* animal and man alike are predicated of an individual man, Socrates (say), where Socrates is an individual substance.[33] It would be a mistake, however, to think that the material conditional is all that is needed here – that it is, in Aristotle's view, just a happy coincidence that where animal is predicated of man, there is some individual substance of which both alike are predicated. As Aristotle's subjunctive reasoning suggests ("*were* animal predicated of none of the individual men it *would not be predicated* of man at all"), animal's being predicated of man in some sense *requires* its being predicated of some individual man. Plausibly, Aristotle means that the one kind of predication is *grounded in* the other. And in general, I take it, he is offering a *reductive* account of certain kinds of (metaphysical) predica-

---

33 "at a minimum": here we must first take account of the nature of the connective, which I argue is more than just the material conditional. But if, as I suggest, Aristotle is concerned with how to *analyse* the fact that man is an animal, the full account will be more complicated than he suggests here; details are given in Section 4. Similar comments apply to the other examples discussed in this section.

tion, such that the various (metaphysical) predications his scheme allows that do not obviously have an individual substance as subject are to be analysed in terms of (metaphysical) predications that do. Accordingly, animal is predicated of man *only because* there is some individual substance of which both animal and man are predicated. (The full account is: animal is said of* man, only because (i) there is some individual substance of which both animal and man are said (no asterisk), and (ii) necessarily, animal is said of *any* individual substance of which man is said. But I shall defer details of this and other examples to Section 4.) Comparably, man Has grammar only because there is some individual substance that Is (a) man and Has grammar.[34] Or, again, body (a *secondary* substance) Has colour only because some individual substance Is (a) body and also Has colour.[35] Thus, continuing the quotation from the passage at the beginning of this section:

> Again, colour is in body and therefore also in an individual body; for were it not in some individual body it would not be in body at all. (5, 2b1–3; Ackrill's translation)

A similar account can be given of the claim that pallor is a colour: pallor Is (a) colour only because (roughly) some individual substance Has pallor and also Has colour.[36]

In all such cases, I take it, Aristotle directs us from the original relation, between animal and man, for example, to relations involving each of these two singly *and some individual substance.* And in general, an item is predicated of something other than an individual substance only if, and only because, there is some individual substance of which both items together are predicated.[37]

In this story, the relations of (metaphysical) predication that do *not* obviously involve an individual substance as subject are the *derived* cases, and they are grounded in the undefined, or *core*, cases, in which an individual substance *is* overtly the subject. For example, in the

---

34 Cf. 5. 3a4–6, quoted earlier in this section.

35 But see the discussion of the reservations by Ackrill later in this section. The preliminary account of the different sentence kinds given in this paragraph is filled out more exactly in Section 4.

Ackrill (1963), p. 83, with regret finds that Aristotle "speaks as if, because colour is in body, colour is in an individual body," while Owen (1965), p. 101, holds that Aristotle means exactly what Ackrill fears he says; beyond their disagreement, however, both get the 'because' in the wrong place. From the fact that colour is in body, *we can infer that* it is also in a particular body; but the fact that colour is in body is explained by, or grounded in, the fact that it is in a given body, and not vice versa. The difficulty with Owen's and Ackrill's use of 'because' is also noted by Moravcsik (1967b), pp. 94–5.

36 See note 35.

37 Again (see notes 35 and 36), Ackrill's reservations regarding this account are discussed later in the Appendix to this chapter; see also notes 40 and 47.

jargon I introduce formally later, animal is said of* man: here no individual substance is obviously involved as subject, and the said-of* relation is to be analysed in terms of the core said-of relation (no asterisk) that holds directly between each of animal and man on one side and some individual substance or other on the other.

We come now to the special play Aristotle makes of the role of individual substances as "subjects for everything else." Why does this fact about them specially qualify them as primary substances? An answer is contained in two theses. The first involves the points just made about Aristotle's scheme of *metaphysical predication;* the second focuses on the various *relations of ontological dependency* to which categorial items other than individual substances owe their existence. Recall that in Aristotle's categorial scheme, everything other than an individual substance is a predicable. Then we claim, first, that

(a) For any predicable, x, and for any y, x is (metaphysically) predicated of y, only if *either* (i) y is itself an individual substance and x stands in one of the core relations of (metaphysical) predication to y, *or* (ii) where y is not an individual substance, there is some individual substance, z, such that x and y alike stand in one of the core relations of (metaphysical) predication to z. Where (ii) is the case, moreover, x is (metaphysically) predicated of y *only because* there is some individual substance, z, such that x and y alike stand in one of the core relations of (metaphysical) predication to z. *Without individual substances as subjects for the core relations of (metaphysical) predication, (metaphysical) predication would not be possible at all.*

Thesis (a) will have to be supported in more detail later (Section 4). For now, to illustrate (i), recall that man is said of (no asterisk) Socrates; to illustrate (ii), animal is said of* man (with asterisk), only if, and only because, there is some individual substance of which both animal and man are said (no asterisk in these last two cases). Thesis (a) is an elaboration of the *monolithic* conception of the subject of (metaphysical) predication already discussed. Thesis (a) by itself makes the existence of individual substances, and of them alone, the foundation of Aristotle's whole system of (metaphysical) predication. On this showing, metaphysical predication is possible in general only if, and only because, individual substances exist and are the subjects of the core relations of metaphysical predication.

This interpretation is hardly trivial, however, for it is inconsistent with one influential reconstruction of Aristotle's theory of (metaphysical) predication in the *Categories*. Ackrill suggests that "strictly . . . it is not colour, but this individual instance of colour, that is in this individual body."[38] On this view, the universal colour is predicated of some (Ackrillian) instance of colour, and that instance in turn is in some

38 Ackrill [1963], p. 83.

individual substance, but properly speaking colour is not itself in any individual substance. That is, while Ackrill is willing to allow a "relaxed sense" in which colour is IN (uppercase) Socrates,[39] still in the strict use it cannot be the case that colour is in (lowercase) him. So Ackrill has this picture of how things stand between colour and this individual body:

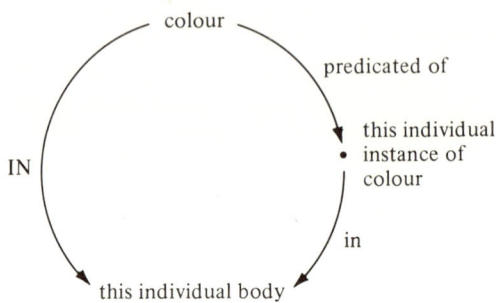

This view runs counter to thesis (a), which requires that if colour or anything else can be predicated at all, it can be predicated directly of an individual substance, this individual body (say), by way of one of the core relations of metaphysical predication. Not surprisingly, Ackrill has harsh words for the passage at *Categories* 5, 2a34–b6c, cited at the beginning of this section, which is the primary evidence for (a). Aristotle says here that colour's being in body rests on the fact that it is in some individual body, but according to Ackrill, Aristotle's formulations are "compressed and careless" and part of "an almost complete neglect" of individuals in nonsubstance categories after *Categories* 2.[40]

Despite this opposition, suppose that we accept thesis (a). Some further argument shows that the existence of individual substances also underwrites the very *existence* of everything else; for given (a), together with some ancillary assumptions, we will be able to show that

(b) If individual substances did not exist, nothing would exist. Things other than individual substances exist only if, *and only because*, individual substances

---

39 Ibid.
40 Ibid. Although Ackrill, I believe, gets the worst of the account of *Categories* 5, 2a34 ff. – see Owen (1965), pp. 100–1; Frede ([1978] 1987), pp. 58–9 – he is able to claim perhaps the more natural reading of 1, 1a24–5: "By 'in a subject' I mean what is in something, not as a part, and cannot exist separately from what it is in" (Ackrill's translation). On Ackrill's reading of these lines ([1963], pp. 74–5), Aristotle supposes that if x is IN y, then x is not a part of y, and x cannot exist apart from y. This last clause has two corollaries: (i) that where x is IN y, x is unique to y (x is not also in something z, where $z \neq y$) (for the reasoning to this conclusion, see Frede ([1978] 1987), p. 58), that is, in Ackrill's terminology, it is an *individual instance* of a property, Callias's generosity, for example; and (ii) that anything that is *not* unique to y in this

exist. Moreover, *things other than individual substances owe their existence to individual substances, thanks to relations of ontological dependency on individual substances, in one step.*

Again, the "only because" requires comment. It is not Aristotle's view (merely) that man, for example, exists *only if* some individual man does, Socrates (say). The existence of individual men in addition to that of man itself is no coincidence, for the existence of individual men is what *grounds* the existence of man, but not vice versa.[41] The requirement, further, that the relevant ontological dependencies all be *in one step* guarantees that the ontological primacy of individual substances is *absolute*. Everything else is ontologically dependent on the existence of individual substances in one step, so that where x is an individual substance and y is ontologically dependent on x, there is no z such that y is ontologically dependent on z, and z in turn is ontologically dependent on x. There are no such "intermediate" items in Aristotle's categorial scheme that ground the existence of something else, while they themselves in turn are grounded in the existence of some primary substance.[42]

way *cannot* "properly be in" y. That is, "general attributes are not in individuals, particular attributes are not in more than one individual" (Owen [1965], p. 100). Corollary (ii) gives Ackrill his conclusion that the items SAID OF a given particular nonsubstance cannot also "properly be in" the very subject that the particular nonsubstance is in ("Strictly, however, it is not colour, but this individual instance of colour, that is in this individual body"; Ackrill [1963], p. 83), and more broadly, general items in the nonsubstance categories cannot "strictly be in" any individual substance at all; cf. [*Do] in the Appendix to this chapter. As best as I can tell, however, other passages in the *Categories* cited in support of Aristotle's commitment to particular properties (e.g., Benson [1988] cites 2, 1b6–9, 5, 4a10–20, 8, 11a26–36, although I am less convinced by his discussion of 5, 3b10–18), are quite neutral on both (i) and (ii).

   An alternative to Ackrill's reading of the text at 1a24–25 is set out in Owen (1965), pp. 100–5, esp. 104–5; cf. the discussion in Jones (1972); on this account, x is IN y, only if x is not a part of y, and were there no z such that x is IN z, x would not exist. Yet a different alternative to Ackrill's reading appears in Frede ([1978] 1987), pp. 58–63.

41 The "only because" is also important for preserving the asymmetry of Aristotle's dependency claims. Dependency cannot consist solely in the fact that, for example, a given nonsubstance, pallor (say), can exist *only if* some individual substance or other exists, for this condition on the existence of pallor is matched by an exactly parallel condition on the existence of individual substances: Socrates, for example, can exist only if some nonsubstance or other exists and is in him. On this showing, there will be no grounds for the priority of either kind of entity over the other, given the standard and most nearly relevant definitions of priority at *Categories* 12, 14a29–35; cf. *Metaphysics* Δ11, 1019a1–4. The "only because" in thesis (b) gives Aristotle the asymmetry he needs: an individual nonsubstance can exist only if, *and only because*, some individual substance or other exists, but it is not the case that any given individual substance can exist only because some nonsubstance or other does so. In particular, the existence of things other than individual substances is grounded in that of individual substances by the two core relations of (metaphysical) predication; since these relations are asymmetric, the grounding is also asymmetric, as required. The issue of asymmetry is pressed in Moravcsik (1967b), pp. 89, 93–6.

42 Cf. the discussion of ontological dependency in Chapter 1, Section 4.

Plausibly, the notion of one-step ontological dependencies is not unfamiliar to Aristotle, for it explains why use of the One-over-Many Assumption in the TMA must stop with the introduction of the *first* universal, man, "over" the plurality of sensible particulars that are men (see Section 1). But one-step ontological dependency is again inconsistent with Ackrill's reconstruction of Aristotle's theory. Suppose that, as Ackrill argues, the universal colour (say) cannot strictly be in an individual substance. That is, colour is predicated of some (Ackrillian) instance of colour, and that instance in turn is predicated of some individual substance, but *properly speaking* there is no individual substance of which colour itself is predicated. Equivalently, colour is IN Socrates, but it is not (lowercase) in him. It is implausible in these circumstances to claim that nonetheless colour is ontologically dependent on some individual substance or other, Socrates (say), *in one step* on the grounds that colour is after all IN Socrates. The IN relation between colour and Socrates is a *derived* one, explained in terms of the two relations between colour and some individual instance of colour and between that instance of colour and Socrates. The relation between colour and Socrates, then, is essentially indirect; at best, colour is ontologically dependent on Socrates in *two* steps, not one.[43]

It is worth noting that the rejection of one-step ontological dependencies is shared by some of Ackrill's critics. Furth carefully separates the two states of affairs that bravery (a particular nonsubstance)[44] is in Socrates and that virtue is in him. According to Furth, a particular nonsubstance like bravery "gets its toehold" on existence by way of inhering in some substance or other; more general qualities like virtue get their toehold by way of being said of some lower quality. Furth sees these two claims together as the "interpretive expansion" of Aristotle's assertion that nothing else would exist if primary substances did not. So he is committed to a doctrine of *two*-step ontological dependence. Virtue, for example, has a toehold thanks to its relation to some particular quality, bravery (say), and bravery in turn has its toehold thanks to its relation to some primary substance or other that is brave. But virtue does *not* get its toehold directly from its relation to some primary substance or other in one step.[45]

Furth's account cuts Aristotle off from a doctrine of one-step ontological dependencies, because for Furth *every* case of metaphysical predication in the *Categories,* and not just the core *in* and *said-of* rela-

43 Cf. Moravcsik (1967b), p. 82 (my emphasis): on Ackrill's theory of property instances, universals in the nonsubstance categories will be "*indirectly dependent* [sc., on primary substances] by being directly dependent on nonsubstantial particulars."

44 On Furth's account, a particular nonsubstance is predicable of many and is *not* an Ackrillian property instance; see note 47.

45 Furth (1988), pp. 9–10, 25–6, and 28.

tions, is a relation of ontological dependence. Similarly, Moravcsik argues that "Aristotle takes predication to be showing the ontological dependence of the entity denoted by the predicate on the entity denoted by the subject."[46] But again, if the fact that animal is predicated of man, or that colour is predicated of pallor, indicates that animal is to some degree ontologically dependent on man, or colour on pallor, we must abandon the idea that the ontological dependencies Aristotle envisions in the *Categories* are all in one step.

To obtain thesis (b), we must make an assumption about the existence conditions for every predicable in Aristotle's scheme. We assume that a predicable exists only if (and only because) there is some subject of which it is in fact predicated. That is, predicables in general exist "through" their subjects. Equivalently, if every predicable in Aristotle's scheme is a universal,[47] their subjects "give existence to universals."[48] Now by thesis (a), we know that items other than individual substances are predicated of each of their subjects only if (and only because) there is some individual substance of which they are predicated. If, then, items other than individual substances exist only if (and only because) there is some subject of which they are predicated, it follows that they can exist only if (and only because) there exists some individual substance of which they are predicated. Thus, the existence of individual substances, and of individual substances alone, supports the very existence of the various predicables in all ten categories, and if individual substances did not exist, nothing would exist.[49] More than this, the existence of everything else is grounded in

46 Moravcsik (1967b), p. 82.
47 The point has been hotly debated for predicables that are the lowest members of the various nonsubstance categories, which on one account are not universals but *particulars*. (The debate was opened by Owen [1965], replying to Ackrill [1963]; later contributions include Moravcsik [1967b], Matthews and Cohen [1967–8], Frede [(1978) 1987], Heinaman [1981], and Benson [1988].) I will not discuss the various issues in any detail here. But notice that even if the lowest members of the nonsubstance categories are particulars, not universals, it is a separate question whether each is also *unique to* a given particular primary substance, or, instead, predicable of many. (For the difference between these questions, see Frede [(1978) 1987], pp. 58 ff.; Heinaman [1981], p. 295; and Benson [1988], p. 290.) If they are of the latter sort, we will also need a revision of the traditional account of the notion of a universal, along the lines proposed in Benson [1988]. Similarly, if the lowest members of the nonsubstance categories are particulars, it is again an independent question whether not only these but also the higher items in the same category that are SAID OF them can properly be in a primary substance, or whether, as Ackrill alleges, only *particular* nonsubstances can properly be in a primary substance, while the higher items from the same category cannot. Cf. note 40.
48 The phrase is borrowed from Wisdom (1934), p. 26. The similar view, that a Platonic form exists only if there exist objects that fall under it, is discussed in connection with Plato's *Sophist* in Frede (1967), p. 55.
49 In the list in *Categories* 4, Aristotle recognizes nine nonsubstance categories in addition to the category of substance, for a total of ten categories (see also *Topics* A9); other lists elsewhere, e.g., at *Metaphysics* Δ7, 1017a22–30, give a lesser number.

the existence of individual substances *by way of the two core relations of metaphysical predication,* which are relations of one-step ontological dependency. The connection with (metaphysical) predication is prominent in Aristotle's summary of his argument at the end of the passage we have been quoting:

Thus all other things are either said of primary substances as subjects or in them as subjects. *So if the primary substances did not exist it would be impossible for any of the other things to exist.* (*Categories,* 5, 2b3–6c; Ackrill's translation, my emphasis)

If the two theses (a) and (b) together can be sustained, they will furnish Aristotle with a powerful alternative to the Platonic account of primary substance. When Plato decides what to count as primary substance, he must choose between *two classes of subjects* – sensibles, which Have their predicables, and forms, which Are what they are.[50] His choice rests on the way in which a subject is connected to its predicables. He concludes, of course, that there exists *a single class of Izzers* that are the primary substances: a sensible exists and Has a given predicable, *F*-ness, thanks to a relation of ontological dependency on the relevant form, which Is (an) *F.* On Aristotle's account, however, Socrates as well as man Is various of his predicables, so the appeal to Izzing is no longer enough to fix what will count as primary substance. The work is done instead by the very notion of being a subject. For Aristotle, in the core theory there is *just one class of subjects,* namely, individual substances, and their role as subjects makes them primary for the two reasons set out in (a) and (b). Since individual substances are subjects, predication in general is possible – everything else is predicated of a subject, or is a subject of predicables, thanks to core relations of (metaphysical) predication involving some individual substance as subject. More than this, without individual substances as subjects for the core relations of (metaphysical) predication, nothing else would exist. On this account, the core relations of metaphysical predication are *relations of one-step ontological dependency,* thanks to which the existence of everything else is anchored in the existence of individual substances in one step. Fittingly, then, individual substances, and individual substances alone, are the primary substances.

On this account, the point separating Plato and Aristotle is not disagreement over the truism that without primary substances, noth-

50 Here I diverge from the traditional view that while Aristotle thought of subjects as prior, *predicables* get top billing in Plato's ontology. For the traditional view, see, e.g., Moravcsik (1967b), p. 94: "In viewing predication as somehow showing the dependency of the various predicates on their subjects, Aristotle came to the opposite conclusion from the one at which his teacher, Plato, arrived. . . . It is interesting historically to ask why predication should be viewed as showing any kind of dependency at all, either for subject or for predicate."

ing else would exist (this is analytic, as Dancy points out).[51] Nor do they disagree over whether primary substances are in some way the basic subjects.[52] Where they do disagree is whether the primary substances are a single class of Izzers (Plato), or whether (as Aristotle insists) they are subjects to the core relations of (metaphysical) predication – that is, on Aristotle's account, they are subjects to the core in and said-of relations thanks to which everything else exists.

4 SAID OF and IN: The Detailed Theory

A crucial part of the argument for the primacy of individual substances offered in Section 3 is the idea in thesis (a) that a predicable is (metaphysically) predicated of something other than a primary substance only if (and only because) there is some primary substance of which both items alike are (metaphysically) predicated. The defence of (a) has been partly textual, based primarily on *Categories* 5, 2a34–b6c, quoted at the beginning of Section 3. But the very fact that (a) helps explain the primacy Aristotle claims for primary substances also speaks in its favour: concerns about primacy give Aristotle good motivation for the view of predication that (a) attributes to him. In particular, (a) helps support an especially strong notion of primacy, according to which everything else exists thanks to relations of *one-step* ontological dependency on primary substances. In this final section, I defend the account of (metaphysical) predication that I take to be at the heart of Aristotle's view of the primacy of primary substance in a different and more limited way by setting out what I take to be his views regarding predication as a *formal theory* that I argue is consistent and also preserves the interesting properties Aristotle claims for his notions.

A scholarly note may first be in order. A frequent concern among commentators has been Aristotle's use of one and the same relation, '*x* is SAID OF *y*', both for the relation between animal and man (say) and for that between man and Socrates. The worry has been that, to all appearances, Aristotle has assimilated the relation of class membership, suitable for the relation between Socrates and man, and that of class inclusion, relating man and animal.[53] A typical response to these objections has been that Aristotle's SAID-OF relation is not simply to be identified with either class membership or class inclusion (more strictly, with their converses), or with any modern notion. Rather, the relation is sui generis: it is a primitive notion in Aristotle's theory, which defies any modern counterpart, and is simply stipulated to be a

---

51 Dancy (1975), p. 346.   52 See note 50.
53 See, e.g., the doubts of Ackrill (1963), p. 76, and Vlastos (1973), pp. 333–4.

relation that can properly stand *both* between Socrates and man *and* between man and animal, without obvious absurdity.[54]

The account to be offered here is in a way the composite of these two views. We concede that in the final analysis, there is a different relation between Socrates and man and between man and animal. But there is also a *single* relation between them. Thus, the (generic) SAID-OF relation *includes* both the core said-of relation between Socrates and man and the said-of* relation, about to be introduced, between man and animal – and in addition to these, the said-of** relation between colour and pallor (say) as well. Thus, a *single* generic relation encompasses three *distinct* subrelations. Meanwhile, the SAID-OF relation is not primitive, for it is defined in terms of its three subrelations. But the said-of relation (lowercase and without asterisks) *is* primitive in Aristotle's theory.[55]

In setting out the theory that I argue underlies Aristotle's remarks about (metaphysical) predication, I take as primitive versions of the SAID-OF and IN relations restricted to the case where the subject is a primary substance. I use lowercase letters to separate the core notions under discussion here from the respective generic notions:

(A1) x is said of y, only if x is a member of the same category as y and y is a primary substance.[56]
(A2) x is in y, only if x and y belong to different categories and y is a primary substance.[57]

(A1) and (A2) tell us the kinds of entity that can stand in the two core relations, but they do not pretend to *define* the relations in question. We define other cases in terms of the undefined ones. First,

(D1) x is *said of* * y if and only if (i) both x and y are secondary substances, (ii) necessarily, for any primary substance z, y is said of z only if x is said of z, and in fact (iii) there is some primary substance w such that y is said of w.

54 Following a suggestion of Moravcsik (1967b), pp. 92 ff.
55 On this view, then, Aristotle is not guilty of a logical mistake; cf. Duerlinger (1970), pp. 196–7. This paper contains formalizations of a number of principles involved in Aristotle's theory of (metaphysical) predication in the *Categories*, but I have not tried to record detailed similarities or differences between his account and mine.
56 (A1) leaves open the possibility that Socrates is said of Socrates, for example – that is, Socrates Is Socrates (cf. Code [1986], n. 11). Accordingly, individual substances are distinguished by the fact that they are not IN any subject whatever, and they are not SAID OF anything *else*, that is, not of anything other than themselves. But (A1) can easily be reformulated so as to rule even this out, by requiring that where x is said of y, x must be a higher member of the same category as y.
57 Things are more complicated, however, if Ackrill is right that, for Aristotle, *only individual instances* of a property can "properly be in" an individual substance. The changes needed to accommodate this view are discussed in the Appendix to this chapter.

For example, animal is said of* man just in case there is some primary substance of which man is said, and necessarily, *any* primary substance is such that man is said of it only if animal is said of it. (Thus, as we saw in Section 3, "animal is predicated of man and therefore also of the individual man; for were it predicated of none of the individual men, it would not be predicated of man at all"; *Categories* 5, 2a36–2b1.) It follows from (D1) that where one thing is said of* another, both the predicable and its subject are members of the category of substance, but the subject is not a primary substance. Notably, however, by (D1), cases of the said-of* relation are to be understood in terms of the core said-of relation (without asterisks). In a sense, then, a subject of the said-of* relation turns out to be not really a subject after all – not, at any rate, a subject in the core theory. If animal is said of* man, then upon analysis animal and man alike are predicables and are said of (without asterisk) *some individual substance* as subject. On this story, man's role as a subject on the left-hand side of instances of (D1) has disappeared: according to the analysis given in the definiens, the only subjects required are individual substances.

Next, say that

(D2) x is *said of*** y if and only if (i) both x and y are members of the same nonsubstance category, (ii) necessarily, for any primary substance z, y is in z only if x is in z, and in fact (iii) there is some primary substance w such that y is in w.

According to (D2), colour is said of** pallor, just in case pallor is in some primary substance, and necessarily, any primary substance is such that pallor is in it only if colour is in it. It follows from (D2) that where one thing is said of** another, both the predicable and its subject are members of the same nonsubstance category. The subject may be a lowest member of its category, but once more, it will not be a primary substance. But as (D2) makes clear, upon analysis pallor *loses* its role as a subject; both pallor and colour are in (without asterisk) some individual substance, and again the only proper subjects are individual substances.[58]

Next, we introduce a version of the inherence relation for the case in which a predicable is a nonsubstance and its subject is a substance but, again, not a primary substance. We have this definition:

(D3) x is *in** y if and only if (i) x is a member of a nonsubstance category and y is a secondary substance, and (ii) for some primary substance z, y is said of z and x is in z.

---

58 For the changes to (D2) needed if Ackrill is right that only individuals in nonsubstance categories can "properly be in" an individual substance, see the Appendix to this chapter.

For example, body (again, a secondary substance) has colour if and only if body is said of some primary substance, and this last has colour. (As we saw in Section 3, "colour is in body and therefore also in an individual body; for were it not in some individual body, it would not be in body at all"; *Categories* 5, 2b1–3.) It follows from (D3) that where one thing is in* another, the subject is a member of the category of substance, but (as before) it is not a primary substance. Once again, however, a subject of the in* relation is not a subject in the core theory at all: on the analysis (D3) gives, if colour is in* body, body and colour alike have some individual body as subject.[59]

We can use (D3) to license the inference Aristotle makes at 5, 3a4–6: "You will call the individual man grammatical, hence, you will call man and animal too grammatical." For suppose that grammar is in Socrates, and supply the further premiss that man and animal are said of Socrates. It follows that there is some primary substance *z* such that both man and animal are said of *z* and grammar is in *z*. We know also that man and animal are secondary substances and grammar is a member of a nonsubstance category. Accordingly, by (D3), grammar is in* man and in* animal, as required.

Aristotle does not expressly distinguish the different said-of relations set out here. The relation he discusses is the union of the three we have outlined. A similar remark applies to his notion of inherence. The two generic relations are defined as follows:

(D4) *x* is SAID OF *y* if and only if *either x* is said of *y or x* is said of* *y or x* is said of** *y*.

(D5) *x* is IN *y* if and only if *either x* is in *y or x* is in* *y*.

We can complete the theory by noticing formally the idea that the IN and SAID-OF relations together exhaust the available kinds of (meta-physical) predication:

(D6) *x* is (*metaphysically*) *predicated of y* if and only if *either x* is IN *y or x* is SAID OF *y*.

That is, (metaphysical) predication is the union of the SAID-OF and IN relations.[60]

---

59 The changes in (D3) needed to make room for Ackrill's view of inherence are given in the Appendix to this chapter.

60 To forestall objections, it is worth noting various *exclusions* from the theory just sketched. (i) At *Categories* 1a25–b2, Aristotle says that this grammatical knowledge (*hē tis grammatikē*) is in the *soul* and that this white (*to ti leukon*) is in the *body;* but he does not discuss the extent to which these examples take us away from the paradigm according to which individual nonsubstances are in *individual substances,* this man, for example, or this horse (2. 1b4–5; cf. 5. 2a13–14). (For this point, see Dancy [1975], pp. 372–3.) Notably, in the *Categories* he shows no interest in the notions of matter and form. He also seems to allow that a (spatially determined) *part* of a substance – a man's hand or foot, for example, is also a substance, contrary to his

Finally, the theory just sketched can be tested against the traditional idea that on Aristotle's account of predication in the *Categories*, both of the following are valid arguments:

I. Man Is (an) animal.   *aliter*   Animal is SAID OF man
    Socrates Is (a) man.   Man is SAID OF Socrates.
    Hence,   Hence,
    Socrates Is (an) animal.   Animal is SAID OF Socrates.

II. Blue Is (a) colour.   *aliter*   Colour is SAID OF blue.
    Aquamarine Is (a) blue.   Blue is SAID OF aquamarine.
    Hence,   Hence,
    Aquamarine Is (a) colour.   Colour is SAID OF aquamarine.

To prove I, suppose that animal is SAID OF man and that man is SAID OF Socrates.[61] Then since man is a nonlowest member of the category of substance, we know by (A1) and (D2) that animal is not said of man and that it is not said of** man; accordingly, by (D4), animal is said of* man. By (D1), then, for any primary substance z, man is said of z only if animal is said of z. By hypothesis, man is SAID OF Socrates: Socrates is a lowest member of his category (in fact, he is a primary substance), so that by (D1) and (D2), man is not said of* or said of** Socrates; rather, by (D4) again, man is said of Socrates. But by our previous result, man is said of a primary substance only if animal is said of it; hence, animal is said of Socrates. Accordingly, by (D4), animal is SAID OF Socrates, as required.

To prove II, suppose that colour is SAID OF blue and that blue is SAID OF aquamarine. Then since colour, blue, and aquamarine are all members of the same nonsubstance category, colour is said of** blue and blue is said of** aquamarine, by (A1), (D1), and (D4). By (D2), then, for any primary substance z, blue is in z only if colour too is in z. And by (D2) again, for any primary substance z, aquamarine is in z only if blue is in z, and in fact there is some primary substance w such that aquamarine is in w. It follows that for any primary substance z, aqua-

later views in, for example, *Metaphysics* Z16. (ii) With items like chalk pale (*to ti leukon*) as his example of a lowest nonsubstance, he shows no sign of worry that, strictly, pallor is in surface, which is a quantity (cf. 6. 5a38–b2), and not an individual substance. (iii) It is also unclear how the theory of the *Categories* is related to Aristotle's account of the four predicables (five, if we count differentiae) in the *Topics*. The four predicables are defined by reference to two ways in which a predicable may be related to its subject: the definition is both essential to and counterpredicated with its subject; an accident is neither essential nor counterpredicated; an *idion* is counterpredicated but not essential; and the genus is essential but not counterpredicated. It is not clear how these different notions relate to the twofold distinction in the *Categories* by which a predicable is either SAID OF or IN its subject. In particular, an *idion* is not essential, and so must be IN rather than SAID OF, its subject; but it is hard to know what to make of counterpredication in such a case, for where x is IN y, it is never the case that y is IN x. (iv) As already noted (note 10) differentiae do not have a ready place in the theory sketched.

61 For I, see *Categories* 3, 1b10 ff., 5, 2a19 ff. Both I and II follow the procedures also described at 3a17 ff., 37 ff., b4–5; see *Topics* Δ2, 122a3 ff., a31 ff.

marine is in z only if colour is in z. Hence, since there is some primary substance w, such that aquamarine is in w, by a final use of (D2), colour is said of** aquamarine, so that by (D4), colour is SAID OF aquamarine, as required.[62]

Individually, these two arguments show that the relations 'x is said of* y' and 'x is said of** y' are transitive. The primary relation 'x is said of y' (without asterisks) is also transitive. For suppose that x is said of y and y is said of z. Then by two applications of (A1), both y and z are primary substances; in these circumstances, given that y is said of z, plausibly, $y = z$.[63] Putting equals for equals, then, x is said of z. Related arguments will show that the generic relation 'x is SAID OF y' also is transitive.

Similarly, if x is in y and y is in z, then by (A2), y will be both a primary substance and a member of some *non*substance category, and if x is in* y and y is in* z, then by (D3), y is both a secondary substance and a member of some nonsubstance category, each of which is impossible. Accordingly, the antecedents in the definitions of transitivity and intransitivity are never satisfied, and the relations 'x is in y' and 'x is in* y' are vacuously transitive and intransitive. And by a similar argument, the same also holds for their union, 'x is IN y.' These results should be compared with the familiar claim that Aristotle's intracategorial relation in the *Categories* is transitive,[64] but that the crosscategorial relation is not transitive.

Appendix. How to Make Room for Ackrillian Property Instances

The account of Aristotle's theory just given will require extensive changes if, as Ackrill suggests,[65] Aristotle holds that only individual instances of a given property, that is, nonrecurrent particulars, can properly be in an individual substance. Setting out at least the first stages of how such an Ackrillian theory must go will, I hope, bring out

---

62 Cf. the references to Aristotle's text in note 61.

63 A fuller axiomatization of the theory that contains (A1) in the main text will add as an axiom the requirement that, where x and y are both lowest members of the category of substance and x is said of y, $x = y$. Things will go rather differently, however, if (A1) is modified in the way contemplated at the end of note 56: where x is said of y and y is said of z, it will turn out that both y and z are primary substances and that y is a higher member of the category of substance than z, which is impossible; on this showing, the antecedents in the definitions of transitivity and intransitivity are never satisfied, and the relation will be vacuously transitive and intransitive. But I omit these complications from the version of Aristotle's theory given here.

64 Moravcsik (1967b), pp. 91–2, says that Aristotle tells us this, but this is surely an overinterpretation. Ackrill (1963), p. 76, has doubts about the transitivity condition, possibly with difficulties over the distinction between class membership and class inclusion in mind (see note 53 and the remarks at the beginning of this section).

65 Ackrill (1963), pp. 74–5; cf. notes 40 and 47.

the advantages of the simpler account in the preceding text. In Ackrill's account, the primitive said-of relation is subject to the same condition as before:[66]

[A1] x is said of y, only if x is a member of the same category as y and y is a primary substance.

The account of inherence, however, is considerably more complicated. The core notion of inherence in Ackrill's theory, which is undefined, is subject to this condition:

[*A2] x is in y, only if x is an (Ackrillian) individual in some nonsubstance category and y is a primary substance.

Because what is in a subject is an Ackrillian individual, or an individual instance of a property, we suppose, further, that

[*A3] x is in y and x is in z, only if $y = z$.

Given [*A3], no universal can stand in the in relation to its subjects. To say what relation does hold between a universal property, generosity (say), and an individual substance, Callias, we must first take account of the relation between the relevant property instance, Callias's generosity, and the universal, generosity. For reasons that will emerge shortly, this relation is undefined; we suppose simply that

[*A4] x is an Ackrillian individual instance of y (y is said of' x) only if x is a lowest member of the same nonsubstance category as y.[67]

Given [*A4], we have the following defined notion of inherence:

[*D0] x is in' y if and only if (i) x is a universal in some nonsubstance category and y is a primary substance, and (ii) for some (Ackrillian) instance z of x, z is in y.[68]

For example, generosity is in' Callias, just in case generosity has Callias's generosity as an instance and Callias's generosity is in Callias.

Two comments are relevant here. First, on this account, generosity has Callias as its subject, only because it has Callias's generosity as its

66 Where a principle in the formalization of Ackrill's account directly replaces a principle in the official reconstruction of Aristotle's theory offered in the main text, or has no immediate counterpart in the official account, I use square brackets in place of parentheses and an asterisk preceding the numeral. Principles taken over without change from the official account are enclosed in square brackets but have no asterisk.

67 As with the other SAID-OF relations, I allow here for the possibility that a thing is said of' itself. It is a harmless consequence of this that in some cases an item said of' an Ackrillian instance will also be in (lowercase) some primary substance; in such cases, the item in question will be identical with that Ackrillian instance. But as Ackrill's theory requires, where x is said of' an Ackrillian instance y, *and $y \neq x$*, it will not be the case that x is also in some primary substance.

68 [*D0] defines the "relaxed sense of 'in'" recognized in Ackrill (1963), p. 83.

subject and Callias's generosity in turn has Callias as its subject: as a subject, then, Callias is at two removes from the predicable generosity. On Ackrill's view, we cannot *eliminate* the property instance as an intermediary between the universal property and the individual substance. Accordingly, as already noted in Section 3, generosity is dependent on Callias in *two* steps, contrary to the doctrine of one-step ontological dependency for which I have been arguing.

The fact that we cannot properly predicate the universal directly of the individual substance, bypassing the property instance, also helps explain why the relation between the property instance and the universal was left undefined earlier. It is tempting to understand the relation between these two along the lines of the extended cases of the said-of relation, where no individual substance is obviously involved as subject but the relation is defined in terms of core relations that do have individual substances as subjects. For man to be an animal, for example, is (roughly) for animal to be said of every individual substance man is said of. If this idea is to help in defining the relation between Callias's generosity and the universal generosity, we must already understand the relation between generosity and Callias (say). But, of course, to understand this last relation, we must already understand the relation between Callias's generosity and generosity, by [*Do]. The two would-be definitions, then, form a tight circle. And in general, it seems that any likely attempt to define the relation 'x is an Ackrillian instance of y' threatens to make the theory circular.

This is far from a complete account of the theory of Ackrillian property instances. From what we have seen so far, however, the theory has two systematic defects: it violates the doctrine of one-step ontological dependencies; and it requires an additional primitive relation, connecting property instances with the relevant universal, while an apparently natural strategy for defining the relation fails.

The remainder of the theory of property instances requires other changes in the account developed in the main text, which I cite briefly here for the sake of completeness. (D1) remains unchanged:

> [D1] x is *said of* y if and only if (i) both x and y are secondary substances, (ii) necessarily, for any primary substance z, y is said of z only if x is said of z, and in fact (iii) there is some primary substance w such that y is said of w.

But on the view that only individuals in nonsubstance categories may properly be in an individual substance, a replacement for (D2) will be needed. Where (D2) dealt with relations among all nonsubstances, there will now be two sets of cases: side by side with the undefined notion in [*A4], we have

[*D2] x is *said of''* y if and only if (i) both x and y are nonlowest members of the same nonsubstance category, (ii) necessarily, for any primary substance z, y is in' z only if x is in' z, and in fact (iii) there is some primary substance w such that y is in' w.

For example, pallor Is (a) colour if and only if (i) both pallor and colour are from the same nonsubstance category, and (ii) necessarily, some (Ackrillian) instance of pallor is in some primary substance only if some instance of colour is in that same primary substance, and in fact, (iii) some instance of pallor is in some primary substance.

Changes in (D3) will also be necessary. (D3) too splits into two cases:

[*D3a] x is *in''* y if and only if (i) x is an (Ackrillian) individual in some nonsubstance category and y is a secondary substance, and (ii) for some primary substance z, y is said of z and x is in z.

For example, suppose that Callias's generosity is in'' man; then man is said of Callias, and Callias's generosity is in him.

[*D3b] x is *in'''* y if and only if (i) x is a universal in some nonsubstance category and y is a secondary substance, and (ii) for some instance z of x, z is in'' y.

For example, timorousness is in''' the cat, for some individual instance of timorousness is in'' the cat – some individual cat, Felix (say), is timorous.

Less plausibly, Ackrill himself prefers to quantify universally over instances of x: thus, in place of [*D3b],

[*D3c] x is *in''''* y if and only if (i) x is a universal in some nonsubstance category and y is a secondary substance, and (ii) for *every* instance z of x, z is in'' y.

That is, by [*D3a], for every instance z of x, there is some primary substance w such that y is said of w and z is in w. For example, "to say that colour is in body is to say that every instance of colour is in an individual body" (Ackrill [1963], p. 83; cf. 74–5). But timorousness is not in'''' the cat: instances of timorousness are not confined just to cats.

The remainder of the theory is as expected:

[*D4] x is *SAID OF* y if and only if *either* x is said of y, *or* x is said of' y (y is an Ackrillian instance of x), *or* x is said of* y, *or* x is said of'' y.

[*D5] x is *IN* y if and only if *either* x is in y, *or* x is in' y, *or* x is in'' y, *or* x is in''' y (or possibly, x is in'''' y).

[D6] x is *(metaphysically) predicated of* y if and only if *either* x is IN y *or* x is SAID OF y.

The theory just outlined is tailored to the idea that the lowest-level items in the various nonsubstance categories are *individual instances* of the relevant items above them in the same category. Unexpectedly at first sight, if we reinterpret Ackrillian property instances as particular (but repeatable) qualities, in the style recommended by Frede and Furth, we get a formalization of something along the lines of the theory attributed to Aristotle by Furth. (In particular, to suit Furth's account, we must drop the axiom [*A3] that is distinctive of the theory of property instances and replace the references to Ackrillian property instances throughout by references to repeatable particular qualities.) According to Furth, eight distinct types of states of affairs need accounting for; the eight are constructed by means of the eight different subrelations collected in [*D4] and [*D5] in the reconstruction of Ackrill's theory just sketched. The difference between Furth's account and that offered in the main text centers around the treatment of the "nonsubstantial atoms" (Furth's term). For Furth, these are not Ackrillian property instances; but they are particulars and, on this account (Furth may reason), sufficiently different from the general items above them in the same category that the difference must be reflected in the different predication relations they are involved in.[69] Accordingly, the relation between colour and *chalk pale* (the nonsubstantial atom) must be kept separate from that between colour and *pallor;* similarly for the relations between *colour* and Socrates and *chalk pale* and Socrates; and finally, the relations between *colour* and animal and between *chalk pale* and animal. In this respect, Furth's theory can be seen as the smile that stays after the rest of the cat – the Ackrillian theory of property instances – is long gone.

69 According to the argument I am imagining on Furth's behalf, animal and man (say) are universals, while Socrates is a particular, so that the relation animal has to man cannot possibly be the same as the relation each of these singly bears to Socrates. (Comparably, in the official theory I offer in this chapter, animal is said of* man, but both are said of [no asterisk] Socrates.) By the same reasoning, then, the relation of colour to pallor cannot be the same as that which colour and pallor have singly to chalk pale, if colour and pallor are universals but chalk pale is a particular. This argument seems to show that if chalk pale is a particular, then we will need *more* inherence relations than those recognized in the official theory, and we must also give up the doctrine of one-step ontological dependencies. One response I will not attempt here would be to reassess the issue of particularity discussed by Frede and Furth (the contrary position to theirs is spelled out, e.g., in Code [1985], p. 103). A more modest alternative is to think that *repeatability,* not particularity, is the issue here. After all, Socrates differs from man and animal in that he alone is not *kata pollōn,* that is, not a repeatable. With respect to repeatability, however, on the non-Ackrill line there is no difference between chalk pale and the items above it in the same chain: chalk pale, pallor, and colour are all alike *kata pollōn.* So far as this goes, then, we will not need to separate the relation between colour and pallor from that between each of these singly and chalk pale.

PART II

Accidental Compounds

Accidental Compounds and Accidental Sameness

For the arguments of the sophists deal, so to speak, above all with the accidental; for example, the question whether musical and grammatical are different or the same, and whether musical Coriscus and Coriscus are the same.

Metaphysics E2, 1026b15–18

For if it is not the job of the philosopher, who is it who will inquire whether Socrates and Socrates seated are the same?[1]

Metaphysics Γ2, 1004b1–3

In this part, I supplement the survey of Aristotle's earlier metaphysical theory given in Part I with an account of his notion of *accidental compounds:* Socrates seated, the generous one, and the rest. Accidental compounds are not identical with individual substances, and they are not identical with accidents. Instead, they are *per accidens* beings, constructed out of individual substances and accidents, each of them beings *per se,* and an accidental compound stands in the relation of *accidental sameness* to its parent substance. On this account, an accidental compound is an entity of the form $a + \phi$, where a is an individual substance, ϕ is an accident of a, and the '+' notation introduces the primitive operation of *compounding:* a is *accidentally the same as* $a + \phi$, but at the same time, $a \neq a + \phi$.

Accidental Compound Theory (ACT) requires an ontology of individual substances and their accidents, but nothing more. But in an extension of Core ACT, Aristotle also admits such entities as musical just Coriscus; he can imagine that an accident, musicality, is an accident, not just of an individual substance, Coriscus, as in Core ACT, but of the compound, just Coriscus; and he can suppose that just Coriscus is in a sense accidentally the same as, not the parent substance

---

1 A "repudiating question": Aristotle means that it is, of course, the philosopher, none other, who will do the job mentioned.

Coriscus, but another compound, musical Coriscus. These ideas go well beyond what is provided for in Core ACT, but it is important to see that they can all be explained in terms of Core ACT and its apparatus of individual substances, accidents, and the core accident-of relation between an accident and an individual substance. On this view, even the most elaborate extravagances of Extended ACT stay ultimately within the limited resources required for the account of Core ACT.

The relation of accidental sameness between an accidental compound and its parent substance also requires attention. It is one of two sameness relations, each different specifications of the generic relation of numerical sameness,[2] that Aristotle plays off against one another. Of the two relations, one counts things the same if they are *accidentally* the same; the other counts them the same if they are the same *in being*. Corresponding to these two relations of sameness, Aristotle considers two different sameness principles. First, anything is true of one thing just in case it is true of the other, *if they are accidentally the same.* In the *De Sophisticis Elenchis,* the modal and epistemic paradoxes offer counterexamples to this principle, and Aristotle corrects it accordingly to incorporate instead the second variety of numerical sameness: anything is true of one thing just in case it is true of the other, *if they are the same in being.* Aristotle's two paradoxes themselves have a remarkably modern ring, and it will be a useful corrective to see just how large a distance there really is between Aristotle's treatment of them, which is tied inextricably to the conceptual apparatus of ACT, and various familiar treatments of comparable puzzles in contemporary discussion.

That accidental compounds are not identical with individual substances – that Socrates seated is not identical with its parent substance, Socrates – is not the least striking fact about them. But the relation between a compound and its parent substance again resists assimilation to any easy contemporary notion. Accidental sameness is not the same, for example, as so-called contingent identity. At the same time, odd though the relation between Socrates and Socrates seated may seem from a contemporary standpoint, the distinction between the

---

2 *Topics* A7, 103a25–31, and see Chapter 4. According to *Topics* A7, there is also a third specification of numerical sameness, numerical sameness rendered by proprium, but for all practical purposes, we may treat this as a special case of accidental sameness. The crucial point, at any rate, is that this is *not* numerical sameness rendered by definition, that is, sameness in being, or "essential" sameness.

None of the different varieties of numerical sameness is the same as our identity. Sameness in being, I suspect, is more restrictive than identity. Accidental sameness, by contrast, is far weaker, to the point that, as we shall see, it is not even an equivalence relation. As already suggested, then, things that are accidentally the same will still be *distinct* items in Aristotle's ontology.

two is not an *intensional* one. A further point concerns the fact that Socrates is a substance but Socrates seated is not; equally, Socrates seated is an accidental compound but Socrates is not. On the assumption that contrary to what is argued here, Socrates and Socrates seated are identical – that is, 'Socrates' and 'Socrates seated' are different names for the identical thing – the examples show that inserting different names for the identical thing into the contexts ' . . . is a substance' and ' . . . is an accidental compound' does not preserve truth value, so that these and perhaps other major classificatory predicates in Aristotle's ontology are *referentially opaque*. In fact, however, Socrates and Socrates seated are not identical in the first place, and there is no support for a conclusion of referential opacity.

Finally, the notion of *compounding* is also crucial. A notion of compounding figures not only in the kinds of compound to be discussed in this part, but also in the form–matter compounds discussed in Part III that are distinctive of Aristotle's later metaphysical theory. The latter kind of compound, however, is not a part of Aristotle's earlier theory. Accidental compounds, then, and the complementary notion of accidental sameness together make up a fragment of a larger theory of compounds, different parts of which appear at different stages in Aristotle's work.

The basic ontology of ACT is set out in Chapter 3; the same chapter also contains the formalization of Core and Extended ACT, in which the real ontological commitments of the different versions of ACT are shown to best advantage. Next, in Chapter 4, I discuss various principles of accidental sameness and the modal and epistemic paradoxes in the *De Sophisticis Elenchis* that Aristotle uses to force the shift from a sameness principle built around accidental sameness to one featuring the stronger notion of sameness in being. In Chapter 5, finally, I return to the distinction between an accidental compound and its parent substance and contrast what I take to be Aristotle's view of the relation between them with various rival accounts, in particular the view that they are contingently identical and the view that the distinction between them is in some sense intensional, or accomplished only by the use of predicates that are referentially opaque.

3

Accidental Compound Theory:
The Basic Notions

The contrast between substances, on the one hand, and members of the nonsubstance categories or accidents, on the other, already prominent in previous chapters, is one of the most familiar and also most persistent features of Aristotle's ontology, from his earliest surviving works to the latest. Somewhat less attention has been given to a third class of entities, in addition to substances and accidents, which are again a part of Aristotle's ontology from the *Categories* all the way through to the central books of the *Metaphysics*. These are the entities I shall call "accidental compounds."[1]

Accidental compounds begin life in the first chapter of the *Categories*, where Aristotle introduces the closely related notion of a paronym:

When things are called after something in accordance with ‹its› name, but differing in ending, they are said to be *paronyms*. Thus, for example, the grammarian ("the grammatical ‹one›," *ho grammatikos*) gets his name from grammar (*grammatikē*), the brave ‹one› (*ho andreios*) gets his from bravery (*andreia*).[2] (1, 1a12–15)

Expressions of the form 'the grammatical ‹one›' and 'the brave ‹one›', which appear in this passage, are constructed out of the definite article together with an adjectival or sometimes participial[3] form, usually in

---

1 The three chapters of this part are a corrected and expanded version of F. Lewis (1982). My interest in accidental compounds was spurred by a remark in K. Fine (unpublished). The same entities are also studied in Matthews (1982), where they appear under the name "kooky objects." Dissenters include Peterson (1985), Williams (1985), and Spellman (1990), and the topic is also discussed in Matthen (1983) and White (1986).

2 The translation of this passage is discussed in Jones (1972), pp. 117–21. Notice the use-mention confusion in Aristotle's characterization here: the participle *diapheronta* and the relative pronoun *hosa* agree, so that literally Aristotle says that it is *things* that differ in ending from the name of the object they are called after.

3 "Participial" here is to take care of verbal forms, 'the ‹one› approaching' and the like; see *Categories* 7, 6b11–14, and note 9.

the masculine gender, but also occasionally the neuter.[4] These are *paronymous referring expressions,* and Aristotle calls their referents "*paronyms.*"

I will argue that a paronym is not simply the person or thing that is grammatical, brave, and the rest. Nor is it the accident, grammar, bravery, and so on. Instead, as we shall see, paronyms are *accidental compounds,* which are neither simply substances nor simply accidents, but rather *compounds* of an individual substance with an accident. Our account of accidental compounds starts with Aristotle's concept of a paronym and with the difference between paronyms, on the one hand, and accidents and substances, on the other.

1 Substances, Accidents, and Accidental Compounds

We begin, then, not with accidental compounds themselves, but with the closely connected topic of paronyms. Now a paronym is a paronym *of something,* so our proper starting point is the relation 'x is a paronym of y'. It is worth emphasizing that the relation 'x is a paronym of y' is a relation between *entities,* not between expressions.[5] Paronyms too, therefore, are entities, and not linguistic items. Nonetheless, Aristotle sees a close connection between paronymy and matters of language. Thus, according to Aristotle, a is a paronym of b only if there is a designator, α, of a and a designator, β, of b such that α is derived "with a difference in inflection" from β. The grammatical one, for example, is a paronym of grammar in virtue of the fact that he is *called* 'grammatical' and that grammar is called 'grammar'.[6]

This mixture of linguistic and metaphysical considerations in Aristotle's notion of paronymy is an uneasy one. The claim is sometimes made that one thing is a paronym of another *under one designation,* but *not* under others. For example, a thing is a paronym of bravery under the designation 'the brave one', but not under the designation 'the musical one' (say) or 'Socrates'. Alternatively, the sentence 'The brave

---

4 Examples are given in Section 1.

5 The view that paronymy is a relation between expressions is advanced by Ross (1936), p. 559.

6 This can hardly be a point about which expression, for example, 'grammarian' or 'grammar', comes first *morphologically.* It is unlikely that the Greek *andreios* (brave) is morphologically derivative from *andreia* (bravery), and quite certain that *grammatikos* (grammarian) is not so derivative from *grammatikē* [sc., *technē*] ('grammar'). So Aristotle's point must be a semantic one: the use of an adjective to pick out a thing can be explained in terms of a relation between that thing and some entity named by a noun that in the ordinary case is syntactically related to the adjective in some suitable way. Although the phenomenon Aristotle is drawing our attention to here is at bottom an ontological one, however, he expresses himself in terms of the accidental syntactic relations between given adjectives and nouns in which that phenomenon is often reflected; see the next but one paragraph in the main text and note 8.

one is a paronym of bravery' is said to be *referentially opaque* at its subject position.[7] On one reading, these claims are harmless, or almost entirely so. The status of a thing as a paronym, according to Aristotle's definition, involves not just metaphysics, but also how things are *called;* on this line of thought, as we shall see, the opacity reduces to that of quotation-mark contexts, and nothing more. On other accounts, however, the opacity is less tractable and is essentially involved in making the distinction between Socrates and the brave one. We shall return to these different treatments of paronymy and opacity later in this section.

Even the minimal role of language in paronymy sketched in the preceding paragraph is problematic, however, for it threatens to limit needlessly the utility of paronymy. Aristotle presents linguistic facts of the kind quoted – for example, that the brave one is called 'brave', while at the same time bravery is called 'bravery' – as logically necessary conditions for paronymy so that, for him, paronymy is essentially tied to matters of language.[8] But the fact that bravery has the name 'bravery', while the brave one is called 'brave' ("with a difference in inflection"), is a mere accident of language, which can (and in various cases does) fail, in contrast to the abiding metaphysical fact that the brave one exists only because there exist the accident, bravery, and some individual substance appropriately related to bravery. It is these underlying metaphysical ideas Aristotle will want to concentrate on.

How, then, are we to understand the metaphysical ideas underlying the notion of paronymy? As Aristotle's examples make clear, one important ingredient in paronymy is his notion of an *accident*. The paronym the generous one, for example, is a paronym of, or is named after, the accident generosity. But a paronym is *not identical with* an

7 A context, *A*, is *referentially opaque* at a given position, if and only if for expressions α and β, such that α and β denote the identical entity, a context, *A'*, is like *A* except that *A* contains α in that position but *A'* contains β there, and *A* and *A'* do not denote the same thing (or if *A* and *A'* are sentences, *A* and *A'* do not have the same truth value).

8 "logically necessary": see *Categories* 8, 10a32–b9. As defined by Aristotle, therefore, paronymy appears to be a matter of mere grammatical accident; cf. Owen (1960), p. 175, and Dancy (1975), pp. 362–3. Where the syntactic conditions for paronymy are satisfied, however, they are the symptom of some deeper metaphysical point. But the moral can be different in different cases. A compound of form and matter is a paronym of its constituent matter (*Physics* H3, 245b9), a fact that here provides a criterion for distinguishing the genuine coming-to-be of a substance from mere alteration. The same phenomenon (but without the jargon of paronymy) yields a different moral at *Metaphysics* Z7, 1033a5–23, and yet a third moral emerges at *Metaphysics* Θ7, 1049a18 ff., esp. 36–b3, where perhaps we find Aristotle's final thoughts on the subject. Still different varieties of paronymy appear at *Eudemian Ethics* Γ1, 1228a36, and *Physics* Γ7, 207b9. In the *Categories* and *Topics*, paronymy draws attention to a single underlying metaphysical relation between an accident and the compound of that accident with a given individual substance. But this relation is only accidentally reflected in syntax, and sometimes syntax fails to reflect the metaphysical facts altogether (*Categories* 8, 10a32–b9).

accident. The difference between accidents and paronyms is reflected in Aristotle's chapter on quality (*Categories* 8), in the contrast between "qualities" (*poiotētes*) and "things qualified" (*poia*), where the latter are "spoken paronymously after" the former (*ta kata tautas* [= *poiotētas*] *parōnumōs legomena; Categories* 8, 10a29; cf. 7, 8b25). A similar contrast is implied by Aristotle's remark (*Categories* 7, 6b11–14) that a paronym from an accident in the category of position is not itself a position.[9] It is plausible to assume that if an item is not a position, then it is not a member of the category of position. In this case at least, then, a paronym is not a member of the same category as the accident from which it is constructed. If this result holds generally, then again a paronym is not the same as an accident.[10]

A more difficult question concerns the relation between paronyms and *substances*. A first reaction is that substances just are paronyms. For example, we know that the generous one is so-named after generosity. Now it is false that Socrates is so-named after generosity. But we cannot use this fact in order to conclude that Socrates is not identical with the generous one or, in general, that substances are not paronyms, for this would be to overlook the demonstrative in the predicate, ' . . . is *so*-named after –'. In the claim,

The generous one is so-named after generosity,

we need only replace the demonstrative with the quotation-mark name of the predicate it refers back to:

The generous one is named 'generous' after generosity,

and the conclusion that substances are paronyms is ready to hand. For example, if Socrates is the generous one, then *he, Socrates,* is named 'generous' after generosity, and *he* is a paronym.

This argument is modelled after a well-known example of Quine ([1960], 153). We know that Giorgione is so-named because of his size. Now it is false that Barbarelli is so-named because of his size. But we cannot use this fact to conclude that Giorgione is not Barbarelli, for

9 Aristotle says: "To lie or to stand or to sit (*to de anakeisthai ē hestanai ē kathesthai*) are not themselves positions, but they are spoken of paronymously from the positions mentioned (= lying, sitting, standing [*hē anaklisis, hē stasis, hē kathedra*])." The infinitives here, 'to lie', 'to stand', and so forth, stand in for uses of the verb to form singular predications, '*a* is lying down', '*a* is standing', and the like. In this respect, therefore, Aristotle supposes that verbs as well as adjectives are implicated in paronymy; see Jones (1972), p. 121, and Dancy (1975), p. 361.

10 This conclusion goes against the view attributed to Aristotle by Simplicius and Dexippus (Ross [1952], p. 106) and picked up by Dancy (1975), pp. 368–9 and n. 41; cf. Code (1976a), n. 11, and (1976b), p. 179, that a paronym is ("from a certain point of view," Dancy [1975]) a member of the same category as the accident from which it is constructed. For similar reasons, we should avoid the characterization by Woods (1974–5), p. 171: "composites *in* other categories" (my emphasis).

this would be to overlook the demonstrative in the predicate, ' . . . is *so*-named because of – '. In the claim

> Giorgione is so-named because of his size,

we have only to replace the demonstrative with the quotation-mark name of the term it refers back to:

> Giorgione is named 'Giorgione' because of his size,

and it is possible once more to suppose that, in fact, Giorgione and Barbarelli are one and the same.

The treatment of paronymy on the model of Quine's Barbarelli example is also instructive for what it suggests about the connections between paronymy and referential opacity. We can reasonably assert that

> (1) The generous one is a paronym of generosity,

while denying that

> (2) Socrates is a paronym of generosity,

even though it is Socrates who is generous. This may seem enough to show that the two claims are referentially opaque at subject position, and for those who find this line of thought attractive, the Barbarelli example will suggest that the opacity ultimately is that of quotation-mark contexts. On this account, we can replace the opaque idiom '*x* is a paronym of generosity' by the locution, '*x* is a paronym of generosity with respect to the (true) description, 'generous' ', which contains the quotation-mark name ' 'generous' ' (where this last is known to be referentially opaque), but which otherwise we stipulate to be referentially *transparent*. Claims of paronymy can now be put into this form:

> (3) Socrates, a.k.a. the generous one, is a paronym of generosity with respect to the (true) description 'generous'.

Here, apparently, the opacity is confined to the quotation-mark context, where its presence is routine and unsurprising.

An unexpected complication stands in the way of reducing the opacity involved in paronymy to that simply of quotation-mark contexts in this otherwise attractive way. In the circumstances at hand, in which it is Socrates who is generous, it is true that

> (4) The generous one is a paronym of generosity with respect to the (true) description 'generous'.

But in those same circumstances, still (I shall want to argue) it is *not* the case that

(5) Socrates is a paronym of generosity with respect to the (true) description 'generous'.

It can be agreed on all sides that the quotation-mark context in both (4) and (5) is referentially opaque. Beyond this lies disagreement. One possible explanation of the difference in truth value between (4) and (5) requires us to abandon our assumption of transparency and suppose that the sentences are opaque still one more time, at subject position in each case. On this account, Socrates and the generous one are *identical;* hence, the difference in truth value must come from the fact that (4) and (5) are after all referentially opaque at subject position.

In contrast to this, I shall argue that (4) and (5) have different truth values, but for reasons that have nothing to do with referential opacity. The explanation lies instead with *Accidental Compound Theory,* according to which straightforwardly 'the generous one' in (4) and 'Socrates' in (5) name *different* things, even though by hypothesis it is Socrates who is generous in the circumstances in question.

On this account, (4) and (5) are referentially transparent at subject position, and the opacity is only that of the quotation-mark name ' 'generous' '. But the moral is quite different from that in Quine's Giorgione–Barbarelli case, in which a similar treatment of the opacity clears the way for saying that Giorgione and Barbarelli are identical. On the interpretation to be developed here, Socrates and the generous one are straightforwardly nonidentical.

The point that Socrates and the generous one are not identical, even where it is Socrates who is generous, deserves special emphasis. We find a clear reason for taking them to be distinct in the fact Aristotle notes at *GC* A4, 319b25–32: they come into existence and go out of existence at different times. For Socrates, the change of becoming ungenerous is mere alteration; but for the generous one it is sheer extinction. In the same vein at *An. Pr.* A33, 47b29–37, Aristotle criticizes the inference from the premises

(i) Musical Mikkalus will perish tomorrow,

and

(ii) Mikkalus is musical Mikkalus,

to the conclusion

(iii) Mikkalus will perish tomorrow.

The premises can be true, Aristotle remarks, but the conclusion false. Musical Mikkalus and Mikkalus can exist at different times, then, for Mikkalus can continue to exist after musical Mikkalus has perished.

But as before, this fact shows that even if the two are in some sense the same, as (ii) suggests, they are not identical.[11]

If these conclusions about ontology are right, they will force a corresponding shift in the interpretation of referring expressions like 'the generous ‹one›' in Aristotle. If there were nothing out of the ordinary about the use of such phrases in Aristotle, we could assume that 'the generous ‹one›' can be co-referential with the proper name 'Socrates', for example, and that they *will* be co-referential if the circumstances are right, that is, if Socrates is the one we have in mind who is generous. This is to give paronymous referring expressions the logic of our definite descriptions.[12] Thus,

> the generous one

becomes

> the *x* such that *x* (alone) is generous.

And then in a wide range of cases, the ordinary apparatus of reference allows us to interchange expressions of this form for proper names of substances, 'Socrates' and the like.[13]

A preferable view, I think, is that Aristotle's expression 'the generous ‹one›', for example, does not after all have the logic of a definite description, but is a name of some entity *other than x*. What entity might this be? I suggest that paronyms can be identified with what in

11 Premiss (i) cannot be a slightly more elaborate way of saying what is said in (iii) if (i) and (iii) have different truth values. But could (i) be a somewhat arch way of saying the following?

> (iv) Mikkalus will no longer be musical tomorrow.

The possibility cannot be ruled out that (i) is a mere *façon de parler* for (iv), but on the interpretation offered here, (i) carries genuine ontological commitment to an entity over and above Mikkalus himself. (As we shall see later in this section, however, musical Mikkalus and compounds like him are in an important sense *derived* entities, and not basic in Aristotle's ontology.)

It is hard to see the relevance of Aristotle's own comment on why the inference fails (cf. Ross [1949], pp. 401–2, and Smith [1989], p. 163). But the style of argument here, with a premiss connecting an accidental compound with its parent substance, is of crucial importance in the theory of accidental compounds and of the related notion of accidental sameness, to be developed in this part. The question of how two things can be "in some sense the same, . . . but not identical" is discussed later in this section.

12 Here I oversimplify the state of current discussion about definite descriptions. For example, the remark in the previous sentence in the main text correctly identifies the *semantic* reference of the definite description 'the generous one', but I omit complications to do with issues of *speaker's* reference; see Kripke (1977), pp. 14–15.

13 Again, I oversimplify here. Strictly, this remark holds only for something like the "weak" Russell language described in Kripke (1977), p. 16, in contrast to the *intermediate* Russell language, in which definite descriptions are not terms, are not assigned a reference, and have no meaning in isolation, and the *strong* Russell language, in which a policy of contextual paraphrase is in force and definite descriptions do not appear at all.

the *Metaphysics* Aristotle calls alternatively "compounds by way of the other categories"[14] or "things spoken of in virtue of an accident."[15] Examples of the latter kinds of entity are the referents of such expressions as 'musical Socrates', '‹the› pale man', 'Socrates seated', and so on. I shall suppose that paronymous referring expressions refer to exactly these same kinds of entities.

On this account, expressions of the form 'the generous ‹one›', which direct us fairly immediately to a given accident but are silent about the identity of the substance with which that accident is caught up, are merely elliptical for expressions in which the underlying substance is explicitly identified. Here are examples from Aristotle's text of both kinds of expression:

Nonelliptical

pale man (*Topics* E4, 133b17–24, 34–6; *Metaphysics* Z6, 1031a19–28, Z12, 1037b17–18, M2, 1077b4 ff.)[16]
musical Coriscus (*SE* 22, 178b39–179a1; *Metaphysics* E2, 1026b15–18)
musical Socrates (*Metaphysics* Δ9, 1018a2–3, Δ29, 1024b29–31)
Socrates seated (*Metaphysics* Γ2, 1004b1–3)

Elliptical

the seated ‹one›, the musical ‹one› (*Topics* A7, 103a30–1)
the approaching ‹one› (*SE* 24, 179b1–4)
the musical ‹thing› (*to mousikon*) (*Metaphysics* Z11, 1037b5–7)

Aristotle's remarks at *Metaphysics* Z1, 1028a25–8, suggest that the elliptical reading of expressions in the second group is the correct one:

These [sc., the walking ‹thing›, the seated ‹thing›, the healthy ‹thing›] are evidently more of the nature of beings, since there is such a thing as a definite subject underlying them (and this is the substance, that is, the particular), "which is plainly implied in the use of such a designation" [Ross's phrase]; for the good ‹thing› or the seated ‹thing› is not said without this.

For example, suppose that Socrates is generous. Then both 'the generous ‹one›', in a suitable context of utterance, and 'generous Socrates' have the same denotation.[17]

---

14 *kata tas allas katēgorias suntheta, Metaphysics* Z4, 1029b22–7; cf. M2, 1077b4–9, 10–11 – *not* "compounds *in* other categories" (Woods [1974–5], p. 171, my italics); see note 10.
15 *tōn legomenōn kata sumbebēkos; Metaphysics* Z6, 1031a19, b22–3; cf. Δ7.
16 See note 20.
17 Giving such similar treatment to phrases of these two kinds may sit oddly with contemporary sensibilities: for while the phrase 'the stately, plump one', for example, looks very much like a definite description, there seems no chance that 'stately,

Accordingly, I will replace both of these Aristotelian names with the single name 'Socrates + generous'. The notation '*x* + *y*' here is meant to express the notion of *compounding,* first brought to my attention by Kit Fine, which I take to be primitive in Aristotle's theory: other associations that the same notation may have in other contexts should be disregarded. The name 'Socrates + generous' is intended to denote the *compound* of the substance Socrates and the accident generosity. This last entity, finally, Socrates + generous, is an *accidental compound.*

As I mean to use the designator 'Socrates + generous', therefore, the expression is not a slightly roundabout way of naming Socrates (supposing it is Socrates who is generous). It names a different entity: not the substance, but the compound of that substance and the accident generosity.[18]

plump Buck Mulligan' can be seen in this way. Statements containing either phrase, however, are open to paraphrase ("Buck Mulligan was stately and plump, and he . . . ," "Exactly one thing was stately and plump, and he . . . "); interpretations of Aristotle will then differ over whether (i) both the original statement and its paraphrase refer to the same entity, namely, just Buck Mulligan himself, or whether (ii) the original statement refers not to Mulligan, but to an entity of a very different kind, namely, an accidental compound.

The elliptical reading of 'the generous ‹one›' and similar expressions proposed in the main text and in F. Lewis (1982) has been disputed in White (1986). According to White, the approacher (White's example) is not itself a compound, so that there is no *x* such that the approacher is identical with the compound of *x* with the accident, approaching, as the elliptical reading requires; instead, it is a simple, along the lines suggested in *Physics* A7 (see note 27) and, *together with* the man (say), makes up the complex the approaching man. This alternative account fits well Aristotle's division between simple and complex in *Physics* A7 (note 27), but I find it otherwise mysterious. In particular, White says that the approacher is neither a compound nor an attribute – but not what it *is.* It does not seem right to say that it is an individual substance or, even less likely, a *variable* substance, varying with whomever happens to be approaching. Pending a clearer alternative account of the approacher, I shall keep to the elliptical reading in the text, according to which the difference between the approacher and approaching Socrates (where Socrates *is* the relevant one approaching) is only a difference in how each is specified: they are the same thing, only more or less completely specified.

18 The difference between Socrates and Socrates + generous is clearly stated again at *Topics* E4, 133b15–24, 31–6. Here Aristotle distinguishes "that to which something belongs as an accident" (*tini hōi sumbebēke ti*), for example, a man, and "the accident taken together with that to which it belongs as an accident" (*tōi sumbebēkoti . . . lambanomenōi meta tou hōi sumbebēken*), for example, a pale man: more simply, a thing can be made out to be one thing taken "in itself" (*kath' hauto*), another thing taken "with its accident" (*meta tou sumbebēkotos*). The terminology at *Metaphysics* Δ29, 1024b29–31, is even more succinct: *auto* and *auto peponthos* – for example, Socrates and musical Socrates. See also the passages at *Physics* A7, 190a20–1, and B3, 195a16–21, and the discussions in White (1972), pp. 71–7, Code (1976b), pp. 174–82, and Cohen (1978), p. 391.

Finally, in a strong statement of the view I mean to oppose here, C. Williams (1985), p. 68, writes concerning the musical thing and the man that "the difference is a difference, not between two things, but between two ways of picking out one and the same thing." Williams sees himself as shifting Aristotle's statements from the material to the formal mode, shedding various ontological implications of the former as he goes; he is candid at one point that it may not be that Aristotle "saw his own work in this light" (p. 65), although later parts of his article seem less cau-

A word is in order here about the choice of *compounding* as a primitive in Aristotle's theory. The notion of compounding appears at virtually every stage in Aristotle's metaphysics, not only in connection with compounds of an accident with a substance, but also in his later works, as we shall see, in which Aristotle introduces compounds of form with matter. Aristotle also speaks of one item's being *in* another. In the *Categories*, for example, as we have seen, Aristotle says that an accident is *in* a substance, and this same way of talking survives in the later works, where he will say both that (again) an accident is in a given substance and also that a form is in a given matter. In general, the two ways of talking – that one item is *in* another or that something is the *compound* of one item with another – exist side by side in Aristotle's text, and I take them both to stand for primitive notions in his theory.[19] The two notions differ most obviously in that the notation '+' is a connective that inserted between a term for an individual substance and a term for an accident, in that order, yields a term for an accidental compound, while the expression '*x* is in *y*,' as Aristotle uses it in the *Categories*, is a two-place predicate that joins a term for an accident and a term for an individual substance, in that order, to make a sentence. The notions are related, for the relevant sentence is true, just in case the corresponding compound exists; for example, pallor is in Socrates if and only if Socrates + pale exists.[20]

Ultimately, the notion of an accidental compound in Aristotle supersedes his earlier notion of a paronym. As it happens, the compound Socrates + generous, for example, is a paronym of generosity, even by Aristotle's linguistic criterion, for its name, 'Socrates + generous', is derived at least in part, and with a "difference in inflection," from the name 'generosity'. Underlying this accident of syntax, however, is the ontological fact that the compound has both Socrates

---

tious. For what I believe is an apt comment on the "sanitizing" tendency in this article, see White (1986), p. 478.

19 Cf. Chapter 2, Section 2, and Chapter 6, Section 4.

20 Aristotle says more about accidental compounds in *Metaphysics* M2 in the course of making a point about priority. Prior in definition, Aristotle argues, is not necessarily prior in substance. His example involves the accident pale and the compound, pale man: "For those things are prior in substance which when separated ‹from other things› surpass ‹them› in being, but one thing is prior in definition to others, if the definitions of the latter ‹are compounded› out of the definition of the former. . . . For if attributes do not exist apart from the substances – for example, something in motion, or pale – then the pale [= pallor] is prior to the pale man in definition, but not in substance: for it cannot exist separated, but always exists simultaneously with the compound [*hama tōi sunolōi*] (and by the compound, I mean the pale man). . . . it is by addition to the pale (*ek protheseōs . . . tōi leukōi*) that we speak of the pale man (*ho leukos anthrōpos*)" (*Metaphysics* M2, 1077b2–4, 4–9, 10–11; following Ross's translation; cf. *Metaphysics* Δ11, 1018b34–7). This example again suggests that Aristotle's talk of "compounding" in this context is not to be taken in any literal sense: it is not part of our ordinary notion of a compound that one of the two ingredients in a compound exists or does not exist simultaneously with the compound itself.

and the accident generosity as constituents. Ontological facts of this sort for Aristotle are what count in the end, while paronymy fades from his attention. Similarly, at *Metaphysics* Z4, 1029b27–9, Aristotle recognizes that the question 'Is a pale man a metaphysical unity?' is not settled by whether the language we use to refer to it is itself complex ('pale man') or simple (the coinage 'cloak'). Thus, paronymy too, as Aristotle defines it, is in the last resort unuseful because it is too closely tied to matters of language. With Aristotle, then, I will leave the notion of a paronym largely to one side hereafter and talk instead of an accidental compound (a "compound by way of an accident"; *Metaphysics* Z4, 1029b22–7).[21]

As with paronyms, I shall suppose that accidental compounds are not identical with individual substances. How, then, *are* accidental compounds and substances related? In an instructive passage at *Topics* E5, 133b15–36, Aristotle insists that a man and a pale man are not "simply different," or "different without qualification" (*heteron haplōs*), but different *because their being is different (allo legetai tōi heteron einai autois to einai)*. Here I take him to say that the two are *distinct*, while at the same time leaving open the possibility that they are *accidentally the same*. The relation of accidental sameness, which is *not* the same as our identity, will be the subject of later sections in this chapter.

But if Aristotle admits accidental compounds to his ontology and if accidental compounds are not identical with, but merely accidentally the same as, individual substances, how can he avoid the charge of ontological extravagance? For each individual substance, there are as many accidental compounds having that substance as their underlying subject as that subject itself has accidents. If Socrates (say) is pale, and musical, and generous, then in addition to Socrates, there exist pale Socrates, and musical Socrates, and generous Socrates, and so on. This proliferation of entities is tolerable for reasons having to do with the *status* these different items have in Aristotle's metaphysical theory. A preliminary point involves Aristotle's distinction between beings *per se* and beings *per accidens*. In the *Posterior Analytics*, Aristotle singles out individual substances as *per se* beings: roughly, they are subjects for predicables *in their own right*, and *not* in virtue of their relation to some further entity.[22] Accidental compounds, by contrast, are *per accidens*

---

21 Under certain conditions, however, an accidental compound will also be a *paronym of* a given accident. For example, Socrates + generous is, but cloak is not, a paronym of generosity, even if 'cloak' is a a name for the generous one. Paronymy, then, will still be useful in helping identify a compound's constituent accident. For example, Socrates + generous is both a compound and a paronym: from the name 'Socrates + generous' (but *not* the name 'cloak', say), we can read off the identity of the constituent accident, generosity.

22 At *An. Po.* A4, 73b5–10, A19, 81b25–9, A22, 83a1–23; cf. *An. Pr.* A27, 43a34–6, Aristotle sets out a contrast between what he calls *per se* ("natural") and *per accidens* ("unnatural") predication. Thus,

beings: they are what they are in virtue of a relation to something
else. In particular, an accidental compound is a subject for predicables
in virtue of a relation to its parent substance. For example, the musical
‹thing› is white only because the man who happens to be musical is
white.[23]

An accidental compound is a being *per accidens* because it is not a
subject in its own right. These reservations about how compounds
figure in the theory of (metaphysical) predication reflect the more
fundamental fact that an accidental compound is *ontologically dependent
on* the individual substance out of which it is generated. Pale Socrates,
for example, a *per accidens* being, is generated out of the individual
substance Socrates, a being *per se*, and pale Socrates stands in a relation
of ontological dependence on Socrates. More accurately, once Aristotle has enlarged the list of beings *per se* to include (lower) items
in nonsubstance categories,[24] the *per accidens* being, pale Socrates, is
generated out of *two* beings *per se:* Socrates himself and the accident

> *y* is *predicated per accidens of x* if and only if (*x* is (a) *y*, only because for some *z*,
> *z* ≠ *x*, *Rzx* & *z* is (a) *y*).
> *y* is *predicated per se of x* if and only if *x* is (a) *y* and *y* is not predicated *per accidens*
> of *x*.

For example, log is predicated *per accidens* of the white: the white is a log only
because some individual substance is white (the substance is accidentally the same as
the white) and it is a log. Something is a *per se* being, next, if nothing is predicated
of it *per accidens;* otherwise, it is a being *per accidens:*

> If there is no *y* such that *y* is predicated *per accidens* of *x*, then *x* is a *per se* being.
> If there is a *y* such that *y* is predicated *per accidens* of *x*, then *x* is a *per accidens*
> being.

An. Po. A4, 73b5, together with the examples elsewhere in the *Analytica Posteriora*
suggest that individual substances are *per se* beings. But according to *Metaphysics* Δ7,
1017a22–30, the list of *per se* beings apparently includes members of all the nonsubstance categories as well; cf. Kosman (1987), pp. 364 ff. This is problematic if Aristotle is using the same criteria for *per accidens* and *per se* beings, for on the *monolithic*
account of (metaphysical) predication given in the *Categories* in Chapter 2, white
comes out a *per accidens* being: colour (say) is predicated *per accidens* of white – white
is a colour, only because some substance is white and that substance Has colour. But
it is not out of the question that in *Metaphysics* Δ, Aristotle has a different account of
per se and *per accidens* beings. He is arguing that there are different uses of 'is' for
each of the different categories and as many kinds of *per se* beings as there are
different relevant uses of 'is'. This suggests that there is a privileged use of 'is'
associated with each category such that if for some *y*, *x* is (Is?) (a) *y* in that privileged
use, then *x* is a *per se* being of the relevant kind. (But otherwise, *x* is a being *per
accidens.*) On this revised account, both Socrates and white will count as *per se* beings.
For more and less restrictive accounts of what may count as *per se* beings, see also
Kosman (1987), p. 365.

23 *An. Po.* A22, 83a10–12. For accidental compounds as beings *per accidens,* see also
    Metaphysics Z6, 1031a19–25, b22–8, and E2 and Aristotle's disparaging remarks in
    that chapter (partially quoted in the epigraph to the Introduction to this part), and
    the contrast between accidental unities and the unity of the objects of definition in
    Metaphysics Z12, 1037b10–27.

24 Cf. the remarks at the end of note 22. To avoid misunderstanding, I should empha-
    size that while pallor is an accident, it is *not* a *per accidens* being by the lights of
    Metaphysics Δ7; cf. Kosman (1987), pp. 364–5.

pallor.[25] It follows that in admitting accidental compounds into his ontology, Aristotle is not as profligate as might at first appear. First, pale Socrates and the rest are not *substances* – by letting these into his ontology, Aristotle is not adding to the stock of entities he will count as *basic*.[26] But also, the new entities are *derived* entities. They are constructed out of individual substances and their accidents, and talk involving accidental compounds can in every case be replaced by talk that demands the existence of no more than substances and accidents.

We can now state our results formally.[27] Compounding is a primitive or undefined notion in Aristotle's theory and is subject to this type restriction:

25 In light of this, is pale Socrates ontologically dependent on the individual substance Socrates in *one* step or in *two*? We already know that pallor is dependent on Socrates in one step; if pale Socrates in turn depends on pallor, then there is apparently a relation of *two*-step ontological dependence between pale Socrates and Socrates. At *Metaphysics* M2, Aristotle *denies* that the accident pallor is prior in substance to pale Socrates on the grounds that the two exist simultaneously (M2, 1077b4–10, quoted in note 20). Despite *Metaphysics* M2, it is hard to be sure that two-step ontological dependence is not the right relation here. After all, pallor is in some sense a constituent of pale Socrates and also one of the arguments for the operation of compounding. If the dependence is in two steps, then (very speculatively) we have a reason that accidental compounds do not appear in the *Categories*, which on the account given in Chapter 2, is concerned only with primary substances and items that stand in relations of *one*-step ontological dependence on them.

26 Cf. Matthews (1982), p. 237. Pale Socrates, for example, is also an *accidental* unity (see, e.g., *Metaphysics* Δ6, Z11, 1037b5–6) and hence exhibits a weaker degree of unity than the individual substance enjoys; see the Postscript to Part III and note 23.

27 The theory we are about to present can be called "Accidental Compound Theory" after the fact that it is concerned with the relation of compounding solely as it holds between an individual substance and an accident. ACT is part of a general theory of compounds in which the relation of compounding holds also between matter and a form (see the comments on (A1) later in the main text); this other half of the more general theory is the subject of Part III.

There are some respects in which ACT, as it is presented here, is an idealization of the theory that underlies the scattered references to accidental sameness and accidental compounds in Aristotle's text. In writing (D1) in the text, for example, I help myself to the modern notion of identity, but it should not be inferred from this that such a notion has any direct counterpart in Aristotle's own theory of the different kinds of sameness. More serious is the occasional lack of fit between ACT and Aristotle's text. First, in some places (e.g., in discussing the so-called fallacies of accident at *SE* 5, 166b28–32, 24, 179a27–31, and 35–7; see also 22, 178b39–179a3 and Peterson [1969], p. 118, n. 40), Aristotle is willing to speak of entities such as the pale one as *accidents*. In fact, however, such entities are clearly of the form $a + \phi$ and are *accidental compounds* in the sense of (D1). Second, at *Physics* A7, 189b32–190a5, Aristotle draws a distinction between entities that are simple (*ta hapla*, b33), for example, the musical or the man, and entities that are compound (*ta sugkeimena*, b33–4), for example, the musical man. At first sight, this fits nicely the distinction between accidental compounds of the form $a + \phi$ and their several ingredients a and ϕ (cf. A7, 190b20–3: "For, the musical man is a compound of (*sugkeitai*) ‹the› man and ‹the› musical, in a way: for, you can break it down (*dialuseis*) into the definitions of these"). But Charlton and others have argued that by ‹the› musical' at 189b32 ff., Aristotle means 'the thing which is musical' (Charlton [1970], pp. 71 ff., esp. 73), or better, 'the musical ‹thing›'. On my account, therefore (but not on Charlton's [1970,

(A1) If $x + y$ exists, then x is a(n individual) substance and y is an accident.[28]

The axiom (A1) tells us the category (in both the modern and the Aristotelian sense) of the objects x and y that make up an accidental compound, $x + y$. But the reader is warned that (A1) is part of Aristotle's earlier theory, namely, ACT, which later is absorbed into a general theory of compounds that makes room for compounds of form and matter as well. In the general theory, (A1) will have to be revised to allow for compounds of form and matter in addition to the accidental compounds under discussion here.

Next, we define the notion of an accidental compound:

(D1) x is *an accidental compound* if and only if for some substance a and accident ϕ, $x = a + \phi$.

A compound in the sense intended here belongs in no single category but is a cross-categorial hybrid compounded from a substance and an item from some nonsubstance category.

Some last words about paronyms. As suggested earlier, all paronyms are compounds: the required sense of 'compound' is now spelled out in (D1). But no substance is itself a compound of a substance with an accident. Hence, no substance is a paronym. It is true, then, that the generous one is a paronym (it is a paronym of generosity). But as before, Socrates is not a paronym, even if he is correctly called 'generous'.

p. 73], since he adopts the Russellian reading of such expressions), the musical, like the musical man, is an entity of the form $a + \phi$, although the first is only implicitly compound, and the parent substance is expressly identified only in the second case. Perhaps Charlton's unpacking of '‹the› musical' here is wrong, and we should not adapt his account to find a reference to accidental compounds. But if this line of approach is not wrong, then the distinction drawn in *Physics* A7 must mark off two cases *within* the notion of an accidental compound as intended here. Third, at *Metaphysics* Z6, 1031b22–5, Aristotle notes the ambiguity of the Greek *to leukon* (the pale), which, he says, can refer alternatively to the quality pallor or to the substance that is pale (*kai gar hōi sumbebēke leukon kai to sumbebēkos*, b24–5). Perhaps Aristotle means to correct himself two lines later, where in place of "that to which pale is an accident," we have – as possibly two *different* options? – "the man *and the pale man*" (*tōi men anthrōpōi kai tōi leukōi anthrōpōi*, b27, my emphasis). Nevertheless, the passage seems to support the view that expressions like 'the pale ‹one›' in Aristotle can function as Russellian definite descriptions, denoting the substance – let it be Socrates – who is pale, rather than as names for some distinct entity, Socrates + pale. At the same time, as we have seen, there is solid evidence that at least in some cases, Aristotle does intend this latter reading of the expressions in question (some of that evidence comes from earlier parts of Z6 itself, 1031a19, b22–3). We must conclude either that Aristotle allows two readings of such designators or that he is speaking loosely in the latter part of Z6, but these complications in Aristotle's account are systematically excluded from the formalization of ACT offered here.

28 In (A1) and throughout this part, 'substance' will ordinarily mean '*individual* substance' – what in the *Categories* Aristotle calls 'primary substance', the individual man or the individual horse, later analysed in the *Metaphysics* as a compound of matter and form (where *form* becomes Aristotle's choice for primary substance).

2   Accidental Compounds: The Core Theory

We have these principles of ACT from Section 1:

(A1) If $x + y$ exists, then x is a(n individual) substance and y is an accident.[29]

(D1) x is *an accidental compound* if and only if for some substance a and accident ϕ, $x = a + \phi$.

As (D1) makes plain, accidental compounds are compounds of a substance with an accident. An accidental compound is not identical with an individual substance; instead, it is *accidentally the same as* its constituent substance. We shall also be interested in the relation between an accident and an individual substance. Again, an accident is not identical with a substance; rather, it is *an accident of* a given substance. These two relations form the backbone of Core ACT to be developed in this section.

The relation 'x is an accident of y' is undefined, but subject to this type-restriction:[30]

(A2) x is an accident of y, only if x is an accident and y is a substance.[31]

The relation 'x is an accident of y' holds, for example, between Coriscus and the accident to be approaching, or between Socrates and the accident pallor.

I take it that the relation 'x is an accident of y' is primitive in Aristotle's theory. It is related to a second basic notion, namely, the notion of compounding introduced in (A1). We assume that

(A3) ϕ is an accident of a if and only if $a + \phi$ exists.

As predicted in Section 1, then, whether or not ϕ is an accident of a is exactly coordinate with questions of the existence or otherwise of the corresponding accidental compound $a + \phi$.

I shall also suppose that the identity of an accidental compound uniquely fixes the identity of both its parent or underlying substance and its constituent accident:

---

29 See note 28.
30 The term 'type restriction' is perhaps tendentious here, since it is impossible to be sure that Aristotle would regard an assertion of, for example, the relation 'x is an accident of y' between an accident and an accident, in violation of (A2) immediately following, as without significance, rather than simply false; see Chapter 1, note 35.
31 In (A2) again, by 'substance' we mean '*individual* substance'; see note 28. The requirement in (A2) regarding the accident-of relation and (individual) substances harks back to a dominant theme in the *Categories*, that substance is the subject par excellence; see esp. Chapter 2, Section 3. (A2) is also a key ingredient in Aristotle's argument in favour of the distinction between substance and accident and against the view that "everything is said accidentally" at *Metaphysics* Γ4, 1007a33–b18.

(A4) $a + \phi^1 = b + \phi^2$ only if ($a = b$ & $\phi^1 = \phi^2$).[32]

For example, even where Socrates is both musical and bald, still musical Socrates ≠ bald Socrates: the two compounds share the same underlying substance, but they are distinct, since they are constructed out of different accidents. Exactly symmetrical reasoning tells us that bald Cicero ≠ bald Socrates, for Cicero ≠ Socrates. (But bald Cicero = bald Tully, given that Cicero = Tully.)

We can now define the relation 'x is accidentally the same as y':

(D2) x is *accidentally the same as* y if and only if (i) exactly one of x and y is a substance and exactly one is an accidental compound, and (ii) *either* there is a ϕ^1 such that x is of the form $y + \phi^1$, where ϕ^1 is an accident of y, *or* there is a ϕ^2 such that y is of the form $x + \phi^2$, where ϕ^2 is an accident of x. [33]

According to this definition, accidental sameness is a relation between a substance and an accidental compound. We know by (D1) that an accidental compound may be unpacked as a compound of a substance with an accident; accidental sameness is defined accordingly in (D2) in terms of the relation 'x is an accident of y'. For example, suppose the generous one is accidentally the same as Socrates. Then we know by (D2) that for some ϕ, the generous one is of the form Socrates + ϕ – equivalently, the generous one = Socrates + ϕ – where ϕ is an accident of Socrates. A little more argument shows that the generous one is of the form Socrates + generous, where generosity is an accident of Socrates.[34] Similar arguments show that Coriscus is

32 Here I continue to suppose that ϕ can function indifferently as a nominal or an adjectival form. But $a + \phi$ can still be counted a paronym of ϕ; see note 21.

33 On clause (i) in (D2): Most often, the relation of accidental sameness holds between a substance a and an entity b named by expressions of the form, for example, 'musical Socrates': thus, I take b to be of the form $a + \phi$ (where ϕ is an accident of a). Some examples: man is accidentally the same as pale man (*Topics* E4, 133b15–24, 31–6; *Metaphysics* Z6, 1031a22–3), Coriscus as musical Coriscus (*SE* 178b39–179a1; *Metaphysics* E2, 1026b15–18), Socrates as musical Socrates (*Metaphysics* Δ9, 1018a2–3, Δ29, 1024b29–31), and Socrates as Socrates seated (*Metaphysics* Γ2, 1004b1–3).

In a minority of cases, the relation is between entities a and b, where a is a substance and b is named by an expression like 'the approaching ‹one›' or 'the musical ‹one›' (*Topics* A7, 103a30–1, the seated ‹one› or the musical ‹one› is accidentally the same as Socrates; *SE* 24, 179b1–4, Coriscus is accidentally the same as the approaching ‹one›; *Metaphysics* Z11, 1037b5–7, Socrates is accidentally the same as the musical ‹thing›). As explained in Section 1, I take expressions of the sort 'the musical ‹one›' to be elliptical for expressions like 'musical Socrates', in which the parent substance is explicitly mentioned.

34 Assume that for some individual substance x, the generous one = x + generous. By transitivity, then, x + generous = Socrates + ϕ; by (A4), accordingly, x = Socrates, so that the generous one = Socrates + generous. That is, the generous one is of the form Socrates + generous, as required.

accidentally the same as the pale one just in case the pale one =
Coriscus + pale and pallor is an accident of Coriscus.[35]

In the remainder of this section, I note some of the more obvious
properties of the two relations under study. By (A2), the relation '*x* is
an accident of *y*' holds between a substance and an accident. The
relation '*x* is accidentally the same as *y*,' by contrast, holds between a
substance and an accidental compound, for example, Coriscus and the
one approaching, by (D2). It follows from these two conditions that '*x*
is an accident of *y*' and '*x* is accidentally the same as *y*' are both
irreflexive relations, given the assumptions that no substance is an
accident and that no substance is an accidental compound.[36] (D2) also
shows that the relation '*x* is accidentally the same as *y*' is symmetric, for
'or' in the definiens is commutative. This suggests that the relation is
also not transitive. For by symmetry we may have both

35 (D2) is supported by Aristotle's examples at *Metaphysics* Δ9, 1017b29–30: " . . . and
    man and musical [sc., are said to be accidentally the same] because the one is an
    accident of the other, but the musical ‹is› a man because ‹it› is an accident of the
    man." Aristotle writes awkwardly here, however, since 'musical' and 'the musical'
    must occur ambiguously (cf. Miller [1973], p. 485, and Kirwan [1971], pp. 149, 134).
    On my account, the ambiguity is resolved by distinguishing between (i) a name for
    the compound the musical one, and (ii) a name for the accident musicality. In the
    second half of the passage, for example, 'the musical' must refer to the compound
    ‹this› man + musical, while the pronoun 'it' refers back to the component accident
    musicality. Similar remarks hold for the use of 'musical' in the first half of the
    passage. This reading of the passage is not uncontroversial, however. The ambiguity
    described is especially harsh, for in each case, the word used ambiguously occurs
    only once. Accordingly, the postulated second sense either must be evoked by a
    pronoun (*thateron*, b29) or is left unexpressed altogether, since Greek does not
    require an immediate grammatical subject for the verb ("‹it› is an accident of,"
    sumbebēke, b30). Writing of a similar case in the two lines immediately preceding
    (1017b28–9, cited in Section 3), Code ([1976b], p. 175) argues that the ambiguity
    suggested is not harsh, but impossible: a similar ambiguity, however, apparently
    occurs at Z3, 1029a23–4, where on my account, *tēs ousias* must mean the compound
    substance, while the pronoun *hautē*, which has *tēs ousias* as its antecedent, must refer
    to substance in the sense of form (on the reading of this part of Z3, see Chapter 10,
    Section 3). Code's own reading of 1017b29–31 depends on a different ambiguity,
    which in the long run may be no easier to accept. One undisputed use of Aristotle's
    phrase, '*x* is-an-accident-of (*sumbebēke*) *y*', is to express a relation between an accident
    φ and a substance *a*, which together make up the compound *a* + φ. Code suggests
    that in addition to this standard use, the phrase can also express a relation between
    an entity like the pale one and the substance, for example, Socrates, with which the
    pale one "coincides" (Code's term). In our jargon, then, the relation can also hold
    between a compound, *a* + φ, and its parent substance, *a*. On the surface, this
    proposal makes a tidier job of the opening lines of *Metaphysics* Δ9. But the tidiness
    (as well as the untidiness of the contrary picture) can be exaggerated. My own view
    is that there is no gain in clarity or economy in the hypothesis that Aristotle uses the
    single phrase '*x* is-an-accident-of (*sumbebēke*) *y*', for both the standard accident-of
    relation and the relation '*x* coincides with (or is accidentally the same as) *y*' (on this
    point, see also C. Williams [1985], pp. 78–9). Accordingly, I stand by the reading of
    the opening lines of *Metaphysics* Δ9 sketched here.
36 For the irreflexivity of the accident-of relation, see *Topics* B6, 112b21–6.

(6) The pale one is accidentally the same as Socrates

and

(7) Socrates is accidentally the same as the pale one.

Yet we cannot use (6) and (7) as premises in order to conclude that

(8) The pale one is accidentally the same as the pale one,

for (8) is false in view of (i) in (D2). (There should be no doubt that (8) *is* unacceptable; the intuition that, on the contrary, (8) is *true* is explained in Section 3.)

A little more argument shows that the relation is *in*transitive. Suppose that an item, x, is accidentally the same as y and that y is accidentally the same as z. By (D2), x is either a substance or a compound. If x is a substance, then by two applications of (D2), y is a compound and z is a substance. By (D2) again, therefore, and supposing once more that nothing can be both a substance and an accidental compound, x cannot be accidentally the same as z. Alternatively, x is a compound. But then y is a substance and z is a compound, by (D2). Again, therefore, x is not accidentally the same as z. Hence, the relation is intransitive.[37] Finally, the fact that the relation is intransitive entails that it is also irreflexive, as we have already suggested.

These results show just how great the distance is between accidental sameness and the contemporary notion of identity. For unlike our identity, accidental sameness is not even an equivalence relation.

The relation 'x is an accident of y' behaves somewhat differently. First, it is irreflexive but *a*symmetric, by (A2) and the assumption that nothing is both a substance and an accident. It is also vacuously both transitive and intransitive. For suppose that an item, x, is an accident of something, y, and that y is an accident of something, z. Then by (A2), y is both a substance and an accident, which is impossible. Hence, there are no "accident chains" with more than two members – any sequence defined by the relation 'x is an accident of y' has at most two members (*oude gar pleiō sumpleketai duoin; Metaphysics* Γ4, 1007b1–2). So the relation 'x is an accident of y' is vacuously transitive and intransitive.[38] For the antecedent in the definitions of transitivity and intransitivity is never satisfied:

Transitivity. $(\forall x)(\forall y)(\forall z)((Rxy \ \& \ Ryz) \rightarrow Rxz)$.
Intransitivity. $(\forall x)(\forall y)(\forall z)((Rxy \ \& \ Ryz) \rightarrow \quad Rxz)$.

37 This conclusion appears to be contradicted at *Topics* H1, 152a31–2. I argue in Chapter 4, Section 3, that this passage does not represent Aristotle's final view.
38 But the relation is not, for this reason, particularly exotic; compare, for example, the relation 'x is the husband of y'.

3   Extended Accidental Compound Theory:
Accidental Sameness*

It may seem that there are counterexamples to the type restrictions in
(i) of (D2) for accidental sameness if there can be true sentences of the
following sort:

(8) The pale one is accidentally the same as the pale one,
(9) The pale one is accidentally the same as the musical one.

Sentences (8) and (9) appear to be assertions of accidental sameness
that violate (D2) by relating an accidental compound to an accidental
compound. Violations of (A2) follow in short order: if we apply
(D2)(ii) to (8) and (9), then the pale one = the pale one + pale (!), and
the pale one = the musical one + pale (or the musical one = the pale
+ musical), so that pallor is an accident of the pale and of the musical
(or musicality an accident of the pale), contrary to (A2).[39] In fact,
however, I shall suppose, sentences like (8) and (9) are assertions of a
different kind of accidental sameness, which I shall call "accidental
sameness*." We define the relation in terms of the core notion of
simple accidental sameness previously outlined:

(D3) x is *accidentally the same* as* y if and only if (i) x and y are both
accidental compounds, and (ii) for some z, x and y are both accidentally
the same as z.

For example, at *Metaphysics* $\Delta 9$, 1017b27–8, Aristotle writes:

The pale ‹thing› and the musical ‹thing› are ‹accidentally› the same because
they are accidents of the same thing.[40]

As we have seen, (D3) defines accidental sameness* in terms of plain
vanilla accidental sameness (no asterisk), relating an accidental compound directly to an individual substance. Plain accidental sameness,
in turn, is defined in (D2) in terms of individual substances and their
accidents. In the final analysis, then, relations of accidental sameness*
between two accidental compounds can be explained in terms of the
core accident-of relation between individual substances and their accidents. And in general, the various extensions of the Core theory in
Extended ACT contemplated in this and the remaining section of this
chapter require no essential additions to the metaphysical commitments already in force in the Core theory.

---

39 The arguments for these two results will be along the lines of the argument already
sketched immediately following the statement of (D2) in Section 2.
40 The continuation of this passage is cited in note 35. On the account adopted here,
Aristotle's expressions, 'the pale ‹thing›' and 'the musical ‹thing›', are again ambiguous in the way explained in note 35; a contrary view appears in Code (1976b),
pp. 175 ff., also previously discussed. See also the discussion in Section 4.

It follows immediately from (D3) that accidental sameness* is an equivalence relation. The relation is reflexive given the 'and' in the two halves of the definiens, for the same reason that conjunction can be accounted reflexive.[41] It is symmetric by the commutivity of 'and'. Finally, the relation is transitive. For suppose x is accidentally the same* as y and y is accidentally the same* as z. Then by (D3), for some substance u, x and y are accidentally the same as u, and for some substance v, y and z are accidentally the same as v. It follows by (D2) that for some ϕ^1, $y = u + \phi^1$, and for some ϕ^2, $y = v + \phi^2$. By transitivity, then, $u + \phi^1 = v + \phi^2$, so that $u = v$, by (A4). Accordingly, there is a single substance, namely, u ($= v$), such that both x and z are accidentally the same as u. Hence, by (D3), x is accidentally the same* as z, as required.[42]

41 Quine (1951), p. 138, n. 1.
42 Aristotle is not explicit on the distinction between accidental sameness and accidental sameness*. But there are clear dangers in not distinguishing between these two.
Even if we adopt a single relation, call it "ACCIDENTAL SAMENESS," defined as the
union of accidental sameness and accidental sameness*, it is still important to keep
separate the different subrelations from which ACCIDENTAL SAMENESS is composed.
(This is done quite correctly in Code [1976b], pp. 177–8.) An example of how these
may be confused is the argument by Pelletier (1979) for the conclusion that the
relation 'x is accidentally the same as y' is symmetric, irreflexive, but not transitive.
Pelletier argues that the claims

    (i) This pale man is accidentally the same as this educated man

and

    (ii) This educated man is accidentally the same as this pale man

can both be true. Indeed, they are both true if either is, for the sameness relation
they involve is symmetric. Yet the further claim

    (iii) This pale man is accidentally the same as this pale man

is surely false; for Aristotle's relation seems to be irreflexive. Hence, it is also not
transitive. These conclusions suffer from a number of difficulties. Taken as expressions of accidental sameness in the strict sense, the claims (i), (ii), and (iii) are ill
formed by the type restrictions on accidental sameness in (i) of (D2). If, on the
contrary, we suppose with Pelletier that (i) and (ii) can both be *true*, we must read
them as expressions of accidental sameness* (it will follow that they are also expressions of ACCIDENTAL SAMENESS):

    (iv) The pale one is accidentally the same* as the musical one,
    (v) The musical one is accidentally the same* as the pale one.

But if (iii) is to be false, we cannot interpret it in a similar fashion:

    (vi) The pale one is accidentally the same* as the pale one,

for (vi) must be *true* if either (iv) or (v) is true, by elementary logic and the definition
of accidental sameness*. Given that either (iv) or (v) is true, (iii) can be false only if
we read (iii) as an expression of the irreflexive relation, accidental sameness *simpliciter*. (But [iii] will be true if it is read as an assertion of the relation ACCIDENTAL
SAMENESS.) So there is no single notion of sameness underlying Pelletier's evaluations
of the three claims, and his argument equivocates on different senses of 'same'.
Pelletier concludes that there is a relation of accidental sameness that is irreflexive,
symmetric, and not transitive. This successfully characterizes the core relation of
accidental sameness, with one qualification: "not transitive" in his account can be

4 Extended Accidental Compound Theory: Some Troublesome Principles in the *Topics*

At a variety of places in the *Topics*, Aristotle puts forward principles of accidental sameness that again are in conflict with the provisions of Core ACT. One response will be to say that the principles in question are outright false, and in one celebrated case, this appears to be Aristotle's final reaction too. At the same time, scattered remarks elsewhere in Aristotle provide evidence for further extensions to Core ACT that will allow the troubling principles to be rewritten so that they are not only harmless, but actually theorems of the Extended theory. So it will be worth considering here what the shape of such an expanded theory will be.

One puzzling passage appears at *Topics* E4:

> For what belongs to something of which something is an accident, will also belong to the accident taken along with that of which it is an accident; for example, what belongs to a man will belong also to the pale man, if he is a pale man, and what belongs to the pale man will belong also to the man. (133b17–21)

Aristotle's examples here suggest that in his view both of the following principles hold:

> (10) ϕ^1 is an accident of a & ϕ^2 is an accident of $a \rightarrow \phi^2$ is an accident of $a + \phi^1$,
> (11) ϕ^2 is an accident of $a + \phi^1 \rightarrow \phi^2$ is an accident of a.

This suggestion raises severe difficulties, however. To generalize the idea of the passage, Aristotle apparently allows us to construct a sequence of accidents and subjects of the form,

> ϕ^1 is an accident of a,
> ϕ^2 is an accident of $a + \phi^1$,
>
> .
>
> .
>
> .
>
> ϕ^n is an accident of $(\dots (a + \phi^1) \dots) + \phi^{n-1}$.

Such a sequence is in direct conflict with provisions in the Core theory, for entities of the form $(\dots (a + \phi^1) \dots) + \phi^{n(n>1)}$ do not exist, by (A1). The *Topics* passage is also apparently inconsistent with other

firmed up to "intransitive." Someone who confuses accidental sameness and accidental sameness* may be tempted to use the weaker description because he or she perceives, correctly, that sentences such as (iv), (v), and (vi) may all be true together. But it is important to see that this possibility reflects a property of accidental sameness* rather than of accidental sameness *simpliciter*. Accidental sameness *simpliciter* is firmly intransitive, while accidental sameness* is equally firmly transitive.

parts of our reconstruction of Aristotle's Core theory; for if any steps beyond the first in the sequence indicated are possible, this appears to conflict with either the claim in (A2) that wherever x is an accident of y, y is a substance, or the idea that nothing is both a substance and a compound. In line with this, at *Metaphysics* Γ4, 1007b1–10, Aristotle himself expressly prohibits sequences of the kind just exhibited on the grounds that an entity of the form $(\ldots (a + \phi^1) \ldots) + \phi^{n(n > 1)}$ is not a proper subject for accidents: "for, not everything makes up one thing" (1007b10).[43]

In these circumstances, the proper conclusion is no doubt to reject (10) and (11) as they stand. At the same time, however, it may also be appropriate to consider further extensions in ACT, featuring additional cases of the accident-of and accidental sameness relations defined in terms of the core cases already given. These additions to the Core theory will not rescue (10) and (11) and other troubled principles as they stand, but they will allow us to rewrite them in a form that is acceptable within the Extended theory. At the same time, as we shall see, we will also be able to explain how there is room for "reiterated" compounds within the Extended theory and how such entities are related to other, more basic items in Aristotle's ontology.

Aristotle explicitly warns us that there will be an extended case of the accident-of relation:

An accident (*to sumbebēkos*) is not an accident of an accident, *unless because both are accidents of the same thing*, I mean for example that the pale may be musical and it [= the musical] pale because both are accidents of the man. . . . and at the same time, we have made the distinction that, while some things are accidental in this way, others are accidental in the way in which the musical ‹is accidental› to Socrates; for in none of the latter cases is the accidental (*to sumbebēkos*) an accident of the accidental, *but this is so in the former cases.* (*Metaphysics* Γ4, 1007b2–5, 13–17; my emphasis)

Unfortunately, however, the language in which Aristotle describes the new relation is equivocal at best. In particular, the Greek phrases *to leukon* and *to mousikon* (the pale, the musical) can mean either 'the pale (musical) thing' (the accidental compound) or 'pallor' ('musicality'); similarly, his technical term *to sumbebēkos* can be translated either as 'the accident', pallor (say), or 'the accidental', namely, the accidental compound, the pale one. So it is hard to know whether the new relation holds between accidents,[44] between accidental compounds, or between an accident and an accidental compound. I shall suppose that the new relation relates an accident to an accidental compound: this is the notion that will do us the most good in dealing with the passages

43 Cf. *De Int.* 11, 20b18–19, and the references in note 23.
44 This was the account I gave in F. Lewis (1982).

cited from *Topics* E; at the same time, it seems to fit best the context in *Metaphysics* Γ4, which is a primary source for the new notion.

The new notion has this definition:

(D4) *x* is *an accident* of* y if and only if (i) *x* is an accident and *y* is an accidental compound, such that for some *z* and *w*, *y* = *z* + *w*, where *w* is an accident of *z*, and (ii) *x* is an accident of *z*.

Allowing for the ambiguities already noted, this appears to be the notion Aristotle has in mind in the first half of the passage at Γ4, 1007b2−5, quoted in the preceding paragraph. Thus, as I understand it, musicality is an accident* of the pale ‹one› because the man is not only pale but also musical. A similar definition appears in two other passages:

Whenever we call . . . the pale ‹thing› musical or it [= the musical] pale, in this case it is because both are accidents of the same thing. (*Metaphysics* Δ7, 1017a15−16)

For then [sc., whenever I say that the musical ‹thing› is pale] I say that the man to whom it is an accident that he is musical, is pale. (*An. Po.* A22, 83a10−12)[45]

Given the way in which one thing can be an accident* of another, we can introduce a new kind of compound, featuring the operation '*x* +* *y*' as a variant on the primitive operation of compounding in Core ACT. We assume that

(A5) *x* +* *y* exists only if *x* is an accidental compound and *y* is an accident.

I take it that the *per accidens* unity, musical just Coriscus (*Metaphysics* Δ6, 1015b20), is an example of a compound of this new kind. The existence of compounds of the form *x* +* *y* is connected with cases of the accident-of* relation in exactly the way that the accident-of relation and the existence of compounds of the form *x* + *y* are tied together in the Core theory:

(A6) ϕ^2 is an accident* of $a + \phi^1$ if and only if $(a + \phi^1) +^* \phi^2$ exists.

(With (A6), cf. (A3) in the Core theory in Section 2.) (A5) and (A6) together show how, given the appropriate derived cases of the accident-of relation and the appropriate extended notions of compounding, we can legitimize sequences of the form contemplated earlier in this section, with asterisks added as required:

---

45 The passage from *Metaphysics* Δ exhibits shifts in 'the pale' and 'the musical' between a name for the compound and for the accident pallor or musicality along the lines already argued for in notes 35 and 40. The passage from the *Analytica Posteriora* comes from Aristotle's discussion of *per accidens* predication featured in note 22.

φ¹ is an accident of a,
φ² is an accident* of $a + φ^1$,
φ³ is an accident** of $(a + φ^1) +* φ^2$,

.
.
.

Arguably, Aristotle has something like this sequence in mind at *Metaphysics* Γ4, 1007b6–10, where he claims that using the core accident-of relation, we cannot construct "upward" sequences of the kind exhibited earlier in this section, but leaves wide open the possibility that other sequences, using other, nonstandard cases of the accident-of relation (*ta d' ekeinōs . . . sumbebēkota*, b7), are after all admissible.

It is clear from (A5) that the existence of "reiterated" compounds of the kind just illustrated requires the existence of nothing beyond the items already available in Core ACT. (A5) suggests that talk of musical just Coriscus, for example, comes down to talk of the accident musicality and the compound just Coriscus; just Coriscus, in turn, can be analysed in terms of the individual substance Coriscus and the accident justice. At bottom, then, the kinds of reiterated compounds distinctive of Extended ACT require the existence of nothing over and above individual substances and their accidents, which are both *per se* beings.[46]

Meanwhile, the passage at *Topics* E4, 133b17–21, with which we began in this section, can be read as supporting not the troubled (10) and (11), but these unproblematic variants:

(10*) φ¹ is an accident of a & φ² is an accident of a → φ² is an accident* of $a + φ^1$.
(11*) φ² is an accident* of $a + φ^1$ → φ² is an accident of a.

(10*) and (11*) are straightforward consequences of the definition of the accident*-of relation in (D4). But it must be noted that Aristotle himself nowhere expressly distinguishes these trouble-free principles from their troubling originals.

Comparable moves are appropriate in dealing with another troublesome passage at *Topics* H1, 152a31–2. Aristotle says:

Again, look and see if, supposing the one to be the same as something, the other is also the same as it: for if they are not both the same as the same thing, clearly neither are they the same as one another. (From the Oxford translation)

These remarks seem to suggest the following principle:

(12) x is accidentally the same as y → (x is accidentally the same as z ↔ y is accidentally the same as z).

46 Cf. the discussion in Section 1.

This principle seems to show that Aristotle is willing to regard accidental sameness as not merely symmetric, but in fact an equivalence relation, contrary to the argument in Section 3 that the relation is both irreflexive and intransitive. That earlier argument was based on the type restriction on accidental sameness included in (i) of (D2). But if (12) is correct, those type restrictions must also go by the board. For, let x be the substance a and y the compound $a + \phi^1$, so that the antecedent of (12) is well formed by (D2). Then as an instance of (12), we have (for different values for 'z') either

(13) a is accidentally the same as $a + \phi^1 \rightarrow$ (a is accidentally the same as $a + \phi^2 \leftrightarrow a + \phi^1$ is accidentally the same as $a + \phi^2$),

or

(14) a is accidentally the same as $a + \phi^1 \rightarrow$ (a is accidentally the same as $b \leftrightarrow a + \phi^1$ is accidentally the same as b).

And in general, every instance of (12) is a counterexample to the type restrictions in (D2).

Again, however, we can construct an extension of ACT, featuring derived notions of accidental sameness that do not appear in the Core theory, that will support counterparts of (13) and (14). The extension of ACT suggested in Section 3 already allows a notion of accidental sameness* between an individual substance and an accidental compound. Principle (13) can be reworked accordingly:

(13*) a is accidentally the same as $a + \phi^1 \rightarrow$ (a is accidentally the same as $a + \phi^2 \leftrightarrow a + \phi^1$ is accidentally the same* as $a + \phi^2$).

Principle (13*) follows directly from the definition of accidental sameness* in (D3).

Other instances of (12), however, apparently require a relation of accidental sameness between individual substances. To my knowledge, we have no direct evidence that Aristotle himself recognized the existence of such cases. But it is easy to construct a definition on his behalf. The definition again ties the new notion to the basic apparatus of Core ACT:

(D5) x is *accidentally the same*** as y if and only if (i) both x and y are individual substances, and (ii) there is an accidental compound, z, such that both x and y are accidentally the same as z.

Where one substance is accidentally the same** as another, we can show that they are *identical*. Suppose that both x and y are accidentally the same as the accidental compound z. Then by two applications of (D2), for some ϕ^1, $z = x + \phi^1$, and for some ϕ^2, $z = y + \phi^2$. By transitivity, then, $x + \phi^1 = y + \phi^2$, so that by (A4), $x = y$, as required.

(D5) allows this reworking of the problematic (14):

(14*) a is accidentally the same as $a + \phi^1 \rightarrow (a$ is accidentally the same** as $b \leftrightarrow a + \phi^1$ is accidentally the same as b).

Principle (14*) follows immediately given (D5) and (for the L–R direction of the consequent of (14*)) the lemma constructed around (A4) in the preceding paragraph, that where a is accidentally the same** as b, $a = b$. Again, however, Aristotle himself does not draw the distinction between (14) and (14*).

Finally, one further principle must be mentioned here that I shall reserve for fuller discussion in Chapter 4. A single principle of accidental sameness underlies the other troubling principles we have been considering so far in this section. According to Aristotle's first statement of the principle at *Topics* H1, 152a33–5, the principle has this form:

(S1) a is accidentally the same as $a + \phi^1 \rightarrow (\phi^2$ is an accident of $a \leftrightarrow \phi^2$ is an accident of $a + \phi^1$).

The applications he makes of the principle elsewhere in the *Topics* suggests that (S1) should be understood as a special case of a principle whose consequent is indistinguishable from the indiscernibility condition that appears in the modern Leibniz's Law:[47]

Strong (S1) a is accidentally the same as $a + \phi^1 \rightarrow (\phi^2(a) \leftrightarrow \phi^2(a + \phi^1))$.

We can use Strong (S1) to prove the troubling principles (10) and (11); meanwhile, the troubling principles (12), (13), and (14) are instances of Strong (S1). The most important applications of Strong (S1), however, come not in the *Topics* but in the *De Sophisticis Elenchis,* where it gives rise to the modal and epistemic paradoxes. In response to the paradoxes, Aristotle expressly rejects Strong (S1) in favour of a principle based not on accidental sameness, but on the stronger relation of sameness in being. As with the troubling principles, (10) and the like, considered earlier in this section, however, an alternative reaction will be to rewrite Strong (S1) within Extended ACT; in this weaker form, as we shall see, the principle is not only entirely benign but, like (10*) and the rest, follows directly from basic principles of Extended ACT.

The various versions of Aristotle's principle (S1) and related developments in the *De Sophisticis Elenchis,* including the modal and epistemic paradoxes and Aristotle's reaction to them, are taken up in Chapter 4.

47 It is far from clear, however, that the principle is *identical with* Leibniz's Law, and if, as I suppose, Aristotle's accidental sameness is not the same as our identity, the two principles are certainly *not* the same. These issues are discussed in Chapters 4 and 5.

Appendix. Some Principles of Accidental Compound Theory

Core ACT

(A1) If $x + y$ exists, then x is a(n individual) substance and y is an accident.

(A2) x is an accident of y, only if x is an accident and y is a substance.

(A3) ϕ is an accident of a if and only if $a + \phi$ exists.

(A4) $a + \phi^1 = b + \phi^2$, only if $a = b$ & $\phi^1 = \phi^2$.

(D1) x is *an accidental compound* if and only if for some substance a and accident ϕ, $x = a + \phi$.

(D2) x is *accidentally the same as* y if and only if (i) exactly one of x and y is a substance and exactly one is an accidental compound, and (ii) *either* there is a ϕ^1 such that x is of the form $y + \phi^1$, where ϕ^1 is an accident of y, *or* there is a ϕ^2 such that y is of the form $x + \phi^2$, where ϕ^2 is an accident of x.

Extended ACT

(A5) $x +^* y$ exists, only if x is an accidental compound and y is an accident.

(A6) ϕ^2 is an accident* of $a + \phi^1$ if and only if $(a + \phi^1) +^* \phi^2$ exists.

(D3) x is *accidentally the same** as y if and only if (i) x and y are both accidental compounds, and (ii) for some z, x and y are both accidentally the same as z.

(D4) x is *an accident* of* y if and only if (i) x is an accident and y is an accidental compound, such that for some z and w, $y = z + w$, where w is an accident of z, and (ii) x is an accident of z.

(D5) x is *accidentally the same*** as* y if and only if (i) x and y are both individual substances, and (ii) there is an accidental compound, z, such that both x and y are accidentally the same as z.

4

Paradoxes of Accidental Sameness

The theory of accidental compounds and of accidental sameness developed in the body of Chapter 3 is directly threatened by various principles involving accidental compounds that Aristotle endorses but that violate provisions of Core ACT. As we saw, these troubling principles must be rejected as they stand; at the same time, however, there are suggestions in Aristotle's text of an Extended version of ACT within which the principles can be reformulated so that they are not only harmless, but also theorems in the Extended theory. Similar options exist with respect to Aristotle's prime principle of accidental sameness, which in the *Topics* apparently takes the following form:

Strong (S1). *a* is accidentally the same as $a + \phi^1 \rightarrow (\phi^2(a) \leftrightarrow \phi^2(a + \phi^1))$.

Strong (S1) entails the different troubling principles in the *Topics* considered in the final section of Chapter 3. And like them, Strong (S1) can be rewritten in a form in which it is not only harmless, but a theorem of Extended ACT. Once more, however, while there is evidence in Aristotle for much of Extended ACT, Aristotle himself nowhere sets out a modified version of Strong (S1) that will be acceptable in Extended ACT. On the contrary, in the *De Sophisticis Elenchis*, under pressure from the modal and epistemic paradoxes, he expressly drops Strong (S1) and replaces it by a principle that is based not on any relation of accidental sameness, but on the stronger relation of sameness in being, and hence lies outside ACT altogether.

The modal and epistemic paradoxes play a decisive role in the shift to a sameness principle based on sameness in being, in preference to a principle of accidental sameness. This view of the paradoxes makes sense, however, only if we suppose that the paradoxes are framed within the ontology of accidental compounds that naturally goes with a principle of accidental sameness. This supposition sets the paradoxes in a very different philosophical context from the one within which a contemporary philosopher is likely to view them. Far from approaching the paradoxes from the vantage point of ACT, a contemporary philosopher is liable to connect the paradoxes with questions concerning Leibniz's Law, and its validity in contexts that are referentially opaque. It is sometimes supposed that Aristotle uses the paradoxes in order to conclude that Leibniz's Law is invalid. But can Leibniz's Law even be correctly applied within the two paradoxes? And is the sameness principle Aristotle appeals to in constructing the paradoxes identical with Leibniz's Law in the first place? The answer to both questions, I argue, is quite resoundingly no; if this is right, then the point of Aristotle's discussion of the paradoxes cannot be to show that Leibniz's Law is invalid. Various familiar means exist for countering the paradoxes while preserving Leibniz's Law, based, for example, on a Fregean or a Russellian treatment of the epistemic and alethic modalities. Aristotle's own solution, however, rests on ACT and the theory of accidental sameness. Aristotle uses the paradoxes to reject a sameness principle based on accidental sameness; but accidental sameness is not the same as our identity, and the sameness principle he rejects is not identical with Leibniz's Law.

In Section 1, I look more closely at the various licensing principles involving accidental sameness that Aristotle proposes in the *Topics*. In Section 2, I turn to the modal and epistemic paradoxes, and the use Aristotle makes of them to reject the licensing principles at work in the *Topics* in favour of a principle based on sameness in being. I also spend some time on the relation between Aristotle's discussion and Leibniz's Law. In Section 3, we see how Aristotle's shift to a more restrictive sameness principle also allows him to drop outright the other troubling principles of accidental sameness already noted in Chapter 3. At the same time, as we have seen, Aristotle also has the option of *reformulating* the troublesome principles within Extended ACT. The reformulated principles will retain reference to "reiterated" compounds like pale musical Coriscus. But Extended ACT preserves what I have argued is the central metaphysical intuition of ACT, according to which the entire cast of characters, musical Coriscus and the like, even pale musical Coriscus, can be constructed out of a basic ontology of individual substances and their accidents, along the lines already discussed in Chapter 3.

1   A Controversial Principle of Accidental Sameness in the *Topics*

At *Topics* A7, Aristotle introduces a notion of "numerical sameness," exemplified in those cases in which there is "more than one name, but only one thing" (103a9–10). Numerical sameness comes in three kinds: numerical sameness rendered by definition (the "most proper and primary" notion of sameness [*kuriōtata . . . kai prōtōs*, 103a25–6]), rendered by proprium, and rendered by accident. Later in the *Topics* (H1), Aristotle refers back to his earlier discussion of numerical sameness[1] and introduces a number of principles based on numerical sameness. Now a modern expectation is that if two things are *the same* in some sense, they will, in some suitable way, *share* their properties. Perhaps the most revealing of Aristotle's principles for us are those that come closest to reflecting this intuition. For example, at *Topics* H1, 152a33–7, Aristotle says:

Moreover, examine them [sc., things alleged to be numerically the same] in the light of their accidents, or of the things of which they are accidents: for, any accident belonging to the one must also belong to the other, and if the one belongs to anything as an accident, so must the other too. If in any of these respects there is a discrepancy, clearly they are not the same.

Aristotle's remarks here are apparently intended to hold for any kind of numerical sameness, including the weakest kind of numerical sameness, simple accidental sameness. If we restrict ourselves to this weakest notion of accidental sameness, we can extract the following sameness principle from the passage:

(S1) a is accidentally the same as $a + \phi^1 \rightarrow (\phi^2$ is an accident of $a \leftrightarrow \phi^2$ is an accident of $a + \phi^1)$.

(S1) can be understood in two ways, depending on what we take to be the logical form of the predicate 'ϕ^2 is an accident of x'. From the applications Aristotle himself later makes of the principle, he apparently understands the predicate to have the form '$\chi(x)$'; on this reading, (S1) is an instance of a principle that places an indiscernibility condition on accidental sames identical to the condition that appears in a modern principle of identity:

Strong (S1) a is accidentally the same as $a + \phi^1 \rightarrow (\phi^2(a) \leftrightarrow \phi^2(a + \phi^1))$.[2]

For the record, however, it is worth noting that 'ϕ^2 is an accident of x' may also be of the form

---

1 *elegeto de kuriōtata tauton to tōi arithmōi hen*, at 151b29–31, refers back to 103a23–4, *malista d' homoloumenōs to hen arithmōi tauton para pasi dokei legesthai* (see, e.g., Waitz [1844–6], p. 507, and Pickard-Cambridge in the Oxford translation) and recalls the notion of numerical sameness in general, as opposed to sameness in species or sameness in genus. Despite the verbal echo, Aristotle does not mean to restrict his discussion in *Topics* H1 to the "literal and primary use" (*kuriōtata kai prōtōs*), namely, numerical sameness by definition, referred to at 103a25–6. Cf. Peterson (1969), pp. 98–9.

2 But if the consequent of Strong (S1) looks like the consequent of Leibniz's Law, the same is hardly true of the antecedents of the two principles; accidental sameness, which appears in the antecedent of Strong (S1), is not the same as our identity.

'Accident-of (ϕ^2, x)',

so that Aristotle's principle will assert instead that

a is accidentally the same as $a + \phi^1 \rightarrow$ (Accident-of (ϕ^2, a) $\leftrightarrow$ Accident-of (ϕ^2, $a + \phi^1$)).

If his principle has this form, finally, it will be tempting to make one further change to bring the principle into line with Extended ACT:

Weak (S1) a is accidentally the same as $a + \phi^1 \rightarrow$ (Accident-of (ϕ^2, a) $\leftrightarrow$ Accident*-of (ϕ^2, $a + \phi^1$)).

In contrast to Strong (S1), as we shall see (Section 3), Weak (S1) is harmless and indeed trivially true.

It is plain from Aristotle's own discussion in the *Topics* that he takes (S1) to be equivalent to Strong (S1). Later in the first chapter of *Topics* H, (S1) is expanded to hold generally, without the restriction to accidents (152b25–9). Suppose that two things are numerically the same. Then in general, Aristotle says,

one ought to consider if there is any discrepancy among *what is predicated of each in any way whatsoever (tōn hopōsoun ... katēgoroumenōn)*, and among what these are predicated of. For everything that is predicated of the one must be predicated of the other, and everything the one is predicated of, the other must be predicated of too. (H1, 152b25–9, my emphasis)[3]

This gives us Strong (S1).

Other developments in the chapter make it unmistakable that Aristotle intends this stronger principle to hold where 'ϕ^2' is a *modal* predicate. The principle at 152b34–5, for example, is equivalent to the instance of Strong (S1) where '$\phi^2(x)$' = '$\Box$(x exists)'. Aristotle writes:

Moreover, see whether the one can exist without the other: for, if so, they could not be the same. (H1, 152b34–5; cf. possibly 151b36–152a4)

Equivalently,

As a matter of necessity, if x is numerically the same as y, then necessarily, x exists if and only if y exists.

Suppose that in fact x and y are numerically the same. Then by the principle at 152b34–5,

$\Box$(x exists $\leftrightarrow$ y exists).

But from this it follows that

$\Box$(x exists) $\leftrightarrow$ $\Box$(y exists),

3 Cf. Alexander, *In Topica* 501.19–502.6, cited by Peterson (1969), p. 80, n. 9, for the broad sense of 'is predicated of' here (equivalent roughly to 'is true of', and hence meant to include any true linguistic predication).

by the modal principle,

$$\Box(P \to Q) \vdash \Box P \to \Box Q.$$

That is, the principle of numerical sameness, Strong (S1), can be applied where '$\phi^2(x)$' is of the form '$\Box(x \text{ exists})$'. Clearly, this result for the predicate 'x exists' can be generalized for all predicates '$\phi(x)$' within the scope of the necessity operator:

$$\Box(x \text{ is numerically the same as } y \to (\Box(\phi(x)) \leftrightarrow (\Box(\phi(y))))).$$

This is the same as saying that Strong (S1) holds wherever '$\phi^2(a)$' has the form '$\Box(\chi(a))$'.

Next, at 152b22–4, Aristotle takes discernibility in counterfactual situations as sufficient grounds for denying numerical sameness:

By a supposition, which may be true *or may be false (it makes no difference which)*, one character is annulled and not the other, showing that they are not the same. (My emphasis)

Thus, if x is numerically the same as y, *it is impossible that* one should have an attribute that the other lacks. That is,

$$\Box(\phi(x) \leftrightarrow \phi(y)).$$

But from this it follows that

$$\Box(\phi(x)) \leftrightarrow \Box(\phi(y)),$$

and by the modal principle, again, that

$$\Box(P \to Q) \vdash \Box P \to \Box Q.$$

Finally, the principle at 152b10–15 too can be interpreted as implying that where a is numerically the same as b, a is necessarily ϕ if and only if b is necessarily ϕ. Aristotle writes:

Furthermore, you must note the result of an addition and see whether each added to the same thing fails to produce the same whole; or whether the subtraction of the same thing from each leaves the remainder different. Suppose, for example, someone has stated that a double of a half and a multiple of a half are the same, then, if 'of a half' has been subtracted from each, the remainders ought to signify the same thing: but they do not. (*Topics* H1, 152b10–15)

"Adding the same thing" to each and "subtracting the same thing" from each here must be understood as a linguistic rather than a metaphysical operation. Suppose a is said to be numerically the same as $a + \phi$. Then, in a test by addition, Aristotle claims, one and the same name or sentential context,

$$C \dots,$$

can be added to the terms 'a' and '$a + \phi$' to verify whether a and $a + \phi$ are numerically the same. For example, where a is numerically the same as $a + \phi$, the sentence

$C \ldots a \ldots$

has the same truth value as

$C \ldots a + \phi \ldots ,$

where the second results from the first by replacing the denoting expression 'a' by the denoting expression '$a + \phi$'. Aristotle's remarks here are sufficiently vague that they can easily include reference to *modal* properties in testing for numerical sameness. To adapt a familiar example, suppose that 9 and the number of the planets are numerically the same. Then if we "add the same thing" to each, the resulting whole should also be the same. In particular, the context '$\square$(... is greater than 8)' can be added to '9' and to 'the number of the planets', and the whole must have the same truth value in both cases. Thus, if

9 is numerically the same as the number of the planets and $\square$(9 > 8),

then by the principle Aristotle appears to have in mind at 152b10–15,

$\square$(the number of the planets > 8).

Aristotle does not explicitly say that the principle applies in modal contexts; but nothing he does say rules out such an application. Again, therefore, Aristotle seems to hold a principle involving numerical sameness that can be applied in modal as well as nonmodal contexts.[4]

Most if not all of the examples considered in the preceding paragraphs suggest that Aristotle is committed to holding that (S1) and Strong (S1) hold in intensional as well as extensional contexts.[5] In the *De Sophisticis Elenchis*, however, under pressure from the modal and epistemic paradoxes, Aristotle comes to doubt (S1) and its expansion, Strong (S1).[6] In their place, he proposes the following rule:

For, only to things that are one and indistinguishable in being is it generally agreed that all the same attributes belong. (*SE* 24, 179a37–9)

Similarly, at *Physics* Γ3, 202b14–6:

4 There is, however, a major difference between the principle at 152b10–15 and the principles discussed earlier in this section: see note 5.
5 In all but the last case, the connection with (S1) or Strong (S1) seems clear. The last case, however, from *Topics* H1, 152b10–15, seems to involve not a principle of sameness along the lines of (S1) or Strong (S1), but a principle of substitutivity in the sense of Cartwright (1971) (see Section 2): as Cartwright suggests, a principle of this kind raises problems of its own, but it is quite different from a principle of sameness.
6 *SE* 6, 168a34–b11, and 24, 179a26–b7. On these arguments, see most recently K. Barnes (1977), Matthews (1982), and White (1986). Earlier treatments are in Peterson (1969) and White (1971b).

for all the same ‹things› belong not to what is the same in any old way, but only to those whose being is the same.

More formally,

(S2) If x is numerically the same in being in as y, then ϕ is an attribute of x if and only if ϕ is an attribute of y.[7]

The relation 'x is numerically the same in being as y' is different from 'x is accidentally the same as y': both are restrictions (but different restrictions) on the relation of numerical sameness *simpliciter* introduced at *Topics* A7, 103a25–31. These various developments are the subject of Section 2.

2   The Modal and Epistemic Paradoxes

In this section, we look more closely at the paradoxes that motivate Aristotle's shift between the different sameness principles, Strong (S1) and (S2), discussed in the preceding section. First, at *SE* 6, 168a34–b10, we find this modal paradox:

(1) The triangle necessarily has the sum of its interior angles equal to two right angles.
(2) The triangle is the starting point.

Hence,

(3) The starting point necessarily has the sum of its interior angles equal to two right angles.[8]

And later at *SE* 24, 179a26–b7, Aristotle sets out the epistemic paradox:

(4) I know that Coriscus is Coriscus.
(5) Coriscus is the masked one.

Hence,

(6) I know that the masked one is Coriscus.[9]

7 A different reading of 179a37–9 appears in Kneale and Kneale (1962), p. 42, and Peterson (1969), pp. 77, 107–8, and 131–4. Later writers favour the version given in the text; see White (1971b), p. 179; K. Barnes (1977), p. 50; Pelletier (1979), p. 287.
8 The argument given here is an idealization of the one that appears in Aristotle's text; cf. K. Barnes (1977), pp. 56 ff. The notion of a *starting point* that appears in this argument is drawn from Aristotle's idea that the different kinds of figure make up an *ordered series* of a special kind in which each later element is in some sense dependent on, and even constructed out of, its immediate predecessors; on Aristotle's view, the triangle is the *first* in the series of figures. See *De Anima* B3, 414b20–5, where Aristotle compares his views about figure with his similar doctrine about the different kinds of soul. These kinds of series (under the name "P-series") are discussed in Lloyd (1962).
9 This is again an idealization of the argument given in Aristotle's text; cf. Peterson (1969), pp. 18 ff.; K. Barnes (1977), pp. 60 ff.

Both arguments are paradoxical because in each case the conclusion is derived from the premises by an apparently valid application of an apparently valid licensing principle, namely, Strong (S1), and moreover, apparently, both the premises can be true yet the conclusion false.

Of these various assumptions about the two arguments, which should we give up in order to be rid of the paradox? A common conclusion in contemporary discussions of the arguments is that they offer a genuine challenge to Leibniz's Law.[10] This conclusion is naturally glossed by the assertion that crucial contexts in both arguments are *referentially opaque* while, notoriously, Leibniz's Law fails in such contexts. On this account, Coriscus and the masked one really are identical, and likewise with the triangle and the starting point – but a stronger relation than mere identity is needed to license inferences based on sameness in epistemic or modal contexts. So Aristotle uses the paradoxes to discard Leibniz's Law in favour of a more restrictive sameness principle.

This analysis of the two arguments rests on some crucial assumptions. It assumes not only that the paradoxes rely on the correct application of a licensing principle, but also that the licensing principle itself is faulty. Finally, it assumes that the principle in question, identified as Strong (S1) in Aristotle's discussion, is in fact the same as Leibniz's Law. This last assumption at least is highly questionable, for the antecedent of Strong (S1) makes use of Aristotle's notion of accidental sameness, and this, as we have seen, is quite different from the notion of identity that appears in the antecedent of Leibniz's Law. It is also questionable, however, even if the licensing principle in both arguments is Leibniz's Law, that that law has been validly applied in the two arguments.

Provisionally, let us leave unchallenged the identification between Leibniz's Law and Aristotle's original sameness principle, Strong (S1). Even so, it is open to doubt that Leibniz's Law has been correctly applied in either argument. Following Cartwright,[11] we distinguish between a principle of identity and a principle of substitutivity. Leibniz's Law is a principle of identity, for it says that if two *things* are identical, then they share all and only the same properties. A principle of substitutivity, by contrast, says only that if two *designators* designate the same thing, then either may be substituted for the other without

---

10 The conclusion is discussed and rejected in Smullyan (1948); see also Cartwright (1971). Scholars who attribute doubts about Leibniz's Law, or closely related principles, to Aristotle include White (1971b) (but not White [1986]) and K. Barnes (1977).

11 Cartwright (1971), p. 121; K. Barnes (1977), pp. 52–3, also notes the relevance of much the same distinction that Cartwright makes to the discussion of Aristotle.

change of truth value. The attempted inference in both paradoxes certainly violates a principle of substitutivity: both arguments are testimony to the failure of substituting for each other 'Coriscus' and 'the masked one', or 'the triangle' and 'the starting point', even when it is agreed that the two expressions in each pair designate the identical thing. But what guarantee do we have that in the argument given, the designators 'Coriscus' and 'the masked one' are functioning as (on this account) they usually do, as designations of the identical thing, Coriscus? Key contexts in both arguments are said to be referentially opaque, which is just to concede that the ordinary principles of reference are not in effect there. But if referring expressions are not working in the ordinary way in those contexts, what assurance is there that we are successfully referring to Coriscus, or to the masked one, as needed for a principle for identity? The modal and epistemic paradoxes, then, successfully demonstrate the invalidity of a principle of substitutivity; if they make use of Leibniz's Law, however, they are guilty of an improper application of a licensing law that, for all we have been shown so far, in itself is quite blameless.

The arguments of the preceding paragraph rely heavily on the idea that a referring expression cannot be counted on to work invariably in precisely the same way, regardless of the context in which it occurs. This idea is central to two ways of looking at the two paradoxes that are, I shall argue, at once quite foreign to how Aristotle understands the paradoxes and, in one form or another, well-nigh irresistible to a contemporary philosopher.[12] It is worth having these two views out in the open, for once they are made explicit, it may be easier to see that there is also room for yet another account that is radically different from either of them.

A Fregean treatment of the paradoxes fastens on the idea that in certain contexts, which Frege calls "oblique," names name not their ordinary denotation, but an *oblique* denotation, which he identifies with the entity he regards as their ordinary sense. This reference shift shows vividly why the usual principle of subsitutivity must fail.[13]

---

12 One commentator who cannot resist the second, Russellian treatment of the paradoxes sketched below is C. Williams (1985); see note 17.

13 Here I disregard various strengthenings of the principle of substitutivity with the aid of the notions of L-equivalence and intensional isomorphism in Carnap (1947). It may be worth noting here that Aristotle's shift from Strong (S1), the antecedent of which has to do with accidental sameness, to (S2), for which the antecedent instead features sameness in being, cannot really be compared with the injection by Carnap of successively stronger conditions into the antecedent of the principle of substitutivity: Aristotle's two principles are concerned with different relations between items in the ontology, while Carnap's principles have to do with different relations between *linguistic* items, so that the two philosophers are dealing with principles that fall on different sides of Cartwright's distinction between a principle of identity and a principle of substitutivity.

Meanwhile, Leibniz's Law, which is a principle of identity in the full-blooded sense, will not apply within the paradoxes. If, for example, in claim (4), 'I know that Coriscus is Coriscus', the proper name 'Coriscus' is functioning as a name of the (ordinary) sense of the name 'Coriscus', then the fact that the man Coriscus is identical with the masked one is irrelevant to any inferences based on the application to (4) of Leibniz's Law. What is needed, rather, will be identities involving not Coriscus, but the *sense of the name* 'Coriscus', or alternatively, in Church's terminology, the *concept* of Coriscus. Both paradoxes, then, are inconsequent.

The idea that a designator may work very differently in different contexts appears in a very different form in a Russellian account of the paradoxes. In Russell's theory, the Fregean reference shift is replaced by a variety of *syntactic* devices. Instead of Frege's idea of the *oblique* occurrence of a designator, Russell supposes that a designator may have a *secondary* occurrence, that is, it has narrow scope as compared with the scope of some other operator within the sentence. In line with this, the modal paradox contains various syntactic ambiguities, which we can resolve by writing out the different readings of its ambiguous components:

(1′) □(the triangle has interior angles equal to two right angles).[14]

(2′) For some x, x alone is a starting point, and x = the triangle.

(3a) For some x, x alone is a starting point, and □(x has interior angles equal to two right angles).

(3b) □(for some x, x alone is a starting point, and x has interior angles equal to two right angles).

On the Russellian view, the paradox is disarmed by pointing to the different readings of (3) in the original argument. On one reading, as (3a), the conclusion (3) follows from (1′) and (2′), but it is harmless.[15] Under a different reading, as (3b), (3) is false, if we assume that no starting point exists necessarily; but it cannot be obtained from (1′) and (2′).[16]

14 Here we take 'the triangle' as a proper name, and so insensitive to differences of scope.

15 The argument is given in Smullyan (1948), pp. 33–4. By (1′) and (2′) we know that

> for some x, x alone is a starting point, and x = the triangle, and □(the triangle has interior angles equal to two right angles).

Putting equals for equals, then, and simplifying, we have

> (3a) for some x, x alone is a starting point, and □(x has interior angles equal to two right angles).

16 Notice that (3b) can be obtained from (1′) and a strengthened form of (2′), namely,

> (2a) □(for some x, x alone is a starting point, and x = the triangle)

(see Smullyan [1948], p. 34). But we have no grounds for asserting (2a), unless perhaps if (2a) is mistaken for the different formula,

Whichever way we read the conclusion of the argument, then, as (3a) or as (3b), no paradox exists.[17]

In fact, however, neither of the ways of handling the paradoxes reviewed so far, I think, is true to Aristotle's treatment of them. The solution I regard as Aristotle's invokes the theory of accidental compounds set out in Chapter 3. On this account, premiss (2) in the modal paradox, 'The triangle is the starting point', expresses a relation of accidental sameness between the triangle and the accidental compound, the triangle + starting point. And Aristotle uses the paradoxes to conclude that accidental sameness is too weak a relation to warrant application of a principle of accidental sameness in every context. That is, he comes to doubt the principle Strong (S1), which is based on accidental sameness, and adopts instead (S2), which features the far stronger relation of sameness in being.

On this account, the proper reading of the modal paradox becomes this:

(1) The triangle necessarily has the sum of its interior angles equal to two right angles.
(2c) The triangle is accidentally the same as the triangle + starting point.

Hence,

(3c) The triangle + starting point necessarily has interior angles equal to two right angles.

And the argument fails, because the move from (1) and (2c) to (3c) rests on the sameness principle Strong (S1), which Aristotle decides is invalid.

A number of points emerge from this analysis of the paradoxes. First, the sameness premisses (2) and (5) in the two arguments involve only accidental sameness, *not* identity. Hence, Leibniz's Law is never at issue in the paradoxes. (For the same reason, as we shall see in Chapter 5, the question of referential opacity is irrelevant to the two arguments.) So it is not correct that Aristotle starts out with Leibniz's Law in *Topics* H1 and elsewhere and, subsequently, under pressure from the modal and epistemic paradoxes, trades it in for some more

(2b) For some x, x alone is a starting point, and $\Box(x = $ the triangle$)$.

(2b) follows from (2) given the necessity of identity,

$(\forall x)(\forall y)(x = y \rightarrow \Box(x = y))$,

but it does not support the unwanted (3b).

17 For this kind of solution to the modal paradox, see K. Barnes (1977), pp. 57–60. But Barnes agrees that this solution is not Aristotle's, contrary to C. Williams (1985), esp. pp. 71–3, who argues that for Aristotle, the paradoxes are motivated by problems concerning substitution for definite descriptions with secondary occurrence.

restrictive principle. The principles at *Topics* H1 and elsewhere are not even remotely versions of Leibniz's Law.

It is implausible too to press on Aristotle the syntactic subtleties of the Russellian account. At the same time, Aristotle's treatment is also quite distant from the Fregean treatment sketched. Admittedly, Aristotle's account, like Frege's, depends on introducing a *second* set of entities, over and above individual substances: Coriscus + masked and the like, in addition to Coriscus himself. But this ontological move is only superficially similar to Frege's. Accidental compounds are not intensional objects in the way that Fregean senses are. More than this, Aristotle makes no use of a Fregean "reference shift." The expressions that pick out accidental compounds in the problematic contexts in the two paradoxes pick out those same compounds in regular, nonmodal contexts as well. So Aristotle's treatment of the paradoxes is at least as different from any of the alternatives sketched as these last are from one another.

3   Alternatives to the Controversial Sameness Principle

Aristotle's rejection of Strong (S1) in the *De Sophisticis Elenchis* on the basis of the modal and epistemic paradoxes brings an unexpected bonus, for it also supports the rejection of the troublesome principles (10) and (11) obtained from *Topics* E4, 133b17–21, and cited at the beginning of Chapter 3, Section 4. Renumbering the two principles for discussion in this chapter, we have

(7) ϕ^1 is an accident of a & ϕ^2 is an accident of $a \rightarrow \phi^2$ is an accident of $a + \phi^1$.

(8) ϕ^2 is an accident of $a + \phi^1 \rightarrow \phi^2$ is an accident of a.

Like (7) and (8), (S1) and Strong (S1) alike recognize entities of the form $a + \phi$ as subjects of accidents, in conflict with the claim in (A2) that if x is an accident of y, then y is a substance. More importantly, (S1) is *a consequence of* (7) and (8), given only the definition (D2). Thus, (7) is equivalent by (D2) and elementary logic to

(9) a is accidentally the same as $a + \phi^1 \rightarrow (\phi^2$ is an accident of $a \rightarrow \phi^2$ is an accident of $a + \phi^1$).

And given (8), by elementary logic we have

(10) a is accidentally the same as $a + \phi^1 \rightarrow (\phi^2$ is an accident of $a + \phi^1 \rightarrow \phi^2$ is an accident of a).

Principles (9) and (10) together give (S1). At the same time, we can use (S1) together with the definition of accidental sameness in (D2) to prove both (7) and (8). Since he rejects (S1) and, with it, the more general principle Strong (S1) as well, Aristotle must also reject the problematic principles (7) and (8).[18]

A similar treatment can be given to the principle (12) derived from *Topics* H1, 152a31–2 and also discussed in Chapter 3, Section 4. Renumbering again, we have

(11) x is accidentally the same as $y \rightarrow$ (x is accidentally the same as $z \leftrightarrow y$ is accidentally the same as z).

Principle (11) is an instance of the principle Strong (S1), for '$\phi^2(x)$' = 'x is accidentally the same as z'. Since Aristotle rejects Strong (S1) in the *De Sophisticis Elenchis*, he is no longer committed to (11). By the same token, he will also no longer be committed to the troubling instances of (11) (= (13) and (14) in Chapter 3, Section 4) already noted.

Once Strong (S1) is discredited, Aristotle turns for its replacement to a quite different sameness principle, (S2), which drops accidental sameness altogether for the very different notion of sameness in being. At the same time, however, although Aristotle himself is silent on the point, it is still open to him to reformulate (S1) and Strong (S1) within Extended ACT along the lines of the reformulated versions of the other troublesome principles discussed in Chapter 3. The new principle will have this form:

Weak (S1) a is accidentally the same as $a + \phi^1 \rightarrow$ (Accident-of (ϕ^2, a) $\leftrightarrow$ Accident*-of (ϕ^2, $a + \phi^1$)).

Weak (S1) follows almost immediately by the definition of the accident*-of relation in (D4). At the same time, Weak (S1) is *not* a licensing principle for the masker paradox or similar paradoxes. Thus, if ϕ^2 is the property of being known by me to be identical with Coriscus, we can use Weak (S1) to show that where Coriscus is accidentally the same as masked Coriscus:

(12) Accident-of (ϕ^2, Coriscus) if and only if Accident*-of (ϕ^2, masked Coriscus).

But the constituent claim in (12) that

(13) Accident*-of (ϕ^2, masked Coriscus)

comes down to just

18 Strictly speaking, since (7) and (8) together are required to obtain (S1) and (S1) is false, it follows by Modus Tollens that he cannot hold *both* of (7) and (8); but (S1) also entails (7) and (8), and he surely has no other reason to hold either singly if he no longer holds (S1). Aristotle himself explicitly rejects (8) in the same chapter in which he rejects (S1) (*SE* 24, 179a27–31, 35–7): sometimes what holds of the 'thing' holds of the 'accident' too, sometimes not. (Note that in the *De Sophisticis Elenchis*, Aristotle calls an entity of the form $a + \phi$ an "accident"; see 179a1–2 and Chapter 3, note 27.)

(14) Accident-of (being masked, Coriscus) & Accident-of (ϕ^2, Coriscus),

by (D4), so the result in (12) is evidently harmless.

It may be helpful, finally, to collect our results so far. Among the various principles of accidental sameness he sponsors in the *Topics,* Aristotle's discussion of the modal and epistemic paradoxes in the *De Sophisticis Elenchis* focuses attention on the problematic Strong (S1). Aristotle explicitly rejects Strong (S1). Although he nowhere explicitly rejects the other troubling principles of accidental sameness that appear in the *Topics,* his attitude towards Strong (S1) and the logical relations between Strong (S1) and those other principles virtually guarantee that he will drop the latter principles too. It is also open to Aristotle, as we have seen, to reformulate all these various troubling principles within Extended ACT. As it happens, however, the only principle he chooses to recast is Strong (S1), and the new principle he proposes in its place, (S2), takes us away from ACT altogether. If, as it appears, Aristotle chooses to reject the troubling principles without finding benign counterparts for them within Extended ACT, then the modal and epistemic paradoxes and the sundry violations of Core ACT simply melt away. But the sporadic use Aristotle makes of Extended ACT is enough to show that it offers an equally effective alternative for dealing with these same difficulties. Now Extended ACT features "reiterated" compounds, pale musical Coriscus and the rest, and this large new cast of characters in itself may seem problematic. But the provisions of Extended ACT guarantee that Aristotle is not about to expand his ontology beyond the basic commitments of the Core theory. Like the plain compounds of Core ACT, "reiterated" compounds are derived entities, constructed ultimately out of individual substances and their accidents. And the various asterisked relations typical of Expanded ACT – the two asterisked relations of accidental sameness and the accident*-of relation – are all defined in terms of notions present in Core ACT. The components of the Core theory, meanwhile – plain vanilla accidental sameness, without asterisks, the plain accident-of relation, the basic notion of compounding, even accidental compounds themselves – all require an ontology of *per se* beings, namely, individual substances and their accidents; but they require nothing more.

5

Compounds and Substances: The Ontological Project

As we have seen in previous chapters, accidental compounds are constructed out of other, more fundamental items in Aristotle's ontology: they are *per accidens* beings, put together out of individual substances and their various accidents, all of which are beings *per se*. To appreciate this picture of accidental compounds fully, we must set to one side various familiar ideas that are virtually "hard wired" into our contemporary ways of thinking. Accidental compounds are accidentally the same as, but emphatically *not* identical with, individual substances. As we have already seen in Chapter 4, then, the theory of accidental compounds offers a resolution to the modal and epistemic paradoxes markedly different from the kinds of treatment, Fregean or Russellian, that come most naturally to a contemporary philosopher. In this chapter, I discuss other ideas from contemporary theory that again threaten to cloud the distinction between an accidental compound and its parent substance, Socrates seated and Socrates (say).

I begin in Section 1 with the relation between Aristotle's accidental sameness and our notions of identity and (especially) contingent identity. On the view that the relation of accidental sameness between an accidental compound and a substance is that of contingent identity, a substance and an accidental compound have exactly the same properties in the actual world, hence are identical in this world, and they diverge only in other nonactual worlds that are possible relative to our own. A suggestion with somewhat the same effect (Section 2) involves the connection between the sameness principles Strong (S1) and (S2), discussed in Chapter 4, and the distinction between Socrates and Socrates seated. The obvious counterexamples to Strong (S1) involve modal and epistemic predicates, which apparently bring out differences between Socrates and Socrates seated that remain undetected in "ordinary," nonintensional contexts. Meanwhile, (S2), which apparently holds also for examples involving modal or epistemic contexts, features a notion of sameness that counts Socrates and Socrates seated as *not* the same from the start. Are there grounds here for concluding that the distinction between them is in some sense an "intensional" one? I will suggest that we should return a negative answer to this question. In Section 3, finally, I consider a further line of argument that again makes the distinction between compounds and substances problematic. This is the idea that a whole raft of classificatory predicates, ' . . . is a substance', ' . . . is an accidental compound', and many others, are referentially opaque; if this were right, then categorial differences between Socrates and Socrates seated would again not point to any *real* differences between them.

I take exception to these different views, at bottom because they do not allow us to make sense of Aristotle's ontological project. His idea that we can use the stock of *per se* beings in order to construct other, *per accidens* beings is hard to fathom if the distinction between a compound and its parent substance emerges only in some nonactual possible world. It is all but unintelligible, if the basic predicates of Aristotle's ontological talk are referentially opaque and yield only "different ways of looking at" individual substances and no clear difference between items in the ontology.

1   Accidental Sameness, Identity, and Contingent Identity

I begin with the philosophical characterization of accidental sameness. Does accidental sameness have any immediate counterpart in modern theory? More particularly, what is the relation between Aristotle's notion and modern notions of identity?

First, clearly enough, accidental sameness is not identity in the strict sense. For example, if Coriscus is pale, then Coriscus is accidentally the same as Coriscus + pale, by (D3). But Coriscus is not identical with Coriscus + pale, for the same reason that any compound is nonidentical with one of its constituents. And further, as Aristotle recognizes, Coriscus may still exist when Coriscus is no longer pale, that is, when Coriscus + pale has passed out of existence.[1]

But are Coriscus and Coriscus + pale perhaps *contingently* identical?[2] Contingent identity is said to hold between objects that have all their 'obvious' (i.e., nonmodal and, in general, extensional) properties in common. For example, it is said, Hesperus and Phosphorus are one planet in the actual world, since whatever is in fact true of the one is true of the other. But they might not have been the same, the contingent identity theorist will argue, for in other possible worlds they have

---

1 See *GC* A4, 319b25–32, and the Mikkalos example at *An. Pr.* A33, 47b29–37, both quoted in Chapter 3, Section 1.
2 For this suggestion, see J. Barnes (1979), discussed in Matthews (1982), pp. 228–9, and White (1986), pp. 477–8.

divergent properties and are distinct. Hence, they are merely contingently identical.[3] At first sight, a notion of contingent identity sits well with Strong (S1), which is a principle based on accidental sameness and apparently limited to extensional (nonmodal, nonepistemic) contexts. And, of course, the very label 'accidental sameness' recalls the modern term 'contingent identity'.

In fact, however, the comparison with contingent identity is quite misleading. It is quite true that when Aristotle concludes in *De Sophisticis Elenchis* that Strong (S1) is invalid, his counterexamples involve *intensional* predicates, so that it is possible for us to think that Strong (S1) survives as a principle for *extensional* contexts. As we shall see, however, there are other counterexamples to Strong (S1) that do not involve intensional predicates. More importantly, the principles of ACT commit Aristotle to thinking that *no* instance of Strong (S1) is true, even in extensional contexts. The type restrictions on accidental sameness in (i) of (D2) show that Strong (S1) cannot hold in *any* context: all instances of Strong (S1) are false, by (D2). For these reasons, Strong (S1) cannot function as a "principle of extensionality"; as a result, a major reason for finding the analogy between accidental sameness and contingent identity attractive disappears.

But in any case, accidental sameness and contingent identity are not the same. If Hesperus and Phosphorus are contingently identical, they must at least be identical in the actual world, as we saw. But, of course, Coriscus and Coriscus + pale are not the identical entity in *any* world, actual or otherwise. Coriscus and Coriscus + pale are accidentally the same, but they are not contingently identical. So accidental sameness is not contingent identity.

2   Sameness and Ontology

I turn now to connections between the theory of sameness and ontology. A good starting point is the difference between the two sameness principles Strong (S1) and (S2) and the consequences this difference may have for ontology.

Aristotle's rejection of Strong (S1) in the *De Sophisticis Elenchis* is based on counterexamples involving modal or epistemic predicates. This leaves open the possibility that without modal and epistemic predicates, no counterexamples to Strong (S1) will be found.[4] Sup-

---

3 A notable expression of scepticism regarding this account of the Hesperus–Phosphorus example occurs in Kripke (1971, 1972). The best defence of contingent identity known to me is by Gibbard (1975).

4 The argument here will require us to suspend for a while the counterexamples discussed in the penultimate paragraph of the previous section. Counterexamples to Strong (S1) in extensional contexts will reappear at the end of the present section.

pose that Strong (S1) has no counterexamples in the absence of modal or epistemic predicates. Then outside modal or epistemic contexts, no difference will come to light between Socrates (say) and Socrates + pale. For according to Strong (S1), two objects are accidentally the same only if any attribute of the one is also an attribute of the other. Any set of contexts, then, that produces no counterexamples to Strong (S1) will also fail to separate Socrates and Socrates + pale.

The new principle (S2), by contrast, is constructed around the stronger notion of sameness in being. This is a stronger kind of sameness in part because it purports to allow substitution in contexts for which Strong (S1) is said to fail. That is, (S2) is thought to be immune to counterexample even when exposed to contexts that are not purely extensional. The other side of this coin is that (S2) also introduces a refinement in our view of what should be included in Aristotle's ontology. According to (S2), two objects are the same in being only if they share all the same attributes. So it must treat Socrates and Socrates + pale as *different* objects because they are not indiscernible with respect to various modal and epistemic predicates. In reaching this conclusion, we assume that (S2) *holds in intensional contexts*, and use intensional counterexamples to distinguish Socrates and Socrates + pale.

The difference in ontology associated with Strong (S1) and (S2) can be illustrated by Aristotle's resolution of a puzzle concerning propria described at *Topics* E4, 133b15–36. Suppose that the attribute of being one who laughs is a proprium of man, that is, that all and only men are laughers. Suppose also that some object that is a man is also pale. Then being a laugher belongs not only to any man, but also to the pale one. Hence, apparently, being a laugher is not a proprium of man after all. Aristotle's solution to this puzzle is to point out that the man in question is not without qualification other than the pale one (*heteron haplōs*, b31–2). They are not identical, but at the same time, they are *accidentally the same*. There are contexts, then, in which they are *not* discernible one from the other. They are not, for example, distinguished if we ask whether what is a proprium of the one is also a proprium of the other. For example, suppose that Socrates is the pale one in question. Then by Strong (S1), apparently, from the sentence

(1) φ is a proprium of Socrates,

we can validly infer that

(2) φ is a proprium of Socrates + pale.

In fact, the sameness principle Strong (S1) appears to hold good in the presence of all contexts of the form 'φ is a proprium of . . . '. But the apparent success of Strong (S1) with respect to these contexts does not show that Socrates and Socrates + pale are identical. In other contexts, application of Strong (S1) fails, as the modal and epistemic paradoxes testify. Aristotle concludes that (S2) is the correct sameness principle to adopt, and this choice commits him to the finer-grained view that (S2) brings of what counts as the same entity.

But can we remain comfortable with the disparity in the view of 'what there is' that Strong (S1) and (S2) suggest? As we have seen, Strong (S1) is free of counterexamples (if at all) only in extensional contexts, while (S2) purports to be immune to counterexamples involving intensional contexts as well. This view of the matter has led to doubts about the nature of the distinction (S2) permits between Socrates and Socrates + pale. Dancy, for example, concedes that Aristotle distinguishes Socrates and Socrates + pale. At the same time, however, according to Dancy, the difference between them is not the concern of ontology, if ontology is a matter of "taking a census of the universe" or is an "inventory by the way of response to the bare question 'What is there?'." In distinguishing Socrates and Socrates + pale, then, "Aristotle is not doing ontology." Dancy's views deserve to be quoted more fully:

A substance (and) a quality . . . are just plain different, no holds barred. But a substance (and) a quale . . . are formally distinct; in particular cases they might be numerically one. For the most part, the last point is not relevant; it becomes relevant only when some sophist produces confusion by ignoring it, and argues, say, that the census-taker must note down two citizens, Callias and Callias educated. . . . For the most part, talk of substances [and] qualia . . . has to do with formal distinctions, and all that is meant when one says that a quale is not a substance . . . is that for something to be a man is not for it to be pale or six feet tall, even where the something is a six-foot pallid man. This suggests that, if doing ontology is a matter of taking a census of the universe, or an inventory by way of response to the bare question 'what is there?,' *Aristotle is not doing ontology*. (Dancy [1975], p. 368, my emphasis)

In Dancy's view, then, making the distinction between Socrates and Socrates + pale a part of ontology is akin to the fallacy committed by the sophist who argues that Socrates and Socrates + pale are two separate items for the census taker to count.[5] In fact, he thinks, the distinction between the two is only "formal" (by this, I take him to mean that the distinction is an *intensional* one); hence, it has no place in ontology.

On this last point, that intensional distinctions do not count in ontology, Dancy is surely at odds with contemporary orthodoxy. On the prevailing view, two things are identical only if they share *all* their

---

5 Compare the fallacy of supposing that φ is not a proprium of man if it also belongs to Socrates + pale (*Topics* E4, 133b15–36) discussed earlier in this section. Aristotle refers to similar "sophistical" difficulties involving Coriscus in the Lycaeum and Coriscus in the marketplace at *Physics* Δ11, 219b20–1.

properties, including the intensional ones. All identity is *necessary* identity, and there is no place for a restricted notion of contingent identity, so-called, that will count things identical if they share only all their ordinary, *non*modal properties.[6]

Setting this issue aside, however, is the distinction in any case really an intensional one? I believe that it is not.[7] Dancy argues that the census taker is indifferent to the distinction between Socrates and Socrates + pale, and so perhaps, in a sense, he is. At least he will always count exactly one citizen, no more, when he counts Socrates, whether or not Socrates is pale – that is, whether or not Socrates + pale also exists. In this respect, then, a substance and a compound are indistinguishable in the actual world. From the standpoint of ontology, the proper conclusion is, I think, so much the worse for the census taker. When we do ontology, we can set Socrates down as one, single object and discover later that there remains a second object to be counted, namely, Socrates + pale. This discovery may result from a hypothesis about how things *might have been*. If Socrates might not have been pale, for example, then Socrates and Socrates + pale are not identical. (This is why we should not concede that intensional distinctions have no place in ontology.) But the discovery that they are two may also come from changes in how the world *actually* is. At those times when Socrates exists but is no longer or not yet pale, the census taker still records one citizen: Socrates. But he does not count Socrates + pale, for Socrates is not pale, so that Socrates + pale does not exist. In this sense, the census taker is *not* indifferent to the distinction between Socrates and Socrates + pale. His counting shows that Socrates is not identical with Socrates + pale. The one is not counted exactly when the other is, for they do not exist at the same times.

These same facts also falsify Strong (S1). Socrates is accidentally the same as Socrates + pale, for Socrates is sometimes pale. But there can

---

6 For the controversy over contingent identity, see the references in note 3 and also the remarks in Marcus (1976).

7 This view, which I argued for in F. Lewis (1982), has since been controverted in White (1986). White has two arguments for the conclusion that Aristotle's way of distinguishing accidental sames is *modal* or *intensional:* (i) if definition is a modal notion, then Aristotle's preferred way of distinguishing accidental sames, namely, distinguishing them by definition, involves modal considerations; (ii) it may be that two things that are accidentally the same have all the same actual properties; but they *must* differ in some nonactual possible world. Against this last, if two things have all the same properties in the actual world but there is at least one property with respect to which they differ in some nonactual possible world, then I count the distinction between them modal; if there is at least one property with respect to which two things differ in the actual world, then the distinction between the two is nonmodal. What if two classes of entities are invariably distinguished with respect to their modal properties, but not always with respect to their "regular," nonmodal ones? My preference would be to call the distinction nonmodal if entities of the two kinds are sometimes distinguished nonmodally, and modal only if – not, as White argues, they are *always* distinguished *modally,* but – they are *never* distinguished *non*modally.

be ordinary, nonmodal properties – *being counted at t,* for example – that Socrates has but Socrates + pale lacks. The natural emendation to Strong (S1) is to say that it treats two objects, a and $a + \phi$, as the same, *provided they both exist.* But this concedes the crucial point that a and $a + \phi$ are sometimes distinguished in the actual world, when one exists and the other does not, even though Strong (S1), as emended, fails to separate them.

The upshot of our discussion is this. The failure of Strong (S1) in the face of various intensional counterexamples forces Aristotle to look for a sameness principle involving a variety of sameness that does confer indiscernibility with respect to modal and epistemic predicates. The result is (S2), which he claims is immune to intensional counter-examples, but which features a notion of sameness that makes Socrates and Socrates + pale to be *distinct.* Strong (S1), meanwhile, which purportedly has no counterexamples if we restrict ourselves to exten-sional contexts, treats them as indistinguishable. The appearance that the distinction between Socrates and Socrates + pale is an *intensional* one is nonetheless an illusion. For Strong (S1) has counterexamples even when it is applied in extensional contexts. Socrates and Socrates + pale are distinguished also by certain of their regular, nonmodal properties, even though they are accidentally the same. So the distinc-tion between them is not an intensional one.

3   Sameness, Ontology, and Referential Opacity

A second line of argument also attempts to cloud the distinction between (say) Socrates and Socrates + pale. According to these argu-ments, the predicates ' . . . is a substance' and ' . . . is a compound', along with many other classificatory predicates in Aristotle's ontologi-cal talk, are referentially opaque. If so, then there is no simple distinc-tion, if there is any clear distinction at all, between the substance Socrates and the compound Socrates + pale. We may begin by consid-ering once more the moral of the modal and epistemic paradoxes. The paradoxes teach us that putting 'Socrates + pale' for 'Socrates' in a true sentence of the form

$$\#(\phi(\text{Socrates})),$$

where '#' is any modal (alethic or epistemic) operator, may lead to a false sentence of the form,

$$\#(\phi(\text{Socrates} + \text{pale})).$$

It is a complex matter to assess the failure of substitution in this case. In general, failure of substitution in contexts of the form

$$\#(\phi(x))$$

is put down to the opacity of the position occupied by the variable '*x*'. It is natural to suppose, then, that the failure of substitution that the modal and epistemic paradoxes dramatize is due to the referential opacity of modal and epistemic contexts. But is this the moral Aristotle draws from the paradoxes?[8] From Aristotle's point of view, it seems, the paradoxes depend on taking to be the same *in being* entities that are in fact only *accidentally* the same. Two points are relevant here. First, as we have seen, accidental sameness is not identity. Coriscus and Coriscus + pale are accidentally the same, but they are not identical. Second, our notion of referential opacity, as developed by Quine, is built around our concept of identity, and not around any loose substitute for that notion. As before (note 7 in Chapter 3), a context, *A*, is referentially opaque at a given position if and only if for some expressions, α and β, such that α and β *denote the identical entity*, a context, *A'*, is like *A* except that *A* contains α in that position but *A'* contains β, and *A* and *A'* do not denote the same thing (or if *A* and *A'* are sentences, *A* and *A'* do not have the same truth value). Referential opacity, then, is defined around our notion of identity. Without identity as we conceive it, there is no opacity.

The implication of these two points is clear. The epistemic and modal paradoxes do not demonstrate that in general Aristotle regards modal and epistemic contexts as referentially opaque. That question is moot, for his examples in the paradoxes do not test those contexts with entities that are properly identical.

The paradoxes of the *De Sophisticis Elenchis* do not show, then, that Aristotle recognizes the opacity of contexts that we ourselves are disposed to regard as opaque. It has also been claimed, however, that Aristotle treats as referentially opaque contexts that we would ordinarily suppose were routinely referentially *transparent*.[9] Indeed, in some sense these contexts could be expected to serve as paradigms of the referentially transparent. These further claims, then, are certainly surprising, and it is worth asking if they are also true.

In essence, the claim is that contexts such as

. . . is a substance

are referentially opaque. For example, the sentence

---

8 The terms 'referentially opaque', 'referentially transparent', and the like are, of course, of modern manufacture. But it is still proper to ask whether in considering the paradoxes, Aristotle treats certain contexts as referentially opaque, that is, whether his treatment of the paradoxes fastens on features that for us would count towards referential opacity. An affirmative answer for the epistemic paradoxes is given in Peterson (1969); my own answer will be negative.
9 This view of Aristotle derives from Peterson (1969), who credits D. C. Bennett with the idea. Peterson's views are endorsed by Pelletier (1979), p. 290, and there are also perhaps reflections of it in Dancy (1975), pp. 365–8, (1978), pp. 386, 406, and Code (1976a), p. 364, (1976b), pp. 180–1.

(3) Socrates is a substance

is true, but the sentence

(4) The generous one is a substance

is false, even though it is Socrates who is generous.[10] Hence, it is argued, the locution ' . . . is a substance' contains an opaque context, and things are substances only relative to an appropriate general term or "substance predicate." An obvious extension of the same argument will purport to show that the context

. . . is an accidental compound

is referentially opaque; and similarly for other contexts like it.

These arguments recall a parody offered by Kaplan (1969) in a discussion of oblique contexts and indirect denotation in Frege. Consider

(5) Although F. D. R. ran for office many times, F. D. R. ran on television only once.

Kaplan (1969) writes:

The natural analysis [of (5)] involves pointing out that the name 'F. D. R.' is ambiguous, and that in the second clause it denotes a television show rather than a man. Substitution or any other logical operations based on the assumption that the name has here its usual denotation are pointless and demonstrate nothing. (p. 117)

Hence, "only the fanatical mono-denotationalist" would argue that the context

. . . ran on television only once

is referentially opaque. Kaplan's example turns on the idea that opacity can be traded here for ambiguity (an idea developed at a deeper level by Frege), but his point can apply as easily to our arguments

10 The falsity of sentences such as (4) is suggested by some perhaps rather equivocal evidence in *Metaphysics Zeta*. At Z4, 1030a4–6, Aristotle appears to say that substances (i.e., individual substances, e.g., Socrates?) satisfy a condition regarding essences that Socrates + pale (say) does not:

The pale is not just-what a this ‹is›, since in fact ‹being› a this belongs to substances only.

A similar point is perhaps made at the end of the chapter at 1030b6–13, esp. 12–13. Similarly, Aristotle argues in Z6 that in contrast to substances (*ta kath' hauta legomena*), an entity like the pale man (one of *ta legomena kata sumbebēkos*) is not the same as its essence. The earlier evidence in the *Organon* is somewhat less controversial. At *SE* 178b39–179a2, for example, Aristotle declares that musical Coriscus is a such, as opposed to Coriscus himself, who is a this (a condition that is the hallmark of the individual substance; *Categories* 3b10–23). And in the *Categories* at 3b33–4a2, Aristotle argues that substance does not admit of degrees, in contrast to *to leukon* (= the pale ‹thing›) and *to kalon* (= the beautiful ‹thing›). Clearly, then, the pale ‹thing› (an entity of the form *a* + pale) is *not* a substance.

concerning Aristotle. A tacit assumption in ascriptions of opacity is *identity;* hence, the charge that ' . . . is a substance' is referentially opaque can be dropped in favour of the view that (e.g.) Socrates and Socrates + generous are not identical.

The latter view is surely the preferable one to hold if we take seriously the suggestion that the pale one is a *compound* of a substance with an accident. Coriscus, for example, has a clear place in the category of substance, while Coriscus + pale is a cross-categorial hybrid that fits cleanly into no single category. Surely, then, such a compound is not the same entity as a substance.

This argument will not impress those who find the context ' . . . is a substance' and Aristotle's other ontological predicates referentially opaque. Coriscus and Coriscus + pale may be classified differently in Aristotle's categorical scheme, but this is *not* a sign that they are not identical, for the usual apparatus of reference breaks down when combined with the relevant categorial predicates. In short, these predicates are referentially opaque. How strong is this line of argument?

The argument has little force if we adopt the account of compounds and (especially) accidental sameness offered here. Consider this argument:

    (6) Coriscus is a substance,
    (7) Coriscus is the pale one,

so

    (8) The pale one is a substance.

This argument is said to show that the context ' . . . is a substance' is opaque, on the grounds that (6) and (7) are both true, while (8) is false. (Without opacity, however, (8) must be true if (6) and (7) are true.) On the account of compounds and accidental sameness given here, however, the argument becomes

    (6) Coriscus is a substance,
    (9) Coriscus is accidentally the same as Coriscus + pale,

so

    (10) Coriscus + pale is a substance.

This argument is valid if we trust Strong (S1). But we should not trust Strong (S1), for Aristotle has discarded it in *De Sophisticis Elenchis,* as we saw. There seem to be no other grounds for supposing that the argument is valid. And if there are not, then our motive for treating the predicate ' . . . is a substance' as referentially opaque is gone. So the conclusion that the predicate is opaque has not been demonstrated.

As these last arguments show, a crucial part of the argument for referential opacity in Aristotle's ontological predicates concerns what entities we admit into Aristotle's ontology and the accompanying account we give of accidental sameness. The different ontological choices are reflected in the differing interpretations we can give to paronymous referring expressions like 'the generous (one)'. Suppose that these do *not* refer to compounds, as is done explicitly by the term of art introduced here,

Callias + generous,

but that they have the logic of ordinary (Russellian) definite descriptions:

the x such that x (alone) is generous.

This reading makes it altogether reasonable to use (6) and (7) as premises to reach the conclusion that, once more, ' . . . is a substance' and many other classificatory predicates in Aristotle's ontological talk are referentially opaque. But to look beyond the label, what does this conclusion *mean*? Why should the ordinary apparatus of reference fail, of all places, in contexts where, if anywhere, Aristotle means to talk about *objects*?

Alternatively, paronymous referring expressions have the form '*a* + φ', as explained, and ' . . . is a substance' and the other workhorse predicates in Aristotle's ontological talk are straightforwardly transparent. On this account, his notion of accidental sameness has no immediate counterpart in modern theory. It is not clear that this is a disadvantage. And at least in doing *ontology* (his way of putting it: talking about *ta onta*), Aristotle is doing what we should expect him to do: talking about objects.[11]

---

11 I have argued against the view that the context ' . . . is a substance' is referentially opaque, that if this view were correct, then in our assertions that make use of such contexts, we should no longer be talking about objects. I conclude that we should prefer a non-Russellian reading of expressions such as 'the pale one' so that they refer to accidental compounds, and not to substances. Against this, it may be objected that the arguments used to show that ' . . . is a substance' and similar contexts are referentially opaque rest solely on the alleged failure of substitution within those contexts. This may seem to leave open the possibility that Existential Generalization is still valid in such contexts, so that the conclusion that they are referentially opaque is mistaken. In fact, we may conclude, they are neither referentially opaque nor referentially transparent, but rather, in Loar's terminology, nonextensional but referential: nonextensional, since substitution fails, but referential, since Existential Generalization succeeds (Loar [1972], pp. 47 ff.). (Cases in which these two criteria, substitutivity and accessibility to Existential Generalization, pull apart are discussed in Loar [1972], and the possibility of applying these ideas to the interpretation of Aristotle is discussed inconclusively in Peterson [1969], chapter 2.) If the context ' . . . is a substance' is nonextensional but referential, then the truth of our assertions involving such contexts will depend in part on how we refer to the

objects we do. But the singular term in subject position in such a context still occurs referentially, and Existential Generalization is still permitted. Manifestly, then, we are still talking of objects, and the ontological revisions for which I argue in the main text are strictly unnecessary. Does this counterargument succeed? It is easy to think of examples of nonextensional but referential occurrences of singular terms in connection with intentional notions (with a '*t*') – for example, knowledge contexts:

> Jones knows that the Evening Star is a planet with a shorter period of revolution than the Earth.

Here, as Loar notes, the singular term 'the Evening Star' contributes to its containing sentence in two distinct ways. One contribution is referential, but the other in Loar's account has to do with reporting the details of Jones's representational state and the description under which he thinks of the object referred to by the singular term. It seems reasonable to require that the claim that a term occurs referentially but nonextensionally in a given context should be accompanied by some explanation of this or some other suitable kind. But I have not seen how any such explanation is appropriate to occurrences of singular terms in the context ' . . . is a substance'. What connections, for example, could we draw between this case and the cases involving propositional attitudes that Loar describes? I shall continue to suppose, therefore, that if the context ' . . . is substance' is not referentially transparent, then it is, simply, referentially opaque. And as before, I find this conclusion intolerable and prefer the simple revision in our view of Aristotle's ontology proposed in the text.

PART III

Form–Matter Compounds

Aristotle's Later Theory of Metaphysical Predication

In his earlier works, as we have seen, Aristotle recognizes the existence of a single kind of compound constructed out of an individual substance and each of its various accidents: this is the accidental compound, accidentally the same as its parent substance, discussed in Part II. By the time of the *Metaphysics,* however, with the introduction of the dual notions of form and matter, Aristotle comes to think of the individual substance as itself a compound constructed out of these two. In such a compound, a form is predicated of matter (and matter is subject to that form) in a way that, broadly speaking, runs parallel to that in which an accident is predicated of an individual substance (and the substance is subject to that accident). And having analysed the individual substance in terms of form and matter, he holds that, not the individual substance itself, but its *form* is primary substance.

The larger theory within which these new ideas belong is usefully approached by way of a reprise of the earlier theory it replaces. As we have seen in earlier chapters, Aristotle's theory of (metaphysical) predication in the *Categories* is in large part anti-Platonic in its motivation. In Aristotle's earlier theory, first, an individual like Socrates both Has certain of his properties, which are his accidents, and Is others, which are essential to him. In Plato's theory, by contrast, Socrates is the subject of only one kind of (metaphysical) predication – Socrates Has or participates in various forms – and the idea that a subject Is its various predicables applies only in the case of forms, which alone Are what they are. At the same time, Aristotle also holds that the universal man too both Is certain of its properties – it Is, say, (an) animal – and at the same time Has other properties; for example, man Has pallor if some individual man is pale. The idea that universals too can be the subjects of two different kinds of (metaphysical) predication again distances Aristotle from the Platonic account. For according to Plato, the form man Is whatever it is, and only sensibles can Have their various properties.[1]

Aristotle's theory challenges Plato's idea that *uniform* theories of (metaphysical) predication prevail both at the level of sensibles and at the level of forms. He also argues that in certain cases, the *same* relation can hold between a sensible and certain of its predicables and between a universal and those same predicables. Socrates, for example, both Has pallor and Is (an) animal, while man too Has pallor and Is (an) animal. This is the *cross*-level notion of *homogeneity* discussed in Part I.

It is worth repeating here the special motive Aristotle has for insisting that Socrates not only Has his various accidents, but also, like man, Is (a) man, Is (an) animal, and the rest. Aristotle holds a principle of "Izzing before Having": Socrates can Have his various accidents, only because he is first a member of his appropriate kinds. That is – borrowing a measure of the stability that Plato reserves for Platonic forms – he Is (a) man, Is (an) animal, and so on.

Aristotle diverges from Plato again over the *subject* of predication. In the *Categories,* Aristotle apparently argues for the view that in the last resort, primary substances are the subjects of *every* (metaphysical) predication. This is the *monolithic* view of the subject of predication, and it is based on the idea that either a (metaphysical) predication overtly has a primary substance as its subject – Socrates Is (a) man or Has pallor – or it can be analysed ultimately in terms of (metaphysical) predications whose subjects are primary substances; for example, man (not a primary substance) Has pallor only because some primary substance Is (a) man and Has pallor. Plato, meanwhile, would argue that sensibles and forms are two irreducibly different kinds of subject.

Largely under the influence of the monolithic view of the subject of (metaphysical) predication, finally, Aristotle abandons Plato's view that one among *two* different classes of subjects, namely, Izzers or Platonic forms, are the basic realities, for the idea that in the core theory there is just *one* class of subjects, namely, individual substances, which are "subjects for everything else," and hence the primary substances. Individual substances are subjects to everything else, because they are subjects to the two core relations of metaphysical predication, (roughly) core Izzing but also core Having, involved directly or indirectly in every case of (metaphysical) predication. The two relations are also relations of one-step ontological dependency; accordingly, Aristotle can argue, everything else exists thanks to a relation of one-step ontological dependency on individual substances (Chapter 2).

1 In line with the cautions already issued in Part I, however, in later dialogues like the *Sophist,* Plato introduces a variety of complications in how forms can be related to other forms that we will not try to consider here.

In the *Metaphysics,* strikingly, Aristotle reverses himself on virtually all the points just noted. The most obvious revision, perhaps, is Aristotle's new choice for primary substance: the primary substances are now (Aristotelian) forms. And the individual substance – Socrates, Callias, and the like – undergoes a corresponding demotion. Socrates is analysed as (in some sense) a compound of form and matter, and not Socrates himself but his form is now primary substance.

In addition to their role as primary substances, forms also have a part to play in the new *Metaphysics* theory of (metaphysical) predication. In the *Metaphysics,* Aristotle clearly *abandons* the monolithic view of the subject of (metaphysical) predication in the *Categories,* in which individual substances are subjects for every predicable, in favour of a version of the old idea that there are *two* irreducibly different kinds of subject for (metaphysical) predication. Either an individual substance is subject to accidents, or (a portion of) matter is subject to a form. Aristotle nowhere allows that there are *more* than these two kinds of subjects.[2] Likewise, he nowhere suggests that the subjects that his theory does recognize can be subjects to *other kinds of predicables* than those indicated.[3]

At the same time, Aristotle also appears to accept a *uniform* theory of (metaphysical) predication in each of the two kinds of case his theory allows. Exactly one relation of predication holds between an accident and an individual substance: the first is *an accident of* the second; and exactly one relation of predication connects a form with the matter of which it is predicated. I shall say that the first *supervenes on* the second.[4]

2 An apparent exception is that Aristotle calls form a *hupokeimenon* at *Metaphysics* H1, 1042a26–9; this puzzling passage (discussed further in Chapter 10, Section 4) is the closest Aristotle comes in his later metaphysics to closing the gap between two notions that in the *Categories* were inseparable, namely, that of a primary substance on the one hand (recall, however, that in the *Metaphysics* the primary substances are identified with *forms*), and the notion of a subject of predication, on the other.

3 This is controversial. Furth (1988), e.g., p. 199, cf. pp. 176, n. 2, 231, argues that one and the same entity, doing duty as both form and species, *informs* or supervenes on Socrates' matter but is *form of,* or is *exemplified by,* Socrates himself. If these two relations are both meant to be *primitive* relations of metaphysical predication, the view violates the rule I claim governs Aristotle's core theory, namely, that an individual substance can be subject to accidents, but not to anything else. I also reject the identification between form and species: thus, outside the core theory, Aristotle recognizes a sense in which Socrates is subject to the *species* man (see Chapter 7), but it does not follow from this that the *form* man is predicated of him as well. In fact, I will argue, Aristotle's extended theory allows for the existence of kinds or species (although they are not metaphysically basic) and that these can be (metaphysically) predicated of the individual substance. At the same time, forms are metaphysically basic, but they are not (metaphysically) predicated of the individual substance at all, not even in any extended sense of 'predicated of'. On the distinction between form and species, see also Chapter 7 and Driscoll (1981).

4 I use the word 'supervenes' here as a term of art for one half of the relation of metaphysical predication, so my use of the term has nothing to do with its use by Kim,

The discussion in the preceding paragraphs suggests a variety of ways in which Aristotle apparently renounces choices made in the *Categories* and reverts instead to Platonic assumptions he had earlier rejected. The various components of Aristotle's new theory can be organized around three central claims: (i) that forms (and not individual substances) are primary substances; (ii) that forms are (metaphysically) predicated of matter, while as before, accidents are (metaphysically) predicated of individual substances – but these are the *only* cases of (metaphysical) predication there are; and (iii), that forms go together with matter to make up "form–matter compounds," analogous at least in some degree to the accidental compounds studied earlier in Part II.

These three points, both singly and in combination, contribute a whole budget of problems that threaten the very heart of Aristotle's theory. The most notorious, perhaps, involves the two ideas that forms both are primary substances and are (metaphysically) predicated – even predicated universally – of matter. These two claims are distinctive of Aristotle's new theory in the *Metaphysics*, but how do they square with earlier claims in the *Categories*, which Aristotle repeats in the *Metaphysics*, that no primary substance is predicated of a subject and that no primary substance is a universal? To all appearances, the earlier criteria for primary substance, which Aristotle shows every sign of wanting to retain as ingredients in his later theory as well, run head on into the combination of the new choice of forms as primary substances together with the role given to forms in the new theory of (metaphysical) predication.

A related point involves yet another criterion for primary substance from the *Categories*. In the ontology of the *Metaphysics*, either an accident is (metaphysically) predicated of an individual substance, or a form is (metaphysically) predicated of matter. With this theory, Aristotle apparently abandons the view from the *Categories* that a single kind of entity is subject for every predicable and that these are the primary substances. A version of the earlier monolithic view of the subject of (metaphysical) predication is revived briefly in *Metaphysics* Z_3, however, where Aristotle experiments with the idea that *matter* is subject to everything, both to accidents and to forms. The upshot of Aristotle's discussion, as we shall see (Chapter 10), is that the "subject" criterion for primary substance from the *Categories* cannot remain as it is. For the criterion is designed to pick out a single kind of entity as subject for everything, and hence as primary substance; but in the

Teller, and others in the contemporary philosophy of mind. As a gesture towards keeping things straight, I use the noun 'supervention' as opposed to their 'supervenience'. The idea that forms are (metaphysically) predicated of matter has sometimes been doubted, without good reason; see Chapter 6, note 6.

Metaphysics, as we have seen, Aristotle holds that there are two irreducibly different kinds of subject, and no such single subject exists. And in yet another departure from the *Categories,* being a subject will guarantee primacy only in the upper half of Aristotle's new scheme of (metaphysical) predication: in the lower half of the scheme, the direction of ontological priority goes the other way, so that a form is prior to the matter of which it is predicated.

A second set of questions involves the extent of the similarities between the two cases of (metaphysical) predication recognized in the new theory of the *Metaphysics.* Strikingly, in his first introduction of matter at any rate, Aristotle seems to find close parallels between the accident-of relation, connecting an accident and an individual substance, and the relation of supervention between a form and matter. On this view, the "two-stage" theory of (metaphysical) predication that appears in the *Metaphysics* in some ways can seem to be a simple extension of the notion of cross-categorial predication or Having in the *Categories.* But how similar really are the two cases of (metaphysical) predication?[5] They are, perhaps, similar enough that we are justified in representing both in terms of the relation of Having; for example, Socrates Has pallor, and these bricks and mortar Have the form of a house. If this is so, however, then there is now this difference from Aristotle's earlier views, that there is no longer room in the primitive basis of his theory for a variety of (metaphysical) predication corresponding to the notion of Izzing that was so prominent before.[6]

Suppose that this is right and that Aristotle now makes no provision for Izzing among the basic ingredients of his theory. Then he can no longer explain membership by an individual in a kind in terms of that individual's Being (a) man (say). Correspondingly, the old demand that a thing Be first a member of its appropriate kind before it can Have its various accidents cannot be left as it stands. Either, then, incredibly, Aristotle no longer makes room for the notion of the membership by a thing in a kind, and no longer holds that, properly, only members of kinds can be subjects to accidents, or he has an

---

5 The relation of (metaphysical) predication itself is the union of the two subrelations just distinguished: (metaphysical) predication holds either between an accident and its subject or between a form and the matter on which it supervenes. In this sense, it is trivial that *the same* relation holds between the two kinds of predicable and their respective subjects. A more intriguing question concerns the two subrelations. To what extent are these two like one another? And do the two together make up a single unitary notion? These questions are discussed briefly in the Postscript to this part.

6 Here there is the complication that in some cases, where form is soul and the matter is the living body of the animal or plant, it is often thought that the form supervenes *essentially* on the matter: if this idea is right, it may seem that in these cases, Having takes on some of the features that characterize Izzing. This is difficult, even treacherous, ground, however, and I shall by and large stay clear of it, with the exception of some brief remarks in the Postscript to this part.

account of membership in a kind that runs exclusively in terms of Having, without any reference to a notion of Izzing.

If, as I shall argue, Aristotle takes the second course and offers an account of membership by an individual in its kind that makes use solely of the notion of Having, then at least on the surface, he has abandoned the nonuniform theory of (metaphysical) predication in the *Categories,* and returned instead to the Platonic picture, on which all predicables alike are Had by their sensible subjects. But in Plato's case, at least, the view that sensibles invariably Have their various predicables, and Are nothing at all, leads to the "bare substrate" view of the *Timaeus.* As we shall see (Chapter 10), Aristotle too must take account of the similar conclusion scouted in *Metaphysics* Z3 that (otherwise featureless) matter is the subject for every predicable.

Aristotle's new theory of (metaphysical) predication precludes the monolithic conception of the subject of predication: neither matter nor any other single kind of entity can be subject for every predicable. His theory makes other equally notable exclusions. It leaves room for two different cases of Having, between matter and a form, and between an individual substance and its accidents – but these are the *only* cases of (metaphysical) predication there are. In contrast to Aristotle's theory in the *Categories,* then, in the core theory of the *Metaphysics,* individual substances are not any longer subjects to their kinds. (Equally, as we shall see below, in the core theory, there is no provision for individual substances as subjects to forms.) This gives added urgency to the question already raised about Aristotle's new treatment of kinds. What account does Aristotle propose to give for those *linguistic* predications in which an individual is assigned to its kind?

We must also come to terms with the place Aristotle seems to find for *matter* in his new theory. In his first discussion of matter in the later chapters of *Physics* A, Aristotle works with an inclusive concept of matter that encompasses not only the bronze that takes on the form of the statue,[7] but also Socrates as he changes from unmusical to musical. Of the relation between Socrates and the unmusical, Aristotle says that they are "numerically the same, but two in form or account": presumably, the same will hold for the relation between the bronze and the statue. The discussion in Part II suggests that the relation between Socrates and the unmusical is the relation that holds between any individual substance and an accidental compound constructed out of it: the two are accidentally the same, in the sense defined in Chapter 3 and discussed in the remainder of Part II. But if these clues do not point us in the right direction, how else are we to understand the

7 This is the narrower and more usual notion of matter. The inclusive notion evidenced in *Physics* A also surfaces elsewhere from time to time, e.g., at *Metaphysics* H1, 1042a32–b8; cf. *CG* A4, 320a2–5.

relation between a thing and its matter? The difficulties are particularly acute if we adopt instead the common assumption that numerical sameness is the same relation as our identity. How can a thing and its matter be *identical*, yet still be *distinguished* from one another in the different ways Aristotle's account of change requires? An answer is often found in the idea that despite the identity, there is still an *intensional* difference between Socrates and the unmusical, or between a thing and its matter. I prefer to suppose that on Aristotle's terms, statements of change are *not* intensional. As predicted, this view is in line with our results in Part II: Socrates and the unmusical are accidentally the same, but not identical, and similarly, a thing and its matter are not after all identical; so the mystery of how they can be distinguished disappears.

Our treatment of these various issues will be distributed between the two remaining parts. Some topics will be best deferred until Part IV, which is devoted to the "fit," or on some accounts the lack of it, between the new choice of form as primary substance and the received criteria for primary substance from the *Categories*.

The topics that remain will be discussed in Part III. In Chapter 6, I present the immediate data of the new theory: the new status of form as primary substance, the new theory of (metaphysical) predication, and the new analysis of the individual substance as (in some sense) a *compound* of form and matter in much the way, apparently, that accidental compounds are compounds of an individual substance with an accident. In Chapter 7, I take a further look at the theory of (metaphysical) predication and its connection with various *linguistic* predications, in particular, the new treatment it provides of the problem of the membership by an individual in a kind. I argue that in the *Metaphysics* Aristotle supposes that kinds or species exist but are not basic in his ontology; instead, they stand in a *derived* relation of (metaphysical) predication to individual substances, where *belonging by an individual in a kind* is now to be understood in terms of a core relation of (metaphysical) predication between the appropriate form and the appropriate matter. (At the same time, I argue that forms are a basic part of the *Metaphysics* ontology, but they are [metaphysically] predicated of matter and *not* of the compound material substance, even in a derived sense of 'predicated of'.) In the two subsequent chapters, I say more about the role of *matter* in form–matter compounds. As a preliminary in Chapter 8, I discuss the nature of the distinction between a form–matter compound and its constituent matter. As with the distinction between an accidental compound and its parent substance, I argue that the two are straightforwardly *not identical*. In particular, the distinction is not merely an "intensional" one. In Chapter 9, I discuss Aristotle's introduction of matter in the latter half of

Physics A: this is the text in which Aristotle presses most the parallel between matter and its relation to form, and the individual substance and its relation to its accidents. The Postscript to this part is reserved for some of the complications and refinements that enter into the account of form and matter that I shall otherwise not discuss here. The complications stem in part from the varied applications Aristotle makes of his theory to an increasingly varied set of cases throughout the natural world, including the analysis of animals and their parts, as well as the idea that the form of an animal is its soul. Other complications include the expanded theoretical apparatus, in particular the different notions of potentiality and actuality with which the initial notions of form and matter come to be surrounded. I also mention briefly some of the interpretive controversies concerning form, matter, and thing that otherwise lie beyond my scope here.

6

Form and the New Theory of
Metaphysical Predication

In this chapter, we examine some of the primary data in the new theory of (metaphysical) predication that appears in its fullest form in the *Metaphysics:* the choice of *forms,* in preference to individual substances, as primary substances; the role given to forms in the theory of (metaphysical) predication; and the analysis of individual substances as in some sense a compound of form and matter (a "form–matter compound," for short), so that it is now appropriate to refer to the individual substance as a "compound material substance." The chapter ends with a sketch of some of the major components in the general theory of compounds, including not only the accidental compounds familiar from Part II but also the new form–matter compounds.

1   Forms as the New Choice for Primary Substances

Can Aristotle really mean to displace the particular substance as primary substance in favour of form? The textual evidence on the point in *Metaphysics Zeta* is unequivocal. We have this bald statement: "By form, I mean the essence of each thing and the [its?] primary substance" (Z7, 1032b1–2). In a number of other places, Aristotle identifies form as substance *tout court* and leaves off the qualification "primary."[1] But the omission does not cast doubt on the identification of form with primary substance: perhaps more often than not throughout *Metaphysics Zeta,* 'substance' is shorthand for '*primary* substance'.[2] In Z3, next, comparing three candidates for "the first underlying thing, which seems most of all to be substance," Aristotle argues that form is prior to matter (see Z10, 1035b20–2) and also prior to the compound of form and matter (Z10, 1029a1–7; 1029a29–31 adds that the compound is prior to the matter). And in Z8, Aristotle

---

1 E.g., Z8, 1033b17–18, Z10, 1035a20 (?), b14–16, Z11, 1037a25, 29 (but see a28!), Z17, 1041b7–9 (Ross [1924], Vol. 2, p. 224).
2 E.g., Z10, 1035a20.

explains how "what we call form or substance" (*to . . . hōs eidos ē ousia legomenon*) and the compound substance are related: "The compound ‹substance› (*hē sunolos*) ‹is› *that which is spoken of in accordance with* ["gets its name from," Ross (1924)] it [= the form]" (Z8, 1033b17–8). In H3, finally, Aristotle explains that kind terms in general – for example, 'house' or 'animal' – are often ambiguous between terms for the compound substance and terms for the form. Such uses are to be explained by the notion of focal meaning (H3, 1043a36–7), where (presumably) the use to pick out the form is primary and the other peripheral uses are to be explained in terms of it.

What stands *against* the identification of (Aristotelian) forms as primary substances? A major source of difficulty, as we have seen in the Introduction to this part, is the role that forms also apparently play in the new theory of (metaphysical) predication. (Aristotelian) forms are predicated of a subject, for in the new theory they are predicated of matter. Equally troubling is the thought that apparently the *same* form is (metaphysically) predicable of *different* examples of matter, from which it seems to follow that forms are *universal to,* or *predicated universally of,* matter. The difficulty in both cases lies with some of the old criteria for primary substance from the *Categories,* which Aristotle still seems to honour in the *Metaphysics:* that no (primary) substance is a universal, indeed, that no (primary) substance is (metaphysically) predicated of a subject at all. I discuss how these difficulties may be resolved in Part IV. For present purposes, it will be sufficient to satisfy ourselves of the immediate data: that whatever the further consequences of such ideas may be, Aristotle is indeed committed in his new theory to holding that forms are (metaphysically) predicable of a subject and that a form is universally predicable of matter. These new ideas are our next topic.

2 Forms and the New Theory of (Metaphysical) Predication

The principal passages are these:

For, the rest are predicated of the substance (*ousia*), but it ‹is predicated› of the matter. (*Metaphysics* Z3, 1029a23–4)[3]

3 For further discussion of this passage, see Chapter 10, Section 3. *Metaphysics* Z3 offers good evidence (corroborated elsewhere in *Metaphysics Zeta, Eta,* and *Theta*) for the point that matter is a subject for Aristotle. But thanks to Aristotle's special purposes in that chapter, much of what is said there about matter as a subject is not typical of his views elsewhere. For example, his argument at Z3, 1029a20–6, seems to imply that the following inference is valid: accidents are predicated on the *ousia,* but the *ousia* is predicated of the matter; hence, the matter is subject for everything. But *ousia* here is ambiguous between 'individual substance' and the notion of 'substance of' or form, so that the passage is not evidence that the predication relation is transitive. (In fact, I shall argue [Chapter 10, note 46], it is vacuously both transitive and intransitive,

‹The subject› is subject in two ways (*hupokeitai dichōs*), either being a this, as the animal ‹is subject› to its affections, or as the matter ‹is subject› to the actuality.[4] (Z13, 1038b4–6)

For that of which and the subject (*to kath' hou kai to hupokeimenon*)[5] differ in this, by being either a this or not being ‹a this›: for example, what is subject to the affections is ‹a› man, both ‹his› body and ‹his› soul [= the compound of body and soul], and the affection is the musical or ‹the› pale. . . . In all cases of this sort, the subject (*to eschaton*) ‹is a› substance; but in the cases that are not like this, but what is predicated is a certain form and a this (*eidos ti kai tode ti to kategoroumenon*), the subject (*to eschaton*) is matter and matter-like substance. (Θ7, 1049a27–30, 34–6)[6]

In these passages, the relations '*x* is (metaphysically) predicated of *y*' and '*x* is subject to *y*' are the converses of one another; that is, *x* is predicated of *y* if and only if *y* is subject to *x*.[7] Aristotle tells us, then, that one thing, *x*, is (metaphysically) predicated of another, *y* (*y* is subject to *x*), only if *either x* is an accident and *y* is an individual substance, *or x* is a form[8] and *y* is matter.[9]

since premises of the form, '*x* is predicated of *y*' and '*y* is predicated of *z*', are never jointly true.) But these reservations about Z3 should not cast doubt on the role of matter as a subject in the *Metaphysics* in general; see note 6, this chapter.

4 With the opening phrase *hupokeitai dichōs*, I take Aristotle to be saying that two different kinds of entity can be subject to predicables, either matter or the individual substance. Alan Code has pointed out to me that the Greek can as well suggest that *one and the same thing* is a subject in two different ways: the most obvious way of spelling out the consequences of this reading will be to suggest that one and the same thing, Socrates (say), *qua* a this is subject to his accidents and *qua* matter is subject to form. I take it that the approach to ontology at work here amounts to much the kind of proposal advanced by Sellars and others and criticized in Chapters 8 and 9.

5 This is the text printed by Ross and Jaeger; there is an attempt to revive the reading of Π, A^b, and Alexander in Gill (1989), p. 159.

6 With the passages quoted, see also *Metaphysics* B1, 995b35; cf. B4, 999a33–4, H2, 1043a5–6. Some have doubted, in the teeth of the textual evidence, that Aristotle really means to say that matter can be a subject for predication (e.g., Rorty [1971]); these doubts are answered in Kung (1978). More recently, the sense in which form is predicated of matter is reevaluated in Kosman (1987); cf. note 25 in the Postscript to this part and Gill (1989); I regret that the latter reached me too late to be discussed properly here.

7 Frede and Patzig (1988), Vol. 2, p. 38, however, deny that this biconditional holds in *Metaphysics Zeta*.

8 On this clause: *x* = *ousia* (Z3, 1029a23–4), *x* = *entelecheia* (Z13, 1038b6), *x* = *energeia* (H2, 1043a6), *x* = *eidos ti kai tode ti* (Θ7, 1049a35). But while *x* is a form, it is important that on the interpretation I mean to offer, an *eidos* as form is *not* the same as an *eidos* as species; the distinction between the two seems to me certain, given the analysis of species or kinds as "compounds of this form and this matter, taken universally" at *Metaphysics* Z10, 1035b27–30; cf. Chapter 7.

9 In *Metaphysics* Z3, Aristotle argues that there are *three* kinds of subject – form, matter, and individual substance; cf. H1, 1042a26–31. I do not think that the inclusion of form here requires any modification in the account of (metaphysical) predication in the main text. But the classification of form as a *hupokeimenon* remains puzzling; I discuss the matter further in Chapter 10, Section 4.

This new theory of (metaphysical) predication in the *Metaphysics* clearly abandons the monolithic view of the subject of predication in the *Categories,* according to which individual substances are subjects for every predicable. In the "two-tier" theory Aristotle erects in its place, there are two irreducibly different kinds of subject for (metaphysical) predication. At the same time, Aristotle does not silently think that there are other fundamental kinds of (metaphysical) predication too. It is worth emphasizing this point from the very beginning, for in general, as we shall see in Chapter 7, Aristotle's theory is notable as much as anything for what it *excludes.* As least as far as the primitive basis of Aristotle's theory is concerned, there is no room for the idea that a kind may be (metaphysically) predicated of the individual member of the kind. This idea was a staple of the metaphysical theory of the *Categories,* but in the later theory, the relation of predication between an individual and its kind is at most a *derived* notion constructed out of other, basic components of the theory. Aristotle also excludes from both the core and extended theories the possibility – simply substituting forms for kinds – that Aristotelian forms can be (metaphysically) predicated of the compound material substance.

Aristotle's theory also rules out the idea central to the *Categories* that a single class of entities are subjects for *every* predicable and that these entities are the primary substances. In the *Metaphysics,* Aristotle has changed his mind about what the predicables are – a predicable is either an accident or a form – and of these, accidents are (metaphysically) predicated of individual substances, and of them alone, and forms are (metaphysically) predicated of matter, but (again) not of anything else. In a very vivid sense, then, the two tiers of Aristotle's system are *isolated* one from the other. Nothing, that is, can be subject to *both* an accident *and* a form. A fortiori, then – contrary to the monolithic view of the *Categories,* which is refurbished and brought briefly into play in *Metaphysics* Z3 – no one thing can be subject to all of a thing's accidents, and subject also to all the forms that help make it up. These points are discussed further in Chapter 10.

In the two-tier theory of predication in the *Metaphysics,* on the usual account, an accident is a universal because it is predicated of different individual substances.[10] In the same way, I take it, a single form is predicable of different portions of matter – Socrates and Callias, for example, have different matters but the same form (*Metaphysics* Z8, 1034a5–8, quoted in Section 3; cf. *De Caelo* A9, 278a15–21) – so that a form too is a universal.

The philosophical ramifications of this view of forms as universals will be discussed in Part IV; here, as before, we will concentrate largely

10 For the possible complications here, see Chapter 2, esp. note 47.

on the textual data. Direct evidence for the view of forms as universals is not abundant in Aristotle's text. I know of only two passages in the *Metaphysics* in which Aristotle explicitly calls forms universals. At M8, 1084b5, the reference is only in passing. In Z11, however, Aristotle declares flatly that "definition is of the universal, *that is, of form* (*tou gar katholou kai tou eidous ho horismos*)" (Z11, 1036a28–9; my emphasis). The notion of forms as universals is integral to the argument under way in the surrounding context. In the previous chapter of *Zeta*, Aristotle has set out a *full-expansion* condition on definition:

The definition of a primary definable, *T*, includes the definition of all the parts of *T* that are not definitional primitives.[11]

This condition is satisfied only when *T* has the right kind of parts: in particular, they must be forms, but not matter, for matter is not properly definable. Neither matter itself, then, nor any compound involving matter – the individual compound of form and matter, Socrates, for example, or a compound of form and matter "taken universally"[12] – can have a definition in the proper sense required by the full-expansion condition. Aristotle reinforces these points at the beginning of Z11. Definition, he says, is of the universal, that is, (again) of *form*. So until the difference between parts of the form and parts in the sense of matter becomes clear, how we are to define a thing will also be not clear (1036a26–31); for (Aristotle could have added) only those things whose parts are all *forms* can satisfy the full-expansion condition, and hence are *proper* definables, as opposed to objects of definition in some less strict or secondary way.[13] The main part of Z11 then takes up the task of separating form and matter in the way required.

The passage in Z11 is the only one in which Aristotle explicitly connects the role of form as the primary object of definition with the idea that it must, therefore, be a universal. In general, however, the argument is familiar that if forms are primary substances, and primary substances are the primary definables, and if, finally, primary definables are universals, then (again) forms must be universals.[14]

It is often argued that forms cannot be universal to matter in this way. One motive for this denial is clear: if forms, indeed, are universals and also primary substances, we have yet to square this with

11 The attribution to Aristotle of a condition on definition along these lines is due to Code (1985), p. 119.
12 Z10, 1035b27–30, Z11, 1037a6–7; cf. perhaps Z8, 1033b25–6 (but for a different reading of this remark, see Ross [1924]. Vol. 2, on 1033b16).
13 For definables that are not proper definables, see Lewis (1984), n. 14 and pp. 118–20, and Code (1985), pp. 112–13.
14 This is an adaptation of an argument at *Metaphysics* B6, 1003a5–17; cf. K2, 1060b19–23, and M10, 1087a10–13.

Aristotle's repeated claim that no universal is a (primary) substance. I attempt to show how these three claims may be made consistent in Part IV. For now, I shall try simply to rebut one common argument for the conclusion that contrary to the texts just cited, a form cannot be a universal. It is often assumed that to be predicated universally, an entity must be predicated of a plurality of *objects* or of *individuals*[15] or of *countable particular substrates*.[16] The emphasis here is on countability or sortability and on what it would take to count or sort different portions of matter. A form cannot be universal to different portions of matter, the argument goes, because these last *cannot be counted or sorted independently of the very form that is predicated of them*. This at least appears to be the objection Woods has in mind:

To speak of a plurality of objects I need some means of marking off each member of the set from other things; I do this, according to Aristotle, by recognizing occurrences of a certain form in matter. Thus I must already regard things as possessing the form before I can think of objects as a genuine plurality.[17]

The shortest counter to this is that even if we grant that we must have some form in mind in order to refer to a given portion of matter, it does not follow that this must be the very same form that is (metaphysically) predicated of that matter. In the usual case, in which a form is predicated of a given example of matter, the matter is itself a compound of form and matter (prime matter is the single exception). Where a compound material substance, a, is a compound of a form, ψ, and a matter, m, let us say that ψ *supervenes on* m[18] but that ψ is *constitutive of* a. Then while we may pick out a given particular example of matter, bronze (say), by way of its *constitutive* form ('the stuff with *such-and-such a ratio* among its meltable ingredients'), in order to assert that it is the subject for some *supervenient* form (the form of a statue, say), these evidently are not the same form. The distinction between constitutive and supervenient form on which this reply turns is discussed further in Section 4.

At the same time, there is not really any reason to think that in picking out a given particular example of matter, we need to appeal to a form at all – either to a form that supervenes on it or to its constitutive form. For example, in addition to proscribed referring

---

15 Woods (1967), pp. 226, 237.
16 Driscoll (1981), p. 151.
17 Woods (1967), p. 237.
18 The reader is cautioned again that the use of the "supervenes on" jargon here is *not* the same as that familiar from the contemporary philosophy of mind; cf. note 4 in the introduction to this part.

expressions of the form 'the bronze of this statue', where, arguably, supervenient form is involved by way of the reference to the statue, we have also 'the bronze that once constituted Myron's *Discobolos*' (a statue known only through its Roman [marble] copy, so that at most, the reference is by way of a once-supervenient form) or even 'the bronze sitting outside in my truck', where the reference is not achieved by an appeal to supervenient form at all. On this showing, it is hard to sustain the picture of matter as capable of being marked off or sorted as a subject for (supervenient) form only by virtue of that very form itself. For similar reasons, it is unlikely that we can successfully pick out an example of matter only by way of its *constitutive* form: 'the *bronze* of the statue' and 'the stuff with *such-and-such a ratio* among its meltable ingredients', for example, both involve constitutive form, but 'the stuff now in my truck' or 'the heaviest material my truck has ever carried' evidently do not.[19]

Why should anyone ever have supposed otherwise? One further line of argument has to do with the concept of matter as matter *for* some given particular kind or kinds of thing. If matter is essentially *for* something, does it not follow that it cannot be directly identified, independently of that which it is for?[20] In many, even the majority, of cases, I think, the premiss is well founded; but it does not even come close to supporting the conclusion. Aristotle suggests in *Metaphysics* Θ7 that the matter of a thing is properly its *proximate* matter, which is *potentially* that thing in (again) some suitably immediate sense. For example, bricks and the like are the proximate matter of a house: they have the passive capacity, or *dunamis,* for being made into a house under the appropriate conditions of realization, in particular in the presence of an efficient cause with the suitable active *dunamis.* On Aristotle's view, it is *essential* to the bricks that they be the proximate matter of a house, and hence essential to them that they be capable of being built (if they have not already been built) into a house. The connection between the matter of a thing and the thing itself is stronger still – and more problematic – in the case of biological matter if, as Ackrill argues, the flesh and bones that are the matter for the living animal are themselves essentially alive, and hence themselves are characterized by the same form that is also the constitutive form of

19 For more discussion of this topic, see Kung (1978), pp. 145 ff.
20 Compare, for example, this passage from Schofield (1972): "According to Aristotle only things or forms have absolutely determinate identities, and only they can be directly identified; whereas the matter (always the matter *of a thing* or *for a form:* see e.g. *Phys.* II 2.194b8–9) has to be identified *via* the relevant thing or form, since there are no such things as 'matters'. So if one takes matter just on its own, without specifying any form or thing for it, there is nothing definite one can say about it" (p. 101, his emphasis).

the animal.[21] Even without this difficult second set of cases, however, it is clear that, for Aristotle, matter is frequently, even usually, matter *for* a given kind of thing or suitable for a given supervenient form. But there is no good reasoning that will take us from these metaphysical points about bricks, or about matter in general, to a conclusion about reference.[22] If a man is metaphysically ignorant, for example, he may not even *know* that it is (part of) the essence of a brick to be built or buildable into a house; but it would be bizarre to conclude that in the absence of the required reference to houses, he cannot refer to or reidentify bricks. Or to adapt an example from Smart, it may be that necessarily lightning is a certain kind of electrical discharge – that this is the essence of lightning. Yet even an "illiterate peasant . . . can talk about lightning though he knows nothing of electricity."[23]

3   The Analysis of Individual Substances: Form, Matter, and Form–Matter Compounds

The new theory of predication in the *Metaphysics* permits a view of the individual substance that is radically different from that available earlier in the *Organon*. In the *Categories*, the criteria for determining what is most of all substance are tied to two canonical forms of (metaphysical) predication, relating a subject to its kinds (including, when the subject is a substance, to its substantial kinds) or, in the case of a substance, to its accidents. The conceptual apparatus that the *Categories* provides offers no technique for inquiring after the inner structure, if any, of the items it identifies as basic: individual substances such as the individual man or the individual horse (*Categories* 2, 1b4–5) or their parts (*Categories* 5, 3a29–32, 7, 8b15; cf. *Metaphysics* Δ8, 1017b11–13, Z2, 1028b9–10, Z16, 1040b6). Individual substances are basic in the ontology of the *Categories* precisely because by the *Categories*' lights,

---

21 Ackrill (1972–3)
22 Ackrill apparently draws the conclusion I mean to argue against here; as Modrak (1985), p. 96, explains the point, "Aristotle is unable to pick out the matter of an organism by a description which is logically independent of the form of the organism." With Ackrill (1972–3), p. 124, Modrak takes this to be an objection against the very notion of compounding itself, but she also argues that short of a way to individuate matter, the view that form is universal in relation to matter cannot be sustained (p. 93). Modrak also has an independent line of argument against the view that form is universal to matter (pp. 93–4): form is (metaphysically) predicated of matter, but it cannot be *universal to* matter, on the grounds that matter does not *exemplify* the form that is predicated of it; on this view, however, Aristotle's notion of a universal purchases an association with the notion of exemplification only by dint of losing its tie with (metaphysical) predication. As in Loux (1979), p. 20, I prefer to give up the connection between exemplification and universals.
    The inference I am objecting to is well criticized in Charles (1988), pp. 36–7.
23 Smart (1959), p. 147. The issues discussed in this section surface again; see the Postscript to this part and Chapter 11, Section 4, p. 329.

they cannot be analysed in terms of anything further: they are, to adapt a phrase of Furth's, *opaque* to further analysis.[24]

The picture we are given in the *Metaphysics*, however, is quite different. There, an individual substance is seen as an organized, structured entity of a certain sort and is analysed accordingly as a compound of matter and form. And of the three, matter, form, and compound, *form* is now primary substance, as we have seen. But a form itself is *not* a compound of matter and form. So a primary substance – that is, a form – may *have* a subject or substratum, but it is not itself a compound of form and substratum: no primary substance is "spoken of by way of one thing's being in another, that is, in something which is its subject as matter" (Z11, 1037b1–4).

The idea that form is, in some sense, a *constituent in* the individual substance, which is thus (again, in some suitable sense) a *compound of* matter and form, requires some comment. The view of an individual substance as a compound dominates Z8, for example, where Aristotle argues that everything that comes to be must be a compound of form and matter. The craftsman, for example, who makes the bronze round makes neither the bronze nor the round, but something else, namely, this form in something else (1033a32–4; cf. b8–10, 18–19, Λ3, 1069b35–1070a4). Again:

What generates is sufficient for the making, and cause of the form's being in the matter. But once we have the whole, such-and-such a form (*eidos*) in these flesh and bones, this is Callias or Socrates; and they are different on account of their matter (for that is different), but the same in form (*eidos*) (for the form [*eidos*] is indivisible). (Z8, 1034a4–8, following Furth's translation; cf. Mansion [1971])[25]

In the same vein, Aristotle uses the phrase *to sunolon* (the composite) or *hē sunolē ousia* (the composite substance) to denote the compound of matter and form.[26] The concrete substance can also be described as

24 Furth (1978), p. 631. Furth's own phrase is *"methodologically* 'atomic' and opaque" (his emphasis), so that the phrase is consistent with Aristotle's having the analysis of individual substances into form and matter to hand in the *Categories* and choosing not to activate it for merely methodological reasons. I do not myself believe that the notions of form and matter are part of Aristotle's conceptual arsenal in the *Categories*, suppressed or otherwise, and so I would not agree that the opacity in question is methodological alone.

25 But those who find a doctrine of individual form in Aristotle will translate Aristotle's word *eidos* by 'form' only in its first occurrence in this passage; if Aristotle holds that forms are individuals, the last two occurrences must be rendered instead by 'species': Frede and Patzig (1988), Vol. 1, p. 87; see also Vol. 2, pp. 147–8.

26 E.g., *Metaphysics* B1, 995b35, B4, 999a33–4, Δ24, 1023a31–2, b1–2, Z10, 1035a20–1, b19, 22, 32–3, 1036a2, Z11, 1037a26, 29–30, 32, Z17, 1041b11–12, H3, 1043a30, K2, 1060b24–5, Λ3, 1070a14; cf. *PA* A1, 640b26 (but contrast the use of the word *sunolon* for the compound of a substance with its accident [M2, 1077b8], for the compound of genus and final differentia [*An. Po.* B13, 97a39], or for the compound of

what is "out of" matter and form (*to ek toutōn*)[27] or as a "this-in-this" (*tode en tōide*), this form in this matter[28] – hence too the frequent comparisons between natural substances and Aristotle's favourite example, the snub, which unlike mere concavity, is a "this-in-this" and involves not just a property by itself, but also its appropriate subject, namely, noses.[29]

But how are we to understand the notion of *compound* that is involved in this language? Sometimes Aristotle speaks of forms as straightforwardly an ingredient or "element" (*stoicheion*) in the compound substance (Λ4, 1070b10–19). In a notable passage at the end of *Metaphysics Zeta*, however, he protests against such talk and calls form a "principle" (*archē*), as distinct from an element (Z17, 1041b11–33, H3, 1043b4–14 [Ross's (1924) text]). In the same spirit, he will say that matter is a *part* of the compound substance (Z10, 1035a2–9; cf. Δ25, 1023b19–22) but is not usually willing to talk of form as such a part.[30] So the precise way in which the concrete substance is a compound of form and matter remains mysterious.

The mystery, though deep, is not perhaps unique to Aristotle. As Lukasiewicz suggested some time ago, Aristotelian form can be regarded as in some respects like a function from matter to a compound – in the favoured cases, to a compound which is also a substance.[31] If we interpret functions in a Fregean style, similarities open up between Aristotle's views and those of Frege. For Aristotle, matter is itself a material object, but one that lacks the right kind of unity to count as a substance (Z16, 1040b8–10, Z17, 1041b11–33, H3, 1044a2–9; cf. H6). Form, meanwhile, is not itself a material object,[32] just as for Frege a function is nonmaterial. But in much the way that for Frege a function is "unsaturated," so for Aristotle form in the

form and this matter, "taken universally" [Z10, 1035b29]). Aristotle also uses the expression *hē sunthetē ousia* (the composite substance) or *to suntheton* (the compound); e.g., Δ24, 1023a31–2, b1–2.

27 *Metaphysics* Z3, 1029a3–5, Z10, 1035a1, 2, b32–3, H2, 1043a18–19, 28; cf. *De Anima* B1, 412a9.

28 *Metaphysics* Z11, 1036b23; cf. *ta ge en hulēi*, K2, 1060b25, and *De Anima* Γ4, 429b14; *PA* A1, 640b27; *GC* A5, 321b20–1, *tōn en hulēi eidos echontōn*.

29 *Metaphysics* E1, 1025b28–1026a7, Z10, 1035a25–6 (cf. the discussion in Z5); *Physics* B2, 194a5; *De Anima* Γ4, 429b13. For other references to the combination of matter and form in the compound substance, see Bonitz (1870), 786a15–23, and Hicks (1907) on *De Anima* A1, 403b11.

30 He does so talk, however, at *Metaphysics* Δ25, 1023b19–22.

31 Lukasiewicz (1953), pp. 80–2. This suggestion is developed further in K. Fine (unpublished). To forestall misunderstanding, I should add the qualification that the comparison between Aristotelian form and the modern notion of a function, especially as it is understood by Frege, is meant to illustrate only one facet of Aristotle theory. If Aristotelian form shares some of the formal features of a Fregean function, it surely also has many other properties that the comparison with Frege leaves untouched; cf. note 34.

32 For the contrary suggestion, see Charlton (1970), pp. 70–3.

sublunary world is of such a nature[33] as to combine with one material object, namely, matter, to make up a second object, which under the right circumstances will be a substance. Now Frege holds that there are functions whose value for an appropriate material object as argument is itself a material object (e.g., the function *the capital of x*). So the structure of a form–matter compound can be much like the result of "saturating" a Fregean function with an object as its argument, and the mystery of how one material object can combine with a nonmaterial entity to compose a second material object is, in some respects at least, the same in both cases.[34]

I have suggested that form is something like a Fregean (singulary) function whose value for a given matter as argument is the appropriate form–matter compound. On this account, the use of compounding to construct an Aristotelian form–matter compound will be something like the operation of application of function to argument in Frege's scheme. And if we suppose that accidents in Aristotle's theory can also be treated as singulary functions, we can construe compounding in general – in connection both with form–matter compounds and with accidental compounds – along the lines of the application of function to argument. If we follow out the comparison with Frege, it is best to regard compounding as a primitive notion of Aristotle's theory, so that form and matter are constituents of the relevant compound, and it is a compound of them – but in a way that, by and large, his theory itself leaves unexplained. This way of treating the notion has some support in Aristotle's remarks on the problem of the "unity of definition" in *Metaphysics* H6, where his solution involves the relation between matter and form:

But if, as we say, the one is matter, and the other form, and the one ‹is› potentially, the other actually, the object of our inquiry would no longer seem to be a puzzle. . . . The difficulty disappears, because the one is matter, the other, form. What, then, causes this – that which was potentially to be actually – except, in the case of things which are generated, the agent? For there is no other cause of the potential sphere's being actually a sphere, but this was the essence of each of them. . . . But as has been said, the proximate matter and the

33 Cf. *Metaphysics* H6, esp. 1045a30–3 (quoted in the next paragraph in the main text), and Λ10, 1075b34–7.

34 But (as predicted in note 31) there are limits to how far the analogy can safely take us. For example (I owe the example and the point to Alan Code), the father of John is not a compound of John and the function *the father of x* in precisely the way that, according to Aristotle, my table (say) is a compound of certain materials and the appropriate form. For example, there is an obvious sense in which the father of John could still have existed, even if he had been forever childless, but the table can hardly exist in the absence of the form of a table. Nor is the father of John created by combining function and argument in the way that the craftsman creates the table by imposing a certain form on a given matter (again, the example and the point are Code's).

form are the same and one, the one potentially, and the other actually. Therefore it is similar to ask what is the cause of the ‹thing that is› one, and ‹to ask the cause› of the fact that it is one [= these come down to the same question]; for each thing is one thing of a certain kind (*hen gar ti hekaston* [b20]), and the potential and the actual are somehow one. Therefore there is no other cause here, unless there is something which caused the movement from potency into actuality. (1045a23–5, 30–3, b17–22)[35]

Here Aristotle treats the unity of form–matter compounds side by side with questions about the development of an actual so-and-so from a potential one. On this idea, the matter of a thing has the passive power or *dunamis* for being made to constitute that thing by the agency of something with the corresponding active *dunamis;* accordingly, matter and form are "combined" to make a unified and single member of a kind, just in case the relevant active and passive *dunameis* perform as advertised and are jointly realized in the specified way. So the question 'Why do matter and form join up to make *one* thing?' is on a par with asking, 'Why are passive *dunameis* actualized as they are by the appropriate corresponding active *dunameis?*' But while these two questions are in some sense equivalent, I am not inclined to think that either kind of talk – Aristotle's potentiality talk or his talk of form and matter – can be defined in terms of the other. Aristotle does not mean to *explain* the realization of active and passive *dunameis* in terms of the compounding of matter and form to make a compound material substance, and the second is not explained in terms of the first. In the absence of any other means for defining either set of notions, both sets of notions remain undefined in Aristotle's theory. Faced, then, with the question 'Why do form and matter make up one thing?' or 'Why does the potential so-and-so become an actual so-and-so?' for want of any better answer, we can only drop a level and abandon the metaphysical question for a material/efficient one: *Who* made the bronze into a sphere? *What* allowed the fire to realize its *dunamis* for upward motion? – where the appropriate answer will cite the relevant moving cause that has the requisite corresponding active *dunamis,* or the removal of some hindering factor.

Aristotle also rejects unequivocally the possibility of any help from *outside* his theory. In the same chapter of *Eta,* for example, he dismisses the metaphors of Plato and others as attempts to supply an explanation of a sort that is neither needed nor possible:

Owing to the difficulty about unity some speak of 'participation', and raise the question, what is the cause of participation and what is it to participate; and

---

35 Cf. Λ10, 1075b34–7; *De Anima* B1, 412b6–9. The translation of H6 in the main text follows Ross's translation, but with corrections, especially in the translation of b19–20.

others speak of 'communion', as Lycophron says knowledge is a communion of knowing with the soul; and others say life is a 'composition' or 'connexion' of soul with body. Yet the same account applies to all cases; for being healthy, too, will on this showing be either a 'communion' or a 'connexion' or a 'composition' of soul and health, and the fact that the bronze is a triangle will be a 'composition' of bronze and triangle, and the fact that a thing is white will be a 'composition' of surface and whiteness. (H6, 1045b7-16; Ross's translation)

Presumably, the last part of this passage means to ridicule the idea that there is anything *explanatory* in any of this talk.[36]

Frege too makes no bones about his inability to define a function or the operation of application of function to argument. In "What Is a Function?" Frege writes:

The peculiarity of functional signs, which we here called 'unsaturatedness,' naturally has something answering to it in the functions themselves. They too may be called 'unsaturated,' and in this way we mark them out as fundamentally different from numbers. Of course this is no definition; but likewise none is here possible. . . . I must confine myself to hinting at what I have in mind by means of a metaphorical expression, and here I rely on my reader's agreeing to meet me half-way. (Geach and Black [1980], p. 115)

In this and other passages, Frege shows an evident tolerance for the use of metaphor to help explain the notions he cannot define.[37] In contrast to Frege, however, Aristotle has no time for the use of metaphor to help us understand the primitive notions in his theory.

4   The General Theory of Compounds

As the discussion in the preceding section shows, Aristotle assumes that the theory of (metaphysical) predication inevitably contains at least one notion – in practice, more than one notion – that remains undefined within that theory. He also rejects the attempt to explain the primitives in his theory of predication by reference to notions that come from *outside* the theory. Aristotle's choice of primitives begins with the notion of *compounding*. Two kinds of compounds are to be considered: accidental compounds, familiar from Accidental Compound Theory (Part II), but also the new form–matter compounds distinctive of Aristotle's later work. In this section, I sketch the general theory of compounds within which the two kinds of compound belong.

36 See *An. Po.* B13, 97b37-9, and J. Barnes (1975), p. 239; *GC* A10, 327b13-22; *Metaphysics* A9, 991a20-2, 992a26-9, Z14, 1039b5-6, M5, 1079b24-7; cf. also *De Caelo* Δ3, esp. 310b16-24, together with the comments in Mourelatos (1967), p. 102, esp. n. 23, and Ackrill (1972-3), p. 122.

37 Compare the similar remarks in "Function and Concept," p. 32, and "On Concept and Object," pp. 42-3, 45, 54-5 (references are to the translations in Geach and Black [1980]).

I shall use the notation '$x + y$' to denote the result of compounding x with y ("the compound of x with y," for short).[38] As before, the '+' notation is meant to express the primitive notion of compounding in Aristotle's theory, and any other associations the same notation may have in other contexts should be disregarded. Aristotle uses the primitive operation of compounding in two quite separate contexts to obtain two different kinds of compound, but I shall use the same notation for compounding throughout and defer until later a discussion of any differences between the two kinds of case.[39] Aristotle assumes that

(A1) $x + y$ exists, only if *either* x is an individual substance and y is an accident, *or* x is matter and y is a form.

Let us use the letter a as a variable ranging over individual substances, m as a variable over portions of matter (for reasons that will emerge shortly, 'matter' here will include compounds of matter and form if they fall below the level of substances), and x and y as unrestricted variables. The variable ϕ will range over accidents, and ψ over forms. Then we can define the two kinds of compound as follows:

(D1) x is *an accidental compound* if and only if for some individual substance a and accident ϕ, $x = a + \phi$.

(D2) x is *a form–matter compound* if and only if for some matter m and form ψ, $x = m + \psi$.

Form–matter compounds include not only the individual substances, which we may now call "compound material substances," but also those compounds of form and matter discussed later in this section that fall below the level of substances.

We come next to the relations 'x is an accident of y' and, relating form to matter, 'x supervenes on y'.[40] These two relations, like the notion of compounding, are undefined in Aristotle's theory. They are subject to the following conditions:

(A2) x is an accident of y, only if x is an accident and y is a (compound material) substance.

(A3) x supervenes on y, only if x is a form and y is matter.

38 What follows is a formalization of only a small fragment of Aristotle's theory of substance. A full-scale formalization is brilliantly done by Kit Fine (unpublished), and some of the principles in my account are descendants of principles due to him. The general theory of compounds formalized in this chapter will contain the account of ACT set out in Part II as a proper part; still further portions of Aristotle's theory are given in the Appendix to Chapter 11. The propositions that make up the theory are numbered continuously within each part, but not across parts.

39 The extent to which the two kinds of case are really parallel is discussed briefly in the Postscript to this part.

40 Compare the cautions issued in note 18 and in the Introduction to this part, note 4.

The relation of (metaphysical) predication is defined as the union of these two:

(D3) *x* is (*metaphysically*) *predicated of y* (*y* is *subject to x*) if and only if *either* *x* is an accident of *y or x* supervenes on *y*.

Finally, it is worth comparing the three primitives assembled so far as part of Aristotle's theory. They are, of course, *different* notions. Most obviously, the notation '+' is a connective that joins terms to make terms – for example, it joins terms for an individual substance and for an accident respectively to make a term for an accidental compound, and it joins terms for matter and form respectively to make a term for a form–matter compound. But the expression '*x* is an accident of *y*' is a two-place predicate that joins terms for an accident and an individual substance respectively to make a sentence, and the expression '*x* supervenes on *y*' is similarly a two-place predicate.[41] The two sets of notions are related in that we can use the accident-of relation and the relation of supervention to say exactly when there exists the result of compounding a given matter with a given form or the result of compounding a given individual substance with a given accident:

(A4) ϕ is an accident of *a* if and only if $a + \phi$ exists.
(A5) ψ supervenes on *m* if and only if $m + \psi$ exists.

I note next a complication peculiar to form–matter compounds, in contrast to accidental compounds. It is an oversimplification to say just that individual substances are compounds of form and matter, without further elaboration. Properly articulated, Aristotle's theory allows for the existence of a whole hierarchy of coincident matters within a single material substance. Socrates, for example, is composed of a hierarchy of coincident matters, starting from prime or altogether unformed matter, all the way up to the proximate matter of the finished substance. This picture is reflected in the fictitious example in *Metaphysics* Θ7: going "downwards" from an artefact to prime matter, Aristotle imagines,

the box is (not wood but) wooden
wood is (not earth but) earthen
earth is (not air but) air-en
air is (not fire but) fire-en.[42] (1049a18–27)

---

41 The distinction between supervention and the operation of compounding applicable to form–matter compounds is slurred by the notation ' $\frac{F}{M}$ ' in Furth (1988), which serves indifferently as an open sentence and an open singular term; see, e.g., his pp. 192, 198, and 264.

42 I have followed Furth (1988), p. 190, in combining the two sequences Aristotle mentions. It is worth noting that from the sequence of matters given in the text, we can construct an account of the metaphysical composition of the box by means of successive applications of different forms to increasingly complex matters, which

Here, the box is "wooden," so-called after its matter, wood, and the wood in turn is "earthen," after its matter, earth. Similarly, earth is "air-en," and air in turn is "fire-en." But, finally,

> there is no x such that fire is x-en.

Accordingly, fire is prime matter.[43]

Despite the fanciful details in the box example in Θ7, similar sequences of matter exist in the real world of living animals and plants. In the biological works at *PA* B1 and *GA* A1 and elsewhere, Aristotle describes how the elements or simple bodies are the matter for the uniform parts, and these in turn are the matter for the nonuniform parts, until finally we reach the completed animal.[44] So we shall need not one but two notions relating matter to the compound. First,

> (D4) x is *the matter of y* if and only if x is matter and y is a form–matter compound, and for some form ψ, $y = x + \psi$.[45]

For example, this bronze is the matter of this statue, but also (given a more complex form) a certain quantity of water is its matter "if everything meltable is ‹composed of› water" (*Metaphysics* Δ4, 1015a7–10, Δ24, 1023a28–9). In writing 'x is *the* matter of y', therefore, we must not take the 'the' too seriously, for in most cases, y will not have a

are themselves (with the exception of the initial, prime matter) compounds of form and matter:

$$\text{the box} = \text{wood} + \text{some form } \psi^1$$
$$\text{wood} = \text{earth} + \text{some form } \psi^2$$
$$\text{earth} = \text{air} + \text{some form } \psi^3$$
$$\text{air} = \text{fire} + \text{some form } \psi^4$$

But, finally,

> there is no x, y, such that fire $= x + y$.

43 On this story, Aristotle's philosophy of nature also makes room for prime matter at the very bottom of the hierarchy of coincident matters. I will not pursue the controversy over prime matter here, either against those who doubt that the notion is really present in Aristotle or against those who find the notion of prime matter in Aristotle but doubt that it is coherent (see the references in note 2 to the Postscript to this part). On the view I adopt, however, prime matter is a genuine part of Aristotle's metaphysical theory. More than this, the distinction between a certain quantity of elemental fire (say) and the quantity of prime matter that is its matter need be no less coherent from the metaphysical point of view than the distinction between an ordinary compound material substance, Socrates, for example, and his matter. In each case, the matter (prime or otherwise) is *the matter of* the relevant compound, but the matter and the compound are *nonidentical*. For the nonidentity of a thing with its matter, see Chapter 8 and, for prime matter, see Chapter 10, note 55.

44 *PA* B1, 646a13–24; *GA* A1, 715a9–12; cf. *Meteorology* Δ12, 389b23–8; *Metaphysics* Δ4, 1015a7–11, Δ6, 1017a5–6, Δ24, 1023a26–29, H4, 1044a15–25, b1–3. These various stages in the complexity of matter are discussed briefly in the Postscript to this part; cf. F. Lewis (forthcoming).

45 Given the stipulation in (D4) that y is a form–matter compound, the matter-of relation in question here is *not* a relation between matter and form by itself; that is, it is *not* the converse of the supervention relation. An alternative version of the matter-of relation that does take it as the converse of supervention is contemplated briefly in Chapter 10, note 55.

unique matter. Among the various matters of a thing, however, its *proximate* matter is usually uppermost in Aristotle's mind (*Metaphysics* H4, 1044b1–3, Θ7, 1049a1–18, *Physics* B3, 195b22–7). A second notion relates proximate matter to its parent compound:

(D5) *x* is *the proximate matter of y* if and only if *x* is the matter of *y* and there is no *z* such that *x* is the matter of *z* and *z* is the matter of *y*.

Complementary to the notion of the proximate matter of a form–matter compound, next, is that of its "last" form: the form that, in combination with the appropriate proximate matter, makes up the compound in question:

(D6) ψ is *the last form of x* if and only if there is a proximate matter, *m*, of *x* such that $x = m + ψ$.

And where ψ is the last form of a compound material substance, we say that ψ is the substantial last form of that substance:

(D7) ψ is *the substantial last form of x* (ψ is *the form of x*, for short) if and only if ψ is the last form of *x* and *x* is a compound material substance.

At the other end of the spectrum, meanwhile, there is prime matter, which, as I have already suggested, is altogether unformed. But the sense in which prime matter lacks form requires careful handling. I shall suppose that what is meant is that prime matter is not itself a compound of form and matter. As a first and only partial characterization, then,

m is prime matter only if there is no matter, m^1, and form, ψ, such that $m = m^1 + ψ$.

The force of this claim is perhaps best appreciated by considering the differences between it and the following, which Aristotle would certainly reject:

m is prime matter only if there is no matter, m^1, and form, ψ, such that $m^1 = m + ψ$.

Contrary to this claim, Aristotle will hold that prime matter *always* has some supervenient form: prime matter is invariably a part of some form–matter compound. At the same time, it has no constitutive form (this is the jargon of (D9), to be introduced subsequently). So we have this definition of prime matter:

(D8) *m* is *prime matter* if and only if *m* is matter and there is no matter, m^1, and form, ψ, such that $m = m^1 + ψ$.

At the same time, Aristotle assumes that

(A6) *m* is prime matter only if for some *y*, *m* is the matter of *y*.

If both (D8) and (A6) are right, some important points emerge about the sequence of matters that coincide with a given compound material substance.[46] Such a sequence begins with an entity that is the matter of something else but is not a form–matter compound (this is prime matter); it ends with an entity that is a form–matter compound but not the matter of anything further (the compound material substance itself). Prime matter appropriately begins the sequence, since it cannot itself be analysed as a compound of form and matter: it is matter pure and simple. The compound material substance appropriately ends the sequence, since it is not itself the recipient of any further form: the compound material substance has assumed its full quota of form, and any further modifications of it must be accounted its accidents.[47]

One final definition will be of use later. As we saw previously, supervention is a relation between the form and matter that together make up a given form–matter compound. We will also need to talk about the relation between the form and the compound in such a case. We define the relevant notion as follows:

(D9) ψ is *constitutive of* x if and only if for some m such that m is the proximate matter of x, $x = m + \psi$.

For example, suppose that this meltable stuff, m, is the proximate matter of this bronze, and for some ψ, the bronze $= m + \psi$. Then by (D9), ψ is constitutive of the bronze, that is, of $m + \psi$. At the same time, ψ *supervenes on* m by itself (cf. (A5)). Again, the form ψ^1 is constitutive of this statue, just in case this bronze, m^1 ($= m + \psi$), is the proximate matter of the statue, and the statue $= m^1 + \psi^1$ ($= (m + \psi) + \psi^1$). (Again, ψ^1 is constitutive of $m^1 + \psi^1$, but it supervenes on m^1 by itself.)

We have also this theorem:

(T1) ψ is constitutive of x if and only if ψ is the last form of x.

(T1) follows from (D9) by (D6).[48]

---

46 Cf. note 43.
47 The boundary between forms and accidents at the upper end of Aristotle's scheme of (metaphysical) predication is discussed in *Metaphysics* I9.
48 The notion of the constitutive form of a thing is designed to single out the *thinnest* form that, compounded with the thing's proximate matter, will produce exactly that thing itself. For example, if water is the proximate matter of bronze, the form of bronze is the constitutive form of the bronze: the bronze in question = water + the form of bronze. But it may happen that other, "thicker" forms also supervene on the water; for example, if the bronze is itself the matter of a statue, then the form of a bronze statue also supervenes on the water. But we do not want to count this last form as constitutive of the bronze. It is important to notice also that the notion of the constitutive form of a thing defined in (D9) is "thin" in yet another way: by stipulating that the form be compounded with the *proximate* matter of the thing, we ensure that the constitutive form of the statue is the form of a statue, which supervenes on the proximate matter of the statue, namely, the bronze, and *not* the form

(D9) stipulates that a thing has a constitutive form only if it also has a proximate matter. But by (D8) and (D4), we know that prime matter has no matter at all. Accordingly, we have this result concerning prime matter:

(T2) m is prime matter only if there is no form ψ such that ψ is constitutive of m.

(T2) should be carefully distinguished from its counterfeit, which claims that

m is prime matter only if there is no form ψ such that ψ supervenes on m.

Unlike (T2), this claim is clearly *false* for Aristotle.

Our discussion in this section has taken us well beyond Accidental Compound Theory, presented in Part II, to consider a portion of the general theory of compounds of which ACT is only a part. Both ACT and the general theory are themselves fragments of a larger theory governing Aristotle's notions of substance and predication; details of this larger theory will be deferred until the Appendix to Chapter 11. More immediately, I shall try to suggest the power of the general theory sketched in this chapter by applying it to the problem of the membership by an individual in a kind. The notion of a kind is to all intents and purposes Aristotle's invention in the *Categories,* where it is clear that he will account for the truth of the *linguistic* predication

of a bronze statue, which supervenes on the water, lower down in the sequence of matters involved in the composition of the thing. This point is brought out in theorem (T1) in the main text. A looser notion of constitution will drop the reference to proximate matter:

ψ is loosely constitutive of x if and only if for some matter, m, of x, $x = m + \psi$;

but this is not the notion of constitution we shall be using here.

It is also worth commenting on why the relation 'x is (thinly) constitutive of y' is *defined* in (D9), while the relation 'x supervenes on y' is left primitive in Aristotle's theory. After all, we know that

ψ supervenes on x if and only if for some compound y, $y = x + \psi$

(cf. (A5)); why resist taking this as a definition, if (D9) can be a definition of constitutive form? Or if supervention is left undefined, why not take constitution as primitive? Two points are relevant here. First, the notions of supervention and compounding featured in the biconditional just given seem to me to be *simultaneous* in Aristotle's theory: neither seems to be truly explanatory of the other, and since neither is usefully defined in terms of any other set of notions, I regard both alike as primitive. But, second, once we have decided to leave supervention as primitive in Aristotle's theory, it is not plausible to extend the same line of thought and remove the definition of constitutive form offered in (D9). Possibly, an alternative way of structuring Aristotle's theory might be to take constitution (better, loose constitution) as primitive and make supervention defined, instead of the other way around, as in Aristotle's actual theory; but there can be enough of a good thing, and once one of the two sets of notions is taken as primitive, on a par with the notion of a form–matter compound, the other can safely follow along as one of the derived components of the theory.

'Socrates is a man' by appealing to a relation of *metaphysical* predication – whose converse is Code and Grice's Izzing – between Socrates himself and the secondary substance man. But what analysis will Aristotle give for the same linguistic predication in the *Metaphysics*, where the only two kinds of (metaphysical) predication his theory now permits have Having as their converse and hold either between a compound substance and its accidents, or between form and matter? It should be no surprise that Aristotle's account of kinds in the *Metaphysics* centers around his notion of form; the details of the connection between forms and kinds will be the subject of Chapter 7.

7

Form and Membership in a Kind

Questions of the membership by an individual in a kind are distinctively Aristotelian. In the Platonic theory of (metaphysical) predication, Socrates Has man, for example, and Has pale in precisely the same way, without any hint of difference between the two kinds of case. Aristotle's theory in the *Categories* is constructed in direct opposition to this picture: as we have seen, Socrates must first Be something (e.g., he Is [a] man), before he can be the subject of accidents (e.g., before he can Have pale). Aristotle's theory of (metaphysical) predication undergoes radical alteration in the *Metaphysics;* but his notion of a kind persists. In this chapter, we will trace some of the adaptations Aristotle's theory of kinds undergoes as his larger metaphysical theory evolves.[1]

1   Predication and Kinds

In the *Categories,* as we have seen, Aristotle holds that the primary substances – that is, in the *Categories,* the *individual* substances Socrates, Callias, and the like – are in a strong sense subjects for everything else, and it is chiefly for this reason that they are ranked as substances in the strictest sense of the word. This monolithic view of the subject of predication is replaced in the *Metaphysics* by a two-tier system, which recognizes *two* kinds of subject, at two different levels.

1 In the pages that follow, I argue that Aristotle's theory of individuals and kinds in the *Categories* is explained in the *Metaphysics* in terms of a relation between form and matter. Contrary to what is often supposed, then, the notion of form is in no way a direct descendant of the *Categories* notion of a kind (so, perhaps, Furth [1978], p. 631, and more clearly, [1988], p. 50, n. 2, and 176, n. 2); rather, form is just one element in the larger apparatus Aristotle uses in the *Metaphysics* to analyse the *Categories*-style species or kind (as we shall see, the analysis is that kinds are "compounds of this form and this matter, taken universally"). But it should be noted that the distinction between the earlier kinds and the later notion of form is not made easier by the fact that behind the conventional translations 'kind' and 'form', there lies one and the same already overworked word, *eidos,* in Aristotle's Greek (cf. F. Lewis [1985a], p. 59).

Either an accident is predicated of an individual substance, as in Aristotle's earlier theory, or going beyond the earlier theory, a form is predicated of matter. For all the differences between Aristotle's earlier and later theories, however, one important feature that on the account given here stays constant is the idea that predication for Aristotle is *metaphysical* predication. That is, predication is a relation between *entities*. In particular, what is predicated is always a metaphysical item, and not an item of language. This is something of an idealization of Aristotle's practice in the *Categories*, where he moves back and forth between a linguistic and a metaphysical notion of predication. But it reflects accurately Aristotle's procedure in the *Metaphysics*, where it seems that predication is usually if not invariably *metaphysical* predication.

The divorce between predication in the dominant Aristotelian sense and our standard linguistic notion raises a question that would be unintelligible in the context of a purely linguistic conception of predication. What are the implications of Aristotle's theory of metaphysical predication for what *we* would call predication, and vice versa? That is, what do Aristotle's theory of metaphysical predication and ordinary, garden-variety linguistic predication have to do with one another?

In the *Categories*, the connections between linguistic and metaphysical predication are relatively straightforward. In particular, as we have seen (Chapter 2, Section 2), each core case of metaphysical predication – one thing is said of (lowercase) another, or one thing is in another – has immediate and obvious linguistic corollaries in a true sentence that relates an individual substance to its kinds or that assigns an accident from a nonsubstance category to an individual substance as its subject.

In the *Metaphysics*, by contrast, the connections between the different kinds of metaphysical predication and ordinary linguistic predication are not always so obvious. One connection, in which the theory of the *Metaphysics* is clearly continuous with that of the *Categories*, is easily established. In the *Categories* and *Metaphysics* alike, to the case in which an accident is (metaphysically) predicated of a substance, there corresponds the linguistic predication, for example,

(1) Socrates is pale.

But the remaining case in the *Metaphysics*, where forms are (metaphysically) predicated of matter, seems to lack any ready or natural counterpart in ordinary language. Conversely, there is one linguistic case clearly covered in the *Categories* for which no obvious counterpart exists in the new, metaphysical account:

(2) Socrates is (a) man.

By the lights of the *Categories,* (2) asserts that a substance is related to one of its kinds by the core said-of relation. (2), then, is handled easily within Aristotle's earlier theory of (metaphysical) predication. But it is not immediately clear how (2) is accommodated by the new apparatus of (metaphysical) predication at work in the *Metaphysics*. Sentence (2) clearly does not assert that an accident is (metaphysically) predicated of an individual substance. Nor is it obvious that (2) asserts that a form is (metaphysically) predicated of matter. Again, then, how will Aristotle deal with (2) within the scheme of the *Metaphysics* – if we are not to say that that scheme is incomplete and simply leaves sentences like (2) unaccounted for?

We saw in the preceding paragraph that there are two problems in need of a solution. In the theory of the *Metaphysics,* apparently, a linguistic predication like (2) has no obvious counterpart in the theory of metaphysical predication; meanwhile, the case in which a form is metaphysically predicated of matter apparently lacks any obvious linguistic counterpart. These two problems can be solved at a single stroke if we suppose that it is the metaphysical relation of predication between a form and matter that underlies the truth of (2) and sentences like it, which assign an individual to its kind. According to this line of thought, the idea that a form is metaphysically predicated of matter is Aristotle's replacement in the *Metaphysics* for the earlier idea that a secondary substance is said of an individual substance. The full account of the different stages in the evolution of Aristotle's theory of kinds will be reserved for Section 5. In the intervening sections, meanwhile, I will sketch further Aristotle's positive theory of forms and kinds in the *Metaphysics* (Section 2) and then discuss some relations between individuals, forms, and kinds that the new theory of (metaphysical) predication apparently *excludes* (Sections 3 and 4).

2 Form and Membership in a Kind

In this section, I consider the details of Aristotle's account of forms and kinds, in particular the treatment his theory gives to sentences like (2) in Section 1.[2] Our main source will be a line of argument Aristotle deploys in *Metaphysics* Z17 in support of his new view that forms are the primary substances or, what Aristotle takes to be equivalent to this, that form is the *substance of* a thing.[3]

Aristotle argues in Z17 that form is the substance of a thing, at bottom because of the part forms play in the analysis of the member-

2 In what follows, I am indebted to the account in Loux (1979).
3 For the equivalence, see (A9) in the Appendix to Chapter 11.

ship by a thing in its kind. Why is this thing a member of its given particular kind? Aristotle takes the answer to point to a *causal* contribution by the form of the thing: *the form is the cause of the being of the thing,* for short. But if we already suppose that *the substance of a thing is the cause of its being,* then if there is only one cause of a thing's being, we can conclude that *the form is the substance of the thing,* as required.

One ingredient in this argument is an idea that Aristotle takes as the keynote of the chapter: that substance is a cause (*aition*),[4] more particularly that it is the cause of being (*aition tou einai*) for a thing.[5] The notion of 'substance' that is to the fore here is undoubtedly that of the substance *of* a thing. As a cause, the substance of a thing supplies the answer to certain kinds of 'why'-questions that may be asked about it. These are 'why'-questions directed to the thing's being – that is, I take it, for some kind *k,* they are directed to the thing's being a *k.*

At the same time, there is work to be done, Aristotle thinks, on the (logical) form that the appropriate 'why'-questions will have. Although its substance accounts for the being of a thing, for example, it does not answer the question of whether the thing *exists,* for this is something we must be able to take for granted (1041b4–5; cf. 1041a15–16, 23–4). Nor are we concerned with answering *why a thing is itself* (1041a14–20, 22–3, b2–4).

This last point leads Aristotle to a surprising conclusion. For the expected question, for example,

Why is *this,* viz. this man Socrates, (a) man? (classificatory *is*),

he substitutes another:

Why are *these,* viz. these materials, (a) man? (the *is* of constitution)

---

4 1041a9–10; cf. A3, 983a26–9, Z13, 1038b7.
5 1041a31–2, b26, 28; cf. Δ8, 1017b15, H2, 1043a2–4, H3, 1043b13–14 (Ross [1924], Vol. 2). I use the English noun 'cause' throughout as the translation for the Greek *aition.* In many if not most commentaries, this translation is used selectively, for only some occurrences of the Greek *aition,* and in other instances – for example, where Aristotle talks of form as an *aition,* as in the case at hand in the main text – the translation is switched to "explanatory factor" or some other euphemism to cover the embarrassment of seeming to use "ordinary" causal talk in contexts in which this is judged inappropriate. But I prefer not to prejudge interpretive questions of this sort in the very translation of the Greek. In some of the cases in which Aristotle talks of form as an *aition,* he also says that form induces change, or "moves" (*kinei;* e.g., *Physics* B7, 198b1–4) – are we also to find some evasive paraphrase here? Or again, Aristotle says that nutritive soul (also a form) *makes* (*poiei*) growth out of the nourishment or that the *dunamis* of generative soul *makes* the offspring (*GA* B4, 740b19–741a3; cf. *Metaphysics* Z7, 1032b21–3; *Meteorology* Δ12, 390b10–14; *GA* B6, 743a32–4): should this language be toned down to say only that soul or form is an explanatory factor in the making of growth or of the offspring? There is, of course, a great deal of complexity in Aristotle's talk of causes, and the topic lies well beyond the scope of the present discussion. Whatever the proper interpretation of such passages, however, our translations should reflect the Greek directly and stay out of the business of interpretation.

(cf. the examples at 1041b5–7). Thus, Aristotle says, "The question, 'Why?', is always ‹meant› in this way: 'Why does one thing belong to another?' " (1041a10–11; cf. 1041a23, 25–6).

Once the relevant 'why'-questions are cast in this way, Aristotle is in a position to argue for a causal role for form. The appropriate 'why'-questions

have as their target the cause (*aition*) of the matter – that is, the form – on account of which the matter *is* something

– that is, on account of which the matter constitutes a thing of some determinate kind – [6]

and *this* will be the substance ‹of the thing›.[7]

On this story, the appropriate 'why'-question is answered by citing the form whose presence explains why the matter constitutes a thing of the relevant kind. And on these grounds, it is form that is properly the cause of being for the thing: that is, form determines the kind to which the thing belongs. Hence, given the connection between the substance of a thing and its cause, form is appropriately the substance of the thing.

The argument given involves the idea that we answer the appropriate 'why'-questions about the membership by a thing in its kind by citing its form, but unexpectedly the thing's matter enters into the picture as well. I shall have more to say about the place of matter in this story later in this section. But what in the immediate context motivates Aristotle's shift to matter as the subject of the 'why'-questions he has in mind? Suppose someone asks a question in the form 'Why is this man a man?' Then (here I follow a suggestion of Cohen's)[8] Aristotle is embarrassed by difficulties concerning the scope of the question word 'why' in the question. If 'why' is given widest scope, the questioner is asking the triviality 'Why is he who is a man a man?' This treatment cuts all questions from the same cloth, giving short shrift to any differences that may exist among them;[9] to all such questions, there is

6 Distinguish here the thought that a given matter is (i.e., *is classified as*) flesh and bones (say) and the thought that it is (i.e., it *constitutes*) a compound material substance, Socrates (say), where Socrates is a member of the kind man. On the account in the main text, then, Aristotle's claim that "matter is something" (hōi ti estin, 1041b8) says that what matter is (constitutes), is of a definite kind: he is not making the perfectly true but here irrelevant claim that (in the usual case at least) matter itself is of a definite kind, flesh and bones (say), or whatever.

7 *hōste to aition zēteitai tēs hulēs, touto d' esti to eidos, hōi ti estin; touto d' hē ousia* (1041b7–9).

8 Cohen (1978), pp. 402–4.

9 *alla touto koinon ge kata pantōn kai suntomon*, 1041a19–20. In fact, of course, the two examples Aristotle quotes here – Why is the man a man? and Why is the musical ‹one› musical? – require quite different treatment, according to Aristotle. The first is answered by specifying a relation between matter and a form, the second a relation between an individual substance and an accident. In this comment on Aristotle's examples, I follow a hint in Furth (1985), p. 125.

only a single reply, namely, the logical truth that everything is itself. So the question-word must be given narrow scope: concerning this object which is a man, why is it a man? But Aristotle has no clear way of picking out this interpretation of the question. He sees that the questioner cannot be asking, *de dicto*, about the statement that a man is a man, but he fails to see that the question can be about the man, *de re*, asking why *it*, that object, is a man. So he concludes that the question cannot be about the man at all, but must be about his *matter*, asking why *that* is a man. As Cohen puts it, Aristotle imports matter for lack of a device for referring to the man in a "logically independent" way, as the variables in modern notation are able to do: concerning this *x* such that *x* is a man, *why* is *x* a man?[10]

10 Cohen (1978), pp. 403–4. On other matters, Cohen and I are in disagreement. Cohen connects the fact that in the *Metaphysics,* matter is apparently a subject to form with the question 'Is Aristotle an "Aristotelian" or any other kind of essentialist?' He offers this definition of an Aristotelian essence: "An attribute is an Aristotelian essence if and only if it is essential to every individual having it which is a genuine subject for that attribute" (p. 395). But then, "Nothing will count as an Aristotelian essence, so long as matter is held to be the subject for predicates in the category of substance" (p. 396). Cohen concludes that matter is not really a subject for form. My inclination, on the contrary, is to take Aristotle's characterization of matter as a subject for form at face value, and to doubt instead the correctness of the definition of an Aristotelian essence that Cohen gives. For if matter is subject to form, then – if Aristotle is to be an Aristotelian essentialist at all – our account of an Aristotelian essence must allow for the fact that, for Aristotle, an essence is *not* essential to the very thing of which it is (metaphysically) predicated. (For more on this point, see in particular the discussion of the principles of mutual exclusivity in Chapter 11.) Cohen's other attempts to undermine the status of matter as a subject for form seem to me to be unsuccessful. The suggestion (p. 401) that a subject for forms must itself be a *tode ti* (while matter can never be a full-fledged *tode ti*) is clearly unwarranted. And his attempt to import the theory of essential predication from the *Analytica Posteriora* to support his view ("the subject of a substance-predicate has to be *that very thing* that is predicated of it" [p. 401, his italics]), even if it is true to the *Analytics,* will not impress those who think that the *Metaphysics,* with its new views about form, matter, and the individual, will likely contain a theory of (metaphysical) predication that is different from what is found in the *Organon.* In discussing Aristotle's views in the *Metaphysics,* Cohen suggests that matter words can be used to refer to the substance, for example, a house, but *without implying that it is a house* (pp. 404–5). The words 'these bricks and stones', for example, refer to what is *and* is not the completed substance; for the matter constitutes the substance but is not actually it. This attempt to have it both ways is unsuccessful. As Cohen notes, the matter is not identical with the house that it constitutes. If, then, a term refers to the matter, it does not refer to the substance. So Aristotle is not predicating form of the substance when he predicates it of the matter. Elsewhere, Cohen talks of Aristotle's "tendency" to treat form as predicable of matter (p. 402). But what Cohen calls a tendency is in fact settled policy on Aristotle's part (see Chapter 6). So I cannot accept Cohen's version of the theory of predication found in the *Metaphysics:* "It is not as if the bit of gold is the individual of which *being a ring* is predicated (as the ring is the individual of which *being round* is predicated). Rather, the ring is the individual of which *being golden* is predicated" (pp. 399–400). (But in Aristotle's account, note that the matter does not have to be an *individual* to be a suitable subject for a form. Equally, the bit of gold is most likely *not* the matter – this is the gold that [presently] constitutes the bit.)

In *Metaphysics* Z17, Aristotle complicates the argument just sketched for taking form to be the substance of a thing, by presenting the problem about the analysis of membership by a thing in its kind as a problem about definition. As we have seen, the problem of the membership by an individual in its kind brings in questions about *causes;* so we will also need a notion of definition according to which the definition of a thing has to do with its cause. With this conception of definition to hand, Aristotle has a more elaborate argument for the conclusion that the causal role of form makes it appropriately the *substance* of a thing (Z17, 1041a32–b33). For if the definition of a thing gives its cause, and form is the cause of the thing in the sense required, then the form has a primary place in the definition of the thing; it follows, supposing that what has a primary place in the definition of a thing is the substance of that thing, that (again) form is the substance of the thing.

The use that definition is put to in this argument requires a variation on the usual approach to definition. Standardly, a request for definition is couched in the form What is (an) *x*? – for example, What is a man? On the line of thought at work in Z17, the question in this form can be replaced by the appropriate 'why'-question: as before, not Why is (classificatory *is*) this object – this man, Socrates (say) – a man? but rather, Why are these materials a man? (constitutive *is*).

As this reformulation shows, certain features of the thing to be defined are taken as already known – its matter and the fact that it belongs to a certain specified kind. The missing component, on Aristotle's view, and the target of the request for definition, is form. Aristotle's approach to definition in this chapter, then, is one that tends to favour form alone as what determines the *what is it* of a thing.[11]

Aristotle's reformulation of requests for definition as 'why'-questions brings causes into the definition in a way that recalls a technique connecting definition and 'why'-questions first developed in the *Analytica Posteriora* for the definition of event types.[12] In both

11 Hence, Aristotle can identify the *what is it* of a thing with its form; cf. F. Lewis (1984), p. 105, and Ackrill (1973–3), p. 68, n. 3.
12 *An. Po.* B2, 90a14–23, esp. 14–15, a31–4, B10, 93b38–94a7; cf. *De Anima* B2, 413a13–20. In *An. Po.* B2, the conclusion that for a whole range of questions, including requests for definition, a proper answer will say *why one thing belongs to another* is reached by a different route: not the distinction between vacuous and substantive questions pressed in *Metaphysics* Z17, but the argument that our questions always seek *causes,* and causes are middle terms (90a5–30). But how should we apply this view about middle terms, worked out for the account of event types, to the "cause of substantial being" (*tou einai . . . tēn ousian,* 90a9–10)? Ross (1949) offers the difficulty that [a] "substance does not inhere in anything; there are no two terms between which a middle term is to be found" (p. 612). *Metaphysics* Z17 and H2 apparently show how the analysis of event types can after all be extended to that of

places, Aristotle uses the stock example of thunder. Why does it thunder? Even to begin to answer the question, we must already have a preliminary definition of thunder: it is noise present in clouds. Using this partial definition, we can rework the question into the standard form, asking why one thing belongs to another: why is noise present in the clouds? (Z17, 1041a24–6). The answer, according to the *Analytica Posteriora*, can be exhibited as the middle term in the appropriate causal demonstration. In Aristotle's example, if 'Noise belongs to the clouds' is our demonstrandum, 'the extinction of fire' gives the appropriate middle term.[13] Then noise is present in the clouds, *because* fire is extinguished there. Working this explanation into our account of thunder, we get this full-fledged definition: thunder is a noise of fire being extinguished in the clouds (B10, 94a5). Our definition here makes clear *why* a thing is (B10, 93b38–9) and can be read off from the appropriate causal demonstration. In this example, the preliminary definition of thunder, that it is noise in the clouds, is supplemented by a reference to the efficient cause of thunder, so that, in this case at least, Aristotle apparently has a way of working the efficient cause into the definition or *formal* cause of a phenomenon. If this is right, thunder is one of those things that are "by nature," but are not themselves substances (H4, 1044b8), for which the efficient cause is part of the definition.[14] Presumably, then, there is also a unique cause of thunder.

members of substantial kinds, once we reinterpret questions about an individual and its kinds in terms of a question about the matter of the thing and its kind, thus leaving room to insert the *form* as the cause of the matter's constituting a thing of the given kind. (These are the grounds on which Aristotle then concludes that the form is the substance of the thing.) But there are obvious difficulties in pressing the parallel between the account of event types and that of substantial being. For example, suppose there is to hand a syllogism that supplies the extinction of fire as a middle term and indicates successfully that noise is present in the clouds, *thanks to* the extinction of fire there (cf. note 13): what form could the parallel syllogism for substantial being possibly take? Aristotle can argue that (i) the kind k is typified by the form ψ and that (ii) ψ supervenes on a given matter m, so that (iii) m constitutes a k. But while there are structural parallels between the triads noise, extinction of fire, and clouds, on the one hand, and the kind k, the form ψ, and the appropriate matter, on the other, it is far-fetched to think that we can construct a syllogism for the second case with the form as a middle term.

13 The resulting demonstration should be along these lines:

Noise belongs to extinction of fire.
Extinction of fire belongs to the clouds.

Hence,

Noise belongs to the clouds.

For some difficulties with this (e.g., can the second premiss really be an A-proposition?), see J. Barnes (1975), p. 211.

14 In *Metaphysics* H4, Aristotle can be read as making the more modest claim that the definition is "not clear" unless *in addition to* it we also cite the efficient cause. But the *Analytica Posteriora* seems to support the stronger claim that the efficient cause should actually be *included in* the definition; see Ross (149), p. 640.

The discussion in *Metaphysics* Z17 shows how this technique for defining events can be extended to the account of a house or a bed or a man. First, the relevant 'why'-question is put, not in the unarticulated idiom Why is this a man? but rather as Why are these materials a man? (constitutive *is*). The answer here is that the appropriate form is present in those materials. These flesh and bones constitute a member of the kind man thanks to the presence of the relevant form. So a definition that makes clear why a thing is cites the form as what makes the difference between the matter by itself and the full-fledged member of the kind.

On this account, just as with certain event types, for example, thunder, it is appropriate to include the efficient cause in their definition, so in the case of houses, beds, or men, their definition too will include their cause, or *aition*. The relevant kind of cause in this case, Aristotle seems to say at Z17, 1041a29–32, is a *final* cause, which we know brings in the *form* of the thing.

According to Z17, the explanations of why a thing belongs to a certain kind and its definition as a member of that kind both point to the contribution of *form* as what distinguishes the finished member of a kind from its matter, or as the cause of that matter's constituting a thing of that kind, so that once more, the form is approximately the substance of the thing. Aristotle's arguments for this conclusion indicate that membership in a kind requires the supervention of the appropriate form on an appropriate matter. This account is confirmed by a reading of *Metaphysics* H2. There, Aristotle explains again that sentences like

(2) Socrates is (a) man,

in which an individual substance is assigned to a kind, must be understood in terms of a relation between form and matter. He argues that a different sense of 'being' is associated with each new kind of thing and suggests that the different senses of 'is' for each kind are to be given by a paraphrase in which the kind term itself *disappears*.[15] For example, that something *is* a threshold or *is* ice[16] is to be understood

15 A similar suggestion is made by Furth (1985), pp. 127–8, cf. (1988), pp. 250–7. But Furth says that what is being eliminated are "substantial" or "(pseudo-)substantial" terms, not kind terms. Against this, while it is right that (and Aristotle is conscious that) most of the examples in H2 do not involve bona fide substances, Aristotle argues in favour of the very same programme of contextual paraphrase in the case of the bona fide substances too (see 1043a4–7). And as far as the threshold example goes, a threshold is a perfectly good example of a (nonnatural) kind, and so a perfectly good case for demonstrating the new analysis of *being a so-and-so*, even if it is *not* a substance (its analysing differentia is an accident in the category of position), and so not a good case study for the analysis of *substantially-being a so-and-so*, that is, of membership in a kind by something that is a genuine substance.

16 Here, Aristotle repeats another example from the *Analytica Posteriora*: B12, 95a16–21.

to say that a certain form (lying thus or being solidified thus) is (meta-physically) predicated of a thing's matter:

Clearly, then, the word 'is' is used in just as many ways; a thing *is* a threshold because it lies in such and such a position, and its being means its lying in that position, while being ice means having been solidified in such and such a way. (H2, 1042b25–8; after Ross's translation)[17]

Here, Aristotle is clear on the role of form in explaining why a thing belongs to a kind, but he is less helpful on the role of matter.[18] Later passages, however, confirm that reference to the individual substance in such paraphrases can be dropped in favour of reference to its matter:

And as among substances what is predicated of the matter is the actuality itself, so in the other definitions too it is what most resembles the actuality. For example, if we had to define a threshold, we should say, *wood or stone in such and such a position,* or a house, *bricks and timbers in such and such a position, . . .* and ice: *water frozen or solidified in this way.* (H2, 1043a5–10)

(Compare the further examples at 1043a5–11.) Hence, we can con-clude that "an object *is* a thing of some determinate species if and only if the associated form can be truly predicated of the parcel of matter constituting that object." Again: "[A] substance's belonging to a kind is not a brute fact. It is something that requires explanation, and the explanation is provided by pointing to the fact that the associated substance-form is truly predicated of the parcel of matter that makes up the substance."[19]

---

17 Cf. 1042b36–1043a1: "For still others, to be will be to have been mixed, and not to be ‹will be› the reverse" (text as in Ross and disregarding Jaeger's emendation, which is gratuitous); see also *De Anima* B4, 415b13.

18 In fact, matter is not mentioned in this extract; for there to be a threshold is for *it* (*auto*, 1042b27), the threshold, to lie in such-and-such a position. I take this to be a solecism on Aristotle's part; see Furth (1985), pp. 127–8, and for further discussion, Furth (1988), p. 254, n. 7.

19 The quotations are from Loux (1979), pp. 18, 19. I have argued in the text that the truth of the linguistic predication

  (2) Socrates is (a) man

is grounded in the fact that the form of a man is metaphysically predicated of Socrates' matter. It may seem a difficulty in this account that – in contrast with the theory of the *Categories* – it puts so much distance between the linguistic predication and its metaphysical underpinnings. How is it that (2) reflects its underlying ontol-ogy so indirectly? In the *Metaphysics,* Aristotle does not attempt to set out a canonical language in which his ontological theory is directly and immediately reflected in the admissible forms of linguistic predication. In Z17, he contents himself merely with issuing warnings about the inadequacy of ordinary language as a guide to ontology (1041a32–b2). Sentence (2), then, is not part of any canonical language, and we cannot reasonably expect to read straight off from (2) the ontology that in Aristotle's metaphysical theory underlies it.

3   Why Forms Are Not (Metaphysically) Predicated of Individual Substances

If the account given in the preceding section is correct, *Metaphysics* Z17 and H2 show Aristotle attempting to bring his treatment of (2) and sentences like it into line with the official notion of (metaphysical) predication that he sets out in other chapters in the *Metaphysics*. If the attempt is successful, then Aristotle can defend the utility of the *Metaphysics* notion of (metaphysical) predication. The new theory has at least the power of its predecessor in the *Categories*, for both theories alike can handle not only sentences that assert an accident of an individual substance, but also sentences that assign an individual to its kind.

The account of individuals and kinds in terms of form and matter raises a number of questions. In particular, why does Aristotle now construe membership by an individual in a kind in terms of a relation between form *and matter*? In the scheme of predication Aristotle offers in the *Metaphysics*, (metaphysical) predication can be a relation between an accident and an individual substance, or between a form and matter, but never between form *and an individual substance*. Why not? What accounts for Aristotle's restrictive attitude about what he is or is not willing to count as a genuine (metaphysical) predication?

An answer to these questions goes to principles at the heart of Aristotle's motivation for the theory of metaphysical predication I am attributing to him. From the beginning, first, Aristotle holds to some version of the view that *subjects are members of kinds*. In the *Categories*, the view appears as the principle of "Izzing before Having," which applies only to subject to accidents, but arguably the principle is generalized in the *Metaphysics* to require that any subject whatever of (metaphysical) predication must first be a member of its appropriate kind. (The single exception is prime matter, which is not a member of any kind; see Chapter 6, Section 4.) Accordingly, an accident can be predicated of a compound material substance only because that substance is first a member of its appropriate kind; at the same time, in the lower half of Aristotle's scheme (with the exception of prime matter), a form supervenes on a subject only because again that subject is a member of a (suitably lower-level) kind.

On the picture I have been arguing for, next, Aristotle's account of what it is for a thing to be a member of a kind, k, requires a shift in what we are to take as the subject that is a k. His view in *Metaphysics* Z17 is that *matter* is (i.e., constitutes) a k, thanks to *form*, which is as it were the middle term connecting matter and the kind. For something, a, to be a k is for the appropriate form to be predicated of the appropriate matter, and for a to be no longer a k is for the form *not* to be predicated of the matter (in these circumstances, since *a* is the compound of that form with that matter, *a* itself no longer exists). On this account, for *a* to be or to cease to be a *k* is defined in terms of a condition *on something other than a itself.*

Suppose now that contrary to what has been argued here, the form, ψ, that typifies a thing *a*'s kind is (metaphysically) predicated *of a itself,* and that being a subject to ψ constitutes the official account of what *makes a* a member of its kind. If the same rule about subjects and kinds applies, then ψ is (metaphysically) predicated of *a* only because *a* is a member of its appropriate kind – that is, only because ψ is predicated of *a!*

If the rule stands that, invariably, subjects are first members of kinds, a circularity argument along the lines just sketched suggests that the form that typifies a thing's kind cannot be (metaphysically) predicated of that very thing.[20] But can Aristotle safely suppose that the form is *not* (metaphysically) predicated of the thing? In fact, Aristotle has no need to allow into his core theory additional cases of (metaphysical) predication beyond those two in which either an accident is (metaphysically) predicated of an individual substance or a form is (metaphysically) predicated of matter. Suppose Aristotle were to allow that in addition to these two kinds of case, the form is (metaphysically) predicated of *the compound substance.* On the most reasonable understanding of this, this third case of metaphysical predication will be the relation '*x* is constitutive of *y*', relating a form and its parent compound material substance, which is a *defined* notion in Aristotle's wider metaphysical theory. In a certain sense, then, constitution can do no real work – at any rate, no *new* work – there, for the definition of constitution assures us that any work constitution appears to do can also be done by the notions involved in its definition. At the same time, constitution will do no real work in the theory of metaphysical predication. In constructing a theory of metaphysical predication, Aristotle needs to stipulate only that forms are (metaphysically) predicated of (i.e., they supervene on) the matter, and he need never make room for a further relation of (metaphysical) predication, specifically the relation of constitution, holding between a form and the compound material substance itself.

These points can be defended in greater detail by developing further the formalization of Aristotle's theory begun in Chapter 6. In Aristotle's theory, as we saw, there are two kinds of (metaphysical) predication:

---

20 Circularity arguments similar to the one sketched here are discussed in Chapter 11, Section 1.

(D3) *x* is *(metaphysically) predicated of y* (*y* is *subject to x*) if and only if *either* *x* is an accident of *y or x* supervenes on *y*.

These two kinds of metaphysical predication support and explain two kinds of linguistic predication. First, where φ is an accident and *a* is a compound substance, we have the truth conditions

(A7) ⌜*a* is φ (*a* Has φ)⌝ is true if and only if φ is an accident of *a*.

For example, 'Socrates is pale' is true if and only if pallor is one of his accidents. A second set of truth conditions exploits the connection already argued for in Section 2 between kinds and forms. Where ψ is a form and *m* is a portion of matter and '*k*' stands in for some kind term, we have, as a first approximation,

(A8) ⌜*a* is (a) *k* (*a* Is [a] *k*)⌝ is true if and only if, where ψ is the form of a *k* and *m* is the proximate matter of *a*, ψ supervenes on *m*.

For example, 'Socrates is (a) man' is true if and only if the form of a man (i.e., the appropriate variety of soul) supervenes on a certain matter (the appropriate combination of bodily organs).

The right-hand sides of (A7) and (A8) refer to the accident-of and supervention relations respectively, and by (D3), these two are the only kinds of (metaphysical) predication there are. Why? In particular, why does Aristotle not allow that a form can be (metaphysically) predicated also of the individual substance?

The extended theory, in which forms *are* after all (metaphysically) predicable of compound material substances, is easily sketched. We begin with the relation '*x* is constitutive of *y*', which holds between a form and a form–matter compound, including any compound material substance. The definition is given in (D9) in Chapter 6: where *x* is any form–matter compound,

(D9) ψ is *constitutive of x* if and only if for some *m* such that *m* is the proximate matter of *x*, *x* = *m* + ψ.

Constitution presents a natural way of expanding the notion of (metaphysical) predication to include a third case, in which a form is (metaphysically) predicated of a compound substance. In place of (D3), we will have

(*D3⁺) *x* is *(metaphysically) predicated of y* (*y* is *subject to x*) if and only if *either x* is an accident of *y*, or *x* supervenes on *y*, or *x* is constitutive of *y*.[21]

Given (*D3⁺), finally, in place of (A8) we have this alternative account of the relevant linguistic predications:

21 The asterisk in '(*D3⁺)' and elsewhere is meant to warn the reader that this is *not* part of Aristotle's official theory.

(*A9) $\ulcorner a$ is (a) $k \urcorner$ is true if and only if, where ψ is the form of a k, ψ is constitutive of a.

Does the truth of linguistic predications connecting a thing with its kinds require us to recognize the relation of *constitution* between form and thing as yet a third variety of metaphysical predication, over and above the accident-of relation and the relation of supervention between form and matter, as (*A9) and (*D3$^+$) suggest? If the circularity argument can be trusted, Aristotle has reason *not* to add a disjunct to (D3), as in (*D3$^+$). At the same time, there is scant textual evidence in favour of such a move.[22] Finally, Aristotle has no positive motive for adding form–thing predications to the basic scheme in (D3). As (D9) makes plain, constitution is defined in terms of the existence of the appropriate form–matter compound, together with the notion of a thing's proximate matter, itself defined ultimately in terms of the existence of the appropriate kind of compound (cf. (D4) and (D5) in Chapter 6).[23] Accordingly, constitution can be

---

22 Here I am in disagreement with Frede and Patzig (1988), Vol. 1, p. 51, who cite *Metaphysics* Z8, 1033a28–31, in favour of the view that Aristotle accepts that an Aristotelian form may be metaphysically predicated of the compound material substance. The passage is not explicitly about the topic of (metaphysical) predication at all. Instead, Aristotle is using the example of the craftsman who makes the bronze sphere to draw a contrast between form and the compound material substance: "Just as he does not make the subject, the bronze, so he does not ‹make› the sphere [= the *form* of a sphere] either, except *accidentally* (*kata sumbebēkos*) because the bronze sphere is ‹a› sphere, and that [= the bronze sphere] he does make." The passage embodies a familiar form of argument: one thing, *x*, has a given property *accidentally*, or not in the proper sense, because *x* is significantly related to something else, *y*, and *y properly* has the property in question. In particular, on the interpretation for which I am arguing, the form has the property of being made accidentally, because the thing itself is made in the proper sense, and form and thing are related so that the *form*'s being predicated of the matter is what explains how the *thing* is a member of its kind. To sustain the alternative conclusion about form–*thing* predications, Frede and Patzig must make at least two assumptions: (i) that in Aristotle's sentence "The bronze sphere is ‹a› sphere," at a30, the second occurrence of the word 'sphere' is a name for the form, as it is one line back at a29; and (ii) that the significant relation between form and thing brought to light by that sentence, such that the form is made accidentally if the thing itself is made in the proper sense, is that the form *is metaphysically predicated of* the thing. Of course, (ii) is also the conclusion for which Frede and Patzig are arguing. But there would be some independent plausibility to (ii) if we could be sure that (i) was satisfied. Against (i), however, there seems no reason not to think that the occurrence of 'sphere' in question names the species or kind, not the form, unless with Frede and Patzig we take an eliminative rather than a reductive attitude towards kinds in the *Metaphysics* (see notes 29 and 31); without this further assumption, we have been given no reason for accepting (ii), and the Z8 passage hardly supplies decisive evidence for form–thing (metaphysical) predications.

The analysis of sentences like 'This is a sphere', with 'sphere' understood as a name for the kind, is pressed further in Section 4. And for a different, but still, I think, flawed argument in favour of form–thing predications, see the final paragraph of Section 5 and note 32.

23 On the definition of 'constitution', see Chapter 6, note 48.

dropped at any time from Aristotle's theory in favour of the primitive notions in terms of which it is ultimately defined. So it cannot be part of the *core* theory of (metaphysical) predication, which does not go beyond notions that are primitive in Aristotle's wider metaphysical theory. But can constitution perhaps be part of an *extended* theory of (metaphysical) predication? The difficulty is not just that constitution adds nothing new to the wider metaphysical theory; it also adds nothing new to the theory of metaphysical predication. The work that form–thing predications might do is done already by form–*matter* predications in the core theory. Aristotle can reasonably claim that the scheme of metaphysical predication given in the *Metaphysics* is adequate as it is to handle sentences like (2) that assign an object to its kind, and that (A8) rather than (*A9) gives the correct account of such sentences. I suggest at the end of Section 4 that Aristotle has a special motive for including *kind*–thing predications in the extended theory. But in the absence of any such special motive here, I conclude that form–thing predications are not part of either the core or the extended theory of (metaphysical) predication.[24]

4   An Extended Case of Metaphysical Predication: How the Species Can Be (Metaphysically) Predicated of the Compound Substance

I argued in the previous section that, for Aristotle, the membership by an individual in a kind – for example, the fact recorded in (2) that Socrates is a man – is adequately explained by a relation of (metaphysical) predication between form and matter. On this interpretation, Aristotle sees a close connection between the question of kinds and the all-important notion of form, but forms get into his account of kinds *without* our having to suppose that forms are predicable universally of compound material substances. Instead, a form is predicated of the *matter* of a compound substance, as his theory of (metaphysical) predication requires.

But if not its constitutive form, is not the *species* or *kind* (metaphysically) predicated of the compound material substance? Aristotle's account of kinds is consistent with the idea that the species is (metaphysically) predicated of compound material substances, in much the same style already familiar from the *Categories*. This idea, however, need not call into question the official account of (metaphysical) predication in the *Metaphysics*. For if a species is (metaphysically) predicated of an individual substance, this variety of predication can safely be

---

24 An important consequence of this conclusion will emerge later in Chapter 11; see esp. the principle of generalized mutual exclusivity discussed in Chapter 11, Section 1.

analysed in terms of one of the primitive relations of metaphysical predication set out in (D3).[25]

The *Categories*-style species makes an appearance in the *Metaphysics* at Z10, 1035b27–30:

> But as for man and horse and those things that ‹apply› to particulars, but universally (*ta houtōs epi tōn kath' hekasta, katholou de*), they are not substance but a sort of compound from this form (*logos*) and this matter taken universally.

In the same vein, at *Metaphysics* Z11, 1037a5–7 (cf. Z8, 1033b25–6):

> It is clear that the soul is primary substance, and the body is matter, and man or animal is the ‹compound› from them both, taken universally (*to ex amphoin hōs katholou*).

It seems very plausible that, following Ross, a compound of this form and this matter, taken universally, a "universal compound," for short, is an explication in terms of the *Metaphysics* notions of matter and form of the *Categories* notion of a secondary substance or species or kind.[26]

The textual evidence here for a new variety of (metaphysical) predication is slight: Aristotle does not even use the word 'predication' in discussing the relation between species and individual, saying only that the one is *epi* (applies to?) the other. Suppose, however, that we supplement the official account of (metaphysical) predication with a relation of kind–thing predication:

> (D10) x is *metaphysically predicated of* y if and only if *either* x is an accident of y, *or* x supervenes on y, *or* x applies to y (x is *epi* y).

Talk of the *application* of kind to thing in (D10) does not require us to add a new primitive notion to Aristotle's theory. Such talk can be explained instead in terms of the core relation of supervention between form and matter. Thus, let us say that the predicate of (2) names a *Categories*-style species, and let k be a variable ranging over such species. Then as a start on understanding sentences in which we assign individuals to their kinds, we have the truth conditions already given in (A8):

25 On this point, see also Loux (1979), who (contrary to the report in F. Lewis [1985a]) also distinguishes between primitive and derived relations of (metaphysical) predication.

26 Notice, however, that the universal compound, or the *Categories*-style species, is *not* to be identified with the notion of a *genous eidos* (often translated 'species of a genus'), which appears elsewhere in the *Metaphysics* at Z4, 1030a12. For reasons not directly relevant here, I hold that a *genous eidos* as it appears in *Metaphysics* Z4 is identical with an *eidos* as form (cf. F. Lewis [1984], pp. 127–30). So I shall suppose that the predicate of (2), for example, refers to a species in the sense of the *Categories* or to a universal compound that in the *Metaphysics* replaces the secondary substances of the *Categories*. But it does not refer to a *genous eidos* in the sense of *Metaphysics* Z4; that is, it does not refer to a form.

(A8) ⌜*a* is (a) *k*⌝ is true if and only if, where ψ is the form of a *k* and *m* is the proximate matter of *a*, ψ supervenes on *m*.

Alternatively, at the level of metaphysical predication,

(D11) *x applies to y* (*x* is *epi y*) if and only if, where ψ is the form of the kind *x* and *m* is the proximate matter of *y*, ψ supervenes on *m*.

For example, suppose that Socrates is a man. Then there exist the appropriate flesh and bones that are the proximate matter of Socrates and which Have the appropriate form or soul. In this way, we can connect thing–kind predications, both metaphysical and linguistic, with the core cases of (metaphysical) predications involving form and matter.

Sentences like (2) represent at least one kind of case in which we apparently refer to species. Principles (A8) and (D11) suggest that the apparent reference to species in such cases can ultimately be dropped. That is, a species in the *Categories* sense may be seen as a derived entity, constructed out of our more basic talk of matter and form. By them- selves, however, (A8) and (D11) only partly accomplish this reduction. What they principally lack is a means of identifying the form that typifies the species *k* in a way that is independent of *k*. If reference to *k* cannot ultimately be dropped from the right-hand sides of (A8) and (D11), then the project of reducing a *Categories*-style species to the notions of form and matter will have failed. How can we ensure that a given form is in fact the form required? The form we need will include all the structural, behavioural and other features and capac- ities that caused us to group *a* and the other objects that share its form as members of the same species in the first place. Once these details are known, we will have a systematic way of identifying the needed form that is independent of the associated species *k*. Reference to *k* can then finally be dropped from the right-hand side of (A8) and (D11).

In practice, we do often specify a given form by reference to its associated kind: for example, 'the form *of a man*', 'the form *of a house*' – even, abbreviating, simply 'man' (*Metaphysics* H3, 1043b3–4) or 'house' – leaving it to the appropriate special discipline, psychology, biology, or the like, to specify more closely the form in question (such- and-such a soul or a receptacle capable of sheltering man and goods). Aristotle's remarks at the beginning of *Metaphysics* H3 may be relevant to this practice.

Similarly, if in the final analysis we hope to replace talk of com- pound substances belonging to kinds by talk of forms supervening on matter, we must also be able to specify the relevant matter, indepen- dently of *k*. Plausibly, once the proper specification of the form is to hand, the constraints on what will be an appropriate proximate matter relative to that form will follow without difficulty. This in turn will give us a way of identifying the matter independently of its relation to k.

(A8) and (D11) point the way, then, to a reductive account of the *Categories*-style species in terms of the *Metaphysics* notions of form and matter. They also show, again, that the notion of metaphysical predication as defined in (D3) is adequate after all to handle sentences like (2), which record the ways in which individuals are grouped together as members of kinds.

It is worth commenting, finally, on the disparity between the treatments accorded forms and kinds respectively in the present and preceding sections. On the account I have given, species are not basic in the ontology of the *Metaphysics,* but it is not unreasonable to think that they can be (metaphysically) predicated of individual substances in a suitably extended sense of 'predicated of'. By contrast, in the *Metaphysics,* forms are basic in the ontology, *but they are not predicated of individual substances at all,* either in a core or in any extended sense. Why these different treatments? Species or kinds have antecedents in Aristotle's own earlier theory in the *Categories.* If his general attitude towards previous philosophy holds good here, then even when the new theory of matter and form is in place and can take over the work done previously by the theory of kinds, Aristotle will not dismiss kinds out of hand, but will opt instead for the milder conclusion that they are simply no longer basic in the ontology.[27] The idea that the species stands in a *derived* relation of metaphysical predication to the individual substance suggests that the species is not a basic part of Aristotle's philosophical apparatus and simultaneously allows him to show how it is related to the items that are properly basic there. Thus, he has only to spell out how the derivation goes, explaining *belonging to a given kind k* in terms of the core notions of matter, form, and supervention, in order to connect the species to notions that are genuinely basic in his later metaphysical scheme.

Form itself, however, is already a primitive component of Aristotle's core theory and a term in one of the two core notions of (metaphysical) predication. So none of the motives for recognizing a derived notion of (metaphysical) predication in the case of the relation between the species and the individual substance applies in the case of form. Our best conclusion is that Aristotle does not recognize a new, extended notion of (metaphysical) predication connecting forms and individual substances.

5   Aristotle's Different Theories of Kinds

In the preceding section, we saw how Aristotle's notion of a species from the *Categories* is absorbed in the *Metaphysics* into the later theory

27 For a different view of the matter, however, see the references in note 29.

of form and matter. It may be useful to expand a little on the different stages in his account of kinds.

Aristotle's account begins, as we have seen, against a background of Platonic indifference to the question of kinds. There are two distinct phases in Aristotle's own account of individuals and kinds: the *Categories* account and the account that is at work in the *Metaphysics*. On the earlier, *Categories* account, the notions of *belonging* and of a *kind* are not susceptible to further analysis. (Not coincidentally, the notion of an individual substance is also taken as primitive.) As in Plato's story, then, the fact that Socrates is a man involves an *unanalysed* relation – even if it is a *different* relation than Plato's relation – between a particular and a universal. The fact that Socrates belongs to his given kind is a brute fact and not open to further philosophical explanation or analysis.

Even in his earliest account of kinds, however, Aristotle distances himself in a number of ways from Plato. First, as we have seen, the relation between Socrates and man (say) in the *Categories* is *different* from Plato's relation, which for Aristotle is the appropriate relation between Socrates and his accidents. At the same time, Aristotle also purchases insurance against the Third Man Argument (TMA) by insisting, contrary to Plato, that the kind man, for example, is a *secondary* substance and, unlike Socrates and the other individuals that belong to the kind, is a such and not a this.[28]

In the later *Metaphysics* analysis, Aristotle retains reference to the kinds or secondary substances of the *Categories,* but no longer regards them as philosophically primitive.[29] Instead, he analyses them as "compounds of this form and this matter, taken universally."[30] Universal compounds, man, for example, and animal, and all those entities "that apply similarly to individuals, but universally" (*ta houtōs epi tōn kath' hekasta, katholou de,* Z10, 1035b28), are universal to compound material substances. By contrast with the secondary substances of the *Categories,* they are demoted further in the *Metaphysics* to the status of nonsubstances (Z10, 1035b27–30).[31] But it is reasonable to suppose

28 On this, see Chapter 1, Section 4, and Chapter 11, Section 6.
29 The account of kinds that follows is contrary to that in Frede ([1978] 1987); cf. Frede and Patzig (1988), Vol. 2, pp. 189–91, who take an eliminative rather than a reductive attitude towards Aristotelian species or kinds in the *Metaphysics;* see note 31.
30 Universal compounds are discussed further in F. Lewis (1984), pp. 105–12.
31 Frede, and Frede and Patzig, get from this an argument by elimination against the existence of kinds or species in the *Metaphysics:* as Aristotle suggests here, a kind or species cannot be a substance; but since it is not properly speaking a quality either, or a member of any other category, and not even *potentially* a member of the categories, it can have no real existence at all, Frede (1987 [1985]), p. 78, Frede and Patzig (1988), p. 241 and esp. pp. 246–7. Against this, I suppose that Aristotle's notion of "compounds of this form and this matter, taken universally," at Z10, 1035b28, gives him a way of connecting the existence of kinds to that of items that are basic in the ontology, that the argument by elimination fails to take into account.

that, like secondary substances, universal compounds are again universal to thises, but are themselves not thises, but suches (Z13, 1039a1–3, where the TMA is again on Aristotle's mind).

In the *Metaphysics* analysis of individuals and kinds, however, Aristotle shows us how we can, if we wish, drop the reference to kinds and talk instead of form and matter and of the relation of supervention. According to the *Metaphysics* analysis, Socrates is a man if and only if the form of a man supervenes on a given portion of matter. As we have already seen in Chapter 6, this analysis supposes that forms are universals: in fact, they are universal not to compound material compounds, but to *matter*.

In the theory of the *Metaphysics*, Aristotle takes a reductive but not an eliminative attitude towards kinds. He concedes that kinds exist and is willing to talk of kinds, even though at bottom he holds that such talk is best reformulated in terms of the theory of form and matter. This continuing hospitality to kinds, however, should not trap us into confusing truths in the theory of kinds for truths about form. In particular, the view that contrary to what has been argued here, an Aristotelian form is predicated *of compound material substances* derives at least some of its support, I suspect, from the tendency to import features from the theory of kinds into the theory of form and matter.[32]

6   Conclusion: The Parsimony of Aristotle's Theory of (Metaphysical) Predication

On the picture I have argued for in the preceding sections, Aristotle's decision on what kinds of (metaphysical) predication to include in his core metaphysical theory largely comes down to questions of theoretical simplicity and economy. In the *Metaphysics*, Aristotle's theory includes the primitive notion of *compounding*, together with the two undefined relations '*x* is an accident of *y*' and '*x* supervenes on *y*'. Metaphysical predication is then defined as the union of these two, as in (D3), first set out in Chapter 6. Aristotle's treatment of (metaphysical) predication reflects the desire to stay as close as he practically can to the basic notions of his theory and to keep to a minimum the number of defined terms to be added to the theory, at least in its purest form. How, then, are we to handle sentences like (2), which apparently assign an individual to its kind? In the *Metaphysics*, kinds no longer have an independent place in Aristotle's theory: they are analysed in

---

32 Cf. Furth (1988), p. 176, n. 2, who argues in favour of form–thing predications, in part on the strength of what he claims is the identity between the *Categories*-style species and form from the *Metaphysics*.

terms of form and matter and have been dropped from the primitive base of his theory. So there is no longer the need for a special subrelation within core (metaphysical) predication to link an individual substance to its kind. In the theory of the *Metaphysics,* sentences like (2), which at first sight seem to lack any obvious metaphysical counterpart, can be understood in terms of the second of the two primitive relations of (metaphysical) predication, namely, supervention, allowed in (D3). No addition is required to the core theory, beyond what (D3) already provides.

The moral of Aristotle's treatment of sentences like (2), then, is in essence a counsel of parsimony. Such sentences at no point call for an enlargement in his basic metaphysical apparatus – the addition of a *Categories*-style species as a basic item in the ontology or a new primitive notion of (metaphysical) predication connecting things with their kinds. Instead, kinds or species are *derived* entities, to be explained in terms of the basic notions of form and matter. Similarly, the accompanying notion of *belonging to a kind* is analysed in terms of the basic notion of supervention between form and matter. But the account of how things belong to kinds nowhere requires that form can be predicated instead of *the compound material substance.* In general, then, the treatment of (2) and sentences like it is for Aristotle an exercise in staying as close as he practically can to the limits set by the primitive notions in his metaphysical theory.

8

The Role of Matter in Form–Matter Compounds: The Nature of the Distinction Between a Thing and Its Matter

In this chapter, we turn to Aristotle's distinction between a compound material substance and its matter, in particular the hypothesis that these are identical, but "intensionally distinct." In Section 1, I argue that this hypothesis is vulnerable, for at least three different reasons. First, whatever "intensionally distinct" amounts to, the attempt to say that two things are identical, yet differ in some way from one another, is in for some hard sledding; for if it is right that there is some real difference to be found between things that are by hypothesis identical, then we have no choice but to give up the law of the indiscernibility of identicals. Second, however, I doubt that there is any real difference to be found, once "intensionally distinct" has been explained. The claim that things are identical but "intensionally distinct" comes down to this, that in certain exceptional contexts, the normal expectation, that we can substitute a name of the one for a name of the other without change in truth value, can *fail*. I argue that these substitution failures point to differences that are only verbal; if a thing and its matter are truly identical, the failures of substitution in question will not provide the basis for any real differences between them. The argument for this conclusion is pressed further in Sections 2 and 3, in which I discuss some examples from the discussion of change in *Physics* A. I also consider the suggestion that – contrary to what is argued here – the use of '*qua*'-clauses shows how even if we do not eliminate the intensionality entirely, Aristotle can after all be "talking about objects" and drawing real, not verbal, distinctions between them.

Yet a third reason for objecting to the hypothesis that a thing and its matter are "identical but intensionally distinct" is that matter and thing are not identical in the first place. If they are not identical, there is scarcely need for heroic measures, for example, the claim that they are "intensionally distinct," to explain the nature of the distinction between them. More than this, if two things are nonidentical, the fact that truth value is not preserved through the substitution of an expression referring to the one by an expression that refers to the other does not entail that the context in question is referentially opaque, or even that it is (merely) nonextensional but referential. Accordingly, even contexts that we might be inclined to regard as clearly intensional have not, on Aristotle's analysis of his examples, yet been shown to be intensional at all. These points are argued in detail in Sections 4 and 5, in connection with the Paradoxes of Becoming and the Paradox of Persistence. There is a brief summary of our results in Section 6. The positive account of matter and coming-to-be, in terms of Accidental Compound Theory and its extension to form–matter compounds, then follows in Chapter 9.

1   Matter, Sameness, and Intensionality

In the second half of *Physics* A, Aristotle argues that individual substances can be analysed as compounds of matter and form. His argument for this conclusion begins at *Physics* A7 with the topic of change. Suppose that a man comes to be musical. The part played by the man, Socrates (say), in this example of qualified or accidental change suggests that there is also "something underlying" that persists through unqualified or substantial change, in which a substance itself comes to be. Having established the role of "something underlying" that persists through unqualified change, Aristotle draws the corollary[1] that the underlying is also (in some sense) an ingredient in an individual substance once it has come to be:

> It is plain, then, that if there are causes and principles of things which are due to nature, out of which they primarily are and have come to be not accidentally (*kata sumbebēkos*), but each what it is said to be according to its substance, everything comes to be out of both the underlying thing and the form. For the musical man is composed in a way out of man and musical. For you will analyse ‹it› into the accounts of these two. It is clear, then, that things which come to be come to be out of them.[2] (A7, 190b17–23)

In A9, finally, Aristotle identifies the underlying that persists through unqualified change with *matter*. The conclusion is now to hand: indi-

---

1 The conclusion emerges ambiguously or at least awkwardly at 190b10–17 (for an analysis of the difficulties of this passage, see Furth (1988), pp. 218–19), and more plainly at b17–23, quoted in the main text. The difficulty concerns mainly the shift in the use of the term *ek* (from, out of); see note 2.

2 This is the part of A7 in which Aristotle sets aside the technical use of *ek* featured in statements of change and discussed at the beginning of the chapter, in favour of a different use, connecting a compound with the items out of which it is (in some suitable sense) composed; see Furth (1988), pp. 195–8, 217–21. Examples of the latter use are given in Chapter 6, Section 3, note 27; see also Chapter 9, note 18.

vidual substances are *compound material* substances – they are compounds of form and matter.

To make good on this conception of matter, at the very least we must know what kind of distinction we are drawing when we try to separate the matter of a thing from the thing itself. The distinction involves a subtlety in Aristotle's notion of what underlies a given change. In any change, according to Aristotle, there is something underlying, which is "one in number, but two in account." For example, when Socrates becomes musical, both Socrates and the unmusical underlie the change in question. Here Aristotle treats Socrates (but not the unmusical) as *matter;* if, then, Socrates and the unmusical are numerically the same, as Aristotle says, then in general, presumably, the matter and that of which it is the matter are numerically the same. It follows, it is often supposed,[3] that they are identical. But if things are numerically the same, let alone if they are identical, how can this be reconciled with their being in any way *discernible* one from another?

The difficulty persists on a closer look at Aristotle's text. On two occasions in *Physics* A, Aristotle argues that Socrates and the unmusical (say) are one in number, but two in form or account or in being:

In all cases of coming-to-be, . . . there must always be something underlying which is what comes to be ‹something›, and this, granted that it is one in number, is not one in form. (By 'in form', I mean the same as 'in account'.) For the being of a man is not the same as the being of unmusical. (A7, 190a13–17; cf. 191a1–3)

Socrates and the unmusical are distinguished, then, in that by definition the unmusical is ignorant of geometry and the other liberal arts (if this is the definition of being unmusical), while it is *not* the case that by definition Socrates is so ignorant.

To this argument for separating Socrates and the unmusical can be added other differences. There is the difference in "how things are,"[4] that the unmusical and Socrates exist at different times, if the former goes out of existence, but the latter does not, when Socrates becomes musical. (This is the familiar point, highlighted in the Paradox of Persistence discussed in Section 5, that Socrates "remains," while the unmusical does not.) They are also distinguished in "how we talk,"[5] for we say that from the unmusical the musical comes to be, but not

3 Examples are given in Chapter 9, Section 5; cf. Sellars (1967): "The individual matter and form of an individual substance are not *two* individuals but *one*. The individual form of this shoe is the shoe itself; the individual matter of this shoe is *also* the shoe itself, and there can scarcely be a real distinction between the shoe and itself" (p. 118, his emphasis).
4 The phrase is from Simplicius *In Phys.* 209. 8–9, 23.
5 Simplicius *In Phys.* 209. 8, 17, 22.

that it comes to be from Socrates.[6] Now we know that Socrates and the unmusical are numerically the same. If, as is often supposed, numerical sameness is our relation of identity, then we have the problem of saying how things that are identical can also differ in these various ways.

The same problem also emerges from Aristotle's discussion of sameness in *Metaphysics* I3. At 1054a32–b3, Aristotle says this about sameness:

> The same being said in many ways, (i) one way we sometimes mean it is in respect of number; (ii) another way, if ‹the thing› is one both in definition (*logos*) and in number, for example, you are one with yourself both in form and in matter; (iii) again, if the *logos* of the primary substance is one, for example, equal straight lines are the same, and so are equal and equal-angled quadrilaterals; and indeed many more, but in these equality is oneness. (Following Furth's translation)

Aristotle here collects three relations of sameness: (i) where things are the same in number; (ii) where they are the same in number and also the same in *logos;* (iii) where they are the same in *logos* but *not* the same in number. Of these three, (ii) is evidently the "most proper and primary" kind of numerical sameness from *Topics* A7, 103a25–6,[7] and (iii) is not a variety of numerical sameness at all (cf. *Topics* A7, 103a10–13). What now of (i)? If numerical sameness is identity, then the kinds of sameness in (i) and (ii) simply repeat each other, for surely, identity *entails* sameness in *logos*. But – astonishingly, if we think that numerical sameness is identity – 'the same in number' in (i) is most likely elliptical for 'the same in number – but *not* the same in *logos*'.[8] This is the puzzle of *Physics* A all over again: how things can be

---

6 Finally, if Simplicius's reading of Aristotle is right, Socrates and matter in general are *countable* in a way that the unmusical is not (Simplicius *In Phys.* 217. 3–35, on *Physics* A7, 190b23–7; but a quite different account of the passage appears in Ross [1936], p. 493). Charlton puts 'measurable' as his translation for *arithmētē*, showing his discomfort with the idea that matter can be in any sense "countable" (the literal translation of Aristotle's Greek). As Kung (1978), pp. 145–7, points out, however, not all cases of Aristotelian matter are stuffs, and hence impervious to being counted. But even when a thing's matter is a stuff, counting is not out of the question. The bronze that makes up this statue, for example, is distinct from the bronze that makes up that statue, and together they make two distinct quantities of bronze: here we are able to count different quantities of bronze and to distinguish the matter of this statue from the matter of that, and this seems enough to give a sense in which matter is countable. Cf. Simplicius *In Phys.* 217. 7–18.

7 See Chapter 4, Section 1.

8 So Ross (1924), p. 287, following Alexander. The relation in (i), then, combines the two remaining kinds of numerical sameness from *Topics* A7 (numerical sameness rendered by proprium and that rendered by accident) into a single notion of nonessential, that is, accidental, sameness. At *Metaphysics* Δ6, 1016b35–6, Aristotle says that sameness in number *entails* sameness in *logos* (strictly in Δ6, sameness in

the same in number – that is, on the account we are considering, they are *identical* – yet contrary to the Law of the Indiscernibility of Identicals, somehow discernible, indeed, different in *logos*.

A frequent move in the face of these difficulties has been to suppose that the differences between Socrates and the unmusical, or between a thing and its matter, come to light only in *intensional* contexts. Intensional contexts, on some accounts, are precisely those in which the ordinary laws of identity break down.[9] If this is right, then intensionality can seem a natural source of differences between things that are numerically the same – that is, on the present account, identical – and the distinction Aristotle has in mind between them will be accordingly an *intensional* one.

The appeal to intensionality here is the duplicate of the move sometimes made in connection with the *De Sophisticis Elenchis* to explain the apparent differences between Coriscus and the one approaching (where Coriscus is doing the approaching in question). In the *De Sophisticis Elenchis,* the appeal to intensionality was encouraged by the fact that the differences in question show up in epistemic contexts and that similar differences, meanwhile, apparently can be found in modal contexts. Contexts of both kinds are ones we regard as intensional: what more natural, then, than to suppose that the apparent lapses in the laws of identity here are due to the intensionality of the contexts in which those lapses occur?[10]

Provisionally, let us grant the assumption that Socrates and the unmusical are identical. Against this background, the appeal to intensionality can inspire radically different reactions. (a) As we have seen, despite the identity between Socrates and the unmusical, there can still be an "intensional" difference between them. On this account, presumably, modal contexts present us with real exceptions to the Law of the Indiscernibility of Identicals. So Aristotle's distinction between Socrates and the unmusical is sustained, but at the price of a basic law governing identity. (b) Defenders of that law, by contrast, insist that if two things are identical, not even modal differences will exist between them. On this second alternative, the Law of the Indiscernibility of Identicals remains intact, but Aristotle's distinction between Socrates and the unmusical is lost. And whichever alternative we choose – assuming still that Socrates is identical with the unmusical – it seems

eidos, but these two are equated by Aristotle at *Physics* A7, 190a16–17), but in Δ6, he has in mind the "most proper and primary" kind of sameness, namely, variety (ii) from *Metaphysics* I3. Variety (i), however, will *not* entail sameness in *logos.*

9 Cf. E. J. Lemmon, quoted in Cartwright (1971), p. 125. Quine apparently argues that on one construction, modal logic violates Leibniz's Law; see Smullyan (1948), p. 31, and Quine (1943), pp. 113–27, (1961), pp. 139–57.

10 The line of argument sketched here is discussed in Chapter 5, Section 2.

that we cannot *both* accept the indiscernibility of identicals *and* make good on Aristotle's distinction between Socrates and the unmusical.

As a first step in assessing the two options just sketched, it is worth noting the possibility that the two sides are arguing over *different* principles involving identity – that the principle that on (a) is defeated by examples like Socrates and the unmusical is simply not the same as the principle upheld in (b). As before (Chapter 4, Section 2), following Cartwright, we distinguish between the Principle of Substitutivity, which allows the intersubstitution of expressions denoting the same thing, and the Principle of Identity, which is just the Law of the Indiscernibility of Identicals: things that are identical have all and only same properties.[11] It is clear that the Principle of Substitutivity fails in intensional contexts. Suppose, for example, that Socrates is identical with the unmusical. Then putting a name of Socrates for a name for the unmusical will not preserve truth value in every linguistic context. But this does not amount to a failure in the Principle of Identity, since we have not shown that because substitution of a name of the one for a name of the other does not preserve truth value, *different properties attach to Socrates and the unmusical themselves*. And if the Principle of Identity never fails, then we will *never* show that where two things are identical, different properties can attach to each.

The distinction between the Principle of Identity and the Principle of Substitutivity has two important consequences. The first, as we have seen – the good news – is that failures of substitution in intensional contexts do not require us to give up the Principle of Identity. This effectively disposes of alternative (a). The second consequence – the bad news for those who suppose that Socrates and the unmusical are identical and look to intensionality in order to make out some difference between them – is that the substitution failures also do not direct us to any real differences between Socrates and the unmusical.

The upshot is as predicted in alternative (b): if two things are identical, not even the resort to intensional contexts can reveal any real differences between them. An example from Quine helps bring out the relevant point. Suppose that 9 and the number of planets "are the same thing, yet 9 necessarily exceeds 7, whereas the number of the planets only contingently exceeds 7."[12] On Quine's view of the modalities, these premises do not reveal conflicting facts about "the neutral thing itself, the number which is the number of planets as well as 9." Instead, they reflect differences in how that thing may be *specified,* which in turn bring different *de dicto* modal consequences with them.

---

11 Cartwright (1971), pp. 119–33.
12 This and the following quotation are from Quine (1963), p. 103.

Thus, on Quine's view, it is a necessary truth that 9 exceeds 7, but it is only contingently true that the number of the planets does so. Clearly, on Quine's account, no difference comes to light here between 9 and the number of the planets, but only between the two *statements* just cited. This gives a clear sense in which any alleged difference between 9 and the number of the planets is no more than verbal. We can hold, consistent with Quine's examples, both that the two are identical and that no violation of the Law of the Indiscernibility of Identicals occurs. For no real difference has been found between the items in question.

If we assume both that Socrates and the unmusical are identical and that the Law of the Indiscernibility of Identicals is sound, then the only contexts in which we appear to differentiate between them are *de dicto* modal contexts. That is, the differences in question do not concern Socrates or the unmusical themselves, but only the differing modal status of our statements about them. Quite literally, the difference is not one that affects Socrates and the unmusical at all.

These results can be usefully compared with the Fregean analysis of intensional contexts. For Frege, if a context falls within the scope of a modal (epistemic or alethic) operator, then terms contained in that context do not have their ordinary reference, but instead an *oblique* reference, which according to Frege is identical with their ordinary sense.[13] Frege's idea brings out the point Cartwright also stresses, that a referring expression cannot be counted on to behave in precisely the same way, regardless of the context in which it occurs. On the intensionality interpretation of Aristotle, apparently there is hope that we will be able to use intensional or "oblique" contexts in order to make out a distinction between a thing and its matter, which are otherwise identical. As it turns out, however, intensional contexts are precisely those in which we can no longer be sure we are talking in the ordinary way about a thing and its matter at all – and if Frege is right, we are talking about quite different entities. On either story, no real difference between a thing and its matter can emerge after all.

A variation on the account considered so far is worth mentioning parenthetically here. Perhaps the contexts in which substitution fails are not straightforwardly intensional, but rather nonextensional but referential. That is, substitution of names for the same thing fails, but Existential Generalization holds.[14] If this option can be made out, we are still in a real sense talking about (ordinary) objects – but as before, all the difference lies in the talk, not in the objects.

13 Cf, the discussion in Chapter 4, Section 2.
14 For the distinction between intensional, on the one hand, and nonextensional but referential, on the other, see Loar (1972) and Chapter 5, note 11. Peterson's term "translucent," for something lying in between the opaque and the fully transparent, is meant to capture the same phenomenon (Peterson [1969], Chap. 2).

Quite apart from the objections sketched in previous paragraphs, there is yet another, more fundamental reason for supposing that if Socrates and the unmusical differ in some way, considerations having to do with intensionality are not relevant to that difference. Perhaps they differ straightforwardly because they are not after all identical, on the grounds that numerical sameness is not after all identity. The argument for this idea repeats in part the reasoning in the analysis of accidental sameness and of the accompanying ontology in Part II. On this line of thought, Aristotle's distinction can be made out without denying the indiscernibility of identicals, and without making a special appeal to intensionality. Indeed, the whole relevance of intensionality to the interpretation of Aristotle is now called into question. If Socrates and the unmusical, or a thing and its matter, are not identical, the fact that substituting a name of one for a name of the other in a given linguistic context does not always preserve truth value is not a useful premiss in the argument that the context in question is referentially opaque. We will return to these points in connection with the Paradoxes of Becoming and the Paradox of Persistence in Sections 4 and 5.

2   Intensionality and the Account of Change in *Physics* A

As we have seen in the preceding section, there are general philosophical grounds for doubting that Aristotle's distinction between Socrates and the unmusical, or between a compound material substance and its matter, can be an "intensional" one. In this section and in Section 3, I pursue this argument further in connection with Aristotle's discussion of becoming and change generally in *Physics* A.[15] Aristotle's examples here are sometimes thought to contain contexts that are intensional on the contemporary account, and this analysis has helped fuel the idea that intensionality is the key to making out the distinction between Socrates and the unmusical (say), or between a thing and its matter. Before we can come to a final conclusion on this score, however, some prior issues should be addressed, beginning with the *location* of the intensionality, if any exists. Aristotle is concerned with when one thing is the cause of, or comes to be from, another *simpliciter;* for example, does the pale come to be from the not-pale or from the musical, or does the doctor or the housebuilder build a house? We can fairly take Aristotle to be committed to finding intensionality here only if two conditions are met. First, he must suppose that 'the musical' and 'the not-pale', for example, or 'the doctor', 'the housebuilder', and 'Callias'

15 There is a more detailed treatment of the discussion of change in *Physics* A in Chapter 9.

(say), name the identical thing; for the sake of argument, we will simply assume for now that this condition is satisfied. Second, his discussion must contain at least one example of sentences that he thinks differ in content only by containing different names for the identical thing and that he thinks can or do differ in truth value. Aristotle will also say that one thing is the cause of, or comes to be from, another *kata sumbebēkos*, or that it does so *kath' hauto*, or that it does so *qua* this or that qualification; these different locutions may introduce intensionality, even if there is no evidence for it on the other, simpler way of talking.

Even when questions about the existence and precise location of the intensionality have been settled, however, the issue of reference remains. In intensional contexts, the ordinary presumptions of reference slip away: how, then, can we be sure we are still talking about our intended subject matter? It is sometimes suggested that '*qua*'-clauses can be used to insulate the remainder of the sentence from the threatened reference failures – but will the use of this device make room for the kind of "intensional" distinction between Socrates and the unmusical that commentators have been looking for?

Our discussion of these topics will be distributed over this section and Section 3. In this section, I discuss two examples from *Physics* A and a third, non-Aristotelian case for the sake of comparison. Whether we can still sustain an "intensional" distinction between Socrates and the unmusical, once the details of these examples have been understood, will be taken up in Section 3.

(i)   The Coming-To-Be of the Pale

Our first point must be that nothing whatever is by nature such as to do or to undergo any chance thing through the agency of any chance thing, unless you take it accidentally (*an mē tis lambanei kata sumbebēkos*). For how could pale come to be out of musical, unless the musical were an accident of the not-pale or the dark? But pale comes to be out of not-pale, and this not out of every ‹not-pale›, but out of dark or something intermediate, and musical out of not-musical, except not out of every ‹not-musical›, but out of the unmusical, or if there is something intermediate between them. (*Physics* A5, 188a31–b3; after Charlton's translation)

The evidence of this passage at first sight is somewhat equivocal. On the intensionality view, Aristotle is saying in the opening lines of the passage that the sentence

(1) The pale comes to be from the musical

is false, and instead, what is true is the modified claim that

(2) It is accidentally (*kata sumbebēkos*) the case that the pale comes to be from the musical.

Sentence (2) in turn apparently comes down to the conjunction of two claims:

(3) The pale comes to be from the not-pale

(i.e., from the dark or from some intermediate colour), and

(4) The not-pale is the musical.

Here it is especially noteworthy that (3) is both true and an appropriate statement of the change at hand, while on the analysis we are considering, (1) is neither.

If in fact there is a difference in truth value between (1) and (3) and if we assume that 'the musical' and 'the not-pale' function as names for the identical thing, then the case for thinking both statements intensional seems sure. Yet Aristotle's rhetorical question, "How could pale come to be out of musical, *unless* the musical were an accident of the not-pale . . . ?" (my italics), clearly implies that where (3) and (4) are true, (1) too is flatly true, even if misleading. If this is right, then any grounds for thinking that (1) and (3) are intensional disappear. The opening sentence from the passage can be brought into line with this latter interpretation. Aristotle apparently has in mind the idea that an unqualified statement of coming-to-be like (1) has a *default* reading,

(5) It is properly the case that the pale comes to be from the musical,

which is straightforwardly false. Sentence (1) itself, however, without the supplement (5) provides, is misleading, but still true. On this story, for all we have seen so far, sentences like (1) and (3) are extensional throughout. What *will* be intensional, if 'the musical' and 'the not-pale' are names for the identical thing, is the result of embedding (1) or (3) or similar sentences within the larger context 'It is properly the case that . . . ', or 'It is accidentally the case that . . . ' – for example,

(2) It is accidentally the case that the pale comes to be from the musical,

which is true, and

(6) It is properly the case that the pale comes to be from the musical,

which is false.[16]

16 On the extensional account, Aristotle's treatment of (1) is very close to his account of "accidental predication" in the *Analytica Posteriora* (A19, 81b24–5, A22, 83a8, 15; cf. *An. Pr.* A27, 43a34–5), in which he suggests that the sentence, for example,

(i) The white thing is a man,

Despite the reservations of the preceding paragraph, suppose that the contrast between the two statements, (1) and (3), of coming-to-be is after all that (3) is true, but that the rival statement, (1), is (not merely misleading or inappropriate, but) outright false. The natural hypotheses to account for this difference in truth value, if in fact the musical thing in question *is* the not-pale, is that both (1) and (3) are intensional.[17] The appeal to intensionality has a by now familiar but troubling consequence. We are supposed to think that the pale comes to be from the not-pale. On the intensionality hypothesis, however, there is the danger that what the pale has come from is not really the not-pale at all – not at any rate the familiar entity that is the musical. If (3) is intensional in the way we have assumed, we must conclude that the ordinary apparatus of reference is no longer in effect there and that we are not talking in the ordinary way about the not-pale. And strikingly, on a Fregean account, we are referring to quite different objects altogether.[18]

Frege's account should be distinguished from the view offered in earlier chapters that the expression 'the musical ‹one›', for example, everywhere refers to the accidental compound of some contextually given substance with the accident musical – where an accidental

expresses an "accidental predication" and should be unpacked as the conjuntion of

    (ii) A given substance, *a,* is the white thing

and

    (iii) *a* is a man.

Sentence (iii) expresses a proper metaphysical predication. Sentence (i), by contrast, is (true but) inherently misleading. The example in *Physics* A5 is similar: the claim in (1) in the main text that the pale comes to be from the musical is (true but) misleading and is best paraphrased as the conjunction of (3) and (4), which most properly express the facts at hand.

    On the issues involved here, see further Bogen (1974), pp. 21–5. For present purposes, I ignore Accidental Compound Theory (ACT) in interpreting 'the pale' and 'the musical'. ACT will come into play later in Sections 4 and 5.

17 Strictly, failure of substitution shows only that the context is nonextensional, leaving open the possibility that it is still referential; for the context to be fully intensional, Extensional Generalization too must fail there. Contexts in which the two criteria for intensionality diverge include intentional contexts, for example, 'Ptolemy knew that . . . ' and an assortment of other contexts collected in K. Fine (1990). But I am inclined to think that if substitution fails in a context that remains referential, there will be some explanation of why this divergence of the criteria for intensionality takes place, and this to my knowledge has not been given in the case of the alleged examples from Aristotle. In any case, if the two criteria do diverge here, so that the context is not fully intensional, there remains the objection given in note 18.

18 Here I disregard the possibility that the context is not intensional, but rather nonextensional but referential (see note 17): in this case, the objection that we are not talking about objects will fail. But if the context is (merely) nonextensional, the nonintensionality again points only to the existence of different ways of talking about Socrates and the unmusical, not to any real differences between Socrates and the unmusical themselves.

compound is not identical with its parent substance, Socrates (say). Instead, according to Frege, whatever reference 'the musical' has in "regular" contexts, certain contexts, which we label "intensional," force a *reference shift* away from the ordinary referent, to some other, *intensional* entity.

These various modifications of the ordinary apparatus of reference threaten to put an unacceptable distance between Aristotle's discussion of change and its proper subject matter. Possibly, however, Aristotle's device of '*qua*'-clauses offers the means for staving off the threat.[19] The referring expression 'the not-pale' can be moved from the position it occupies in (3) into a '*qua*'-clause, so that the alleged intensionality attaches to the '*qua*'-clause and the remainder of the sentence is straightforwardly extensional.[20] This frees us to replace the original occurrence of 'the not-pale' in (3) by what (4) apparently tells us is a designation of the same thing, namely, 'the musical':

(7) The pale comes to be from the musical *qua* not-pale.

That is, the pale comes to be from the not-pale (= (3)), and the not-pale is the musical (= (4)). The effect of the '*qua*'-clause in (7) is

19 Peterson (1969), pp. 202–12. Comparable uses of '*qua*'-clauses appear, e.g., in Kirwan (1971), p. 181; Moravcsik (1975), p. 633; and Spellman (1989) and (1990) (the published versions of the last two papers reached me well after the present work was written). But perhaps the most thoroughgoing use of '*qua*'-clauses is in Sellars (1967). An example is worth quoting. Sellars asks about the sense in which a compound material substance is a composite or "whole" that (on Sellars' view) has an individual form and an individual piece of matter as its "parts": his answer, as we have seen (note 3), is that the individual form and the thing, and the individual matter and the thing, are in both cases identical. This answer raises another question. Continuing the quotation begun in note 3:

> What, then, is the difference between individual form and matter of this shoe if they are the same *thing*? The answer should, by now, be obvious. The individual form of this shoe is the shoe *qua*
>
> > (piece of some appropriate material or other – in this case leather) *serving the purpose of protecting and embellishing the feet.*
>
> The individual matter of this shoe is the shoe *qua*
>
> > *piece of leather* (so worked as to serve some purpose or other – in this case to protect and embellish the feet).
>
> Thus, the "parts" involved are not incomplete individuals in the real order, but the importantly different parts of the formula
>
> > (piece of leather) (serving to protect and embellish the feet)
>
> projected on the individual thing of which they are true. (Sellars [1967], p. 118, his emphasis)

Finally, the work of '*qua*'-clauses can also be done by talking instead of "things under a certain description"; see, e.g., Hartman (1977), p. 73; Waterlow (1982), p. 14 (quoted in note 43); Bostock (1982), p. 184. (Waterlow's and Bostock's views are discussed further in Chapter 9, Section 5.)

20 In *Physics* A5, Aristotle does not apply the apparatus of '*qua*'-clauses to this example. But A8, 191a34 ff., makes it clear that he regards the application as appropriate.

to bring in the proper as opposed to the accidental cause of the coming-to-be (cf. *Physics* B5, 196b25–9, quoted later in this section): the pale comes from the musical only because of the connection between the musical and the not-pale, thanks to which the instance of coming-to-be at hand falls into line with the appropriate principle that "all change is between contraries," so that only not-pale things (i.e., only dark things or things of some intermediate colour) come to be pale. But (again) everything in (7) *outside* the '*qua*'-clause is straightforwardly extensional and talks in the ordinary way about ordinary objects, the pale, the musical, and the like.

(ii)   The Doctor and the Housebuilder

The example of the doctor in *Physics* A8 is similar,[21] except that here the device of '*qua*'-clauses is present in Aristotle's account from the very beginning. In A8, Aristotle contrasts two ways of reading sentences asserting that one thing acts on, or is acted on by, or comes from, another. By a sentence of the form

(8) The doctor φ's,

for example, we may mean either that

(9) The doctor *qua* doctor φ's

or that

(10) The doctor *qua* something other than a doctor φ's.

A statement of the form of (8), without '*qua*'-clause, has the *default* reading (9), in which the subject expression in the original sentence is simply reduplicated within the scope of the '*qua*'. When the default reading of a given sentence is true, Aristotle will say that the original sentence is "the most appropriate" (*malista legomen kuriōs*, 191b6–7). For example, the sentence

(11) The doctor heals

has a default reading that is true, for the doctor heals *qua* doctor (191b6); hence, (11) itself will be "most appropriate." In other cases, however, the default reading of a '*qua*'-less sentence may be false, and by implication, the sentence itself, without '*qua*'-clause, is inappropriate. (But Aristotle does not say that the original sentence is – not merely inappropriate, but – outright false.) For example, the sentence

(12) The doctor builds a house

---

21 Cf. also *Metaphysics* E2, 1026b37–1027a5.

has a default reading that is false – a doctor does not build a house *qua* doctor (191b4) – and (12) itself is not appropriate. But a different expansion of (12), with a different '*qua*'-clause, is true, namely

(13) The doctor *qua* housebuilder builds a house.

Suppose now that we say, truly but inappropriately, that

(12) The doctor builds a house.

(Sentence (12) is true, but it is inappropriate since its default reading is false.) On the model suggested by the account of how things come to be pale in *Physics* A5, what is asserted in (12) is a (misleading) compression of the claim that

(14) The doctor is the housebuilder,

together with the point that

(15) The housebuilder builds a house.

Sentence (15) reports the occurrence at hand in a way that directly connects the building of the house with the capacity for housebuilding that is the source of the change (*hothen hē kinēsis,* B3, 195a5–7). Sentence (14), meanwhile, supplies the necessary link between (15) and the doctor: the doctor *is* the housebuilder, and the occurrence recorded in (12) that the doctor builds a house indirectly involves the capacity for housebuilding in virtue of this connection. Claim (13), finally, with '*qua*'-clause, differs from the compressed claim (12) that the doctor builds a house, without any qualifying phrase, for unlike (12), (13) flags the connection between the doctor and the housebuilder that permits the appeal to the relevant capacity.

As before, our account plays two claims off against each other – in this case, the claim in (12) that the doctor builds a house against the claim in (15) that *the housebuilder* does so. On the account offered so far, the one claim is misleading because its default reading is false, while the other is appropriate because its default reading is true; both sentences themselves, however, are *true*. As Aristotle points out:

A thing can also be a cause (*aition*) in this way [sc., either in itself (*kath' hauto*) or accidentally (*kata sumbebēkos*)], for example, the housebuilder is in itself the cause of a house, but the pale or the musical ‹is a cause› accidentally. That which in itself is a cause is determinate, but that which is a cause accidentally is indeterminate: for an unlimited number of things can be accidental to a single thing. (*Physics* B5, 196b25–9; following Charlton's translation; cf. *Metaphysics* E2, 1026b2 ff.)

In line with this, the sentence,

(16) It is accidentally (*kata sumbebēkos*) the case that the doctor builds a house,

is true, while

(17) It is properly (*kath' hauto*) the case that the doctor builds a house

is false. Instead, we know that

(18) It is properly (*kath' hauto*) the case that the housebuilder builds a house.[22]

The difference in truth value between (17) and (18) suggests that the context following the '*kath' hauto*' is intensional, providing as always that the doctor is identical with the housebuilder; a similar conclusion holds for what follows the '*kata sumbebēkos*' in (16).[23] But, of course, this has no tendency to show that the contained sentence, (12) or (15), by itself contains an intensional context.

Suppose, however, that − contrary to what I have suggested and going beyond anything Aristotle expressly says − (12) is not merely inappropriate, but in contrast to (15), outright *false*.[24] Supposing still that the doctor *is* the housebuilder, the difference in truth value seems to show that the statements in question are intensional after all. As before, however, doubts about how referring expressions behave in intensional contexts undercut any hope that the difference in truth value points to a real difference between the doctor and the housebuilder. And as before, we can use a '*qua*'-clause to eliminate the intensionality from the remainder of the sentence; for example, in

(13) The doctor *qua* housebuilder builds a house,

we can at least be sure that outside the '*qua*'-clause, we are talking in the ordinary way about the doctor and his housebuilding.

22 The operators 'It is properly the case that . . . ' and 'It is accidentally the case that . . . ' introduce epistemic rather than alethic modalities; cf. Chapter 9, Section 3.

23 Nothing here, however, advances the project of finding a difference between the doctor and the housebuilder. It could be said that the doctor *is*, but the housebuilder is *not*, a *kath' hauto* cause of the house; but I take the logical form of this to be that the one statement, that the housebuilder did the building, is appropriate, but that its rival, that the doctor did so, is misleading. In the end, then, the difference is only between the two assertions and is not a difference between the doctor and the housebuilder.

24 On this account, presumably, (12) combines a report of the act of housebuilding with the incorrect explanation that the housebuilding was done *in virtue of* the agent's abilities as a doctor. I emphasize that I do not mean to endorse this analysis. On my account, both (12) and (15) are true, and they differ only in that (15) is, and (12) is not, an appropriate statement of the change at hand. As with the examples in (i), then, both (12) and (15) are straightforwardly extensional, and intensionality comes in only when they are embedded in some suitable larger context, for example,

   (12*) It is inappropriately put that the doctor builds a house,
   (15*) It is appropriately put that the housebuilder builds a house.

   Cf. the discussion of (2) and (6).

(iii)   Barbarelli and Giorgione

The '*qua*'-clauses that appear in (7) and (13) confine the intensionality they create to the expression immediately following the '*qua*'. The intensionality is quite readily explained in these cases: it is due to the analytical or explanatory nature of that portion of the statement. One last example, not from Aristotle, illustrates a very different source of intensionality and a different way of confining it within the sentence. Consider the claim

(19) Barbarelli is so-called because of his size.

In marked contrast with our earlier examples, (19) is not merely misleading but, uncontroversially, outright false. Claim (19) is an illegitimate compression of two pieces of information:

(20) Giorgione is so-called because of his size

and

(21) Giorgione is Barbarelli.

What makes (20) true but (19) false, even given the fact in (21) that Giorgione *is* Barbarelli? A natural answer is that the subject position in (20) is intensional, and the attempt to treat it extensionally, using (20) and (21) to derive (19), is illegitimate. In contrast to the cases considered in (i) and (ii), the appeal to intensionality here is uncontroversial and is supported by the evident change in truth value between (19) and (20).

In this case too, however, we can if we want shift the intensionality from subject position in (20) to a different position in the sentence:

(22) Giorgione, that is, Barbarelli, is named 'Giorgione' because of his size.

Here, the quotation-mark name is evidently referentially opaque with respect to the expression immediately contained within the quotation marks, so that the intensionality of (19) at its subject position is assimilated to the intensionality of the quotation-mark construction.

3   '*Qua*'-Clauses and Intensionality

I propose now, at least provisionally, to suppress our earlier doubts in connection with the contested examples in (i) and (ii) in Section 2 and to suppose that the examples in (i), (ii), and (iii) alike involve a failure to preserve truth value through substitution of names for the identical thing, and hence are properly analysed in terms of intensionality. The examples are intended to show that we can talk about the not-pale in a way that distinguishes it from the musical, or about the doctor in a way that distinguishes him from the housebuilder, despite the fact that in each case, by assumption, the members of each pair are identical. Prima facie, as we have seen, this idea faces the difficulty that we are not clearly talking about the not-pale, or about the doctor, at all.[25] If our statements of change or becoming are intensional, we are not talking straightforwardly about the not-pale, that is, about Socrates, who happens not to be pale, in (3). Again, in (15), we are not talking straightforwardly about the housebuilder, that is, the doctor, that is, Callias (say), and saying that *he* builds the house. Philosophers sometimes conclude that we are not talking about ordinary objects at all, but (e.g.) about a Fregean sense. The resort to '*qua*'-clauses promises a way around these difficulties. The professed advantage of '*qua*'-clauses and similar devices is that they allow us to isolate the intensional component of a sentence, as in (7), (13), and (22), leaving a remainder that is an ordinary extensional statement of becoming, or of housebuilding, or of being named. In the part of the sentence that stands outside the '*qua*'-clause, we say of the musical, that is, the not-pale, that the pale comes from *it;* or of the doctor, who is a housebuilder, that *he* builds a house; or of Giorgione, a.k.a. Barbarelli, that *he* has a name (not here further specified) that reflects his size. In each case, we are now talking straightforwardly about objects: the musical (= the not-pale), the doctor (= the housebuilder), Giorgione (= Barbarelli).

Despite this apparent success, '*qua*'-clauses bring problems of their own. It seems unlikely that the qualification '*qua* housebuilder', for example, in (13), 'The doctor *qua* housebuilder builds a house', can be simply paraphrased away in favour of some other, quite harmless locution. We cannot say, for instance, that (13) is simply shorthand for the conjunction of (14) and (15) without any further problems, for by hypothesis, (15) itself is *intensional* at the appropriate position. And in general, I suspect, there is no way simply to paraphrase away the cautionary '*qua*'-clause in (13), unless we are willing to readmit intensionality into our paraphrase.[26]

At the same time, once the extensionality of the remainder of (13), for example, *outside* the '*qua*'-clause, has been secured, the '*qua*'-clause itself cannot be simply dropped from the sentence with impunity. For the remainder that is left is just the sentence (12), which by itself is

---

25 Here I continue to ignore the complication mentioned in notes 17 and 18.

26 '*Qua*'-clauses can sometimes be paraphrased harmlessly away. For example, 'John *qua* basketball player is short, and *qua* fourteen-year-old is tall' becomes 'John is short relative to the class of basketball players and tall relative to the class of fourteen-year-olds'. So '*qua*'-clauses do not always resist elimination. But I have not seen how they can be eliminated in the cases under study in the main text. For more on this topic, see Anscombe (1979).

false on the intensionality account. Or if the remainder left is (15), what prevents us from moving from it straight back to (12), given the fact that the housebuilder *is* the doctor? How are we to make intelligible the supposed contrast in truth value between (12) and (15), if indeed, as Aristotle says, the doctor *is* the housebuilder? If we appeal to intensionality to supply an answer, we have still to say how this hypothesis is to be reconciled with the idea that our statements of becoming, or of housebuilding, and the like, are about ordinary objects. But if the cautionary '*qua*'-clause cannot simply be dropped from (13), then pending some further account of '*qua*'-clauses, the best we can do in our statements of housebuilding is to say that one and the same thing relative to one way of talking about it *does,* and relative to a different way of talking about it *does not,* build a house. And if our talk about the doctor and his efforts at housebuilding has always to be talk about him *qua* so-and-so (with "*qua* so-and-so" not further explained), it is not clear how great an advance this is over the simple-minded opacity view, which frankly concedes that we are not talking straightforwardly about the doctor at all.

The reasons for these failures become clear once we look at the explanation for the intensionality that the different '*qua*'-clauses introduce. In the doctor case, for example, the intensionality is associated with an *explanatory* context: we are saying of the housebuilder, that is, the doctor, that he builds a house *because of* his abilities as a housebuilder. Or in the Giorgione–Barbarelli case, to take a very different example, we say of Giorgione, that is, Barbarelli, that the name 'Giorgione' is suitable to his size: here the source of the intensionality is the quotation marks in the quotation-mark name ' 'Giorgione' '. Once these explanations have been advanced, surely any doubts about whether we are talking in a relatively ordinary way about ordinary objects in the remainder of the sentence will have evaporated. Along with these doubts, however, the apparent differences between the housebuilder and the doctor, between Giorgione and Barbarelli, and the rest will have evaporated as well. The alleged differences are now seen to be mere artefacts of our way of combining explanatory talk into our report of the change, or of subordinating the quotation-mark name ' 'Giorgione' ' to the device of pronominal cross-reference: Giorgione is *so*-called because of his size. The apparent distinction this last way of talking gives between Giorgione and Barbarelli is obviously bogus: it merely fronts for the distinction between the *names* 'Giorgione' and 'Barbarelli'. Similar remarks apply to the apparent distinction between the doctor and the housebuilder (remembering our assumption that the doctor is the housebuilder): for all we have seen so far, there is no real distinction between them at all, but only between the different explanatory roles played by the properties of being a doctor and of being a housebuilder. Likewise, finally, with the not-pale and the musical: the example does not force a distinction between the not-pale and the musical, but rather between the different consequences of being musical and of being not-pale.

On this account, the attempt to find an "intensional" difference between the doctor and the housebuilder, or between the not-pale and the musical, or Barbarelli and Giorgione makes the difference merely the artefact of the familiar kinds of intensional talk associated with explanatory contexts or with quotation-mark contexts. In reality, the difference is no difference.[27] It is at best a difference relative to how we talk; that is, it is a product of *de dicto* modal differences, and thus is no difference *among objects* at all.

But, of course, there is in reality all the difference in the world between the not-pale and the musical or between the doctor and the housebuilder: they are not identical in the first place! I turn to this point in the next section.

4   Some Alternatives to Intensionality: The Paradoxes of Becoming

I argued in the preceding section that the claim that certain contexts are intensional does not support the idea that if Socrates and the un-musical are identical, there is still an "intensional" difference between them. The appeal to intensionality, then, does not help explain Aristotle's claim that these are "one in number but two in account." An objection of a different sort is that on Aristotle's view a thing and its matter, or Socrates and the unmusical, are simply not identical in the first place. On this assumption, Aristotle's examples are not sufficient to show that a given context is intensional. Even more obviously, if Socrates and the unmusical are not identical, the whole appeal to intensionality in order to explain how they can differ is now beside the point.[28] A good test of these rival interpretations is given by the Paradoxes of Becoming and the Paradox of Persistence. The paradoxes use the fact that Socrates and the unmusical (say) are one in number in order to erase the differences that Aristotle's theory of change apparently requires between them. One strategy in combatting the paradoxes is to assume that Socrates and the unmusical are identical, but to block the problematic inferences on the grounds that our statements of becoming, or of persistence, are intensional. But suppose we deny that Socrates and the unmusical are identical, even though they

27 It results from a "mere juggling of words," and the whole exercise is just an "attempt to have it both ways," or (with a slightly different example in mind) "a licence to say contradictory things about identity and existence" (Williams [1982], p. 218).

28 Compare this with the argument of Chapter 5.

are one in number, and thus leave the issue of intensionality to one side – do we still have an effective defence against the paradoxes, as Aristotle wants?

I begin in this section with the Paradoxes of Becoming. At *Metaphysics* E2, 1026b15–21, Aristotle notices briefly a paradox that purports to do away with becoming:

> For the arguments of the sophists deal, so to speak, above all with the accidental; for example, the question whether musical and grammatical are different or the same, and whether musical Coriscus and Coriscus are the same; and whether whatever is, but not eternally, has come to be, so that if ‹someone›, being musical, has come to be grammatical, ‹then› also, being grammatical, he has come to be musical: together with any other arguments of this kind.[29]

The argument about becoming that Aristotle appears to have in mind is this. Suppose that

(23) The musical has become the grammatical,

so that

(24) The musical is now the grammatical.

Aristotle says that the argument the sophist constructs from these premisses takes its force from a fallacious treatment of the accidental, but his other remarks in the paragraph suggest that the fallacy he has in mind may also involve questions of the sort 'Are entities like Coriscus and musical Coriscus the same or different?' In line with this idea, it is plausible to take (24) as an assertion of sameness of some kind between the musical and the grammatical. Suppose that we also accept a *sameness principle* governing things that are the same in the relevant sense: two things are the same in this sense, we can suppose, only if every property of the one is also a property of the other. By (24) and two applications of the sameness principle to (23), there follows the sophist's conclusion

(25) The grammatical has become the musical.

Aristotle warns us that there are other paradoxes along the same lines, and it is easy to imagine the kinds of argument he has in mind. Let us simplify a little, and suppose that it is Socrates who is undergoing change and that he has become musical. That is, we imagine that these two premisses hold:

(26) Socrates has become the musical.
(27) Socrates is now the musical.

29 See also *Topics* A11, 104b25–8. My discussion of the Paradoxes of Becoming is indebted to the treatment in Code (1976b); see also Matthews (1982), pp. 236–7.

Then by the sameness principle just mentioned, we can apparently show that Socrates has become Socrates, or that the musical has become the musical, or even that the musical has become Socrates. All three conclusions are meant to be manifestly absurd, and the sophist presumably takes them to show that in fact nothing comes to be.[30]

The paradoxes just sketched revolve around the use of a sameness principle governing things that are the same in some suitable sense. One ready way of contesting the sophist's sceptical conclusions about becoming is to doubt whether the sameness principle will license substitution at the positions occupied by 'Socrates' and 'the musical' in (26):

(26) Socrates has become the musical.

And to explain why the sameness principle falters in this way, we might suppose that the context '*x* becomes *y*' is *referentially opaque* at both argument places (equivalently, it is *intensional* with respect to designators occurring at those two positions); hence, it is not open to applications of the principle in question.

This claim is not without problems, however, as we have already seen. In the account of becoming, for example, what entities are they that come to be if the opacity view is right? And what are the entities that they become? If intensionality is involved, we are not referring in the ordinary way to Socrates in (26), and perhaps we *are* after all referring, but not to Socrates, but to some unexpected Fregean entity.[31] In either case, what are we to conclude for the received view of Aristotle's theory of change and becoming? Can we still, consis-

---

30 There are other problematic arguments as well. Suppose again that Socrates has become musical. In *Physics* A7, Aristotle sanctions an alternative way of describing the change; in place of (26), we say that

The unmusical has become the musical.

At the same time, as before, we know that

Socrates is now the musical.

There follows, apparently, the undesirable conclusion that

The unmusical has become Socrates.

In addition to the "retrospective" Paradoxes of Becoming, there are also their various prospective counterparts. For example,

Socrates will become the musical.
Socrates will be the musical.

Hence,

Socrates will become Socrates.

Further "prospective" arguments along the same lines are easily constructed, but I refrain from doing so here.

31 Again, this argument assumes that the relevant statements are straightforwardly intensional. For a different possibility, see notes 17 and 18.

tently with the opacity reading of (26), think of Socrates as a three-dimensional object that passes through time, undergoing changes of various kinds while himself remaining one and the same?

A subtler version of the intensionality view attempts to avoid these difficulties by confining the intensionality to '*qua*'-clauses in the way outlined in the preceding section. For example, the initial premiss

(26) Socrates has become the musical

has the *default* reading

(28) Socrates *qua* Socrates has become the musical,[32]

and from (28) together with (27) and the relevant sameness principle, we can infer, harmlessly, that

(29) The musical *qua* Socrates has become the musical.

That is, virtually repeating (26) and (27), the musical is (now) Socrates, and Socrates has become the musical. But we cannot use (28) and (27), together with the sameness principle, to conclude that

(30) Socrates *qua* the musical has become the musical.

Sentence (30) asserts that Socrates is the musical, as before, and erroneously that the musical has become the musical. But the inference to (30) is blocked by the intensionality of the position immediately following the '*qua*'. Despite the apparent success of the use of '*qua*'-clauses in blocking the problematic inferences, however, questions remain about the interpretation of such clauses (see Section 3), in particular whether once more the intensionality they bring into assertions of becoming is ultimately unacceptable.

Yet a different view is in an interesting way *intermediate* between the two intensionality accounts just sketched and the rival view that denies intensionality altogether. On this intermediate view, we continue to suppose that (26), for example, is intensional, but argue that (26) and assertions like it can be reworked in such a way that both the intensionality and the paradoxical inferences alike ultimately disappear. Thus, (26) and its like are not basic in Aristotle's theory of becoming, but can be paraphrased away in favour of locutions that are *not* referentially opaque. On this account, the claim to have found referential opacity in assertions of becoming may not so much indicate a deep truth in the analysis of becoming as suggest that that analysis is incomplete.

Accordingly, suppose once more that

(26) Socrates has become the musical.

32 "default reading": see the discussion of the doctor example in Section 2.

To get the full measure of (26), we must bring out the temporal indicators implicit in the tense of the verb and say how they interact with the expression 'the musical'. If we take 'the musical' as a definite description, subject to the familiar Russellian analysis, then we know already, leaving aside any special problems involving time, that the surface grammar of (26) does not reveal its true logical form. But there is a special bonus from applying Russell's technique for definite descriptions when temporal indicators are also present. A familiar treatment due to Smullyan, shows how various modal paradoxes disappear given the Russellian treatment of definite descriptions. Perhaps, then, given the account by Smullyan of the interplay between modal terms and definite descriptions treated in the Russellian way, we can construct a similar analysis of the interplay between various *temporal* terms and definite descriptions, so that the Paradoxes of Becoming too will finally dissolve.[33] Thus, taking, 'the musical' in (26) as a definite description and giving it *wide* scope, we have the unwanted reading

(31) Something, x, alone is musical, and at some time t prior to now, Socrates ≠ x at t, but now x = Socrates.

That is – if (31) is intelligible at all – since Socrates *is* the musical, at some previous time Socrates *and Socrates* are not identical, but now they are! From this, it follows, apparently, that Socrates has become Socrates, and the musical has become the musical. If the description has *narrow* scope, however, we get this harmless rendering of (26):

(32) For some time t prior to now, Socrates is unmusical at t, but now something, x, alone is musical, and Socrates = x.

With this as our reading of (26), the sophist's puzzle collapses. His argument fails, moreover, without help from the claim that expressions of becoming are referentially opaque. And similar arguments will show that the remaining Paradoxes of Becoming can be similarly dissolved.[34]

But there are disadvantages. First, it is doubtful that Aristotle himself masters the syntactic apparatus needed to bring out the relative scope of definite descriptions and various temporal operators in the

33 Smullyan (1948), pp. 31–7. Smullyan's treatment of the combination of definite descriptions with modal operators is illustrated in connection with the modal and epistemic paradoxes of the *De Sophisticis Elenchis* in Chapter 4, Section 2.

34 For a Russellian move of the sort described in connection with assertions of becoming in Aristotle, see Brody (1973), p. 353. There is also a discussion of this and related issues, with the alternative move to something like ACT clearly signposted, in Cohen (1978), pp. 389 ff.

way required.[35] Second, the analysis also helps itself to the Russellian treatment of the expression 'the musical' and the like. In fact, however, as we shall see, Aristotle's use of expressions such as 'the musical' may not be merely a roundabout – and also somewhat quaint – way of talking about Socrates, and the Russellian treatment may not after all be appropriate to them.

One further disadvantage of the Russellian treatment deserves notice. On the Russellian account, we can make sense of the claims that Socrates does, but the musical does not, become the musical only by recognizing that these are fundamentally *misleading* ways of talking. What they misleadingly say is best understood by means of their paraphrases, in which the full Russellian theory of descriptions comes into play, and our talk about 'the musical' simply melts away before the apparatus of quantifiers, predicates, and bound variables. On Russell's theory, then, the attempted distinction between Socrates and the musical is merely the by-product of a faulty theory of logical form.

To the contemporary interpreter of Aristotle, the Russellian treatment of the paradoxes has a seductive familiarity.[36] But Aristotle's own resolution of the paradoxes, I suspect, takes a very different form. On the interpretation I wish to offer, for Aristotle there is nothing misleading about the distinction between Socrates and the musical. Above all, to say that they are one in number is not to concede that they are identical.[37] On the contrary, they are not identical but, instead, accidentally the same. One sameness relation, then – but not identity – does hold between them. At the same time, they are not essentially the same: they are "two in account." To make good on this, we must give up the interpretation of 'the musical' as a Russellian definite description. For Aristotle, 'the musical' is not a description of Socrates, for it is not a description at all: it is instead the proper name of an *accidental compound,* Socrates + unmusical, which is straightforwardly not identical with Socrates.

In line with this, suppose that (26) is true and that Socrates has become the musical. The sophist's argument now becomes this:

---

35 See, e.g., White (1972), pp. 61 ff. (But for the view that Aristotle is not in the dark about the placement of modal operators in the way that White suggests, see Sorabji [1980], p. 205.)

36 Williams (1985) can again be cited in this connection (see Chapter 4, note 17). Williams's account uses Russell's theory of definite descriptions together with the appropriate scope distinctions to resolve the paradoxes; in contrast to the Russellian account sketched here and in Code (1976), however, his version avoids explicit quantification over times. But it is still essential to his solution that Aristotle master the relevant scope distinctions (or some comparable device), and he does not say enough about how Aristotle himself would represent these distinctions for us to be sure that Aristotle has the syntactic competence the distinctions require; cf. the objection two paragraphs earlier in the main text.

37 Or even à la Russell, that something, x, alone is musical, and x = Socrates.

(33) Socrates has become accidentally the same as Socrates + musical.
(34) Socrates is now accidentally the same as Socrates + musical.

Hence, by a principle governing things that are accidentally the same,

(35) Socrates has become accidentally the same as Socrates.

The crucial question in this argument for Aristotle is the soundness of the principle governing things that are accidentally the same. Aristotle states the required principle in the *Topics:*

Strong (S1) a is accidentally the same as $a + \phi^1 \rightarrow (\phi^2(a) \leftrightarrow \phi^2(a + \phi^1))$.[38]

In light of this principle, if Socrates and the musical are accidentally the same, then (again) it is true of *the musical* that Socrates has become accidentally the same as it just in case it is true of *Socrates* himself that Socrates has become the same as him. In a key move against arguments of this kind, however, in the *De Sophisticis Elenchis* Aristotle comes to think that Strong (S1) is after all unsound; instead, "only to *things that are one and indistinguishable in being* do all the same ‹things› seem to belong."[39] Socrates and the musical are *not* the same in being, so we no longer have any reason to think that anything true of the one must also be true of the other. In particular, there is no reason to think that if Socrates has become accidentally the same as *the musical,* then Socrates has become accidentally the same as *Socrates.* So the sophist's paradox collapses.

What on this account becomes of intensionality as a tool for diagnosing the Paradoxes of Becoming? If we are willing to ignore the distinctive Aristotelian ontology of accidental compounds, it may be tempting to lay failures of a sameness principle like Strong (S1) at the feet of the supposed intensionality of statements of becoming.[40] But this diagnosis is not relevant given the ontology of Accidental Compound Theory. An accidental compound and its parent substance are not identical, and so the failure to preserve truth by substituting a name for the one by a name for the other in a statement of becoming has no tendency to show that statements of becoming are intensional.

5   Some Alternatives to Intensionality: The Paradox of Persistence

A second puzzle of the same general character as the Paradoxes of Becoming discussed in the preceding section again illustrates how

---

38 For Strong (S1), see *Topics* H1, 152a33 ff., b25–9; cf. the discussion in Chapter 4, Section 1.
39 *SE* 24, 179a37–9; *Physics* Γ3, 202b14–16; cf. (S2), discussed in Chapter 4, Section 1.
40 Notice, however, that if intensionality is involved in the paradoxes, the correct conclusion is not that Strong (S1) is unsound, as Aristotle apparently comes to think it is, but rather that it is *inapplicable;* cf. the discussion of Cartwright in Section 1 and, in particular, in Chapter 4, Section 2.

contexts that we may be inclined to treat as intensional may well, for Aristotle, have a quite different analysis in straightforwardly extensional terms. This new puzzle has to do with Aristotle's account in *Physics* A of what does and what does not persist through a given change. The centerpiece of Aristotle's account of becoming in the second half of *Physics* A is the idea that the principles of coming-to-be must include "something underlying" and that this, while one in number, is not one in form (*eidos*) or in account. For example, if Socrates becomes the musical, what underlies – that is, what comes to be the musical – is alternatively the man, Socrates, or the unmusical.[41] Socrates and the unmusical have different persistence conditions, for Socrates persists through the change of becoming musical, but as Aristotle sees it, the unmusical does not. Given this difference between Socrates and the unmusical, how should we understand Aristotle's claim that they are "one in number"? If they are one in number, how will his qualification that they are also "two in account" make room for any difference between them? An easy argument threatens to undo Aristotle's attempt to keep them apart. Suppose that

(36) Socrates persists through the change of becoming the musical,

while at the same time,

(37) Socrates is the unmusical.

Premiss (37) asserts that Socrates and the unmusical are *the same* in some sense. If we also accept a principle governing things that are the same in the relevant way, then from (36) and (37) together it seems to follow that

(38) The unmusical persists through the change of becoming the musical.

A simple-minded response to this difficulty will be to say that in the sentence

(36) Socrates persists through the change of becoming the musical,

the position occupied by the subject term 'Socrates' is referentially opaque, and so not open to arguments based on the sameness principle in question. This raises the familiar difficulty that we are no longer referring in the ordinary way to Socrates when we say that Socrates persists through the change in question.[42]

---

41 In line with this, at *Physics* A7, 189b32–190a13, Aristotle notes that ordinary language permits a variety of ways of describing the change in question; cf. Chapter 9, Section 1.

42 On the Fregean account, assertions of persistence raise some of the same questions as assertions of existence. By saying that Socrates persists through a given change but the unmusical does not, we mean nothing more than that Socrates exists continuously from Friday through Sunday (say), but the unmusical exists on Friday but no

The difficulty can perhaps be met by the resort to '*qua*'-clauses.[43] Thus, we suppose that

(39) Socrates *qua* Socrates persists through the change of becoming the musical,

while at the same time,

(40) Socrates *qua* the unmusical does not persist through the change of becoming the musical.

As before, we suppose that the position *before* the '*qua*' is referentially transparent, so that the usual devices of reference work there perfectly well. This apparently removes any doubt we might have that our assertions are after all about *Socrates,* to the effect that *he,* Socrates, persists *qua* Socrates but not *qua* the musical.

At the same time, the use of '*qua*'-clauses also apparently helps solve the Paradox of Persistence. In *Physics* A8, as we have seen (Section 2), Aristotle notes two broadly different ways of reading sentences asserting that one thing acts on, or is acted on by, or comes from, another, and he offers '*qua*'-clauses as a means of disambiguating the sentences in question. In accordance with this, the unwanted conclusion in

(38) The unmusical persists through the change of becoming the musical

is perhaps *ambiguous.* On one view, (38) can in context be written as

(41) The unmusical *qua* Socrates persists through the change of becoming the musical;

in this form, the conclusion (perhaps) follows from its premises, but is harmless, for it tells us only that Socrates is the unmusical and that he, Socrates, persists through the change of becoming musical.[44] To derive (41), we adopt (39) as our reading of the first premiss, (36), of the paradox:

longer on Sunday. On the Fregean account, 'Socrates exists' is an oblique context, and the usual reference shift occurs away from the usual referent of the proper name 'Socrates' to its oblique referent or sense. If Frege is right, then, as we have seen, we are not only not referring in the ordinary way to Socrates, but referring instead to some very *un*ordinary entity.

43 I take it that the use of '*qua*'-clauses is only verbally different from the language of "under a description" – for example, "Thus the same thing (component) remains under one description though not under the other" (Waterlow [1982], p. 14); see also the references to Bostock and Waterlow in note 19 and the discussion in Chapter 9, Section 5.

44 It is instructive to compare (41) with (40), remembering that, for Aristotle, both sentences are *true.* With the pair formed by these two, compare 'The triangle *qua* isosceles does not have 2*R*' and 'The isosceles *qua* triangle has 2*R*' at *An. Po.* A24, 85b10–13; cf. *SE* 6, 168b2–4. These examples are discussed in Bäck (1988), chap. 2, which the reader should consult for further details.

(39) Socrates *qua* Socrates persists through the change of becoming the musical.

Premiss (39) is the *default* reading of (36), where the subject expression in (36) is merely reduplicated in the '*qua*'-clause in (39). We know, further, that (once more)

(37) Socrates is the unmusical.

Claim (41) apparently follows from (39) and (37) by the appropriate sameness principle. Alternatively, (38) has the default reading

(42) The unmusical *qua* the unmusical persists through the change of becoming the musical.

Claim (42) is evidently unacceptable, but it does not follow from the available premisses.

If Aristotle finds the argument for (41) acceptable,[45] what prevents the inference from (41) and (37) again to (42)? The answer comes easily that in (41) the occurrence of the term 'Socrates', immediately following the '*qua*', occupies a position that is referentially *opaque*, hence not open to applications of the sameness principle at work to produce the inference to (41).

As before, however, other accounts of the paradox are also available. As the classic alternative account by Russell suggests, if the inference from (36) and (37) to (38) fails, as Aristotle wants, this is not because the ordinary principles of reference break down here or because we must deal with a Fregean oblique rather than an ordinary referent. Instead, the problem has a *syntactic* solution, and once the proper logical form of the target sentences is uncovered, there is simply no room any longer for applying our referential principles in the way we had at first expected.[46]

45 Notice, however, that Aristotle may be inclined to doubt even the inference from (39) and (37) to (41), on the grounds that it is an instance of the "fallacy of accident" (see, in particular, *SE*, Chap. 24). If so, then (41) is simply an *abbreviation* for the conjunction of (36) and (37): the unmusical *is* Socrates, and Socrates, we know, persists through the change of becoming the musical.

46 Thus, suppose that, once more,

(36) Socrates persists through the change of becoming the musical.

Bringing out the references to time implicit in (36) gives this result:

(43) For some t prior to now, Socrates is unmusical at t, but something, x, alone is musical now, and x = Socrates, and Socrates exists continuously from t to now.

As (43) shows, if Socrates persists through the change of becoming the musical, then he has become, and now is, the musical. With the second premiss in the argument, then,

(37) Socrates is the unmusical,

we are talking about some *previous* state of Socrates:

On the Russellian account, Aristotle's treatment of persistence and his distinction between Socrates and the unmusical require the explicit use of temporal indicators, suitably combined with Russell's theory of descriptions. Some doubts about the place of these devices in the interpretation of Aristotle have already been mentioned in Section 4. As before, an alternative account of Aristotle's theory of persistence through change is built around the notion of an accidental compound and the related theory of accidental sameness. Suppose, as in (37), that Socrates is the unmusical; the unmusical, then, is identical with Socrates + unmusical. Now Socrates himself is not identical with the unmusical (i.e., with Socrates + unmusical); rather, they are *accidentally the same*. Accordingly, the first premiss of the paradox, (37), becomes

(46) Socrates is accidentally the same as Socrates + unmusical.

Aristotle's opponents may quite reasonably think that if Socrates persists through the change of becoming musical, then Socrates + unmusical must do so too; for as we have seen, Aristotle himself endorses the requisite licensing principle:

Strong (S1) a is accidentally the same as $a + \phi^1 \rightarrow (\phi^2(a) \leftrightarrow \phi^2(a + \phi^1))$.

This use of Strong (S1) dramatizes the threat to Aristotle's attempt to distinguish between Socrates and the unmusical. They are, he says, one in number but two in account: this seems to show that they are *accidentally* the same.[47] And this concession is enough to do the damage, in light of Strong (S1). So the qualification that Socrates and the unmusical are *two in account* seems to be of no help.

That qualification, however, will allow us to distinguish Socrates and the unmusical as Aristotle wants, if we drop Strong (S1) in favour of the more restrictive principle that things are indiscernible, not if they are accidentally the same, but if they are the same *in being*.[48] Socrates and the unmusical are *not* the same in this sense. Hence, the fact that Socrates *is* the unmusical – that is, they are accidentally the same – is not enough to support the conclusion that, like Socrates, the

(44) For some t prior to now and for some x, x alone is unmusical at t, and x = Socrates.

Given (43) and (44), we can show, harmlessly, that what once was the unmusical does persist through the change of becoming the musical:

(45) For some t prior to now, something, x, alone is unmusical at t, and x alone is musical now, and x has existed continuously from t to now.

This falls well short of proving that

(38) The unmusical persists through the change of becoming the musical.

47 The varieties of numerical sameness are discussed in *Topics* A7; cf. Chapter 4, Section 1.
48 Cf. (S2), Chapter 4, Section 1.

unmusical (i.e., Socrates + unmusical) must survive the advent of musicality.

Finally, the fact that Socrates and the unmusical are accidentally the same, but not identical, suggests that this last solution to the Paradox of Persistence, as with the solution to the Paradoxes of Becoming at the end of Section 4, simply sidesteps questions of the intensionality or otherwise of the linguistic contexts featured in the paradox.

6 Conclusion

The resolutions to the Paradoxes of Becoming and the Paradox of Persistence outlined at the close of the two preceding sections indicate two ways in which we can *separate* a substance and the compound of that substance with an accident – Socrates (say) and Socrates + musical – for all that they are accidentally the same. Contrary to the Paradoxes of Becoming, if Socrates becomes musical, the predicate 'Socrates has become … ' is true of Socrates + musical but false of Socrates; the resolution to the Paradox of Persistence upholds a similar conclusion for the predicate ' … persists through the change of becoming musical', which is true of Socrates but false of Socrates + unmusical. (As this example reminds us, Socrates and Socrates + unmusical are also separated by the fact that they may exist at different times if Socrates is not always unmusical.)

These predicates can be added to the growing list of contexts by which Socrates and Socrates + musical may be distinguished. We saw in Part II, in the discussion of the modal and epistemic paradoxes in the *Topics* and the *De Sophisticis Elenchis,* that Socrates and Socrates + musical may be distinguished in modal and epistemic contexts. They are also distinguished from one another by reference to various "metaphysical" predicates. For example, the predicate ' … is a substance' is true of Socrates but false of Socrates + musical. Conversely, the predicate ' … is an accidental compound' is true of Socrates + musical but false of Socrates himself.

Suppose now that both Socrates and Socrates + musical exist at a given time, so that at that time Socrates is accidentally the same as Socrates + musical. Does it follow that (say) Socrates is in the Agora if and only if Socrates + musical is there too? Our first inclination may be, quite correctly, to accept this consequence. But there is a complication. Aristotle denies that anything but an individual substance can be a genuine subject of metaphysical predication: it follows, then, that the accident, being in the Agora, cannot be metaphysically predicated of Socrates + musical, for this is an accidental compound and not a substance. It does not follow from this, however, that the *linguistic* predication 'Socrates + musical is in the Agora' can never be true. It is true, then, that Socrates is in the Agora if and only if Socrates +

musical is. But in the sentence 'Socrates + musical is in the Agora', we must not suppose that there is being expressed a relation of metaphysical predication between Socrates + musical and the accident in question. Rather, *two* relations of metaphysical predication are at work here, one between Socrates and the accident musical and another between Socrates again and the accident being in the Agora. These underlying metaphysical predications are brought out if we reparse the original, linguistic predication in the style recommended in the *Analytica Posteriora:* 'There is a substance, namely, Socrates, who happens to be musical and who is also in the Agora'.[49]

In sum, it is true of Socrates that he is in the Agora if and only if it is also true of Socrates + musical that it is there too, given that Socrates and Socrates + musical are accidentally the same. In contrast to this, however, it is true of Socrates that he is a metaphysical subject to the accident being in the Agora, but it is false of Socrates + musical that he is a metaphysical subject to that same accident.

We have now collected a variety of linguistic contexts that allow us to distinguish between Socrates and Socrates + musical. But (to repeat a moral already urged in Part II) the differences in truth value do not tend to show that the different contexts are intensional, much less that the distinction between Socrates and Socrates + musical is itself in any way an "intensional" one. If two things are accidentally the same, as Socrates and Socrates + musical are, it follows that they are *not* identical. So a principle of accidental sameness is not a principle of identity. But the notion of intensionality is defined around the concept of identity, and not any weaker relation. So a failure of a principle of accidental sameness has no consequences for the intensionality or otherwise of the contexts in question. If Socrates and Socrates + musical are merely accidentally the same, the relation between them is simply not strong enough for us to test for intensionality.

Similar conclusions can also be applied to the distinction between matter and the compound material substance. An individual substance, *a,* is in some sense an ingredient in, and also accidentally the same as, the accidental compound $a + \phi$. Analogously, the matter m is (in some sense) an ingredient in, and also *the matter of*, the compound material substance $m + \psi$. The matter of a compound substance and the substance itself are "one in number but two in account." But like the distinction between Socrates and Socrates + musical, this distinction too is not in any way an "intensional" one. The two are straightforwardly not identical: the fact, then, that what is true of the one is not necessarily true of the other is no occasion for surprise. Still less is it occasion for a diagnosis of intensionality.

49 See note 16 in Section 2 and the discussion in Chapter 2, Section 2, p. 57,

9

The Role of Matter in Form–Matter Compounds: Change and the Introduction of Matter in *Physics* A

After the largely theoretical discussion in Chapter 8, I turn in this chapter to Aristotle's own introduction of matter in the analysis of coming-to-be set out in the later chapters of *Physics* A. Aristotle's account proceeds in two stages, discussed in Sections 1 and 2. Aristotle explicitly claims that the opening parts of his analysis take in all cases of coming-to-be, but his first examples have to do with *accidental* change and run in terms of Accidental Compound Theory (ACT) (Section 1). But the account is quickly extended to take notice expressly of substantial change as well, and here the analysis proceeds in terms of the ontology of form, matter, and form–matter compounds (Section 2). Aristotle also suggests that his analysis of change provides an answer to the sceptical attack on change launched by Parmenides, and in Section 3 I try to say how this answer is supposed to work. The details of Aristotle's rebuttal are notably obscure. It hangs on the idea that one thing comes to be from another either "accidentally" (*kata sumbebēkos*) or strictly (*haplōs, kuriōs*), and Aristotle presses into service '*qua*'-clauses of the kind already considered in Chapter 8 to indicate how the different readings he has in mind will go. In Section 4 I check the reconstruction of his views offered in Section 3 against two quite different ancient accounts, and in Section 5 against one rival contemporary account.

1 A Paradigm for Change: How Socrates Has Become the Musical

Aristotle begins his official account of coming-to-be in *Physics* A7 by warning that his first remarks will apply generally, to all the varieties of becoming (189b30–2; cf. 190a13–14), so we may expect any details distinctive of particular kinds of becoming to be deferred to later in the discussion. Aristotle's first step is to lay out the form that our assertions of coming-to-be standardly take. Suppose that Socrates has come to be musical. Then we have

(1) Socrates has become the musical[1]

and

(2) The unmusical has become the musical

or even

(3) The unmusical man has become the musical man.[2]

At the same time, we can say by way of variation on (2) that

(4) From the unmusical, ‹he› has become the musical.

But there is no similar counterpart to (1); we do *not* say that

(5) From Socrates [or from ‹a› man], ‹he› has become the musical.

The acceptability or otherwise of these different locutions suggests that something does, and something does not, persist through the change in question.[3] If we can say that, from *x*, a thing comes to be musical, then in the usual case at least,[4] *x* does *not* survive the coming-to-be. Thus, we can say that the musical comes to be *from* the unmusical, for the unmusical does not persist through the change in question. But we do not say that the unmusical comes to be from Socrates, for Socrates does persist through the change.

The notion of persistence or not through a given change points to perhaps the central feature of Aristotle's theory. This is the claim that, in every change, there is something that comes to be ‹something› and that underlies the change (*dei ti hupokeisthai to gignomenon*, A7, 190a14–15), and that this is one in number but two in account.[5] There are *two* candidates for what underlies, then, and of these, Aristotle holds, one survives the change of becoming musical but the other does not.

What is the correct account of the ontology in which the distinction between the two kinds of underlying thing, or *hupokeimenon*, is real-

---

1 I have changed Aristotle's example to give 'Socrates', rather than his 'A man', as grammatical subject. I am also regimenting his examples somewhat: the definite article in the predicate 'Socrates becomes *the* musical' is present in some passages, not in others, but I take it to belong in the canonical version of the example. The point of so doing will emerge later in this section.
2 Sentence (3) makes it explicit, in a way that (2) does not, that something, namely, one and the same man, persists through the change in question. Meanwhile, (2) suggests only that change involves the replacement of one thing, the unmusical, by another, the musical. Cf. Waterlow (1982), p. 13.
3 190a9–13, 17–31, esp. 21–31; cf. Code (1976a).
4 Aristotle notes the exception at 190a24–6; cf. Section 2.
5 *Physics* A7, 190a13–17, b23–7, b36–191a3, A9, 192a1–34.

ized? Sentences (1) and (2) suggest appropriate candidates for what underlies: in the example, they are Socrates and the unmusical. As we have already seen in the discussion of the Paradox of Persistence (Chapter 8, Section 5), the difference between these is best understood in terms of ACT. In the case at hand, the unmusical is identical with Socrates + unmusical, where Socrates + unmusical is the accidental compound of Socrates with the accident unmusical and is *accidentally the same as* (but not identical with) Socrates himself.[6]

Aristotle argues that Socrates survives the change of Socrates' becoming musical but that Socrates + unmusical does not. In any change, moreover, we must be able to find entities that play these two parts: something that remains through the change and something else that does not but is succeeded by something newly created as a result of the change. The distinction between the two kinds of *hupokeimenon*, as we shall see in Section 3, gives Aristotle his answer to what he takes to be the argument by Parmenides that either nothing at all persists through a given change or, if anything persists, what emerges as a result of the change is identical with what existed before, so that in either case no change takes place after all.

Suppose that Socrates has now become the musical. On Aristotle's account, two factors contribute to making the change intelligible. The first is the continuing presence of Socrates, who enters into different sameness relations, while himself continuing to exist throughout. *One and the same thing*, Socrates, is both accidentally the same as the unmusical at some earlier time t and accidentally the same as the musical now. But the change is made intelligible also because we know that something gets *replaced* as a result of the change. When Socrates becomes the musical, Socrates + unmusical ceases to exist and is replaced by Socrates + musical. On this account, Socrates is involved at different times in accidental sameness relations that are mutually exclusive. They are mutually exclusive because they hold between Socrates and compounds determined by accidents (musicality and unmusicality, respectively) that are themselves mutually exclusive.

We can give these analyses of the two assertions of becoming, (1) and (2). First,

Socrates has become the musical if and only if
(i) there is an accidental compound, the unmusical, such that the unmusical = Socrates + unmusical,
(ii) the musical = Socrates + musical,
(iii) for some time t prior to now, Socrates + unmusical exists at t,
and
(iv) Socrates + musical exists now.

6 This is in line with the results of Chapter 8. A different view is discussed in Section 5.

Equivalently, Socrates is accidentally the same as the unmusical at t and accidentally the same as the musical now. Second,

> The unmusical has become the musical if and only if
>   (i) for some x, the unmusical = x + unmusical,
>   (ii) for some y, the musical = y + musical,
>   (iii) for some t prior to now, x + unmusical exists at t,
>   (iv) y + musical exists now, and
>   (v) $y = x$.

Equivalently, x is accidentally the same as the unmusical at t, and y is accidentally the same as the musical now, and $y = x$. The right-hand sides of the two definitions are, of course, equivalent if Socrates is the unmusical one in question.

2 Matter and Becoming

Aristotle's general account of change, which gets under way at the beginning of *Physics* A7, turns on the idea that, as we have seen, there are two kinds of thing that underlie any given change, and of these one persists through the change, while the other does not. At A7, 190a31–33, Aristotle finally separates the different kinds of change: qualified change, as when a thing comes to be *this* – for example, Socrates comes to be musical – and unqualified change, in which a substance comes to be. Aristotle emphasizes that there is something underlying in both kinds of change. More than this, in each of the varieties of change, there are again *two kinds* of underlying thing (190b23–7, b35–191a3). Although the point has sometimes been doubted,[7] it is reasonable to think that in each variety of change, the two kinds of thing that underlie are distinguished from one another in exactly the way Aristotle claimed in his general remarks at the beginning of the chapter. That is, the one persists, but the other does not.

Consider first the qualified change of Socrates' becoming musical. Here the two entities that underlie are Socrates himself and the accidental compound Socrates + unmusical. Socrates himself persists through the change in question, but the compound Socrates + unmusical manifestly does not. Consider next an example of unqualified change, in which a substance comes to be. For example, suppose that a bronze statue comes to be. What underlies in this case is, first, the matter by itself and, second, the compound of the matter with the appropriate privative form. Of these, the matter persists, but the compound of the matter and privative form does not.

Let ψ^0 be the privative form of statuelessness and ψ^1 its positive counterpart, the form of a statue, and let m be the bronze that is the

7 Jones (1974), controverted in Code (1976a).

matter of the statue, on which ψ^0 and ψ^1 in turn supervene. It is crucial to distinguish properly between m itself and the two compounds $m + \psi^0$ and $m + \psi^1$. The distinction is analogous to that in the case of qualified change between (say) Socrates and Socrates + unmusical or between Socrates and Socrates + musical. As Aristotle himself notes, the deficiencies of ordinary Greek do not make the distinction any easier. The point is brought out by a minor puzzle involving Aristotle's linguistic criterion for persistence. As a rule, Aristotle points out, if x comes to be from y, then y does not persist through the change in question. But we say that the statue comes to be from the bronze, and the bronze *does* persist through the coming-to-be of the statue.[8] The explanation for the anomaly is that there is in Greek no separate expression for the compound of the matter with the privative form (*Metaphysics* Z7, 1033a13–16). So we speak indifferently of "the bronze," plastering over the distinction between the bronze by itself, m, and the compound of the bronze with the privative form, $m + \psi^0$. There is the temptation, then, to ignore the central distinction Aristotle is labouring to make between the *hupokeimenon* that does persist, namely, m by itself, and the *hupokeimenon* that does not, namely, $m + \psi^0$.

For all the difficulties of marking the difference in ordinary Greek, the distinction between m and $m + \psi^0$ is crucial to Aristotle's account. Plausibly, most of the arguments for the view that contrary to what is being urged here, the matter does *not* persist through the coming-to-be of a substance are based on a confusion between m and $m + \psi^0$, so that the nonpersistence of $m + \psi^0$ is falsely taken to indicate that m by itself also fails to persist.[9]

In cases of qualified change, as we have seen, we may say either that Socrates or that the unmusical has become the musical ((1) and (2) of Section 1). The parallel between qualified and unqualified change for which Aristotle is arguing suggests two corresponding ways of talking in the case of unqualified change. We may say either that

(6) The bronze by itself, exclusive of the privative form, has become the statue[10]

8 *Physics* A7, 190a21–31; *Metaphysics* Z7, 1033a5–23. Other exceptions come to light at *Metaphysics* α2, 994a22–b6: the man comes to be from the boy, or the learned man from the learner, where (Aristotle seems to imply) that from which the coming-to-be takes place is only changed, or perhaps brought to maturity, but not destroyed (cf. a24, 26, with a31).
9 Cf. Code (1976a), pp. 361–3.
10 Cf. A7, 190a25–6, on Code's reading of the text ([1976a], pp. 359–61). Furth (1988), pp. 196–7, denies that the bronze *becomes* a statue on the grounds that this is tantamount to confusing different senses ("vertical" and "horizontal") of 'from which', although he admits that Aristotle himself does not always keep these two clearly apart (pp. 217–21). In any case, I take it that the paraphrase I am about to give for (6) avoids the confusions Furth has in mind.

or that

(7) The non-statue-shaped piece of bronze has become the statue.[11]

(Here the bronze by itself is m alone, while the words "non-statue-shaped piece of bronze" labour to pick out the compound, $m + \psi^0$, of the matter with the appropriate privative form.) We explain these two ways of talking as follows. First,

The matter m of the statue has become the statue if and only if
(i) there is a non-statue-shaped piece of bronze and a privative form, ψ^0, such that the non-statue-shaped piece of bronze $= m + \psi^0$,
(ii) for some positive form ψ^1, the statue $= m + \psi^1$,
(iii) for some t prior to now, $m + \psi^0$ exists at t,
and
(iv) $m + \psi^1$ exists now.

Equivalently, m is the matter of the non-statue-shaped piece of bronze at t and is the matter of the statue now. Next:

The non-statue-shaped piece of bronze has become the statue if and only if
(i) for some matter m and privative form ψ^0, the non-statue-shaped piece of bronze $= m + \psi^0$,
(ii) for some matter n and positive form ψ^1, the statue $= n + \psi^1$,
(iii) for some t prior to now, $m + \psi^0$ exists at t,
(iv) $n + \psi^1$ exists now,
and
(v) $n = m$.

That is, m is the matter of the non-statue-shaped piece of bronze at t, and n is the matter of the statue now, and $n = m$. The right-hand sides of the two definitions are equivalent if it is the same statue that has come to be in each case. As Aristotle predicts, the two definitions are parallel in form to the two definitions at the end of Section 1 for cases of qualified or accidental change.

3   Aristotle's Response to Parmenides

A crucial part of the account of Socrates' becoming musical, given in previous sections, involves the distinction between the two kinds of *hupokeimenon*, Socrates and the unmusical. We can test our account of these two against Aristotle's rebuttal in *Physics* A8 of the sceptical attack by Parmenides on coming-to-be. As we shall see, the main burden of Aristotle's reply will be that we must take account of *both*

---

11 Cf. *Metaphysics* Z7, 1033a8–10: "‹A thing› comes to be from the lack and ‹from› the *hupokeimenon*, which we call the matter (for example, both the man and the sick ‹one› comes to be healthy)."

entities, Socrates as well as the unmusical, if our description of Socrates' coming to be musical is to be fully satisfactory.

Parmenides' celebrated attack is founded on a dilemma. What is comes to be either from what is or from what is not, but of these, neither is possible. Suppose, for example, that Socrates has come to be the musical and that the musical has come to be from *what is*. What is, in this context, apparently, is either Socrates himself or the musical. If the musical has come to be from the musical, this plainly implies that the musical already exists before the change – but how can this be? It is of no help, Parmenides can argue, to say instead that not the musical but rather *Socrates* has become the musical. If Socrates has become the musical, then since Socrates now *is* the musical, it follows by the Paradox of Becoming (Chapter 8, Section 4) that again the musical has come to be the musical, or even that Socrates has become Socrates. That is, the alleged change is no change at all, and the supposedly new thing that results from the change has existed all along (A8, 191a30).[12]

Alternatively, the musical has come to be from what is not, that is, from the unmusical. Equivalently, the unmusical has become the musical. This, however, says no more than that the unmusical existed then but not now, and the musical did not exist but now does. On this showing, Socrates' becoming musical is not a change by a single subject at all, but simply the replacement of one entity by another. But without an account of how the previous existence of the unmusical is relevant to the new existence of the musical, this is the same as saying the musical is created *from nothing*.

The arguments just given flesh out the bare-bones argument by Parmenides reported at the beginning of *Physics* A8 that what is comes to be neither from what is nor from what is not, so that nothing whatever can come to be. Aristotle himself responds equally schematically to Parmenides' argument – not, as perhaps in Parmenides' case, for the sake of generality alone, but so that ultimately he can match up Parmenides' argument with his own generalized metaphysical notions of *matter* and the *lack*.

Against Parmenides, Aristotle argues that a thing *can* come to be from something – but (to this extent apparently agreeing with Parmenides), strictly speaking, *not* from what is and *not* from what is not. This, he claims, is no violation of the Law of Excluded Middle (A8, 191b26–7), as Parmenides would surely complain. What Aristotle denies is that a thing comes to be from what is *haplōs*, 'strictly', or that it comes to be from what is not *haplōs*. Part of his solution, then, must be that even if these are mutually exclusive, they are *not* also exhaustive alternatives. Instead, a thing can also come to be from what is or

---

12 Cf. Simplicius *In Phys.* 236. 21–2, 28–30, cf. 237. 1–2.

from what is not *kata sumbebēkos,* 'accidentally', where this allows two other, more promising possibilities in addition to Parmenides' original two.

There is virtual agreement that Aristotle's solution involves pressing the contributions of two ingredients in any change: broadly, the matter and the lack.[13] That is, there is something that endures through the change and also something that gets replaced as a result of the change. Beyond this lies disagreement. One disagreement involves ontology. Aristotle himself tells us that the matter and the lack are "one in number but two in account." But is it the identical thing that performs both roles? Or are the matter and the lack non-identical, but related by some sameness relation *other than* identity? We have already discussed this issue in the discussion of the Paradox of Persistence in Chapter 8 and reserve final comment on it for Section 5 of this chapter.

Disagreement of a different kind concerns the details of Aristotle's account. How are we to understand the various options that according to Aristotle give not only the two halves of Parmenides' dilemma, but also the two further options Aristotle himself finds acceptable? The difficulties here are so severe, and the different interpretations so radically divergent, that even the syntax of Aristotle's solution is in dispute. For example, what is the scope of the phrase '*kata sumbebēkos*'? Is Aristotle saying that a thing comes *kata-sumbebēkos*-from what is? or that a thing comes from what-is-*kata-sumbebēkos*? Alexander is reported to have considered both alternatives, coming down in favour of the second (Simplicius *In Phys.* 238. 6–14). Or finally, taking the qualifying phrase as a sentential operator, is Aristotle suggesting that *kata-sumbebēkos*, a thing comes from what is? Dogmatically here, I shall suppose that the last of these alternatives is correct. This choice is explained in the remainder of this section, and discussion of rival interpretations, ancient and modern, is reserved for the two sections that follow.[14]

Suppose, then, that Aristotle intends the qualifying phrases '*haplōs*' and '*kata sumbebēkos*' to govern the entire remainder of the sentence in each case:

---

13 Simplicius *In Phys.* 235. 12 ff., 25–6; cf. Aristotle *Physics* A8, 191b33–4, and Ross (1936), p. 497.

14 Comparable questions concern the syntax of the specific qualifications Aristotle applies in each case: '*qua* what is', '*qua* what is not'. I shall not try to settle these questions here. But I shall assume, without argument, that the '*qua*'-clauses should not be treated in isolation, but are best handled by way of a contextual paraphrase applied to the entire containing sentence. I have been helped in thinking about Aristotle's '*qua*'-locutions by the recent account in Bäck (1988), but I have not been able to attempt here anything like the thoroughgoing treatment he gives.

(i) *haplōs* (a thing comes to be from what is),
(ii) *haplōs* (a thing comes to be from what is not),
(iii) *kata-sumbebēkos* (a thing comes to be from what is),
(iv) *kata-sumbebēkos* (a thing comes to be from what is not).

By way of explaining these options, Aristotle tells us that if *haplōs* a thing comes to be from what is not, then it comes from what is not *qua* what is not – this is the *default* reading of the unmodified sentence 'A thing comes to be from what is not', where the filling in the phrase 'from ... ' is reduplicated immediately after the '*qua*': 'from what is *qua* what is not' (A8, 191a34 ff., esp. b6–10, 25–6). But if a thing comes to be from what is not *kata sumbebēkos*, "accidentally," then some *non*reduplicative qualification is needed.[15]

What do these suggestions amount to? First, Aristotle rejects schema (ii). For example, suppose that

(8) The unmusical (= what is not) comes to be the musical.

This claim has the default reading

(9) The unmusical *qua* the unmusical comes to be the musical,

where the subject expression in (8) is reduplicated immediately following the '*qua*'. If its default reading, (9), were true, then (8) by itself would be *appropriate*, or true *haplōs*. That is, contrary to Aristotle and Parmenides alike,

(10) *haplōs* (the unmusical comes to be the musical),

in line with schema (ii).[16] As it is, however, (9) and (10) alike are false, so that (8) is *not* appropriate, or true *haplōs*. Aristotle's new proposal is that, instead, it is true *kata sumbebēkos* (b13–15; cf. 17–18):

(11) *kata sumbebēkos* (the unmusical comes to be the musical).

That is, the preferred schema is (iv). So the proper expansion of (8) via '*qua*'-clauses will need some other, nonreduplicative filling after the '*qua*'; we may guess that the required reading is this:

(12) The unmusical *qua* what is comes to be musical.

The '*qua*'-clause points to the role of what is (i.e., the *matter*, Socrates [say], A9, 192a4–6) in addition to the unmusical, so that ultimately the sentence can be expanded into the full-blown paraphrase

15 Here I follow Aristotle's treatment of the doctor example at A8, 191a36–b10, esp. b4–5, discussed later in this section.
16 For purposes of discussing instances of schemas (i) through (iv), I will not distinguish between sentences of the two forms *x* comes to be from *y*, and *y* comes to be *x* – for example, the musical comes to be from the unmusical (= what is not), and the unmusical (= what is not) comes to be the musical. On this understanding, (10) is an instance of schema (ii), while (11) illustrates schema (iv). Similar conventions govern the later discussion of schemas (i) and (iii).

(13) Socrates (= what is: the "matter") comes to be the musical, and Socrates is the unmusical.[17]

Similarly, the target sentence

(14) Socrates (= what is) comes to be the musical

has the default or reduplicative reading

(15) Socrates *qua* what is comes to be the musical.

But as Aristotle and Parmenides agree, schema (i) is not acceptable; it is not the case that

(16) *haplōs* (Socrates comes to be the musical).

That is, (14) is not appropriate, or not true *haplōs,* and the default reading (15) is false. Instead, according to Aristotle, in line with schema (iii), we must suppose that

(17) *kata sumbebēkos* (Socrates comes to be the musical).

So some different, nonreduplicative filling following the '*qua*' is again called for:

(18) Socrates *qua* what is not, that is, *qua* the unmusical, comes to be the musical.

Sentence (18) in turn comes down to this conjunction of claims:

(19) The unmusical (= what is not: the lack, A8, 191b15–16, A9, 192a5, 6) comes to be the musical, and Socrates is the unmusical.

Aristotle rejects the underlying schemas, (i) and (ii), and so he also rejects (10) and (16), in which the initial statements of becoming, (8) and (14), are embedded. But it does not follow, and Aristotle does not say, that (8) and (14) themselves are false. The modality in (10) and (16) is exclusively *epistemic:* it is not *haplōs* the case that a thing comes to be from what is, or *haplōs* that it comes from what is not, because it is not *most enlightening* from an explanatory point of view, and hence *less appropriate,* to be told (just) that a thing comes from what is (i.e., from the matter), or (just) that it comes from what is not (i.e., from the lack). The most enlightening account, rather, is the one that mentions *both* factors, the matter and the lack, together.

The point that both (8) and (14) are true is crucial, since it secures that the two halves of Aristotle's treatment are not at odds with one another. The fact, for example, that the proper and complete account of the change in (19) contains (8) as a proper part does not force us to

---

17 Cf. note 14. My treatment of (12) here again follows what I take to be the proper resolution of the doctor case to be discussed in the main text.

think that a true sentence, namely, (19), contains a false sentence as a conjunct. But the occurrence of 'The unmusical comes to be the musical' in (19) is not unenlightening, as it is by itself in (8); for in (19), it occurs together with the supplement that Socrates is the unmusical. Similarly, the fact that (13) contains the target sentence (14) as a conjunct is unproblematic: (14) in isolation is unenlightening, but in (13), it is supplemented by the added information that Socrates is the unmusical. In this way, Aristotle's solution to one side of Parmenides' dilemma need not undercut his answer to the other.

At the same time, it seems that Aristotle must be mixing different senses of 'from' in the course of his account – one sense in which a thing comes properly from the matter and another in which it comes properly from the lack (cf. Section 4). But the switch in senses on the present account is harmless. It is precisely Aristotle's point that both senses together must be in play if we are to capture satisfactorily the different ingredients that are necessary to any change. A thing comes from what is, that is, from the matter – but not from this alone. It comes also from what is not, that is, from the lack, but again, not from this alone. The different senses of 'from' here are run inextricably together: using uppercase letters for this "fused" use, a thing comes both FROM the matter and FROM the lack.[18]

On the account given, Aristotle's response to Parmenides turns on the contrast between relatively more and less enlightening statements of change. There is a close parallel to this way of taking Aristotle's qualifying phrases 'haplōs' and 'kata sumbebēkos' in his discussion of the doctor example and cases like it at A8, 191b4–10, and elsewhere in *Physics* A and B. For example, suppose that

The doctor *kata sumbebēkos* builds a house.

The '*kata sumbebēkos*' does not attach to the subject phrase – 'the-doctor-*kata-sumbebēkos*' – nor to the predicate – '*kata-sumbebēkos*-builds-a-house'. Aristotle does not mean, even if it is true, that someone is accidentally a doctor, and he built a house, or that someone built a house accidentally. Nor does he mean even (taking the '*kata sumbebēkos*' to govern the entire remainder of the sentence) that it is an accident that one and the same person is a doctor and built a house. His point is, rather, that from the explanatory point of view, the bare statement

The doctor builds a house

is best expanded (keeping the reference to the doctor) to say that

18 Aristotle finds no difficulty in combining senses of 'from' – for example, at *Metaphysics* Z7, 1033a8–10, quoted in note 11, where a single occurrence of '*ek*' (= our 'FROM'?) is made to do duty for both meanings.

The doctor is the housebuilder, and the housebuilder built a house.

That is, he built the house in virtue of his capacity for housebuilding.[19]

With the doctor case, compare the claim at issue in the discussion with Parmenides that

The musical comes from the unmusical *kata sumbebēkos*.

Aristotle does not mean, even if it is true, that someone is now accidentally musical or that once he was accidentally unmusical. Nor does he mean even that, as a matter of accident, one and the same thing is musical and came from the unmusical. (And since for Aristotle all change is between contraries, it is a matter of necessity, not accident, that *if* a thing has come to be musical, then one and the same thing is musical and has come to be from the unmusical or some intermediate.) Instead, what the sentence comes down to is that

Something, Socrates (say), is the unmusical, and he, Socrates, comes to be the musical.

This is what Aristotle regards as the most revealing statement of the change at hand, and so the qualifying phrase *'kata sumbebēkos'* can be dropped.

It is crucial in this account that the *'kata sumbebēkos'* should introduce an epistemic and not an alethic modality. It is, again, an accidental fact that one and the same thing, Socrates (say), both is the unmusical and comes to be the musical. But this point is irrelevant to Aristotle's present purposes. From Aristotle's present point of view, the statement of change in its final, most revealing form does not warrant the qualification *'kata sumbebēkos'* at all.

According to Aristotle, I have argued, a proper statement of coming-to-be should refer to both the matter and the lack. How does this answer the problems Parmenides set out? Suppose that Socrates has become the musical. It follows that Socrates now *is* the musical; more precisely, he is accidentally the same as the musical. As we have already seen in Chapter 8, the relation of accidental sameness is not strong enough to support the inference to the paradoxical conclusion that the musical has become the musical. But the larger challenge Parmenides issues remains: can we coherently hold that the product

19 The Polycleitus example is similar (*Physics* B3, 195a32–b12). We say that Polycleitus *kata sumbebēkos* sculpts. This, however, is not to say that someone is accidentally Polycleitus, and he made a statue, or that it is an accident of Polycleitus that he built a statue. Nor even is it to say that it is accidentally the case that one and the same thing both is Polycleitus and built a statue. Instead, Aristotle holds that the causally most appropriate statement of the occurrence at hand is not that Polycleitus built the statue, but rather (bringing in his capacity for sculpting) that Polycleitus is the sculptor, and the sculptor built the statue.

of the change is not simply identical with what existed before? If we are to point to something that has been replaced as a result of the change, Socrates' part in the process of becoming must be supplemented by the role played by the unmusical, which in this case is identical with Socrates + unmusical. Thus, the musical comes to be from what is, that is, from Socrates, only in virtue of the fact that Socrates was once accidentally the same as the unmusical and that the unmusical has given way to the musical. In effect, then, we have explained what is new about the change: the unmusical has disappeared, and the musical has emerged to take its place.

Suppose, conversely, that we construct an account of the change that runs solely in terms of the part played by the unmusical. Must this account too be incomplete? This is the point at which Parmenides' other challenge comes into play. If a thing's coming-to-be is a matter of first the unmusical's existing and subsequently giving way to the musical in the way described, why not suppose that in fact *nothing* continues through the change? How is the account given different from the "replacement" theory, in which change is merely the replacement of one entity by another that temporally succeeds it so that, in the proper sense, no real change has taken place at all? Aristotle's response is to show that, after all, something exists throughout the change of coming to be musical and is the single subject of that change. If the unmusical exists at some earlier time, then for some individual substance, x, the unmusical = x + unmusical. Similarly, if the musical exists now, then for some individual substance, y, the musical = y + musical. Finally, since the unmusical has become the musical, $y = x$. That is, there is a single individual substance, Socrates (say), such that both the unmusical = Socrates + unmusical, and the musical = Socrates + musical. The persistence of Socrates across time as an ingredient in both the unmusical and the musical allows Aristotle to defeat the replacement theory and point instead to the existence of a single subject that persists through the change. It is true, then, that the musical comes to be from what is not, that is, from the unmusical – but it does so only insofar as the unmusical is accidentally the same as Socrates and Socrates persists through the advent of musicality.

According to the account given in previous paragraphs, Aristotle's answer to Parmenides turns on his ability to distinguish three distinct entities in the change in which Socrates comes to be musical: the unmusical, the musical, and, finally, Socrates himself. In Parmenides' own ontology, such distinctions are impossible: as Aristotle argues, Parmenides leaves no room for even the distinction between substance and accident (*Physics* A3, 186a28–32). In Aristotle's ontology, by contrast, we can not only distinguish among Socrates, the unmusical, and the musical, but also analyse the unmusical and the musical into their component parts: each is a compound of Socrates with the relevant accident, musicality or unmusicality. Aristotle can also specify the relation between Socrates and the unmusical: Socrates is *accidentally the same as* the unmusical. Comparably in the case of substantial change, where ψ^0 is the privative form and ψ^1 its positive counterpart, the matter m is *the matter of* both compounds, $m + \psi^0$ and $m + \psi^1$. So the results for Socrates' change to being musical hold generally for substantial as well as for accidental change.

4 Some Ancient Alternatives

Historically, Aristotle's qualifying phrase '*kata sumbebēkos*' has been taken to govern not the entire statement of coming-to-be, as suggested in the preceding section, but single words or phrases within the sentence. In this section, we consider two possibilities scouted by the Greek commentators Alexander and Simplicius (Simplicius *In Phys.* 238.6–14) that the phrase governs the 'from' or that it governs the verb 'is' or 'is not'. Both of these nonsentential options, as we shall see, have some support in Aristotle's text.

(i) Kata-sumbebēkos-from

At *Metaphysics* Z7, 1033a19–22, Aristotle says,

since neither would one say without qualification (*haplōs*) that the statue comes to be from ‹the› wood or the house from ‹the› bricks, if one looks at it carefully, since it is necessary that that from which ‹without qualification› a thing comes to be *changes*, but does not remain.[20] (Cf. 1033a11–13)

This passage seems to suggest a use of 'from' such that (a) x comes to be without-qualification-from y (i.e., *haplōs*-from y), only if y itself, changes as a result of the change and does not remain.[21] In this same use of 'from', presumably (b) x comes to be *with*-a-qualification-from y, only if y is matter and remains. Given these distinctions, Aristotle could respond to Parmenides by pointing out that his initial dilemma takes the following form: for any y, *either* a thing comes to be *haplōs*-from y and y is, *or* it comes to be *haplōs*-from y and y is not. This, however, he can rightly say, is not an instance of the Law of Excluded Middle, so it is not logically false to deny both alternatives. By way of a third, more promising option, Aristotle can suggest instead that a

---

20 My translation follows Code (1976a), p. 363. Cf. also *Physics* A7, 190a21–9, with Code's comments.

21 This is also the spirit of Aristotle's examples at the beginning of *Physics* A7 discussed in Section 1.

thing comes to be *kata-sumbebēkos*-from what is. By 'what is', arguably, Aristotle means the matter (*Physics* A9, 192a5–6). Then a thing comes to be only *kata-sumbebēkos*-from what is, since by (b), to say that a thing comes from the matter involves the less appropriate context for the relevant use of 'from'. At the same time, agreeing with Parmenides, a thing cannot come to be *haplōs*-from the matter; for by (a), what a thing comes from-*haplos* is not the matter, but the lack.

This account of how a thing can come to be *kata-sumbebēkos*-from what is, immediately rules out any corresponding explanation of the other half of Aristotle's response to Parmenides. If by 'what is' Aristotle means the matter, then plausibly, by 'what is not' he will mean the lack (A8, 191b15–16, A9, 192a5, 6). What, then, of Aristotle's further claim that a thing comes to be *kata-sumbebēkos*-from what is *not?* Presumably, Aristotle must mean that it comes less-appropriately-from the lack. But in settling the first half of Parmenides' dilemma, we agreed, following (a), that this was the *appropriate* context for the sense of 'from' in question. So getting straight on one side of Aristotle's response to Parmenides' dilemma undercuts our answer to the other.

Similarly, Aristotle concedes to Parmenides that a thing cannot come to be *haplōs*-from what is not, that is (we are supposing), not *haplōs*-from the lack. But according to (a) again, this is precisely the best-favoured context for the use of 'from' under discussion. If the *same* use of 'from' is in effect in both halves of the dilemma, then getting things right in one half seems to entail getting them wrong in the other half. Perhaps we should conclude that Aristotle has in mind a *different* use of 'from' in discussing the second side of Parmenides' dilemma. At *Physics* A7, 190b26–7, speaking of the matter, Aristotle remarks, "What comes to be comes to be not *kata sumbebēkos* from it." Similarly, at A9, 192a31–2: "By matter I mean that which primarily underlies each thing, from which as a constituent and without qualification (*enuparchontos mē kata sumbebēkos*) a thing comes to be." Here, then, we have a use of 'from' according to which (adding asterisks to mark this new usage) (c) *x* comes to be *haplos*-from* *y*, only if *y* is matter and remains.[22] But where the expectation in (c) fails, we say that (d) *x* comes to be *kata sumbebēkos*-from* *y*, where *y* changes and does not remain.[23]

Despite this, it is unlikely that Aristotle can be relying on a shift between 'from' and 'from*' in constructing his anti-Parmenidean alternatives. His argument, on the present account, turns on a contrast between proper and improper contexts in which 'from' can

---

22 This is what Waterlow calls the *constitutive* use of 'out of': Waterlow (1982), p. 11; cf. Chapter 8, note 2.

23 This account is the one apparently recommended by Alexander *apud* Simplicius *In Phys.* 238. 11–14.

occur: surely we have the right to expect that it is the *same* sense of the word whose propriety or the reverse is being considered in these different cases?

(ii) Is-kata-sumbebēkos, is-not-kata-sumbebēkos.

At *Physics* A9, 192a4–5, Aristotle writes,

And of these ‹we say that› the one, the matter, is not being *kata sumbebēkos*, but the lack ‹is not being› in virtue of itself (*kath' hautēn*).

Here he is picking up a point about the lack from his discussion earlier at A8, 191b15–16: the lack "is *kath' hauto* not being, without persisting."[24] In these passages, Aristotle seems to make room for qualified and unqualified uses of 'is' and 'is not'. Parmenides can be seen as arguing that for anything x such that a thing comes to be from x, either x is, without qualification, or x is not, without qualification. In fact, however, Aristotle might point out, we need accept neither alternative, for (again) 'x is without qualification' and 'x is not without qualification' are contraries, not contradictories. This is because in 'x is not without qualification', the 'not' governs the 'is', *not* the verb and the qualifier together ('is without qualification').[25] To provide a third alternative to Parmenides' two, on this account, Aristotle suggests (reworking one of Parmenides' alternatives) that a thing can come to be from what is-not-*kata-sumbebēkos*. An explanation is given by Simplicius, who follows Alexander in his account of how the qualifier *kata sumbebēkos* governs the 'is' and the 'is not'. Simplicius writes, "We say that ‹a thing› comes to be *kata sumbebēkos* from what is not: for a thing comes to be from the matter, insofar as the lack, which is *kath' hauto* not being, belongs to it" (*In Phys.* 238.4–5; cf. 237.24–5). According] to Simplicius, claims of the form 'x is not *kata sumbebēkos*' come to this: that something y is not (*without* the qualifier), and y belongs to x. Now Aristotle is explicit that the lack is-not-*kath'-hauto*. Further, there is a sense in which the lack "belongs to" the matter. The matter *is* the lack, that is, it is *the matter of,* or is *accidentally the same as,* the lack. For

24 In full, Aristotle says this: "We ourselves too say that nothing comes to be without qualification (*haplōs*) from not being, but that ‹a thing› comes to be in a way from not being, viz. *kata sumbebēkos*: for a thing comes to be from the lack, which is *kath' hauto* not being, without its persisting" (A8, 191b13–16). Taken as a whole, then, the passage gives equal support to the rival interpretation just discussed in which Aristotle's qualifiers, '*kath' hauto*' and '*kata sumbebēkos*', seem to modify the 'from' rather than 'is' or 'is not'.

25 Compare the pair 'John runs successfully' and 'John is successful in not running' (= 'Successfully, John does not run'), where the 'not' in the second sentence governs the verb 'runs' but does not include the adverb 'successfully' within its scope. These too are contraries but not contradictories: both, for example, are false if John runs, but does so ineptly or incompetently.

example, Socrates is accidentally the same as the unmusical. The matter, then, is-not-*kata-sumbebēkos*, and a thing comes to be from what is-not-*kata-sumbebēkos*, because it comes from the matter. But a thing does not come to be from what is-not-*haplōs:* that is, it does not come to be from the lack.

At the same time, working the other side of the street, Aristotle says that a thing comes to be from what is-*kata-sumbebēkos* but not from what is-*haplōs* (191b17–18). But if (as we supposed in the preceding paragraph) matter is what is-not-*kata-sumbebēkos* on account of its relation to the lack, then presumably it is our best candidate for what *is-haplōs* (240. 19–20): on its own terms, independently of its relation to the lack, it simply is. Further, we are told that the lack is what is-*not-haplōs;* presumably, then, the lack is what *is-kata-sumbebēkos:* it is, only by virtue of its relation to the matter, which is. Putting all this together, Aristotle's reworking of the second half of the dilemma will be that a thing comes to be from the lack, and not from the matter. As before, however, this claim is defeated by his reworking of the first limb, which seemed to say that the thing came from the matter, and *not* from the lack. On this account, Aristotle again has an answer to each limb of Parmenides' dilemma – but the two answers contradict one another. And once more, the only obvious means in sight of saving him from outright contradiction is to suppose that he has shifted senses of 'from' in moving between the two halves of the dilemma.

It is likely that our discussion so far has not exhausted the possibilities for understanding Aristotle's response to Parmenides on the nonsentential readings suggested by Alexander and Simplicius. It is also likely that similar difficulties in such readings will persist: on all nonsentential readings, I suspect, Aristotle's treatment of one half of Parmenides' dilemma apparently renders inadmissible his treatment of the other, unless we are willing to suppose that he is shifting between different senses of 'from' in different parts of his account.

In contrast to this negative result, on the sentential account given in Section 3 Aristotle contrasts two ways of taking statements of the form '*x* comes to be *y*' and 'From *x*, ⟨a thing⟩ comes to be *y*': they may not be appropriate as they stand and may have to be qualified by means of the suitable nonreduplicative '*qua*'-clause (the cautionary phrase '*kata sumbebēkos*' warns that this treatment is required); or they are true *haplōs* – they are appropriate as is and may be left *without* any qualification or given a merely reduplicative '*qua*'-clause along the lines sketched in Section 3. Even in the first case, however, where a nonreduplicative '*qua*'-clause is needed, the relevant contrast between the original statement of coming-to-be sans '*qua*'-clause and its qualified counterpart is not that the second statement is true, but the first, false. Instead, the original, unqualified statement comes up short *epis-*

temically, in contrast to its qualified counterpart, which with the addition of the appropriate (nonreduplicative) *'qua'*-clause is fully enlightening about the nature of the coming-to-be at hand. This solution, already outlined in Section 3, also admittedly requires a shift in senses of 'from'. But the shift here is unobjectionable. We no longer suppose that Aristotle is discussing the propriety or otherwise of 'from' – presumably, with a single sense of 'from' in mind. On the contrary, he is giving the rationale for why in any fully satisfying statement of coming-to-be, it is relevant to mention what a thing comes to be *from* in *both* senses of the word.

5   A Contemporary Account and the Distinction Between Socrates and the Unmusical Once More

On the account offered here, Aristotle's response to Parmenides gets its main force, not from contrasting true as opposed to false statements of coming-to-be, but rather from playing off against one another relatively more or less informative statements of the change. A similar point of view also appears in the recent account by Waterlow.[26] At the same time, there are some more or less minor differences between her account and that offered here, as well as one difference that is major. This last difference concerns the ontology involved in Aristotle's answer to Parmenides. Since Waterlow's account represents perhaps the majority view, it will be worth taking a separate look at the matter in this final section.

Waterlow holds that the controversy between Aristotle and Parmenides has to do with appropriate and inappropriate occurrences of designators on the two sides of the verb ' . . . becomes – '. If a designator occurs on the left-hand side of the verb, then it is implied that it points to some feature that *remains* through the change. Any occurrence of a designator for which this implication fails is inappropriate, and it earns Aristotle's cautionary phrase *'kata sumbebēkos'*. By these canons,

The unmusical comes to be musical

is not the best expression to the change at hand. The musical comes to be from the unmusical *kata sumbebēkos*, for on Waterlow's assumptions, 'the unmusical' is not the most appropriate description of what the musical comes to be from.

At the same time, if a designator occurs on the right-hand side of ' . . . becomes – ', then it is implied that it identifies the feature that newly emerges as a result of the change – what does the *replacing*. Any

26 Waterlow (1982), Chap. 1.

designator in this context for which the implication fails is inappropriate. By these canons, neither

Socrates comes to be Socrates

nor

The man comes to be (the) man

is the most appropriate expression of the change at hand. The second occurrences of 'Socrates' and '(the) man', respectively, are inappropriate and require the qualifying phrase '*kata sumbebēkos*' in each case.

On this account, Aristotle reworks the two sides of Parmenides' dilemma to provide this choice of alternatives: either a thing comes to be from what is not *kata sumbebēkos* or a thing comes to be what is *kata sumbebēkos*. Here, 'what is not' is a place marker for designators that convey what gets replaced as a result of the change, for example, 'the unmusical'. If 'the unmusical' appears on the left-hand side of an assertion of a thing's coming to be musical, then it occurs inappropriately, that is, *kata sumbebēkos*. Meanwhile, the phrase 'what is' is a place marker for designators conveying what remains through the change, for example, 'the man' or 'Socrates', which appear appropriately on the left-hand side of an assertion of Socrates' coming to be musical. If, on the contrary, '(a) man' or 'Socrates' appears on the *right*-hand side of such an assertion, then it occurs inappropriately, that is, *kata sumbebēkos*.

A number of elements in this account deserve comment. Waterlow supposes that the contrast between the alternatives Parmenides rejects and the more promising alternatives that Aristotle constructs out of them is not between true and false assertions of change, but between assertions that are appropriate and ones that are inappropriate but still (most likely) true. Specifically, for Waterlow, an assertion of coming-to-be is appropriate, if it contains the appropriate *designators*, which correctly signal what remains through the change and what newly emerges as a result of it, and inappropriate otherwise. As we shall see shortly, this is in sharp contrast to the account offered here, which is not at the level of language and runs instead in terms of an ontological distinction between the matter and the lack. But on both accounts, Aristotle attaches the qualifier '*kata sumbebēkos*' to an assertion of change to indicate not that the assertion is false, but only that it is in one way or another not fully appropriate. That is, the modality is largely if not exclusively epistemic.

Waterlow also avoids any shift in senses of 'from'. What a thing comes to be *from*, in her account, is what is appropriately named on the left-hand side of ' . . . becomes – ', and this is invariably the matter. In her account, 'from', then, is invariably 'from*' – what she calls *constitu-*

tive 'from'. On the account I have offered, there are shifts in the sense of 'from', but, I have argued, they are harmless.

But while the sense of 'from' remains constant in Waterlow's account, she accepts instead a shift in the scope of Aristotle's qualifying phrase '*kata sumbebēkos*' governing once the designator to the left of, and once the designator to the right of, the verb ' . . . becomes – '. This, I think, produces an odd result. How are we to understand Parmenides' original dilemma? Aristotle suggests fairly clearly that his two new alternatives to those Parmenides offered are obtained by adding qualifications to Parmenides' original two. If this is right, then on Waterlow's account, we must picture Parmenides' initial dilemma as taking this form: *either* a thing comes to be from what is not *or* it comes to be what is (sans Aristotle's qualification '*kata sumbebēkos*' in each case). It is hard to see why this dilemma is convincing, for the alternatives no longer even seem to be either exhaustive or mutually exclusive.

Finally, some central features in Waterlow's account of appropriateness or inappropriateness in our assertions of becoming are at odds with the account offered here. For Waterlow, appropriateness or the reverse in a given case is a matter of introducing a single entity under different names or descriptions, of which some are appropriate and others, perhaps many, inappropriate. She explains that one and the same thing, Socrates, remains under the description '(the) man' or the name 'Socrates' but is replaced under the description '(the) unmusical'. A similar idea appears in the account published in the same year as Waterlow's book by Bostock:

Before the change we have an object which can be described as a man (as an underlying thing) or as a thing that is not musical (as having a privation); *it is the same thing that is described in these two ways. Qua* underlying thing it persists throughout the change, in the sense that we have the same man at the end as we had at the beginning, but it can now be described rather as a musical thing. (1982, p. 184, my emphasis)

The same view had also been expressed earlier by Charlton:

The underlying thing is not a third factor over and above the opposites: it is the same thing as one of the opposites, *viz.* that from which the change takes place, but under a different description. . . . The man and the thing which is ignorant of music are the same thing under different descriptions. (1970, p. 73; cf. p. 79)

Views of this sort lead to a good many tangles, as we have seen in Chapter 8. Suppose that the two designators 'the unmusical' and 'Socrates' designate the same thing. Then '(the) unmusical' names Socrates, who remains through the change of becoming musical: so how can '(the) unmusical' be the appropriate designator for what is *replaced* as a result of the change? Similarly, 'Socrates' designates the unmusical, which is replaced in the change: how, then, can 'Socrates' be an appropriate designator for what *remains?*

An easy answer is that, for example, 'the unmusical' is an appropriate designator for what gets replaced as a result of the change, not because it *denotes* anything different from what 'Socrates' denotes, but because it has a different and more appropriate *sense.* So to talk of Socrates and of the unmusical is to talk of the same thing twice – but to talk of it differently because of the differing senses of the two expressions. If it is right, Aristotle's distinction between the matter and the lack cannot be an ontological one at all. His distinction instead marks out different ways of thinking or talking about one and the same thing.

Waterlow appears to accept this conclusion. At all events, having suggested that Socrates remains under one description but not under another, she adds the very different, and I think radical, proposal that it is the *description* '(the) man' or the *name* 'Socrates' that remains, and the *description* '(the) unmusical' that is replaced.[27] This new proposal expressly concedes that, on the account at hand, Aristotle's distinction between the matter and the lack is not a question of ontology at all, but is merely verbal.

I prefer to suppose instead that Aristotle's distinction between Socrates and the unmusical, or more generally between the matter and the lack, is after all an ontological one and not just a question of language. So our account of "more or less enlightening" for Aristotle cannot be that statements of coming-to-be can contain more or less appropriate descriptions of one and the same entity. What, then, *does* make an assertion of coming-to-be "most enlightening" for Aristotle? It can be such if it mentions the complete roster of entities immediately involved in the coming-to-be, rather than a partial list, and also indicates how in reality these entities are interrelated. Thus, a coming-to-be is fully intelligible when we are told the matter, the lack, and, finally, the terminus of the change. For example, if Socrates comes to be musical, we need to know the role of Socrates, who persists through the change, and also the parts played by the unmusical (i.e., Socrates + unmusical), which is replaced as a result of the change, and by the musical (= Socrates + musical), which does the replacing. On this account, the relevant contrast for Aristotle is between complete and incomplete lists of the entities immediately involved in a coming-to-be, and not between appropriate and inappropriate descriptions of the same entities.

27 Waterlow (1982), p. 14.

Complications and Refinements in the Account of Matter, Form, and Thing

Aristotle's theory of form and matter hardly stands still after its introduction in *Physics* A, recounted in previous chapters. The theory begins life as a means of extending the analysis of accidental change to the coming-to-be and passing away of an individual substance; the account of substantial change, as we have seen, quickly yields an analysis of the individual substance itself as a compound of matter and form. This analysis of the individual substance is tied immediately in *Physics* B to the theory of explanation, in which Aristotle's scheme of four causes is defended by the way each cause grips onto the form or the matter of the object under scrutiny. The idea that significant portions of the behaviour of a natural substance – a living plant or living animal – can be fully explained by reference to causes built around the twin notions of form and matter gives Aristotle a powerful tool that he puts to work in a bewildering variety of contexts, for example, in biology, cosmology, and psychology, to mention only some. These different applications to these widely different subject matters – which take Aristotle well beyond the terms of the original exposition of the theory on the pattern of accidental change, and well beyond his favoured explanations of matter and form in terms of artefacts, a bronze sphere or statue, for example – introduce considerable strain in the original theory, where they do not threaten to break its limits altogether. In particular, to cite just one example, in the biology and the psychology Aristotle must contend with his notion of *homonymy*, which seems to show that various biological structures that seem to fall on the side of matter must themselves be alive, and must themselves exhibit the form or soul of the living being they help constitute.

At the same time, Aristotle is also concerned with the enlargement of the conceptual apparatus of form and matter, in particular by way of the notions of potentiality and actuality. In the beginning, the notions of form and matter are closely associated with the analysis of change, and in conformity with this, matter can be connected with the potentiality for being made to constitute a product that exemplifies the corresponding actuality or form. These connections are apparently deployed in *Metaphysics* H6 to solve the problem of the unity of the compound material substance – of "what is the cause of the round and the bronze being one" (1045a28). But in *Metaphysics Theta* and in *De Anima* B, Aristotle develops different notions of potentiality and actuality, not connected with change, which he appears to say (*Metaphysics* Θ1, 1045b35–1046a2) are most of all relevant to the analysis of substance in *Metaphysics Zeta* and *Eta*.

Finally, various interpretive complications also press in. I have argued in this part that the distinction among thing, form, and matter is a real, ontological distinction: none of these three is identical with any other, and the distinction among them is not merely the product of various intensional contexts. No better than the intensionality hypothesis I mean to discard here is the idea that Aristotle's distinction among form, matter, and thing is instead an *intentional* one (with a "t"); that is, the distinction is an artefact of how we *look at* or *think of* the individual substance, but it has no counterpart "in the real order." This idea is tied to a passage in *Metaphysics* H6 in which Aristotle is often taken to say explicitly that the form and proximate matter of a thing are identical; further support comes from views about the nature of form, especially the hypothesis of *individual* form discussed throughout Part IV, and also from a reading of *Metaphysics* Z6 on the sameness in certain cases of a thing with its essence or form.

Despite the importance and complexity of these various questions, there is a large body of metaphysical theory in Aristotle that, for long stretches at least, proceeds independently of them, and my primary aim in this book is to get clear on this amount of theory first. But I shall close this part with some very brief and necessarily oversimplified remarks on some of the wider issues noted.[1]

An initial question addresses Aristotle's very first move, from the account of accidental change to views about substantial change and about the analysis of the individual substance itself as a compound of form and matter. This conception of individual substances takes Aristotle well beyond the views of the *Categories*. Aristotle drops the notion of Izzing from the primitive basis of his theory, and instead extends the idea that an individual substance Has its various accidents to say that matter too may Have a given form. How are these two cases of Having related? Are they exactly similar relations, differing only in the two kinds of application, so that the difference between the two

---

1 Some of the questions raised in this postscript are discussed further in F. Lewis (forthcoming).

halves of the new scheme of (metaphysical) predication is carried entirely by the difference between the relata – accidents or forms, individual substances or matter – in each case? Or are the cases so different that no single unitary notion can encompass them both? Or, to stake out a position intermediate between the two extremes, are they very different subrelations, each with its own distinctive features, but within a coherently single, unitary notion? Aristotle himself says only that "things underlie in two ways" (*dichōs hupokeitai; Metaphysics* Z13, 1038b5), which nicely straddles these different options. Of the three, I suspect that the intermediate option is the correct one. In the comparable case of the two kinds of (metaphysical) predication in the *Categories*, we would be willing to say that the relations of Izzing and Having are very different, but still make up a single recognizable notion of metaphysical predication, and plausibly, a single unitary notion also underlies two different specific kinds of (metaphysical) predication in the *Metaphysics*. If this is right, then a similar response is no doubt also appropriate for the notion of compounding thanks to which an accidental compound is constructed out of an individual compound and an accident, or a form–matter compound is obtained from matter and form. The two kinds of compound are very different and feature different specific notions of compounding; but a single generic notion of compounding, which plays a purely formal role in the construction of a single whole out of two disparate components, is also at work in both cases.

On this account, the difference in metaphysical composition between Socrates and Socrates seated has to do as much with the nature of the items from which each is generated as with differences in the relations of (metaphysical) predication that connect Socrates' matter with his form, or Socrates himself with his accidents. But the latter differences still deserve attention. The differences between the two relations form an important part of the argument of *Metaphysics* Z3 (on this, see the Introduction to Chapter 10, this volume). In particular, as I shall suggest here, the relation of (metaphysical) predication between form and matter is vastly more complex than its counterpart between Socrates and his accidents and is subject to a variety of pressures in different philosophical contexts.

The "two-stage" theory of (metaphysical) predication that appears in the *Metaphysics* in some ways can seem like a simple "downward" extension of the notion of cross-categorial predication or Having in the *Categories*. In *Physics* A, where form and matter are introduced, Aristotle himself talks as though the two cases run pretty much parallel to one another: at least as far as the account of becoming is concerned, he feels that he can safely generalize about both before coming down to specifics about either (A7, 189b30–2; cf.

190a13–14). At the same time, Aristotle suggests that we should be able to read off the metaphysical composition of the individual substance from the account of how it comes to be: this gives him his conclusion, that individual substances are compounds of form and matter. So there is also an obvious parallel between the result of predicating an accident of a substance – an accidental compound like the musical, Socrates seated, and the like – and compound material substances, which are the result of predicating form of matter.

But the two cases of (metaphysical) predication also differ in quite fundamental ways. One obvious point of difference is the multistep nature of the model featuring form and matter. What in *Physics* A Aristotle identifies as *the* matter of an individual substance – the bronze, for example, that is the *proximate* matter of the statue – is itself a compound of some further form and some further matter: and this further matter itself, no doubt, can be analysed in turn by reference to still other layers of form and matter, ending only when we reach prime matter.[2] In a partly fanciful passage at *Metaphysics* Θ7, 1049a19–27, for example, he imagines that a box is made out of wood, the wood out of earth, the earth out of air, and so on, down to fire, which for the purposes of this example counts as prime matter (a24–6, 27; cf. Chapter 6, Section 4). These complications by themselves make for a difference with the other half of Aristotle's system of (metaphysical) predication, which contains only a single layer, in which various accidents are predicated of their parent substances.

Still other complications have to do with how the theory of matter and form meshes with the account of change, specifically substantial change, whereby an individual substance comes to be or passes away. On Aristotle's conception of the relation between an individual substance and its accidents, a subject, Socrates (say), can in many cases at least cycle harmlessly through his accidents – for example, he is now pale, now dark, now pale again. If we looked only to *Physics* A, it is as though the same story could also be told about the relations among matter, form, and privation; this bronze, for example, loses its statue-lessness and comes to make up a statue, the statue is then melted down or hammered out of shape, the result is later fashioned once again into a statue, and so on without (in theory) any limit.

But even if, initially at least, the account of substantial change is modelled after that of accidental change, we will get the right results

---

2 Some, e.g., C. Williams (1982), pp. 211–19, have doubted that the notion of prime matter is coherent, others, e.g., Charlton (1970), pp. 129–45, that the notion is present in Aristotle; I believe that the sceptics are wrong on both counts, but the point is peripheral to my present concerns, and I will not try to argue it here. More recent sceptics, with an ingenious alternative account of the transformation of the elements without prime matter, include Furth (1988) and Gill (1989); Furth's account is criticized in Scaltsas (1989), p. 83.

only if we are working from the right variety of accidental change. Of the different kinds of accidental change an individual substance can go through, one is *alloiosis*, change in sensible quality, as opposed to (say) change in place. Some, but not all, cases of *alloiosis*, in turn, also involve *acting and being acted on by*: in this last set of cases, a substance, *a*, becomes actually φ from having been potentially φ, *by the agency of something (else) that itself is actually* φ (*GC* A7) – a thing gets heated up (say), as opposed to turning pale.[3] This gives the appropriate model for substantial change. In the account of substantial change too, in the standard case at any rate, we must be able to insert reference to an efficient cause that appropriately involves the form that will be the constitutive form of the product. The form is appropriately involved in cases of natural coming-to-be, for "it takes a man to beget a man": the efficient cause will be an actual member of the same kind as the offspring and will have the form of the offspring as its own constitutive form. In cases of human craftsmanship, by contrast, the constitutive form of the product is present only in the craftsman's mind.

In other respects, the theory of form and matter and the account of substantial change get worked out in ways that simply have no counterpart in the account of accidental change. In substantial change, significantly, the form of the product is implicated not just with the efficient cause, but also with the matter. In *Metaphysics* H5, Aristotle contrasts a "normal" product, for example, wine, and the "abnormal" product, vinegar, to which the normal one can give way. He continues to suppose that the same matter is present both in the normal product and in its abnormal counterpart. For example, *hudōr*, water, is the matter both of wine and of vinegar. But it is the matter of the one *kath' hexin kai kata to eidos*, "in accordance with the disposition and in accordance with the form," and of the other *kata steresin kai phthoran tēn para phusin*, "in accordance with a privation and a destruction that is contrary to ‹its› nature." Again, the water is *potentially* wine and also *potentially* vinegar, but the two potentialities differ in the same way (1045a1–2): the potentiality the matter has for the abnormal product vinegar is only a degenerate one. Properly, matter is matter *for,* and has the potentiality for, the normal product.[4]

At the same time, if wine turns to vinegar, its matter loses not just the features and capacities typical of wine, but also the capacity for having those features and capacities. If the matter now makes up the

---

3 In cases of accidental change that exemplify *alloiōsis* but *not* acting on and being acted on by – for example, when Socrates becomes pale – there is no efficient cause that is actually pale to transmit its pallor to Socrates, and the accident pallor preexists only in the sense that, before turning pale, Socrates is *potentially* pale; cf. Ross (1924) on *Metaphysics* Z8, 1033b5–6.
4 See also *Physics* A9, 192a16–25.

abnormal or undesirable product, it will have lost two degrees of potentiality at once. Accordingly, Aristotle now rejects the idea that the matter can cycle directly back and forth between the normal and the abnormal product, as Socrates (say) can cycle directly through being now pale, now dark. Wine, alas, may turn straight to vinegar, but the vinegar cannot change straight back to wine. Once the normal product $m + \psi$ has degenerated, it can be obtained again, if at all, Aristotle suggests, only after the degenerate product $m +$ (the degenerate counterpart of ψ) has first reverted to matter.

The addition of the notion of a *power* or *potentiality* (*dunamis*) to the account of matter is crucial. In *Metaphysics* Θ7, Aristotle argues that supposing the matter of a thing to be properly its *proximate* matter, the matter is *potentially* the thing in again some suitably immediate sense. For example, something is the matter of a house only if it has the appropriate passive *dunamis* for being made into a house once it comes into contact with an agent with the corresponding active *dunamis* and once the other realization conditions obtain (1049a5–12); or it must actually constitute a house as a result of the interplay of such *dunameis*. The upshot is a heavily top-down view of matter. According to Aristotle's settled view, matter is always the matter suitable for some *end:*[5] thus, the matter of a house includes rafters, beams, floorboards, and the like but, strictly, not just wood or timber.[6] And the matter of a man is apparently flesh and bone (Aristotle's stock account) or, better, a body with the appropriate organs.[7]

Aristotle's point is not just that something is the matter of a given kind of thing *only if* it can come to constitute (if it does not already constitute) a thing of that kind – that bricks (say) are the proximate matter of a house only if they can be built into, or actually have been built into, a house. Nor is he holding merely that it is a *necessary truth* that bricks are the matter of a house only if they are capable of being built (if they have not actually been built) into a house. More radically, his point is that it is *essential* to the bricks that they be the proximate matter of or for a house, and hence essential to the bricks that they be capable of being built (or actually have been built) into a house.[8]

The tie between matter and the passive power for being made into a thing of a given kind suggests that something is the matter of a thing only insofar as there exists a *process* for actually obtaining a thing of

5 *Physics* A2, 194a27–b9; *PA*, A1, 639b26–40a1, 642a12–14.
6 *lithoi, plinthoi, xula; Metaphysics* H2, 1043a15, *PA* A5, 645a34.
7 E.g., *PA* A1, 642a12–14; *De Anima* B1, 412a28–b6. Some of the complications these biological examples involve are discussed below.
8 Cf. Z15, 1039b9–30: matter has the nature such that it is capable of being and of not being; that is, it has the constitutive power, which may or may not be realized, for being made to constitute a so-and-so.

that kind from that matter.[9] If this is right, then this is a very different conception from the view of matter suggested in *Metaphysics* Z3 (see Chapter 10, this volume), where matter is thought of the way a metaphysician might think of it, as the result of mentally "stripping away" predicables to reveal the underlying subject. In Z3, there is no suggestion that this "thinking away" somehow traces in reverse the actual processes by which the finished thing was obtained from its matter, and the concept of matter seems to work entirely in abstraction from any actual or possible physical processes by which the thing did or could come into existence.

The top-down view of matter gets further support from Aristotle's notion of homonymy. Very roughly, a thing is homonymously a so-and-so, according to Aristotle, when it is not able to behave in the way typical of members of its purported kind. For example:

A corpse has the same shape and form (*tēn autēn tou schēmatos morphēn*),[10] but yet it is not a man. Again, a hand constituted in any old way, for example, a bronze or a wooden one, cannot be a hand except homonymously, like the doctor in a painting. For it will not be able to perform its own work, just as flutes of stone cannot ‹perform› their work, or the doctor in a painting. Similarly to these cases, none of the parts of a corpse is still of such a sort, I mean for example an eye or a hand. (*PA* A1, 640b34–641a5)[11]

In this passage, as often elsewhere, Aristotle's explanation of homonymy comes with examples of two kinds: *either* a thing that has the wrong matter to perform as members of its purported kind should *or* a bodily part that has lost its ability to do its proper work because the animal has died or because the part has been severed from the living animal. But this account of homonymy will require some sharpening. Of the two kinds of example Aristotle gives, eyes of stone and, in general, parts with the wrong matter are not a serious possibility in the real biological world. Imaginary cases such as these successfully illustrate one facet of homonymy – the failure of a thing in such a state to do the work proper to its purported kind. But they fail to capture an asymmetry that I take to be an essential feature of homonymy in the real biological world. In cases where the matter is wrong, there is no chance that the thing ever has performed or ever will be able to

9 Here I have been influenced by a remark in conversation by Michael Frede.

10 These are words that can indicate Aristotle's own notion of form, but as his discussion of Democritus in the lines immediately preceding the passage quoted suggests, the "shape or form" that a corpse shares with a man constitutes too thin, or "Democritean," a concept of form, that is suitable at best for artefacts (and not even for all of these), but that stops well short of a properly Aristotelian conception.

11 Cf. the continuation at a18–33. Other passages in Aristotle that address this topic include *Meteorologica* Δ12, 389b31–390b2; *De Anima* B1, 412b18–22; *GA* A19, 726b22–4, B1, 734b24–7, 735a7–8; *Metaphysics* Z10, 1035b23–5, Z11, 1036b28–32, Z16, 1040b5–16.

perform in the way expected of members of its purported kind; for example, a stone flute never has sounded, and never will sound, a note, and an eye of stone never did, and never will, see. By contrast with this kind of case, a severed hand, for example, or the hand of a corpse, *once had* the ability to perform as hands should but *has now lost* that ability. This asymmetry is an essential ingredient in the biological cases of homonymy.[12]

We have seen that matter essentially has the potentiality *for* some standard product, best of all, for a natural substance. Homonymy gives the other side of the story: it has to do with a falling away from the standard product, where a homonymous man (say) or a homonymous hand is the *lapsed* state of a substance or its parts.[13] These two sides of the story – the passive power in the matter for the product and the homonymous product that has fallen away from its proper state – both contribute to the strongly teleological cast of Aristotle's philosophy of nature.

But the notion of homonymy has also been taken to suggest that, in certain cases, the tie between matter and thing is even closer than anything suggested so far. As Ackrill explains in an influential paper, in the case of living things,

> the matter is itself 'already' necessarily living. For the body is this head, these arms, etc. (or this flesh, these bones, etc.), but there was no such thing as this head before birth and there will not be a head, properly speaking, after death. In short – and I am of course only summarizing Aristotle – the material in this case is *not* capable of existing *except* as the material of an animal, as matter *so in-formed*. The body we are told to pick out as the material 'constituent' of the animal depends for its very identity on its being alive, in-formed by *psuchē*. (1972–3, p. 126)

I am inclined to think that the view of matter Ackrill suggests is correct for the set of cases he discusses here and given a certain conception of matter.[14] But I am less convinced that Aristotle's notion of homonymy plays a role in establishing these conclusions in the way Ackrill goes on

12 The asymmetry is also responsible for the complication noted two paragraphs below in the main text.
13 Cf. *PA* A1, 641a18.
14 The concession is a guarded one. I suppose that what Aristotle identifies as the proximate matter of an animal, namely, its living body, is essentially endowed with the kind of life typical of that animal. But this is not to say that, in general, matter is essentially alive, or even that on *each* of the different possible conceptions of the proximate matter of an animal, the proximate matter essentially has the kind of life typical of the animal itself (on the "different conceptions" hinted at here, see the remarks later in this postscript). I also do not mean to accept the suggestion that there is any particular difficulty about "picking out" or referring to the matter independently of the form, even if the latter is essential to the former in the way Ackrill says; cf. the remarks at the end of Chapter 6, Section 2, and note 18, this chapter.

to suggest.[15] Homonymy shows only that it is essential to the animal's matter that it not have *lost* the relevant form, and it is consistent with this that the matter should exist *before* the relevant form is present. If homonymy is always associated with the decline of a thing rather than its development, we should perhaps allow that flesh as it develops in the fetation is after all flesh, even if it cannot yet fulfil all its functions before the whole creature is fully formed (*GA* B5, 741a10–13).

Even if the notion of homonymy does not support Ackrill's conclusions, however, I suspect that Aristotle's definition of *soul* in the *De Anima* does. For example, imagine an animal whose constitutive form or nature is the capacity for perception, that is, sensitive soul or *psuchē aisthetikē*. Aristotle's definition of *soul* apparently commits him to the view that the matter of sensitive soul is a body with the appropriately functioning sense organs.[16] On this view, the sense organs that help constitute the matter of the animal must themselves, in their own right, have the capacities typical of sensitive soul.[17] If so, two conclusions apparently follow: sensitive soul is *essential to* the sense organs, so that the form is essential to the matter on which it supervenes; and what appears to come to the same thing, the sense organs, and hence the matter of the animal, cannot exist independently of the animal itself. In general, then, in at least a certain range of cases – perhaps artefacts are excluded – the form that supervenes on a given matter is also essential to it, and not only is matter essentially matter *for* a given product, but also in an important set of cases, it cannot exist independently of the product.

---

15 "[Aristotle's] account of the body and bodily organs makes unintelligible, given the homonymy principle, the suggestion that this body or these organs might lack or have lacked *psuchē*" (Ackrill [1972–3], p. 126).

16 The definitions in *De Anima* B1 have a special logical character that Aristotle comments on by implication later in *De Anima* B3. A definition of soul, he says, should not be a common formula, which applies in the same way to all the different varieties of soul, but is proper or peculiar to none (*oudenos . . . tōn ontōn idios logos oude kata to oikeion kai to atomon eidos*, B3, 414b26–7). Instead, the definition he gives in B1 is more properly a definition *schema* and applies *differently* to each of the different kinds of soul. But since the different kinds of soul are arranged in a natural sequence, the way in which the general schema for definition is understood varies systematically according to the place the kind of soul under discussion occupies in that sequence. A given kind of soul, by the lights of Aristotle's definition schema, will be the *relevant* first actuality, paired off with a natural body that potentially has the relevant kind of life, that is, a body characterized by the relevant set of organs. Accordingly, *psuchē aisthetikē*, to take a particular kind of soul, is the first actuality of a body whose characteristic organs are *sense* organs.

17 I take it that Aristotle's view that the matter of sensitive soul must be a body with the appropriately functioning sense organs cannot be the triviality that the matter in question includes the appropriately functioning organs *in virtue of its being matter to sensitive soul;* instead, I take it, it is a *precondition* of being matter for sensitive soul, to be explained independently of being matter to sensitive soul, that the matter be alive in the appropriate way.

It is important to see that this conclusion goes well beyond the points urged earlier, that matter is teleologically driven and that it is essential to bricks (say) that they be capable of being built (if they are not already built) into a house. These claims by themselves come nowhere close to the conclusion suggested by the *De Anima* that the form or soul that supervenes on a given matter is essential to it, so that the matter of an animal cannot exist without that form or soul.

The idea that, in certain cases, a form is essential to the matter on which it supervenes lies behind a number of often puzzling, and at times outright sceptical, conclusions. In particular, according to Ackrill, it follows in such cases that the form supervenes essentially on the matter – that is, the relation of supervention itself is essential.[18] At the same time, there are also reasons for thinking that the relation of (metaphysical) predication holds *accidentally* between form and matter in every case. I shall look briefly at two questions one might raise in this connection.

Is (Metaphysical) Predication in All Cases Alike an Accidental Relation?

Plausibly, an accident is predicated *accidentally* of the compound substance. To the extent that the relation between form and matter is patterned on that between an accident and its parent substance, this raises the possibility that the predication relation between form and matter is also in all cases accidental. A rather more substantial argument for the same conclusion comes from the idea (Chapter 11) that in the *Metaphysics* the relation of (metaphysical) predication and the substance-of relation are *mutually exclusive*:

18 Ackrill (1972–3), pp. 124 ff. There are other puzzling conclusions as well. For example, Ackrill appears to suppose that if the form is essential to the matter, then it will not be possible to pick out or identify the matter in a way that is logically independent of the form; but if the matter cannot be specified independently of the form, he suggests, it is hard to make sense of the idea that the form and the matter together make up a compound in some nonstandard but still recognizable meaning of 'compound' (Ackrill [1972–3], p. 124; cf. Modrak [1985], p. 96). The idea that a thing's matter cannot even be specified without reference to the form is expressly taken to be one of Ackrill's conclusions in Burnyeat (forthcoming), but the shift from metaphysical notions (the form is *essential to* the matter) to epistemological ones (the matter *cannot be identified* independently of the form) is well criticized in Charles (1988), p. 36 (cf. Chapter 6, note 22). Another consequence some have argued for is the idea that Aristotelian matter is not (in our sense) purely material: that the proximate matter of an animal is necessarily *living* matter, while there is no level of matter *below* its living flesh and the like that escapes the animal's form or soul – no matter, that is, that is *not* necessarily living. There is some discussion of this last point in F. Lewis (forthcoming); the case for the overall view of (biological) matter and its negative consequences for the functionalist interpretation of Aristotle's philosophy of mind in particular are spelled out in a trenchant paper by Burnyeat (forthcoming).

x is the substance of y only if x is not (metaphysically) predicated of y.

Now it can be shown that one thing is the substance of another, just in case the first is also the essence of, and the definition of, the second.[19] The narrow notion of mutual exclusivity governing (metaphysical) predication and the substance-of relation, then, can be broadened to become a contrast between (metaphysical) predication, on the one side, and relations involving essence or definition or substance, on the other:

> x is the substance or the essence or the definition of y only if x is not (metaphysically) predicated of y.

At the same time, Aristotle recognizes *reduced* cases of the substance-of relation and also of the relations 'x is the essence of y' and 'x is the definition of y'. For example, a form is in the primary sense the substance of one thing, namely, itself, but in the reduced sense it is the *substance of* *another*, namely, the compound material substance of which it is the constitutive form.[20] One common theme, however, is preserved in all the different cases. In all the secondary cases alike, some counterpart of mutual exclusivity holds. That is, Aristotle is committed to holding that

> x is the substance or the essence or the definition of y, in either the primary or in any secondary sense of these notions, only if x is not (metaphysically) predicated of y.

If this general version of mutual exclusivity holds, then we have a powerful reason for thinking that where a form is (metaphysically) predicated of a given matter, what is predicated is not even in any reduced sense essential to its subject. On this showing, (metaphysical) predication in the *Metaphysics* is in all cases an *accidental* relation between a predicable and its subject, not only when an accident is predicated of a compound material substance, but also when a form is predicated of matter. Thus, where a given matter, m, Has a form, ψ (equivalently, ψ supervenes on m), it is possible that m should exist and yet *not* Have ψ. For example, the bronze that is the matter of this statue, and hence Has the form of a statue, might still exist even if the statue did not; that is, it might exist, yet fail to Have the form of a statue.[21]

The idea that the predication relation between matter and form is accidental runs into an immediate objection based on an application of

---

19 See Chapter 11, note 10, and, for greater detail, F. Lewis (1984).
20 Cf. the references in note 19. The asterisk notation signals that this is a separate, nonstandard case of the relation in question, with its own distinctive properties; see F. Lewis (1984).
21 Cf. *Metaphysics* Z15, 1039b29–30, and Ackrill (1972–3), p. 125.

Aristotle's notion of homonymy to matter. In the biological world, the various parts that make up the matter of an animal are what they are *homōnumōs*, 'in name only', if they have lost the appropriate form or soul. Ackrill argues that this result puts Aristotle directly in conflict with the anti-essentialist principle being defended here: Aristotle apparently is committed to saying that, in the relevant cases, the matter on which form supervenes Has a predicable it could not possibly fail to Have, where by this we mean that it would no longer exist, or would exist only homonymously, if it failed to Have the form in question.[22]

These questions about homonymy and its application to the relation between form or soul and the body on which it supervenes as matter take us well beyond the intended scope of this book. I shall briefly mention two points here. First, I have argued that homonymy applies *a*symmetrically in the biological world: by homonymy, it is essential to a given part that it *not have lost* the form that supervenes on it, and it is formally consistent with this that the part exist but not yet have taken on the form in question. Aristotle's discussion in the *De Anima,* however, does suggest a conception of matter and form on which the form is essential to the matter on which it supervenes, so that the matter can exist only for as long as it Has the relevant form. Second, and more important, even if the results Ackrill describes hold for the cases in the *De Anima* that are his main subject, it is not clear that they hold for matter across the board, or even that they hold on every possible conception of the matter and form of a living animal. I have argued that a prime component of Aristotle's theory of matter is the idea that a thing's matter is what has the potentiality for being made to constitute (if it does not already constitute) a thing of that kind. (This is in line with the initial connection in *Physics* A between matter and the analysis of change.) But the living body clearly does not have the potential for being made to constitute the living animal in the way this idea requires. For a notion of matter that does involve change and process, we must look elsewhere, specifically to the embryology, where (I would argue) the successive varieties of soul – nutritive, locomotive, sensitive – that are introduced at different stages in the development of the fetation create different levels of matter, ready to be transformed by the arrival of the next level of form into an item of a yet higher level, until finally the finished animal is produced. These different embryological stages present an alternative notion of matter that restores the connection with change or process – and one that is free of the troubles we have been considering. Matter at each stage can

22 Ackrill (1972–3), p. 126.

be essentially what it is, *independently* of the form or soul that supervenes on it.[23]

Perhaps, then, the conclusion we should settle for is this. Variant conceptions of matter undoubtedly exist, as divorced from considerations of change as the metaphysician's conception in *Metaphysics Z3*, already mentioned – for example, the idea in the psychology that the body with sense organs, essentially capable of sensation, is as matter to sensitive soul as form, or that the body with a heart and blood vessels, essentially capable of nourishment and growth, is as matter to nutritive soul.[24] It is a topic for another day to ask what purpose these

23 Ibid., pp. 131–2, draws attention to the different kinds of soul involved at the different stages of the embryological development of a human being (say) and notes that (had the development of the creature been suitably frustrated) "the human body might have remained at the merely vegetable or merely animal stage" or "might have failed to develop beyond the animal stage." But, Akrill argues, there is no real comfort here: the relation of sensitive (animal) soul to the body of the human fetation at its animal stage, for example, is open to the old problem that the body at this stage is necessarily living in precisely the way conferred by sensitive soul. My suggestion is that we should look instead at the relation between sensitive soul and *what developed into the animal stage of the fetation*, namely, the fetation in its still earlier, plantlike stage. This is the notion of matter associated with change, and as Akrill himself notes, had things gone differently, it might have stayed merely vegetative; that is, its relation to the form or soul that supervenes on it is accidental.

It is also worth noting the rather different strategy for finding a notion of the matter of an animal that is not in the grip of the animal's substantial form or soul offered in Cohen (1987). Cohen concedes that the body of the animal is essentially living but suggests that there is a different entity, call this the animal's BODY, that has accidentally the properties the body has essentially. Unlike the body, then, the BODY is not essentially characterized by the substantial form or soul of the animal. Having attempted a similar device in earlier versions of the present work, I am now unconvinced that textual evidence exists that Aristotle acknowledged the existence of anything like the BODY, much less the extension that presumably would be required of the BODY–body distinction to the lower levels of matter in the animal. More importantly, the move to the BODY does nothing for what I take to be Aristotle's primary conception of matter, namely, matter associated with change. Cohen complains that, on Akrill's picture, Aristotle's view that the relevant soul or form is essential to the body is based on diachronic or developmental considerations: Aristotle means to deny that there exists a nonliving body that is potentially alive, so that the body takes on life, Frankenstein-like, after a previous inanimate existence (Cohen [1987], p. 119; the original of the Frankenstein objection, more prosaically phrased, is in Alexander, *De Anima Mantissa* 104. 11–17). Cohen himself holds that Aristotle's point has nothing to do with change; accordingly, it is harmless to suppose that there exists such a thing as the BODY that is only accidentally but not essentially living. My own view is that Akrill is correctly answered by pointing out that if Aristotle is concerned with change, the living body is no more a suitable candidate for the matter involved in the coming-to-be of an animal than the BODY is. If the challenge is to find a notion of the matter of an animal suitable for the analysis of change, the right place to look is among the different stages of embryological development, in which each preceding stage is matter for its successor, and there is no question of the matter's being already in the grip of the form or soul that is about to supervene on it.

24 I have similar reservations about the sequence, nonuniform–uniform–simple, in the physiology (Chapter 6, note 44), which again does not seem to recapitulate the stages in the development of an animal.

variant conceptions serve or how they are related to what I take to be the standard conception defined around the notion of change. The variant conceptions of matter involve very different and quite likely problematic views of how matter is related to the form that supervenes on it or to the animal it constitutes. But these are very different notions of matter, and whatever difficulties they may encounter leave the standard conception of matter untouched.

I have been arguing for the idea that on what I have called the standard view of matter and form, a compound material substance is the result of a relation of (metaphysical) predication between form and matter that is *accidental* in every case. Another set of difficulties related to this idea involves the kind of *unity* the compound substance will have on this account. If the form supervenes *accidentally* on the matter, can Socrates (say), who is a compound of matter and form, enjoy a unity any better than that of the accidental compound Socrates seated, which according to Aristotle is only an accidental unity?

Do the Two Kinds of Compound Have the Same Kind of Unity?

Accidental compounds, according to Aristotle, are accidental unities and beings *per accidens*. Individual substances, however, are apparently beings *per se* – must they not also exhibit a greater degree of unity than accidental compounds? Some qualifications about the status of compound material substances must be issued at the start. In *Metaphysics* Z11, Aristotle denies that "anything said by virtue of one thing's being in another ‹which is› its subject as matter" can be *primary* (1037b3–4; cf. Z4, 1030a10 ff.), and a remark in Z6 suggests that what is not primary is also not a *kath' hauto legomenon* (1032a5). And it is clear on other grounds too that there is some backtracking on the standing of individual substances as compared with the account in the *Categories*. For all this, the relation between the matter and form that together make up a compound substance is closer than that between an individual substance and its accident within an accidental compound, where accident and substance are "many whenever the one does not belong to the other, and one only whenever it does belong and when the subject (*to hupokeimenon*) undergoes some modification" (Z12, 1037b14–18). I cannot agree with Kosman that the difference between the two kinds of case is so great that a "relational" account is appropriate only in case of an accidental compound, while – contrary apparently to the evidence of *Metaphysics* Z11 – "the being of a substance is not thus relative to an independent substratum," since there is no "independently identifiable subject."[25] But a compound sub-

---

25 Kosman (1987), pp. 364, 367. On this point, Kosman stands in a tradition of scepticism about the claim that form is (metaphysically) predicated of matter; there is a

stance is still better off as regards its unity than an accidental compound. We expect a greater degree of stability of compound substances than we do of accidental compounds, for they are members of kinds as accidental compounds are not.[26] More significant still, the existence of compound substances *supports* the formation of accidental compounds. The accidental compound Socrates seated, for example, is compounded out of the relevant accident and the compound substance Socrates, where Socrates can exist separated from Socrates seated, but not vice versa, so that the former is prior in substance to the latter (for the notion of priority at work here, see, e.g., *Metaphysics* Δ11, 1019a2–4). So the very idea that the *per accidens* being Socrates seated is constructed out of Socrates and the appropriate accident, both of them beings *per se,* by itself requires that the compound substance exhibit a greater degree of stability and unity than the accidental compound is capable of.

This picture is borne out by a look at the composition of the two kinds of compound. In part, they differ in that different specific notions of (metaphysical) predication or different specific notions of compounding are involved in putting each kind of item together from its metaphysical constituents. Below the level of the generic relation of (metaphysical) predication or the generic notion of compounding the

response to this scepticism in Chapter 6, Section 2. Kosman's views are also based on his reading of Aristotle's discussion of the unity of substance in *Metaphysics* H6 and what he regards as the culmination of the argument of *Metaphysics Zeta* and *Eta* in *Theta*, where, according to Kosman, Aristotle explains a new sense of *potentiality* and *actuality*, not associated with change, that completes the account of substance in the previous two books. Kosman takes Aristotle to say at the end of H6 that the matter and form of a thing are identical; the account of potentiality and actuality in *Theta* is then supposed to explain how they can be the same, yet exist at different levels of actuality. I argue elsewhere that the "identity" reading is not the only or even the easiest reading of Aristotle's Greek in H6. Beyond this, the view that matter and form are identical raises the question of their relation to the thing of which they are the matter and form. Kosman appears to hold that all three are identical and distinguished not "in the real order" (Sellars' phrase [1967], p. 118), but only in different ways of thinking about one and the same thing. Quite apart from the suitability of the appeal to intentionality to distinguish some of the major players in Aristotle's ontology, these views raise questions about the nature of form: they apparently require a notion of individual form such that the form of a natural object is proprietary to that object alone and will not be the form of another object of exactly the same kind. Other questions concern the conception of matter: if (concurrent) matter and thing are identical, then by the Law of the Indiscernibility of Identicals, the same matter cannot persist before or after the thing exists. Instead, in the paradigm cases of substance at least, that is, the living creatures of the biological world, the substantial form of the thing is essential to the matter: the substantial form or soul of the animal has the matter forever in its grip, and the matter cannot exist outside (conceptually *or* physically outside) the living animal. At the same time, there will be no matter in the constitution of the animal *low enough* to escape the animal's form or soul. This is not the place to tackle these issues, but they are discussed in a preliminary way in F. Lewis (forthcoming).

26 See, e.g., *Metaphysics* I9.

relation that ties Socrates' form to his matter is not exactly the same as that linking Socrates himself and the accident being seated. For this reason alone, we should not worry that the looseness of the connection between a thing and its accidents will be reproduced exactly in the relation between form and matter.

The differences between the two kinds of unities can also be traced to differences in the kinds of item entering into their composition. An accidental compound is constructed out of items in different categories, of which just one, the parent entity or subject, but *not* the predicable, is in the category of substance. Compound material substances, by contrast, are put together out of a form, which in the *Metaphysics* Aristotle counts as a substance par excellence, and matter, which is a potential substance (H2, 1042b9–10; cf. 1, 1042a27–8, H6, 1045a29 ff.), or better, which has the potentiality for being made to constitute an individual substance of a given kind. Now Aristotle appears to suggest in *Eta* 6 that the conception of form as actuality to matter as what is only potentially the substance by itself solves the problem of the unity of substance, even if, as is often suggested, many of the needed details are not given until later in Book *Theta*. Quite apart from the details of the positive story, the view at least protects Aristotle against the difficulty, set out at the end of Z13, that we cannot make a substance out of two substances, both of which exist in actuality (1039a3–24). Even without the full positive story, however, it is clear that, for Aristotle, form is a principle of unity for the compound material substance in a way in which an accident cannot possibly be a principle of unity for the accidental compound. In *Metaphysics Zeta* 17 and in *Eta*, Aristotle argues that, in any whole, we can distinguish between an element (*stoicheion*) and a principle (*archē*), thanks to which the elements constitute a thing of a given kind.[27] Now both kinds of compound, whether accidental compound or compound substance, are of the form *x* + *y*, for example, Socrates + seated or the bronze + triangular, and in both cases, Aristotle apparently thinks of the second entity, being seated or being triangular, as somehow providing the principle of unity for the whole.[28] On this view, what unifies a compound material substance is a form, where the form is both a primary substance and also the actuality and the substance *of* the resulting compound (H2, 1042b10–11); and on this account too,

27 In Z17 and H3, Aristotle argues that a principle is not an element, or composed out of elements, and in H6, he ridicules the idea that we need a further principle to account for the unity between the elements on the one side and the principle that unifies them so that they constitute a whole on the other.

28 It is not as implausible to treat the two cases similarly as might at first appear. In *Metaphysics Eta*, Aristotle discusses a wide range of cases in terms of the model of underlying subject and differentia he finds in embryonic stage in Democritus: the list in H2 includes such disparate examples as bundles, books, thresholds and lintels,

the compound substance will exhibit a greater degree of unity than the accidental compound is able to do.[29]

> breakfast and dinner, winds, or ice; and in all of them there is something analogous to form that is a cause (*aition*) and principle of unity for the whole. Similarly, even in the rarefied metaphysical reaches of H6, Aristotle recognizes contact and sticki- ness as causes of a thing's being one (1045a11–12) and, later in the same chapter, lumps together the cases of being healthy (*not* the *sunousia* or *sundesmos* or *sunthesis* of soul and health), the bronze's being triangular (not a *sunthesis* of bronze and triangular), and the white ‹thing›'s existing (not a *sunthesis* of whiteness and surface). In all cases, he suggests, the unity is to be explained instead by the roles of the two constituents of the compound or whole as the one matter, the other form, inter- preted in terms of potentiality and actuality respectively (H6, 1045a25–b23).
>
> 29 In a similar vein in *Metaphysics* Δ6, Aristotle distinguishes between things that are one *per accidens*, for example, musical Coriscus, and things that are one *per se*, in particular, those that are one by virtue of being a certain whole, thanks to form (Δ6, 1015b16–17, 1016b11–17).
>
> For questions concerning the unity of the compound material substance, the reader should also consult the discussions in Gill (1989) and Witt (1989), which reached me only after the present work was written.

PART IV

Substance and Predication in Aristotle's *Metaphysics*

The Old Criteria for Primary Substance and the New Theory of Form

In the preceding three parts, we have documented major shifts in Aristotle's ontology, from the theory of individual substance, accidents, and accidental compounds in the *Categories* and *Topics* to the analysis of the individual substance as a compound of form and matter first set out in *Physics* A and developed in the central books of the *Metaphysics*. But the *Metaphysics* records a change of heart that is all the more enigmatic for being apparently incomplete. In the *Categories*, Aristotle had held that the individual substance – this man or this horse – is primary substance. In the *Metaphysics*, by contrast, with the addition of form and matter to the ontology, he says that not the individual itself, but rather its form, is primary substance. So Aristotle has changed his view in a major way about what to count as primary substance. But he has *not* apparently changed his mind about various of the *criteria* or other ancillary claims governing primary substance. In the *Metaphysics*, as in the *Categories* and other earlier works, Aristotle requires that

(i) no universal is a (primary) substance

and that

(ii) no (primary) substance is predicated of a subject.[1]

At the same time, he repeats the claim that

(iii) every primary substance is a this.

---

1 In the *Categories,* Aristotle holds only that no universal is a *primary* substance, and that no *primary* substance is predicated of a subject; the broader prohibitions, that no universal is a substance of any sort, and that no substance of any kind is predicated of a subject, are typical of the *Metaphysics* (see the references in Chapter 11, notes 6 and 26).

The *Categories* invites a corollary to (iii), that

(iv) *no universal* is a this,[2]

and in the *Metaphysics* the two claims (iii) and (iv) appear side by side.[3] These various ideas are holdovers from Aristotle's earlier metaphysical thinking, but how do they stand up in the *Metaphysics*? Are they still appropriate, given Aristotle's new choice of form as primary substance?

To answer these questions properly, we need to look more closely at some of the other claims Aristotle makes about form in the *Metaphysics*. The *Metaphysics* contains an important new theory of (metaphysical) predication in which form has a role.[4] According to this theory, an accident is (metaphysically) predicated of an individual substance (this repeats a component of his earlier theory in the *Categories*), but also (going beyond the earlier theory) a form is (metaphysically) predicated of matter. The role this new theory assigns to form makes form appear a very poor choice for primary substance, given the constraints on primary substance already noted. In the new theory of (metaphysical) predication, a form is apparently a universal, for it is (presumably) predicated universally of different portions of matter. But by the criteria for primary substance, if a form is a primary substance, it cannot be a universal (= (i)); indeed, it cannot be predicated of any subject at all (= (ii)). Two of Aristotle's earlier criteria, then, lead immediately to trouble in the *Metaphysics*. And even if these difficulties can be overcome, so that a form can somehow be both a primary substance and a universal,[5] a further puzzle remains. By (iii) of the criteria held over from the *Categories*, every primary substance is a this, so that if a form is a primary substance, it too must be a this. Yet at the same time, as Aristotle holds both early and late, no universal can be a this (= (iv)). If, then, a form is a universal, it cannot be a this after all.

2 In the *Categories,* all *and only* primary substances are thises; since Aristotle already holds that no universal is a (primary) substance (= (i) in the text), it follows immediately that no universal is a this. As we shall see, however (Chapter 11, Sections 3–6), various of the ingredients of this argument must undergo considerable revision in the *Metaphysics.*

3 *Metaphysics* B6, 1003a7–9, Z13, 1038a24; cf. b35–1039a3.

4 Predication for Aristotle is often a metaphysical relation between entities, in contrast to what is for us the natural notion of predication, where what is predicated is a linguistic item. In the *Categories*, as we saw in Part I, predication is sometimes metaphysical predication, but in the *Metaphysics*, it is more consistently metaphysical predication. As in earlier chapters, I will always use 'predication' to mean metaphysical predication, unless explicitly noted to the contrary.

5 On some readings of Aristotle, it is a mistake to try to show that one and the same thing can be both a primary substance and a universal: the forms of natural substances that are the primary substances are *individual* forms, belonging to exactly one thing, and not universals at all. This interpretation is discussed in Chapter 11.

The first two difficulties suggest that Aristotle's preference in the *Metaphysics* for form as primary substance, the criteria for primary substance carried over from his earlier works, and the new *Metaphysics* theory of predication together form an inconsistent set. The third difficulty derives a contradiction from these same materials together with the added assumption that no universal is a this. We cannot simply explain away the contradictions on the grounds that the criteria for primary substance given in the *Categories* and the discussion of substance in the *Metaphysics* represent two different strata in Aristotle's thought, for in the *Metaphysics* both strata are present side by side. Must we conclude that in the *Metaphysics* Aristotle's various views on substance·are doomed to pull forever in contrary directions? To help answer this question, I separate the various difficulties just raised into three different puzzles, which I take up in turn in Chapter 11, primarily although not exclusively in connection with *Metaphysics* Z13. I shall argue that the *Metaphysics* does in fact show ways to knit together the earlier criteria on substance from the *Categories* with the new ontology of form and matter and the choice of form as primary substance in the *Metaphysics*. In the Appendix to Chapter 11, I try to support this reconciliationist hypothesis by sketching the theory in which all these various ingredients have their place. As we shall see, Aristotle's rethinking of the topic of substance in the *Metaphysics* is fashioned largely around the role he gives to two key relations, '*x* is the substance of *y*' and '*x* is predicated of *y*'; getting straight on the principles governing these two relations, I argue, is the key to unravelling the puzzles just noted.

One other major conflict with the *Categories* comes to the fore in *Metaphysics* Z3. In the *Categories,* perhaps the most important criterion for primary substance, in Aristotle's view, is tied to a *monolithic* view of the subject of (metaphysical) predication: "It is because the primary substances are *subjects for everything else* that they are called substances most strictly."[6] In *Metaphysics* Z3, by contrast, Aristotle argues that the subject criterion, allied (as in the *Categories* he means it to be) with the monolithic view that a *single* set of items are the subjects to *all* predicables, leads to the absurd conclusion that matter alone is substance. The conclusion is absurd because it conflicts with the idea that a substance above all should be separable and a this (Z3, 1029a27–30) – criteria that matter satisfies only weakly, or not at all. True to his usual attitude towards the received criteria for substance, Aristotle does not conclude that the subject criterion should be abandoned outright; on the

---

6 *Categories* 5, 2b37–3a1, my emphasis; cf. 2a34–5, b15–17. Aristotle's use of this criterion in the *Categories* is discussed in some detail in Chapter 2, Section 4.

contrary, he says in the *Metaphysics* that three prominent contenders for primary substance – matter, compound material substance, and his own best choice, form – in different ways *satisfy* the criterion (H1, 1042a26–31; cf. Z3, 1029a2–3). This further puzzle, of how Aristotle can retain the subject criterion for substance, consistent with the choice of form as primary substance and avoiding the undesirable consequences of the *reductio* argument in Z3, is taken up in Chapter 10.

Finally, this is perhaps the place to make note of a recent account on the market flatly inconsistent with the reconciliationist programme I defend here. Graham (1987) takes a developmental view of the different strata in Aristotle's thought. The form of developmentalism Graham favours is *unabashed:* he would not share my view that the developmental account of Aristotle is best seen as a convenient fiction, which dramatizes the different strains in Aristotle's thought – some of them more complex versions of what elsewhere seems simple and unarticulated, some even in conflict with others – representing them *as if* they were the product of actual changes and even developments in Aristotle's thought.[7] More serious, Graham also favours *radical* developmentalism, for the discontinuities he finds in Aristotle's thought are not minor and, on strictly logical grounds, cannot be patched over, inasmuch as the different views fall into two "systems," S1 and S2, that at one level are logically incompatible and at another are incommensurable in the sense of Kuhn (1970). Yet more serious still, the development that Graham's Aristotle undergoes is *inadvertent,* or even advertent but *confused:* Aristotle is either unaware of the radical discontinuity between S1 and S2 or mistakenly thinks that the differences can be patched over; he is "trying to achieve a synthesis of his two systems – a task that we know is logically impossible to achieve."[8]

The evidence that Aristotle is inadvertent is that he fails to comment on the various discrepancies Graham finds between the two "systems." Rather than inadvertence on Aristotle's part, however, the mistake may instead be ours: we may be wrong about the evidence, for Aristotle may comment on the discrepancies but we fail to see the

7 See also Furth (1988), pp. 4–5, who writes that he ought perhaps to be "disappointed" if what in Aristotle appears to be simple and even unsophisticated were found to be his later rather than his earlier thoughts; the failure will be just a failure in the dramatic story, and not a reversal of any substantive thesis concerning the conceptual issues at stake in the text. At the same time, however, I do not endorse Furth's view of the *Categories* as a "primer," so that some apparent changes between the *Categories,* where the notions of matter and form make no appearance, and other places where they are present are really only by-products of Aristotle's exposition necessary for pedagogical purposes only.

8 Graham (1987), p. 213.

significance of his comment.[9] Or the evidence may not require a conclusion of inadvertence, for Aristotle may not comment unmistakably on the difficulties, but he may still have a solution to them, which we fail to spot.[10] According to Graham, however, even if Aristotle is not inadvertent, he is surely confused, for he juxtaposes elements from the two warring systems, even though they are in Graham's view logically incompatible, even incommensurable. Unless, what is unlikely, Aristotle's earlier views in the *Organon* are essentially about a different set of topics – unless they are narrowly logical, hence only instrumental to Aristotle's metaphysical endeavours and not in competition with them – the only way of marrying the two systems together, Graham argues, will be if the later is a logical extension of the earlier, in the strict sense that the earlier system, S1, is a proper part of the later, S2.[11] On this construal, the task is hopeless if S1 and S2 are logically incompatible. I argue instead that Aristotle is neither inadvertent nor confused; he believes that he has solutions to the difficulties of getting the earlier and later parts of his thought to mesh, and his belief is not unreasonable, for *Metaphysics Zeta* finds him well embarked on the task of *modifying* the old ingredients of his metaphysical thinking from the *Categories* and moulding them to fit the requirements of their new metaphysical context.[12]

9 Contrary to Graham, I argue that in *Metaphysics* Z3 Aristotle comes within an inch of saying outright that he is now abandoning one of the main criteria for (primary) substance as it was formulated in the *Categories;* see Chapter 10, esp. Section 5.

10 This is not an unlikely mistake, especially given the state of the corpus as we have it and if we do not take the sanguine view expressed by Cherniss (1935), p. 270, quoted in Graham (1987), pp. 7–8.

11 Graham (1987), pp. 85–7. On the view I propose, a looser sense of 'extension' is appropriate here, although this is hardly to adopt a unitarian view in any significant sense, as Graham (1987), p. 221, seems to suggest.

12 Against this, Graham argues that the meanings of key theoretical terms change between the two theories and that these shifts in meaning are evidence that the theories are incommensurable. But if key theoretical terms do undergo shifts of meaning between Aristotle's early and later metaphysics, why are these shifts not a sign, rather, that Aristotle is engaged in the project of *preserving* as best he can elements from the earlier theory, suitably modified, in the context of the later one? And even if a conclusion of incommensurability is justified, does incommensurability on every construal rule out the kind of reconciliation I have in mind? Finally, it is none too easy to show that the shifts in meaning on which the incommensurability hypothesis is based do in fact occur. It may be no simpler to individuate meanings than it is to individuate theories. For example, the introduction of form and matter has deep and far-reaching theoretical consequences, and it is plain that under pressure from these consequences, Aristotle shifts the criteria for substance and for primary substance – but does it follow that the *meanings* of the terms 'substance' and 'primary substance' have changed? By way of analogy, Dalton's definition of 'atom' includes the notion of indivisibility, so that by the lights of Dalton's definition, if the atom should turn out to be splittable, then the very meaning of the term has changed; in retrospect, however, Dalton himself might say that the splitting of the

The best test for the reconciliationist view I propose is the text of *Metaphysics Zeta* itself, and this will be our subject in the two chapters that remain.

atom amounts to not so much a change in meaning as the discovery that a deep theoretical principle about atoms is false. (I am indebted to Tyler Burge for the example.) Comparably, the criteria for primary substance work sufficiently differently in Democritus (say) and in the metaphysics of the *Categories* that they pick out different items as primary substance; but it is far from clear that the meanings of 'substance' or 'primary substance' have changed, and Aristotle can still regard himself and Democritus as engaged in recognizably the same enterprise. Equally, the criteria for primary substance pick out different items in Aristotle's earlier and later works; indeed, I shall argue, the criteria themselves have subtly changed in order to make this possible. But Aristotle can rightly think that in some deep sense he and his former self in the *Categories,* as well as his other predecessors in the Greek philosophical tradition, are working on the same perennial question, suitably refined: What is being? – that is, What is substance? (*Metaphysics* Z1, 1028b2–7; see the Introduction to Part I).

10

Matter and the Subject Criterion for Primary Substance

In the *Categories,* Aristotle draws the most important of his criteria for primary substance from the theory of metaphysical predication: "It is because the primary substances are subjects for everything else that they are called substances most strictly."[1] The appeal of this criterion is not merely local, Aristotle thinks, to his own metaphysical theory. Passages in *Metaphysics* A and elsewhere make it clear that, in Aristotle's view, the earlier history of philosophy is shot through with the idea of primary substance as above all, in his term, a *hupokeimenon,* or *subject.*[2] There is also a second part to the subject criterion: according to *Metaphysics* Z3, primary substances themselves "are said of nothing further."[3] In the theory of (metaphysical) predication in the *Categories,* this part of the criterion appears as the requirement that primary substances are neither SAID OF nor IN any subject.[4]

The subject criterion is a powerful weapon in Aristotle's hands in the *Categories.* As we saw in Part I, the first half of the criterion, that primary substances are subjects for everything else, is filled out to require that a predicable is predicable of any subject at all only if (and

---

1 *Categories* 5, 2b37–3a1; cf. 2a34 ff., b15–17.
2 A major theme in Presocratic philosophy, according to Aristotle, is the attempt at a materialist reduction in which things are regarded as modifications of an underlying matter, which is the substance of everything: *Metaphysics* A3, 983b6–984a16, Λ4, 985b11–22, A5, 987a2–7; cf. B5, 1001b32–1002a1, Δ8, 1017b10–14, 23–4 (where the connection with the "primary subject" criterion is expressly made), and *Physics* B1, 193a9–28, esp. 17–28. The central argument in *Metaphysics* Z3 gives Aristotle's own version of the materialist reduction. It is, of course, one of the primary purposes of his theory of predication in the *Metaphysics* and the associated account of kinds to oppose a reduction of this kind.
3 *Metaphysics* Z3, 1028b37, 1029a8; cf. Z13, 1038b15, and *Categories* 5, 2a11–14. For the two halves of the criterion together, see Δ8, 1017b13–14, b23–4, and *Physics* A7, 190a35–b1.
4 *Categories* 2, 1b3–6, 5, 2a11–14, 3a8–9, a37.

only because) there is some primary substance of which it is predicated. So (i) (metaphysical) predication is possible in general only because primary substances exist. Next, assume that a predicable exists only if (and only because) there is something of which it is predicated. In the scheme of the *Categories,* items other than primary substances are all *predicables,* and as before nothing is predicable of any subject unless there exists some primary substance of which it is predicated. It follows that (ii) items other than primary substances exist only if (and only because) primary substances exist. A key ingredient in this story is the existence of core relations of metaphysical predication that are themselves relations of one-step ontological dependence; thanks to these relations, Aristotle can argue, everything else is dependent on individual substances in one step.

Finally, the second half of the subject criterion, that primary substances are (metaphysically) predicated of nothing further, essentially supports the first half by excluding a variety of unwanted possibilities. First and most obviously, Aristotle supposes that a primary substance is the *lowest* in a sequence of subjects in the category of substance, terminating in "this man" or "this horse" (say), which are "indivisible" (*atomon,* 2, 1b6). A primary substance, then, is not (metaphysically) predicated of anything "lower" in the same category. But, more broadly, a primary substance is not predicated of *any* other item in the same category, and not of any item in some nonsubstance category either; and in general, there are no "predication cycles" involving primary substances such that (by hypothesis) a primary substance is "subject to everything else," but at the same time it is itself predicated of one of its own predicables.[5] So the role of primary substances as subjects is undiminished. They are subjects for everything else, but also nothing else is subject to them. Nothing, then, subtracts from Aristotle's grander claims in the *Categories* that primary substances underwrite not only the possibility of (metaphysical) predication, but also the very existence of all items other than themselves.

In the *Metaphysics,* however, where Aristotle reasserts the subject criterion for primary substance from the *Categories,* its use is far from trouble free. One source of worry, which I shall defer until Chapter 11,

5 The existence of predication cycles involving primary substances and within the category of substance is already excluded by the provision that the primary substance is "subject to everything else" if we add the appropriate assumption about *levels.* That is, we assume that where x and y are members of the same category, x is (metaphysically) predicated of y only if x is "higher than" y in its category. Cycles involving primary substances and *across* categories will be blocked by the different assumption that for x and y that are members of different categories, x is predicated of y only if y is a substance. At the beginning of *Categories* 5, however, Aristotle excludes cycles of all kinds involving primary substances, both within a category and across categories as well, in the way indicated in the text. That is, he assumes that a primary substance is not predicated of anything further (it is neither IN nor SAID OF a subject, 2a11–14).

is the claim that primary substance "is not (metaphysically) predicated of anything further" and the trouble this makes, given that forms are (metaphysically) predicated of matter, and forms are primary substances. Our immediate concern here will be how a primary substance can be a subject for everything and not itself predicated of anything further, in the sense in which this is taken in Z3 as introducing the lowest subject in a chain of subjects.

In the *Categories*, as we saw, individual substances are primary because of their special character as subjects: they are subjects to core relations of (metaphysical) predication, thanks to which everything else is ontologically dependent on them in one step. How successfully can the mechanism of one-step ontological dependence be transferred to the new metaphysical context of the *Metaphysics*? For one thing, Aristotle now has the different device of "focal meaning," relating the other categories of what is to what is in the primary sense (*Metaphysics* Θ1, 1045b27–32; see also the Introduction to Part I). Is there room for (metaphysical) predication too as a determiner of ontological priority and dependence? In the core theory of (metaphysical) predication in the *Metaphysics*, there are two cases to contend with: either (as before) an accident is predicated of an individual substance, or (the new part) a form is predicated of matter. Can Aristotle still muster an argument to show, consistent with this new, two-tiered system of (metaphysical) predication, that again there exists a relation of metaphysical predication that is also a relation of one-step ontological dependency between every predicable and a single class of subjects?

Aristotle's discussion in the *Categories* suggests that things are predicated of something *other than* the members of some privileged class of subjects only because, in the last analysis, they are predicated of subjects in that privileged class, and that these privileged subjects are the primary substances. *Metaphysics* Z3 gives his best arguments for thinking a single such privileged class of subjects also exists in the new metaphysical environment that makes room for matter and form. The privileged subjects of the *Categories*, namely, the individual substances, will no longer do. In the *Metaphysics*, an individual substance is no longer "that of which everything else is predicated": if we stay with the primitive notions of Aristotle's theory, only accidents are predicated of the individual substance, while forms are predicated instead of matter (Chapter 7). In the *Metaphysics*, *matter* is now Aristotle's best candidate for the privileged class of subjects: he must show that accidents are predicated of the individual substance only because they are predicated of its matter, so that matter counts as the only substance.

Metaphysics Z3 explains that this result is not after all acceptable, for matter does not satisfy other criteria for substance as well as do other candidates, namely, form and the compound material substance

(1029a27–30). A deeper moral of the Z3 is surely that we have reasons for doubting the continued appropriateness of the primary subject criterion "as is" without significant changes from its earlier use in the *Categories*. In the first place, not every relation of metaphysical predication is now a relation of ontological dependence. Unlike the accident-of relation between an accident and an individual substance, the relation of supervention between form and matter does not establish the dependence of the predicable on its subject; for this reason alone, we cannot expect that the two relations can be put together in the way put under scrutiny in Z3 to compose a single system of metaphysical predication in which ontological priority flows from the very bottom to the very top. At the same time, there is no reason to suppose that any counterpart to the monolithic conception of the subject of metaphysical predication at work in the *Categories* is even possible in the new metaphysical context of the *Metaphysics*. Like the individual substance, matter too cannot be that of which everything else is predicated: in the official theory, only forms are predicated of the matter, while accidents are predicated instead of the individual substance, and of it alone. In the *Metaphysics*, I suspect, in fact *nothing* exactly fits the subject criterion as it is spelled out in the *Categories*. In the *Metaphysics*, the monolithic view of the subject of (metaphysical) predication is gone: the sequence accidents–substance–matter envisioned in Z3 breaks into two separate halves, each with its own proper subjects and its own proper predicables, and a counterpart to the place occupied by the individual substance as "subject to everything else" in the *Categories* simply does not exist.

The general order of attack in Z3 is this. Aristotle acknowledges at the very outset the received idea that the primary subject is most of all substance.[6] He gives this definition of a (primary) subject (the "primary" is included at 1029a2, but is also sometimes dropped, e.g., at 1028b36):[7] it is that of which everything else is said, but which itself is no longer said of anything else (b36–7). Accordingly, substance must satisfy the account given of a primary subject: substance too is what is not said of a subject, but is that of which everything else is said (1029a8–9; cf. Δ8, 1017b13–14). But – looking beyond the mere characterization – what items answer to this description? The answer in the *Categories* is clear: they are the individual substances. In Z3, applying the old criterion as best we can now that our ontology also

---

6 Z3, 1029a1–2, taking *malista* with *einai ousia:* it could as well govern the *dokei*, however, so that Aristotle is posting this as the most commonly received idea.

7 For "primary," in addition to 1029a2, see a16 and *eschaton* at a24 and Δ8, 1017b24, and perhaps also at Θ7, 1049a34. But this is not, I think, the sense of "primary" at *Physics* A9, 192a31.

includes form and matter, we find that, if anything, *matter* is a primary subject. By contrast with this, Aristotle's official view in *Zeta* and *Eta* is that three different items count in rather different ways as subjects, even perhaps primary subjects:[8] the matter, the form, and the compound (Z3, 1029a2–3, 5; cf. Z10, 1035a1–2, H1, 1042a26).

The discussion in Z3 exhibits doubts about what, following the primary subject criterion inherited from the *Categories*, we are now to count as a primary subject and hence as primary substance. These doubts reflect questions about whether the criterion is applicable at all in its original form: what form should the subject criterion now take, and how will any such criterion mesh with others of the criteria for primary substance? Aristotle shows a similar ambivalence concerning the subject criterion in *Physics* A once the analysis of the individual substance as a compound of matter and form is on the scene. Aristotle confidently restates the *Categories* criterion for (primary) substance (it is not said of anything else, but everything else is said of it; A7, 190a35–b1); but he also acknowledges a doubt: "It is not yet clear whether the form or the subject (*hupokeimenon*) is substance" (A7, 191a19–20, where "subject" covers both matter and the individual substance).

In Z3, Aristotle gives arguments that will choose the substance that is primary from the three rival candidates. First, form comes ahead of matter and the compound.[9] But also, form and the compound come ahead of matter in terms of separability and thisness (a27–30), and the compound is *posterior* to form (a29–32). On this reckoning, form seems to be most of all substance, the compound next, and matter last. So matter is substance to the weakest degree among the three.

But as Aristotle argues in the central part of the chapter, the (primary) subject criterion makes matter *alone* substance (1029a10,

---

8 "*Primary* subject," Aristotle might be thought to suggest in Z3, where the *toiouton* at a2 apparently refers directly back to *hupokeimenon prōton* at a1–2 and presumably also invokes the definition at 1028b36–7, but the force of this is diluted immediately by the claim that matter, form, and the compound material substance all count as subjects *in different ways*. Aristotle says only that they are all *subjects*, dropping the "primary" in the summary at H1.

Aristotle is quite emphatic, both in Z3 and in H1, that form, matter, and the compound are subjects in different ways: in Z3, 1029a2–3, *tropon tina* . . . , *allon de tropon* . . . , *triton de* . . . ; in H1, 1042a27–31, *allōs men* . . . , *allōs de* . . . , *triton de*.

9 Z3, 1029a5–7, reading *tou* (Ross and Jaeger's text; see Ross [1924], Vol.2, p. 165), with the consensus of the earlier manuscripts, E (the first hand) and J, as opposed to *to*, in E (the second hand) and A^b. The ancient commentators are divided between the two readings. Among modern scholars, Ross and Jaeger's reading is defended in Frede and Patzig (1988), Vol. 2, pp. 40–1, but the alternate reading is adopted in Gill (1989), pp. 16–18. Notice, however, that as Ross points out, Aristotle repeats the priority of form over the form–matter compound at a29–32.

18–19, 26–7, and for the 'alone', see a19).[10] So we have the discrepancy that other criteria for substance make matter come in third, but the primary subject criterion makes it the *only* substance. Even more striking, it is often thought that the matter the subject criterion favours is not the proximate matter of a compound substance, but rather *prime* matter.[11] (Aristotle himself does not expressly supply the 'prime', and I usually add the word in parentheses here.) The upshot is that the subject criterion leads to contradiction, and the argument is a classic *reductio* argument.[12]

10 See also a10–11: "If it [matter] is not substance, it escapes us what else will be." On this showing, I take it, *at most* matter will be substance. Frede and Patzig (1988), Vol.2, p. 43, however, think that if matter *is* substance, then the present formulation leaves it open that there can be other kinds of substance as well: but this a curiously backhanded way of stating what they take to be the conclusion Aristotle intends at this point, namely, that *aphairesis* gives *three* kinds of substance. For their treatment of the claim that matter *alone* is substance, see note 12.

11 One dissenter is Dancy (1978), who expressly disavows the "prime" (p. 398; cf. p. 408). See also Frede and Patzig (1988), Vol. 2, pp. 46–7, and Furth (1988), pp. 187–8 and n. 4.

12 We have seen that Z3 contains at different points the very different suggestions that entities of *just one* kind count as primary subjects, and hence as substances, and that entities of *three* kinds are primary subjects, and hence substances. On the account I propose, this discrepancy gives Aristotle the contradiction he needs to reject the primary-subject criterion in the strict form in which it is handed down from the *Categories*. But the discrepancy is used quite differently in Frede and Patzig (1988), Vol. 2, pp. 41–5, to call into question the inference from the fact simply that matter is a primary subject to the conclusion that matter alone is substance. Aristotle has already suggested that form and the compound material substance also are (in their own ways) primary subjects, so if primary subjecthood is all we have to go on, we can hardly conclude that matter alone is substance. Frede and Patzig infer that the result that matter alone is substance must come from the fact that it is a primary subject, *supplemented by* the Platonist suggestion that once the inessential properties are gone in the process of *aphairesis*, there is left the body determined by length, breadth, and depth, and that these will be the substance of the thing: against this, Aristotle points out that length and the rest are qualities, not substances; all that can be left as substance, then, on this modified Platonic position, must be the matter that underlies them. But it seems less plausible to give the Platonist a walk-on part in the argument when Aristotle's own views in the *Categories* provide a readier target. The *Categories* gives a quite strict content to the primary-subject criterion, and on this reading, if anything matter alone is substance; in fact, however, on Aristotle's view, not just matter, but also form and the compound material substance, count as primary subjects, and hence as subjects. (Aristotle concedes that the criterion can apply differently in the three cases; if so, they cannot *all* satisfy the criterion in the strict way required by the *Categories*, and most likely none will do so.) So the discrepancy – that at a2 ff., Aristotle announces that *three* kinds of entity count as primary subjects, and hence as substances, but then at a18–19 seems to conclude that (on a certain point of view) matter *alone* is a primary subject, and hence alone is substance – is met by pointing to the different levels at which Aristotle's discussion proceeds. At one level, he is applying a *reductio* to the primary-subject criterion from the *Categories* in the strict sense defined there and repeated in Z3 at 1028b36–7 and 1029a8–9; on this reading of the criterion, *per absurdum* matter alone is primary substance. At the other level, he has in mind uses of the criterion, now suitably relaxed and incorporated into the official doctrine of the *Metaphysics*, that will in different ways pick out the three candidates for substance – not just matter, but also the form and the compound material substance – with which he contests the use of the criterion that is the target of the *reductio*.

A prominent feature of the central *reductio* argument is its use of *aphairesis*, 'stripping off', where (as I shall suppose) we are to *mentally disregard* or *think past* anything that can be counted as a predicable as a way of locating the primary subject, which, by hypothesis, will be substance. (But as we shall see, *aphairesis* is *not* 'thinking *false*': we are not required to imagine that a thing does not have the properties it has.) The argument itself is discussed in Section 1, and the notion of *aphairesis* is defended in Section 2.

The central *reductio* argument is supported by an ancillary argument at a20–6, where Aristotle argues again that the primary subject is (prime) matter, so that on the subject criterion, (prime) matter alone is substance. He also explains the relation between this new choice for primary subject and the theory of categories and concludes that the primary subject has no *per se* properties from any category, and even that it has no *per se* properties in any acknowledged sense that is independent of the categories. The auxiliary argument is discussed in Section 3.

Aristotle's conclusion is that we must not stay with the primary-subject criterion as stated (*dei de mē monon houtōs*, 1029a9), for (i) it is not sufficient (*hikanon*), for (iia) it is unclear, and (iib) it makes matter substance (1029a10), or rather, if it does not follow that matter is substance, it altogether escapes us what is (a10–11).

"Not sufficient" here does not mean "not a sufficient condition," given Aristotle's explanation of the phrase in (iia) and (iib).[13] Here already, however, there is an oddity, for (iia) and (iib) surely pull against each other at least to some extent: if the criterion is unclear, how reliably can it point to matter as (the only) substance? In fact, as we shall see, in the ontology of the *Metaphysics*, *nothing* fits the criterion in its present form. This is in accordance with Aristotle's doubts at a10–11: either matter alone fits the criterion as stated, or nothing does.[14] So the criterion is insufficient on two counts. First, in the context of the *Metaphysics*, it is, quite simply, without application as it

13 The "not a sufficient condition" reading is given in Robinson (1974), pp. 185–6; cf. Kung (1978), p. 149, and Frede and Patzig (1988), Vol. 2, p. 50. But if the condition were "not sufficient" in this sense, then presumably the problem would be that it yields *three* candidates for (primary) substance, where a clearer condition will give just one. If this is the force of Aristotle's complaint of unclarity in (iia), however, how can he go on to say in (iib) that in light of the condition, it seems that necessarily matter alone is substance (a18–19; cf. 10–11)? (This reasoning, however, will not impress Frede and Patzig, who hold that the reference to matter *alone* at a18–19 is not a genuinely Aristotelian conclusion; cf. note 12.)

14 These remarks can be taken to indicate that Aristotle has doubts about the process of *aphairesis* that he is about to introduce as a means for discovering the primary subject. In contrast to this, I shall argue in Section 2 that Aristotle has no doubts about *aphairesis* itself – either that it is coherent or that it can have a coherent end product. He does doubt, however, whether its end product can properly be called a primary subject. But the trouble lies with the notion of a primary subject as defined and not with *aphairesis*.

stands.[15] Despite this, however, Aristotle continues to believe that substances are in some sense subjects, and even that form, matter, and the compound substance are all in different ways subjects and, to this extent, substances. So, second, the criterion must be reworked to capture these intuitions. In fact, Aristotle will want to reformulate both halves of the criterion. The sense in which a primary substance is properly a subject is discussed in Section 4 of this chapter. The second part of the subject criterion, that a primary substance is (metaphysically) predicated of nothing further, and the special problems this makes for Aristotle's choice of form as primary substance, are taken up in Chapter 11.

1   The *Reductio* Argument

The main part of Aristotle's *reductio* argument – that of which everything else is said but which itself is said of nothing else is (prime) matter, so that (prime) matter alone is substance – runs from 1029a11 to a19; an auxiliary argument extends from a21 to a26, and Aristotle completes the *reductio* by arguing for the absurdity of the conclusion that (prime) matter alone is substance at a26–30. We shall start by looking at the main part of the argument from a11 to a19 and its completion at a26–30.

Let us call that of which everything else is predicated but which itself is predicated of nothing else a "primary subject" (cf. 1029a1–2). Suppose further that being a primary subject is a necessary and sufficient condition for being a substance. Aristotle's procedure is first to devise a method for locating primary subjects and then to see what in his own ontology, if anything, corresponds to what his method picks

---

15 The unclarity of the subject criterion from the *Categories* is not that form, matter, and the compound material substance all apparently fit it, as both Schofield and Dancy seem to say (Schofield [1972], p. 97; Dancy [1978], p. 393). First, Aristotle argues that, if anything, matter fits the criterion, so it is hard to see how he can also think that all three kinds of item fit it equally well (cf. notes 12 and 13). Second, the primary-subject criterion includes a *definition* of 'primary subject' borrowed from the *Categories,* and this definition is quite precise. There is no way in the world the phrase "that of which everything else is predicated" could apply to form or to the compound substance, and only slightly more hope that it can apply to matter. This last point indicates the real source of the unclarity Aristotle complains about: how are we to apply the primary-subject criterion, once it is transplanted, word for word, from its original home in the *Categories* into the very different metaphysical environment of the *Metaphysics?* (A very different account of the unclarity appears in Frede and Patzig [1988] 2, p. 41: it is because of uncertainties over whether accidental properties alone, or both accidental and essential properties, are to be stripped away, or because of difficulties in seeing how form can be a subject for everything else. But while I agree that these are legitimate questions, to ask them here draws attention away from the difficulties of the primary-subject criterion as it was formulated in the *Categories,* which in contrast to Frede and Patzig I take to be the focus of Aristotle's concerns here.)

out. His means for identifying primary subjects will be *aphairesis*, or 'stripping off': primary subjects, then, are just the end products of *aphairesis*. And the end product of *aphairesis* is in each case (prime) matter. Accordingly, (prime) matter is a primary subject, so that on the present account, (prime) matter is the sole candidate for substance. But of course, on other grounds, other items in Aristotle's ontology have a far stronger claim to being substances than does matter, let alone prime matter; so being a primary subject, as interpreted in this argument, cannot be a necessary and sufficient condition for substance after all.

In more detail, the steps of the argument are these. We state first the assumption that is the ultimate target of the *reductio:*

(1) Everything is predicated of x but x is predicated of nothing else (x is a primary subject, for short) if and only if x is a substance. (1028b35–6, 1029a1–2, 7–9)

The concept of a primary subject in (1) is part and parcel of the *monolithic* view of the subject of (metaphysical) predication at work in the *Categories*. Aristotle begins his attack on (1) by introducing *aphairesis* as an appropriate method for uncovering primary subjects:

(2) x is a primary subject if and only if x is the end product of *aphairesis*.

As we shall see below, (2) is plausible for Aristotle if he pictures the objects to which *aphairesis* applies as *compounds* of predicables with their subjects along the lines suggested in Accidental Compound Theory (ACT, Part II). On this picture, we can intelligibly *think past*, or *disregard*, the predicables associated with the object and uncover their common subject. And in the cases Aristotle attempts to construct in *Metaphysics* Z3, if we can think past *all* the predicables associated with an object, what we are left with will be a *primary* subject in the sense of (1): all the predicables that get stripped away are, ultimately, predicables of this single subject. At a10–11, Aristotle quietly reserves the right to conclude that *nothing* is to be found as a primary subject.[16] Setting these doubts aside, however, suppose that repeated steps of *aphairesis* lead successfully to an end product. In the example in the text, only two steps are needed; here we give only their result, reserving details for later discussion:

(3) x is the end product of *aphairesis* if and only if x is "what is determined by length, breadth, and depth." (a16–18)

---

16 These doubts about success in the search for a primary subject, however, need not show that the method of *aphairesis* itself is intrinsically flawed; see the discussion in note 14.

Next, the argument requires an assumption about what in Aristotle's own ontology answers to the description in the right-hand side of (3):

(4) *x* is what is determined by length, breadth, and depth if and only if *x* is (prime) matter.

Two inferences now complete the identification of (prime) matter as a primary subject. Given (3) and (4), we can infer that

(5) *x* is the end product of *aphairesis* if and only if *x* is (prime) matter.

And given (5) and (2), we know that

(6) *x* is a primary subject if and only if *x* is (prime) matter

– if in fact, remembering our doubts in connection with (2), anything at all qualifies as a primary subject in the sense defined. But we have supposed in (1) that being a primary subject in the relevant sense is both necessary and sufficient for being a substance. It follows, then, that

(7) (Prime) matter alone is substance. (a18–19, 26–27; cf. 10–12)

This result, as Aristotle is quick to point out, conflicts directly with others of the criteria for substance, which show that

(8) Both forms and compound material substances are substances to a greater degree than is (prime) matter. (a27–30)

Accordingly, contrary to (1),

(9) Being a primary subject in the sense defined cannot be a necessary and sufficient condition for substance after all.

Aristotle's argument is intended to show that the subject criterion for substance assumed in (1) cannot stand, at least not without serious emendation. The argument can support this moral to good effect, however, only if we can be sure that it does not contain other ingredients that are equally or perhaps more open to question. And in fact, critics have found other materials to doubt in the argument. One frequent target has been the notion of *aphairesis* around which the argument is built. Schofield, for example, holds that in Aristotle's view *aphairesis* has no real end product at all. He regards the reference to "what is determined by length, breadth, and depth" in the argument (reproduced in (3) and (4)) as an "inept gloss" intruded into Aristotle's text. Instead, he takes Aristotle's argument to be a disjunctive syllogism: *either* the primary subject is the end product of *aphairesis*, that is to say, it is nothing at all (*ouden horōmen hupoleipomenon*, a17–18), *or* it is matter; hence, on the assumption that a primary subject exists at all, it must be identified with matter.[17]

Aphairesis is also regarded with scepticism by Charlton, who apparently concedes to the argument that *if aphairesis* were possible it would terminate in prime matter, but doubts that there is such a thing as prime matter in Aristotle. For Charlton, accordingly, the whole passage represents an opponent's point of view and is not an expression of Aristotle's own thoughts at all.[18]

In contrast to these sceptical views about *aphairesis*, I argue that *aphairesis* has a genuine and central role in the argument. I argue too that *aphairesis* is in fact a coherent notion, given the assumptions Aristotle makes in the argument about the objects to which *aphairesis* is applied and that, for as long as these assumptions are in force, it is reasonable to suppose that *aphairesis* can have an end product. So the central position *aphairesis* takes in Aristotle's argument does not undermine his attack on his intended target.[19] Further, I argue that the actual steps of *aphairesis* Aristotle sets out, ending in "what is determined by length, breadth, and depth," are plausible and that this description is plausibly satisfied by prime matter. In effect, then, I shall be defending directly steps (3) and (4) in the summary just given; since (5) is a consequence of (3) and (4), it will not need separate defence.

At the same time, Aristotle's argument for the intermediate conclusion that the primary subject is (prime) matter in (6) is undoubtedly flawed. It is flawed, however, not because of difficulties with *aphairesis* as such, but for reasons having to do with the central theme of the chapter, namely, because it incorporates a mistake about the notion of a subject. The argument is, after all, a *reductio* argument, and its target is the use of the subject criterion for substance that Aristotle inherits from the *Categories*. The trouble, as we shall see, is with the *monolithic* view of the subject of predication that is built into the subject criterion in the *Categories*. In the *Metaphysics*, there is no such thing as a primary subject, "that of which everything else is predicated, but which itself is predicated of nothing else." The difficulty first emerges with the notion of a primary subject in (1): it then spreads to the attempt in (2) to identify a primary subject so conceived with the end product of *aphairesis*. Far from undercutting Aristotle's *reductio* argument, however, these troubles are the very ones Aristotle intends his argument

17 Schofield's interpretation is discussed further in Section 2.
18 Charlton (1970), p. 138.
19 This is in contrast to Schofield's account, in which it is argued that *aphairesis* is essentially flawed, but leaves the main argument undamaged because it plays such an unimportant role there.

to expose. In Section 2, I turn to the details of the argument from *aphairesis*.

2 In Defence of *Aphairesis*

Aristotle gives this account of how *aphairesis* proceeds:

For when the other things are stripped off, plainly nothing ‹else› is left;[20] for on the one hand, the other things are affections and effects and powers of bodies,[21] but on the other, length and depth and breadth are particular quantities but not substances (for the how much is not substance), but rather that to which these belong primarily, *that* is substance. But yet length, breadth and depth being stripped off, we see nothing remaining, except if there is such a thing as what is determined (*horizomenon* [a18]) by these, so that necessarily the matter seems to be alone substance to those who look at it in this way. (1029a10–19)

A key feature of the procedures described here is that they take place in two stages.[22] Aristotle strips off first the sensible properties of body (a12–13). He turns his attention next to length, breadth, and depth, which have *not* been removed in the first stage, and looks in turn for that to which these belong primarily (a14–19).

Why have these procedures so often seemed so problematic? One puzzle is how *aphairesis* can even get started. Consider the bust of Aristotle that (we may suppose) sits on the desk before us (see Z3, 1029a5). The bust is heavy, fragile, and (say) reddish in colour. Now *aphairesis* requires us to strip these properties away from their subject. In this spirit, *what* is it that is heavy, fragile, and the rest? The answer we give is supposed to lead sooner or later to a primary subject, which, if things go as intended, is a philosopher's object, far removed from the bust with which we began. The mystery is why the answer should not lead instead to a perfectly ordinary object, namely, simply the bust itself. For example, what is it that is fragile? Surely, the bust itself or, if we like, the thing that is heavy. And what is it that is heavy? Again, the bust itself or, if we prefer, the thing that is fragile. Time and again, the bust itself is apparently the subject. Or – what amounts apparently to the same thing – the different descriptions of the thing can take in one another's laundry: it is the thing that is heavy that is subject to the

20 For the "else," see a18 later in the text; cf. Schwegler (1867), Vol. 4, p. 43, and Dancy (1978), p. 394.
21 " . . . those other than bodies are affections" (Schofield [1972], p. 97), taking *sōmatōn* as governed by the *alla*, rather than following *pathē* and the rest, is a slip: a comment on p. 98 ("Aristotle's reference to *bodies* as what bear properties [a13]," his emphasis) suggests that he takes the grammar as in the text.
22 The point is made clearly in Ross (1924), Vol. 2, p. 165; see also Dancy (1978), p. 395; Sorabji (1985–6), pp. 2–4.

property fragility, and the thing that is fragile that is subject to the property heaviness, and so on.

It is essential to *aphairesis* to disallow virtually all this. We are at liberty to cite the bust itself as subject for the property fragility (say), but only at the very first stage of *aphairesis*. After sufficiently many applications of *aphairesis*, we are meant to end up with something that is pure subject, with no predicables still "embedded" within it that remain for stripping away. We are supposed to come at the end not to the bust of Aristotle we started with, but to something more like Locke's "supposed, but unknown support" of the qualities that have been stripped away: something that (in some sense) lacks all properties altogether.[23] Further, it is *never* admissible to cite this heavy thing (say) as (metaphysical) subject for the property fragility. We are never allowed simply to fall back on a description of the thing in order to specify the subject for one of its properties.

There is an easy argument to show that this last requirement is, quite simply, absurd. By hypothesis, the statue is subject to the property fragility. But in answering the question 'What is it that is fragile?' on the present construal, we are not allowed to say that it is this heavy thing that is subject to the property fragility. Yet we suppose that the statue is indeed heavy; that is, the statue is identical with this heavy thing.

Even more pointedly, we are not allowed to say that it is this fragile thing that is subject to the property fragility. So one and the same thing *is* identical with the fragile thing (for by hypothesis, it is fragile), but it is *not* subject to the property fragility. This surely is the same as saying that one and the same thing both is and is not fragile.

One response to the difficulty is to deny that the statue is after all fragile. Such a move is hardly surprising. If having supposed that the statue is fragile, we are forced right away to the view that it is *not* fragile (for we are not allowed to reintroduce the description 'fragile' in referring to the statue), it is natural to conclude that indeed the statue is not fragile. This line of thinking leads inexorably to the paradox that at every step of *aphairesis* we strip away a predicable that turns out not really to have been there in the first place. The ultimate result of *aphairesis*, so conceived, is a substratum that is truly bare of properties[24] or that is a "featureless bearer of properties" – something that simultaneously does and does not have its various predicables.

23 The quotation is from Locke, *Essay,* 2. 23. 3. The view of substance in Locke as a bare substratum (see, e.g., Bennett [1971], p. 62) is not unopposed; see McCann (forthcoming). Also the sense in which Aristotle's ontology leaves room for a "bare substratum" should be carefully qualified; see note 55.

24 Contrary to what according to Descartes is "manifest by the natural light that is in our souls," that "nothing has no properties"; see *Principles of Philosophy,* Part 1, Principles 11 and 52.

A more likely move, I think, is to continue to hold that the statue is fragile but to deny that it is identical with this fragile thing. This may seem a worse paradox even than before, but in fact it is a trivial truth of ACT set out in Part II. This heavy thing, for example, is identical with the accidental compound of this statue with the accident heaviness, namely, this statue + heavy. But this statue + heavy is not identical with this statue. There is no problem, then, in supposing that it is true of the statue, but false of this statue + heavy, that it is subject to the accident fragility or that fragility is (metaphysically) predicated of it.[25] This account requires us to give up the usual Russellian reading of the designator 'the heavy thing', according to which it designates the one and only thing that is heavy, that is to say, the statue, in favour of the view that it designates something else entirely, namely, the relevant accidental compound.[26] It is no surprise, then, that the statue can be fragile, yet the designator 'the fragile thing' should *not* refer to the statue. And as we shall see, an easy extension of ACT that deals with form–matter compounds establishes comparable results when we reach down below the level of accidents into the very composition of the statue itself out of matter and form.

The appeal to ACT shows how *aphairesis* can take us to a different object from the fragile statue we started with, *without* having to suppose that the new object, the statue itself, is something that is not fragile at all. So we can resist the arguments by Stahl (1981), whose account of *aphairesis* in *Metaphysics* Z3 makes him a sceptic about the notion of matter as something distinct from that of which it is the matter. Stahl writes:

Thinking away all the properties of an *F*, including its *F*-ness, does not make it a non-*F*. Thus, . . . [given the question 'What is it that is potentially all the things I have thought away?'] an answer of the form 'the *F*' or 'that *F*' *will* do.[27]

If this is right, surely the stripping off will end where it began, with the statue, or the fragile thing, or the like. In fact, however, Stahl is not

25 These differences are exactly as the conditions on the notion of predication require: in Aristotle's core theory (Chapter 6, Section 4), where *x* is an accident, *x* is predicated of *y* only if *y* is a compound material substance (and *not* if *y* is an accidental compound). Here, however, there is a complication to be noted, one having to do with the distinction between linguistic and metaphysical predication. It is true that the statue, and that the heavy statue (the statue + heavy), alike are fragile; that is to say, the two *linguistic* predications are alike true. But things are very different when we ask what is and what is not the case at the level of *metaphysical* predications. Very different metaphysical relationships underlie the two linguistic predications. It is in fact the case that fragility is metaphysically predicated of the statue (and the statue in a metaphysical subject to fragility). But fragility is *not* metaphysically predicated of this statue + heavy; rather, both heaviness and fragility alike are metaphysically predicated of a *single* (metaphysical) subject, namely, the statue itself. This kind of case is discussed also in Chapter 8, Section 5.

26 See Chapter 3, Section 1.

27 Stahl (1981), p. 178, his emphasis, responding to a point in Robinson (1974), p. 187.

entitled to the "Thus." The first sentence, I believe, is true, but the second is false: the subject is an F – but it is not identical with the F. Or in the notation of ACT, if ϕ is (metaphysically) predicated of a, it is predicated of something that is ϕ – but it is *not* (metaphysically) predicated of the ϕ, that is, of $a + \phi$.

Again, Stahl writes:

When *in thought* we strip away properties from a thing, we consider that *same* thing without considering its properties. We do not consider a *different* thing, the matter of the original object, a peculiar entity with no properties.[28]

Stahl seems to suppose here that when we strip off ϕ from the ϕ, *either* we stay with the same object, the ϕ, *or* (absurdly) we must move to a different object that is not ϕ at all, ending ultimately with "a peculiar entity with *no* properties" (my emphasis). But this is a false dichotomy. On the account offered here, we start *aphairesis* in each case with a *compound* entity, $x + y$, and end with its underlying subject, x, where $x \neq x + y$. But still, y continues to belong to x, and the view of matter as "a peculiar entity with no properties" is out of court.

Finally, we can agree with Stahl that "surely, if they [length, breadth, and depth] delimit something, what they delimit is something delimited, not undelimited?" But we need not accept his implied conclusion: "How ... could the length, breadth, and depth delimit anything but the statue?"[29] In fact, there is a perfectly acceptable sense in which they delimit not the statue but its matter, so that this last is not "undelimited stuff," as Stahl supposes.[30] In Aristotle's example, the statue is a compound of matter m and the properties of specific dimension ψ. ψ is (metaphysically) predicated of, and hence supervenes on, m, so that indeed m is delimited by ψ. At the same time, ψ is not constitutive of m, but rather of $m + \psi$. There is a sense, then, in which the dimensional properties ψ are essential to the statue, and we cannot imagine the statue without them. But it does not follow that we cannot "think past" ψ to reach m by itself.

The appeal of ACT explains how *aphairesis* gets started, by showing how *aphairesis* is not a matter simply of cycling through the various descriptions of a thing, so that it is the fragile thing that is subject to the predicable heaviness, and the heavy thing that is subject to the predicable fragility, and so on. But once *aphairesis* is properly under way, at what point is it finished? If ACT is any guide, *aphairesis* at this first stage will stop at the statue, but – contrary to what is needed to get the primary-subject criterion up and running in earnest – it will go no further.

28 Stahl (1981), pp. 178–9, his emphasis.
29 The two quotations are from ibid., pp. 177–8.
30 Ibid., p. 178.

For light on some different possibilities for where *aphairesis* might end, we can turn to two arguments, one elsewhere in Aristotle, the other in Descartes, where even at the first stage of *aphairesis* we get back to something more elementary than the statue. In the closely related chapter *Metaphysics* B5, for example, Aristotle offers a reappraisal of some of the best-favoured traditional candidates for substance, the simple bodies earth, air, fire, water. Each of these is a combination of hot, cold, and the like, together with plain *sōma* by itself, the body that is modified by them. Aristotle concludes, in language reminiscent of Z3, "Of these [= the simple bodies], the ‹different› heats and colds and the like are modifications, not substances, and the body that is modified by them alone remains as something that is and as a substance" (B5, 1002a1–4; cf. Z3, 1029a12–16). Aristotle does not use the word *aphairesis* here or elsewhere in B5, but there are enough similarities in language between B5 and Z3 to suggest that some of the same thoughts, including the notion of *aphairesis,* are also at work in both chapters. On this reading, body is our only remaining candidate for substance, because its various modifications, heat and cold and the like, have been stripped away. Notice that in B5, there is also the potential for taking the body in question to be not physical but rather geometrical magnitude, and indeed the next step in the chapter is to consider various geometrical and mathematical candidates for substance, in preference to *sōma,* now construed as geometrical magnitude.[31]

A similar process of stripping off in Descartes also proceeds all the way to body. Why should stripping off proceed so far? And having gone that far, why stop there? Descartes has no hesitation about where stripping off should stop. All the sensible properties of a thing are accidental to it, but extension is essential to it. This gives him his stopping place:

Those things being removed which do not pertain to the wax, let us see what remains: obviously only something extended, flexible and changeable. (*Second Meditation, AT* 7 pp. 30–1)

The nature of matter or of body in its universal aspect, does not consist in its being hard, or heavy, or coloured, or one that affects our senses in some other way, but solely in the fact that it is a substance extended in length, breadth and depth. . . . weight, colour, and all the other qualities of the kind that is perceived in corporeal matter, may be taken from it, it remaining meanwhile entire: it thus follows that the nature of body depends on none of these. (*Principles of Philosophy,* ed. Haldane and Ross, Second Part, Principle 4)

We have only to attend to our idea of some body, e.g. a stone, and remove from it whatever we know is not entailed by the very nature of body. We first

---

31 See Annas (1976), p. 34, on the possible slide from physical to purely geometrical three-dimensional objects.

reject hardness; for if the stone is melted, or divided into a very fine powder, it will lose this quality without ceasing to be a body. Again, we reject colour; we have often seen stones so transparent as to be colourless. We reject heaviness; fire is extremely light, but none the less conceived as a body. Finally, we reject coldness and heat and all other such qualities; either they are not what we are considering in thinking of the stone, or at least their changing does not mean that the stone is regarded as having lost the nature of a body. We may now observe that absolutely no element of our idea remains, except extension in length, breadth, and depth. (AT 8, p. 65, quoted by Kenny [1968], p. 207)

Descartes relies on "clear and distinct ideas" to tell him when he has reached the essential properties of an object, which cannot be stripped off from it. There is perhaps some trace of the same thought in Aristotle, when he suggests in the second stage that length, breadth, and depth *can* be removed, because they are not substances – that is, perhaps, not the substances of, or not essential to, what they are removed from (a14–15; cf. B5, 1002a1–2).

This account of where stripping off must come to an end has let Descartes in for some criticism, however. The claim that length, breadth, and depth cannot be stripped away seems to depend on taking these as determinables – for why should a thing's actual determinate dimensions be essential to it? Yet the argument for allowing the various sensible properties to be stripped away is successful only if these are taken to be fully determinate properties. So Descartes's division between the sensible qualities of a thing and its properties of extension depends on treating them unequally. If these are taken both alike as determinables, both must stay; or if both alike as determinates, both can be removed.[32]

We can avoid this criticism in Aristotle's case if, as we have supposed, the end product of the first stage of *aphairesis* is not sheer body, but rather, the statue. Plausibly, its actual determinate length, breadth, and depth are essential to the statue – unlike its particular weight or colour, for example.[33] On this interpretation, at the first stage of *aphairesis*, Aristotle deals exclusively with determinate properties, whether they stay or get stripped off.

At the same time, it would be a mistake to think that Aristotle's choice of stopping point to end the first round of *aphairesis* relies exclusively on the appeal to a distinction between accidental and

32 The objection is made by Williams (1978), p. 218; the same criticism is noted by Kenny (1968), who also suggests how Descartes might have responded to it (pp. 207–8).
33 The choice of example, then, is especially important. If the example had been instead a jeweler's weight (say), its specific dimensions could well be stripped from it, but its actual weight could not. (I am indebted here to a comment by Greg Jesson.)

essential properties.[34] His choice of stopping place is due at least as much to the philosophical tradition, which he thinks favours the subject criterion in the first place,[35] and in Z3 and in B5 alike, he seems to be motivated by both kinds of reasoning. A dominant strain in the philosophical tradition is that natural bodies are the substances (e.g., in *Zeta* itself at Z2, 1029b8–13), and Aristotle elsewhere in the *Metaphysics* rationalizes this choice for substance in terms of the subject criterion (B5, 1001b32–1002a4, Δ8, 1017b10–14). So natural body is an easy point at which *aphairesis* may stop. But the tradition is vague about what is meant by natural body. Possibly, any natural body or stuff can count as a substance – standardly, the four elements or their parts, or what has them as parts, even the universe as a whole (Z2, 1028b8–13), but also perhaps, stretching a point, a statue (say). Supposing, then, that the first round of *aphairesis* in Z3 ends with the statue (in contrast to the red statue – the statue + red – or the heavy statue – the statue + heavy – or the like), this (forgetting for a moment that the statue is after all an artefact) is at least broadly in line with the tradition that natural bodies are plausibly subjects, and hence plausibly substances as well.

In B5 and Z3 alike, the end of the opening round of *aphairesis* leaves Aristotle in broad terms at one with the majority of earlier thinkers (B5, 1002a8). But later and reputedly wiser minds (B5, 1002a11–12) take the matter further. There is a striking difference, however, between the further steps Aristotle describes in B5 and the continuation in Z3. In B5, after the introductory round of *aphairesis,* essentially *different* criteria for substance are employed (roughly, definitional independence and existential separation) to reach the mathematizing conclusion that, ultimately, numbers are the substances. As in Z3, Aristotle then brings other considerations to bear to show that these cannot be the substances after all. Strikingly in Z3, however, the first round of *aphairesis* is not the last. In contrast to the discussion in B5, the second step of the argument consists in reopening *aphairesis.*

To see what is so striking about this, consider this puzzle about the state of things at the end of the first stage. *Aphairesis* has stopped with a given body, namely, the statue, partly because this (or something comparable) is where the philosophical tradition stops, but also no doubt because, apparently, no accidental properties of the thing now

---

34 Aristotle uses the language of substance in apparently appealing to this distinction ("for the how much is not a substance," a15; cf. B5, 1001b29–32, where he expressly uses the accidental–essential distinction to guide the process of stripping off). This is perhaps harmless, if his argument can rely on an informal notion of essence and accident. But his use of these notions must not seem to presuppose too much substance theory in a supposedly neutral hunt for what is the primary subject, and hence substance.

35 See note 2.

remain to be removed. Aristotle now envisions further applications of *aphairesis* as a result of which, ultimately, any remaining properties too disappear.[36] At this point at the beginning of the second stage, however, by hypothesis, all the accidental properties have already been stripped away, so that there is nothing but essential properties left to go. But how, if only accidental properties can be stripped away, can essential properties too disappear? How, by stripping away accidental properties alone, can we finish with something that has no essential properties?

The answer to this puzzle lies in Aristotle's "shift-of-subject" manoeuvre. In B5, the later and supposedly subtler thinkers had to change their methods if they were to go beyond the choice of natural body as substance. But in Z3, Aristotle has a way of reapplying the same methods of the first stage, thanks to the idea that what is essential to one thing *may be accidental to another*. This is a key idea of Aristotle's own metaphysics, quite apart from the special context of the *reductio* argument in Z3. Consider, for example, the different character of the relation between Socrates' form and Socrates, on the one hand, and between that same form and Socrates' matter, on the other. Socrates' form is constitutive of Socrates, and he is classified as a member of his kind by means of it; but that form (merely) supervenes on, and is accidental to, his matter.[37] Again, these actual dimensions (such-and-such determinate length, breadth, and depth) are constitutive of the statue and are part of what makes it the statue it is; but they supervene on, and are accidental to, the matter of the statue, which can exist as well with some other actual shape.

In the second round of *aphairesis,* then, we are interested in the relation between the length, breadth, and depth of the statue, on the one side, and not the statue itself, but rather its *matter,* on the other. Aristotle argues that the application of *aphairesis* here leads to the primary subject for length, breadth, and depth (a15–16); that is, he adds somewhat doubtfully, to "what is determined (*horizomenon*) by these" (a18) – that is, presumably, the indeterminate extension that is made determinate by actual length, breadth, and depth – which he apparently identifies with (prime) matter (a18–19).

For this result to carry conviction, however, we shall need a defence against the sceptical attack by Schofield, who argues that the second round of *aphairesis* is not coherent. Schofield's doubts about *aphairesis* provide the main impetus for a reading of Z3 substantially different

---

36 It is crucial here, again, that stripping away proceeds in two distinct stages; see note 22.

37 For complications here, see the Postscript to Part III. The point is easier with the artefact example and a conception of form limited to the (Democritean) notion of the *shape* of a thing, as perhaps in the case of a statue; cf. *PA* A1, 640b30–641a17.

from that offered here. On Schofield's view, within the overall *reductio* of the subject criterion for primary substance, the argument does not proceed straight through, identifying the primary subject with what-ever emerges as the result of *aphairesis* (= (2) in Section 2), and then claiming that the actual result of *aphairesis* is in fact identical with (prime) matter (= (3)–(5) in Section 2). Instead, the argument is a disjunctive syllogism featuring two alternative interpretations of the subject criterion. On one alternative, the criterion is interpreted in terms of *aphairesis,* which it turns out is incoherent. On the only remaining alternative, (prime) matter satisfies the criterion.[38] Accord-ingly, either nothing satisfies the subject criterion, or (prime) matter does. So (returning to the main *reductio*) (prime) matter satisfies the subject criterion if anything does, and hence is substance. This result, Schofield thinks, is confirmed in the supporting argument at a21–6, where Aristotle defends his official notion of matter spelled out at a20–1 and argues that it fits precisely the definition of a primary subject given earlier in the chapter.

I have some doubts about this analysis. I argue in Section 4 that we should not concede the crucial point that anything at all can satisfy the primary-subject criterion as it stands. This, if right, invalidates both the argument by disjunctive syllogism and Schofield's interpretation of the supporting argument at a21–6. But if, on the contrary, as Schofield thinks, the argument at a21–26 succeeds in showing that matter is a primary subject, and hence substance, this makes it all the harder to see why on his account *aphairesis* appears in the argument at all. To minimize the role of *aphairesis* in the argument, he supposes that it appears there only as part of a disjunctive syllogism, which offers these two alternatives, matter and "the result of *aphairesis,*" for how to interpret the primary-subject criterion. But if *aphairesis* is as problematic as Schofield suggests, it remains a puzzle why it should come up as a plausible alternative at all, or why an argument by disjunctive syllogism should ever seem a promising strategy in the first place.

On Schofield's account, by cancelling length, breadth, and depth, Aristotle is cancelling "not just a thing's *specific* length, breadth and depth, . . . but the dimensions which constitute extension alto-gether."[39] On this view, it is doubtful that stripping off can have any coherent end product at all. In particular, if, as Schofield supposes, the matter of a thing is identical with its extension, by cancelling the

---

38 On this reading, *hôste*, a18, does not interpret the end product of *aphairesis* in terms of (prime) matter, but instead introduces (prime) matter as an *alternative* to the end product of *aphairesis*.

39 Schofield (1972), p. 98, his emphasis.

extension of the thing, Aristotle must also cancel its matter. So he cannot go on to identify matter with the end product of *aphairesis*. In reality, *aphairesis* leaves no intelligible end product at all.

Dancy argues convincingly against this that in Z3, as in the parallel passage in *Physics* Δ2, Aristotle is stripping off only the determinate length, breadth, and depth of a thing.[40] In *Physics* Δ1, Aristotle argues that length, breadth, and depth are the three extensions that determine a body (209a4–6), and later in Δ2 that when we cancel that by which a given body, a sphere (say), is determined, *matter* is left: "For, whenever the limit and the ‹other› qualities of the sphere are stripped away, nothing is left beyond the matter" (209a9–11; cf. 7–9). Cancelling the three extensions, then, does not cancel the matter. If matter is extension, it is pure indeterminate extension, which remains, and not the specific extension that is removed when limit, surface, and shape are removed.

If this defence of *aphairesis* succeeds, other questions still remain. Above all, what are Aristotle's precise instructions for how to apply *aphairesis* to a thing – to the statue, say? Dancy imagines a process of systematically replacing all the properties of the statue, although he acknowledges it is not strictly a requirement in every case outside Z3 that the stripping off *aphairesis* requires even be physically realizable. According to his account of the example in Z3, however, we are meant to imagine a different state of affairs from what in fact is the case, in which the statue is not red but on the most plausible interpretation, has some other actual colour.[41] The less plausible version of this is to imagine that instead of being red, the statue does not have *any* colour. This last is the kind of hypothesis Aristotle has in mind at *Physics* Δ8, 216b6–8: "For, suppose the magnitude were without qualities (*apathes*, b15) – that it were really to be separated (*ei kai chōristheiē*) from *all* the others, and were neither heavy nor light." The mood of this conditional tells against its being anything but wildly contrary to fact. But even the weaker version of this view, which supposes (simply) that the statue has different properties than those it actually has, misses the point of Aristotle's thought experiment. The point of applying *aphairesis* is to find some metaphysical "ingredient" in the statue that is the true subject of all the properties we associate with the statue. A project of this sort is hardly furthered by imagining something that has *none* of the properties in question. The difficulty remains, however plausible the replacements we find for the properties we remove.

---

40 Dancy (1978), n. 59. For "parallel," see his p. 394.
41 Ibid., pp. 396 ff. esp. p. 398.

A preferable view is that, preliminary to a step of *aphairesis,* we should ask whether, without any changes in how the world actually is, the statue in some other set of circumstances might have been of some other colour. Is it possible that the statue should exist but have some other colour? If this possibility is open, then the statue might exist, but not the red statue. Accordingly, the statue, which is red, is not identical with the red statue, that is, with the statue + red. These facts justify a step of *aphairesis.* Starting with the statue + red, we apply "selective inattention" so as to disregard the predicable, red, and attend instead to the underlying subject, the statue.

In this account, we are not invited to suppose that in the actual world, the statue is, in fact, not red, but rather to ask whether in the world as it actually is, it is possible that the statue should not have been red. As it is intended in *Metaphysics* Z3, then, *aphairesis* should be physically realizable, but we are not required to suppose that it is, in fact, physically realized. On the account given here, *aphairesis* does not require us to suppose that the properties of a thing are actually changed. *Aphairesis* is not "supposing false," but better, selective inattention. But as Frege says, inattention is a strong lye, and we must be sure that it does not lead to absurdity. Realizability supplies the appropriate constraint in Z3. The constraint is a modal one: we require of the properties we strip away that it be possible that they should be changed yet the item to which they in fact belong continue to exist.

Suppose we decide that the statue can remain the same, yet have some colour other than the one it actually has. How does this advance the project of stripping off that actual colour in order to find its subject? If *aphairesis* is a process of *discovering* the subject of properties, how can we identify the subject, *before* stripping its properties away, and determine that it can continue to exist without them? Presumably, our selection of the properties to be stripped away comes together with a hypothesis about the identity of the subject they are to be stripped away from. For example, plausibly the first stage of *aphairesis* in Z3 involves a hypothesis about the sensible qualities and the statue itself. But as we see, there are some properties – length, breadth, and depth – left over. *Aphairesis* continues, then, by postulating some fresh subject for the predicables left over after the first round of *aphairesis.* Thus, we form a hypothesis about the various dimensions of length, breadth, and depth, and their subject – "that which is determined by these" – later identified with (prime) matter.

At each of these two stages, *aphairesis* is performed on an entity that is a compound of a subject with some predicable. For example, the red statue is an accidental compound, this statue + red. But the statue might not have been red, so the property red can be stripped away. The subject, which "remains," is not identical with the compound of that subject with the property in question. But of course, none of this is to imagine that the statue is not in fact red after all. Comparable moves apply in the case of the statue by itself. The statue too is a compound: in the example in Z3, Aristotle thinks of it as a compound of indeterminate extension and specific dimensions of length, breadth, and depth. And as before, we distinguish the subject, indeterminate extension by itself, from the compound of that subject with the appropriate specific dimensions.

The two stages of *aphairesis* in Z3 approximate the same structure as in Aristotle's official theory. According to Aristotle's official account, alluded to also in Z3, the red statue (say) will be analysed by way of, broadly, a two-stage system. In the first, "upper" stage, accidents are (metaphysically) predicated of a compound material substance, and the result is an accidental compound, this statue + red. In the second stage, "below" the first, the statue itself is analysed as a compound of a given matter and form, this bronze + statue-shaped, where again the form is (metaphysically) predicated of the relevant matter. The bronze too is a form–matter compound, and so on through the lower orders of matter all the way down finally to prime matter, which is *not* a compound of any form with any matter.[42]

Despite these similarities, the discussion of the statue example in Z3 parts company with the official theory of the *Metaphysics* in one crucial respect. In Z3, Aristotle imagines that we can somehow put together the two separate steps of *aphairesis* to reach at the end a single, rock-bottom subject that is "subject for everything else" in the way required by the monolithic conception of the subject of (metaphysical) predication from the *Categories*. This paves the way for the further conclusion that the rock-bottom subject in question is (prime) matter, so that (prime) matter alone is substance. But as Aristotle also points out in Z3, matter is not the only, and not even the best, candidate for substance, so that the primary-subject criterion must be rejected. In a sense, however, even this *reductio* argument against the primary-subject criterion concedes too much. For the sake of the *reductio*, in Z3 Aristotle goes along with the fiction that in the new theory of the *Metaphysics* there can be such a thing as a primary subject, subject to *all* the predicables associated with a thing: not only its accidents in the top half of the scheme of predication, but also its form in the lower half as well. This permits the *reductio* to proceed against its immediate target, the view in (1) that a thing is a substance just in case it is a primary subject. Underlying this mistaken view, however, is the more fundamental mistake of supposing that in the new theory of the *Metaphysics* there is room for such a thing as a primary subject in the first place. In fact, Aristotle rejects the monolithic view that a thing's matter is subject not only to the relevant form, but also to the thing's accidents as well. A fortiori, then,

42 The details of this scheme are discussed further in Chapter 6, Section 4.

aphairesis is powerless to deliver a primary subject in the way Aristotle pretends in the body of Z3. But to defend *aphairesis* one more time, the problem is with the monolithic assumption about subjects. It need not suggest that *aphairesis* as such is in any way objectionable.

3 The Auxiliary Argument: Matter and *per se* Properties

After the main argument at a11 to a19, Aristotle appends an auxiliary argument at a21 to a26 designed to support the conclusion that frames it at a18–19 and 26–7, that (prime) matter (alone) is a substance:

(a20) By matter, I mean what *per se* (*kath' hautēn*) is said to be neither of a certain kind (*ti*), nor of a certain quantity, not anything else ‹of those› by which being is defined. (a21) For, there is something of which each of these is predicated, (a22) whose being is different from that of each of the predicables (*tōn katēgoriōn hekastēi*) (a23) (for, the others are predicated of the substance, but it ‹is predicated› of the matter), (a24) so that the ultimate ‹subject› *per se* is neither of a certain kind nor of a certain quantity nor anything else: indeed, not even the negations ‹belong *per se*› either, for these too will belong accidentally (*kata sumbebēkos*).

The supplementary argument proceeds in two stages. First,

(10) Everything else (= items from the various nonsubstance categories) is predicated of the *ousia,* and the *ousia* is predicated of the matter. (a23–4)

Hence,

(11) There is something, namely, (prime) matter, of which each of the predicables from all the different categories is predicated. (a21–2)

Claim (11) differs only slightly from claim (6) in the main argument, identifying the primary subject (if there is one) with (prime) matter. And given (6) (i.e., (11)) in combination with the initial assumption (1), that the primary subjects are the substances, we are already in a position to conclude, as before, that (7) (prime) matter alone is substance. Moreover, the argument for (7) is new, since (7) can be reached in this case without any use of the method of *aphairesis*. Surprisingly, however, Aristotle adds two further steps to the argument before drawing his conclusion.[43] Building on the result that a primary subject exists, he goes on to make an assumption about the relation between the primary subject and its various predicables:

(12) The being of the subject of each of these various predicables, that is, the being of (prime) matter, is different from that of each predicable itself. (a22–3)

---

43 These added steps will be intelligible, however, if Aristotle is unhappy with the move from (10) to (11), criticized in the two paragraphs that follow in the main text; see also note 49.

From this, it follows that

> (13) (Prime) matter (a20), that is, the ultimate subject (a24), does not have any *per se* predicables from any of the categories: it is not *per se* of a certain kind, or *per se* of a certain quantity, and so on for the other categories (a20–1, 24–5); all its predicables belong accidentally to (prime) matter. (cf. a25–6, the negations *too* will belong *kata sumbebēkos*)

Hence, finally,

> (7) (Prime) matter alone is a substance. (a18–19, 26–7)

The initial step of the supplementary argument from (10) to (11)[44] presents Aristotle's argument that in the context of the ontology of the *Metaphysics*, there exists a subject of which *everything* else is predicated. The argument revolves around the claim standard in the *Metaphysics* that accidents are predicated of compound material substances, and forms are predicated of matter. This standard picture, evoked in (10), is radically extended in (11). In addition to the two cases of predication recognized in (10), Aristotle argues in (11) that accidents and forms alike ultimately are all predicated of a single subject, namely, (prime) matter. The move to (11) is apparently accomplished by a transitivity argument: accidents are predicated of the *ousia*, the *ousia* is predicated of the matter, so accidents and *ousia* alike are predicated of the matter. On this account, the inference is defective on at least two counts. First, on this account, the argument requires an equivocation on the term *ousia*, for the accidents are predicated of the *compound material substance*, while it is the *form* by itself that is predicated of the matter.[45] Second, the predication relation is not transitive in the way the argument seems to require.[46]

---

44 I take it that a23–4 (= (10)) supports a21 (= (11)), but not a22–3 (= (12)), which I take to be an independent assumption; see note 48.

45 Frede and Patzig (1988), Vol. 2, p. 48, say that *ousia* here can mean only *form;* this no doubt fits their view that while matter underlies form, *form itself underlies accidents* by virtue of its privileged relation to the compound material substance that does so: see, e.g., their 1, pp. 40–1. They seem to have in mind two different accounts of the privileged relation in question. One is that the individual form of a thing and the thing itself are "identical in a certain respect." I do not claim to understand the notion of *identity in a certain respect*, but it may tempt Frede and Patzig to think that by something like Leibniz's Law, if the thing is a subject to accidents, then its individual form will be too: this is perhaps the argument at Frede and Patzig (1988), Vol. 2, p. 39. The other account of the privileged relation between form and thing is that the form is the cause of the being of the thing, or "that which the thing properly and finally is": hence, what holds for the thing holds in a "mediated" way for the form too (1, p. 40). It is perhaps a mistake, however, to think that Frede and Patzig mean to validate the argument from (10) to (11), since at Vol. 2, p. 38, they seem to say that while Aristotle shows that the matter underlies the accidents, it is not the case that in turn the accidents are predicated of the matter; see Chapter 6, note 7.

46 In fact, the relation is vacuously transitive and intransitive, since in the theory of predication at work in the *Metaphysics*, there are no x, y, and z such that both x is predicated of y and y is predicated of z. Accordingly, the antecedents in the definitions

Finally, not only is the inference to (11) invalid, but also, in the *Metaphysics*, (11) itself is false.[47] According to Aristotle's official theory, as we have seen, the accidents are predicated of the compound material substance, but not of anything else. In particular, they are not predicated of the matter. On these grounds alone, then, contrary to the monolithic view advanced in (1), the accidents of a thing and the forms associated with it are not all predicated of one and the same subject.

The fact that (11) is false is of major importance. The auxiliary argument lets in a good deal of the official metaphysical theory of the *Metaphysics* – not just the mention of matter, as in the main argument, but in (10) the official, "in-house" theory of (metaphysical) predication in effect in the *Metaphysics*. These various notions take us well beyond the metaphysical world of the *Categories,* where the primary-subject criterion was first advanced. In this new context, Aristotle suggests in Z3, either matter alone fits the primary-subject criterion for substance or nothing does. The proper conclusion, as we have seen, is that as the subject criterion is being understood in the body of the chapter – which is no different from how it is understood in the *Categories* – *nothing* fits it in the *Metaphysics* ontology. In Z3, however, Aristotle goes along with the fiction that there is a primary subject of the sort described and asks what in the context of the new theory of predication it must be like. *If* there is such a thing as a primary subject, it will be very different in nature from what fills that role in the simpler world of the *Categories.* The remarks in the second part of the auxiliary argument are intended to deal with these differences.

In the *Categories,* the primary subjects are the individual substances, and these occupy pride of place in Aristotle's categorial scheme. Things are very different in the *Metaphysics,* however. In Z3, Aristotle argues that the primary subject is (prime) matter, and he assumes that the notion of (prime) matter (a20), that is, the primary subject (*to eschaton,* a24), shares its being with none of its predicables from the different categories (= (12)). Accordingly, (13) no predicable from any of the categories belongs *per se* to (prime) matter: (prime) matter is not *per se* of this or that kind, it is not *per se* of this or that quantity, and so on for each of the categories. That is, it falls outside the scheme of the categories altogether.[48]

of transitivity and intransitivity for the relation of predication are never true, and both definitions are vacuously satisfied.

47 But it is apparently endorsed by Schofield (1972), p. 101. Similarly, despite the sharp differences he sees between the metaphysical theories of the *Categories* and the *Metaphysics,* Graham (1987), p. 217 (cf. 223–4), apparently buys the monolithic conception of the subject of predication even in Z3.

48 What are we to make of the initial assumption in (12) that the being of (prime) matter is not that of any of its various predicables from the different catego-

We can put the conclusion slightly differently, in the jargon of Izzing. In the *Categories,* we classify an individual substance, Socrates (say), by the fact that he Is (a) man. A parallel system of classification is at work in the nonsubstance categories: each nonsubstance too Is some predicable that exists above it in the same category. Invariably, then, there is an answer to the question 'What is it?' not only in the case of items in the category of substance, but also for nonsubstances as well. In contrast to all of this, there is no *x* from any category such that (prime) matter Is *x.* In the case of (prime) matter, there is no answer to the question 'What is it?' from any of the categories. But nothing can be a member of a category, yet not Be some predicable from

---

ries? Aristotle here is setting the needed distance between the notion of predication featured in (11), relating (prime) matter and its various predicables, and *per se* predication. (For a different sense of '*per se*' not derived from the theory of categories, in which again prime matter has no *per se* predicables, see note 50.) In *Metaphysics* Δ18, Aristotle considers various *per se* predications, where the notion of predication in question is, I believe, *linguistic* predication. For example, the sentence 'Callias is *per se* an animal' is true just in case the predicable animal (introduced by the predicate 'animal') is either identical with or (as in this case) included in the *what is it* of the subject Callias. Aristotle writes: "For according to one notion of the *per se* (*kath' hauto*), the essence of each thing ‹is *per se* to it›, for example, Callias is *per se* Callias and ‹*per se*› the essence of Callias; in another way, whatever belongs in the *what-is-it* ‹is *per se* to the thing›, for example, Callias is *per se* an animal; for Callias is an animal of a certain kind" (Δ18, 1022a25–9). According to the use of '*per se*' illustrated in this passage, a sentence of the form '*x* is *per se* y' is true just in case either *y* is the essence of *x* (where a thing's essence gives a *complete* answer to the question 'What is it?') or (more liberally) *y* is a *part* of the *what-is-it* of *x;* see F. Lewis (1984), p. 93, and nn. 5 and 6.

Other passages make it clear that there is a whole range of cases in which it is true to say that *x* is *per se* y and a variety of cases of the *what-is-it* of *x,* all differentiated from one another according to what kind of entity *x* is. Primarily, the notion of a thing's *what-is-it* belongs within the category of substance alone (Z4, 1030a18–19). But there are secondary uses in the other categories too (Z4, 1030a19–27; cf. F. Lewis [1984], pp. 92 and 98). Aristotle argues in Z3 that none of these notions of *x*'s being something *per se,* or of the *what-is-it* of *x,* has any application for the case where *x* = (prime) matter. Aristotle assumes that where an item, *a,* is (metaphysically) predicated of (prime) matter, the being of *a* is not the same as, and is not included in, the being of (prime) matter, whether *a* is in the category of substance or in some nonsubstance category (Aristotle says only "not the same as," but "not included in" is also needed to complete the argument). But in general, *x* is (included in) the being of *y* only if the being of *x* is (included in) the being of *y.* In the *Categories,* for example, Aristotle supposes that where *x* is SAID OF *y,* and hence is (included in) the definition of *y,* the definition of *x* is also (included in) the definition of *y* (a similar requirement appears as the full-expansion condition on definition in *Metaphysics* Z10: where *y* is a primary definable, for any *x* that is included in the definition of *y* and is itself a primary definable, the definition of *x* should also be included in the definition of *y;* see Chapter 6, Section 2). Accordingly, if the being of *a* is not (included in) the being of (prime) matter, then *a* itself is not (included in) the being of (prime) matter. But if *a* is not (included in) the being of (prime) matter, then, finally, it is false that (prime) matter is *per se* a. And in general, for any predicable, *x,* from any of the categories, it is false that (prime) matter is *per se* x. Thus, (prime) matter lies wholly outside Aristotle's categorial scheme.

within that category. Accordingly, (prime) matter falls outside the system of categories altogether.

Why, finally, does Aristotle go to such pains to set out the status of (prime) matter, that is, on the assumptions of Z3, the primary subject, within the ontological theory of the *Metaphysics*? On one, perhaps less likely possibility, the claim in (14) that (prime) matter has all its predicables accidentally is meant to support the intermediate conclusion in the main argument at a11–19 that (prime) matter is a plausible end product of *aphairesis,* thus clearing the way for the further conclusion that (prime) matter is the primary subject. This account makes Aristotle's argument remarkably circuitous, if not redundant. He has already argued that (prime) matter is a primary subject in steps (10) and (11) of the auxiliary argument. There seems no need, then, for the further argument that all its properties are accidental to (prime) matter, so that (prime) matter is a plausible end product of *aphairesis,* to facilitate the conclusion, again, that (prime) matter is the primary subject.[49]

A more likely alternative is that in these later steps of the argument, Aristotle is attempting again to support the conclusion already reached in (6) (= (11)) that the primary subject can be identified with (prime) matter. As in (10) through (11) – but in contrast to his very first argument for this conclusion in (2) through (6) – his argument is independent of the *aphairesis* test for uncovering primary subjects. In support of identifying the primary subject with (prime) matter, Aristotle points out that there is a second-order property – that of having no *per se* predicables from any of the categories – that the primary subject, if it exists, must have in common with matter. And in fact, the characterization of matter in (13), according to which it has no *per se* predicables from any of the categories, is surely correct in Aristotle's theory, quite independently of the particular needs and purposes of Z3.[50]

---

49 The apparent redundancy may be acceptable, however, if the appearance of the second argument is a sign that Aristotle himself is dissatisfied with the problematic move from (10) to (11); see note 43. Frede and Patzig (1988), Vol. 2, p. 42, argue that the supplementary argument is meant to buttress the conclusions at a11–19 about the end product of *aphairesis* in a different way. Aristotle urges that if we abstract from all the accidents of a thing, no *thing,* no *this,* is left; but the end product is not nothing at all, but matter. The account of matter needed to support these distinctions is then developed at a20–6.

50 I have argued that matter in general, prime matter included, has no *per se* predicables from any of the categories. There is, however, a source alternative to the theory of categories thanks to which in the ordinary case, matter can and does have *per se* predicables in a different sense of '*per se*': the source is the theory of constitutive form. Thus, where *m* is matter, we assume that

(i) For any ψ, *m* is *per se** ψ if and only if ψ is constitutive of *m*.

In contrast to this, however,

(ii) For any ψ such that ψ supervenes on *m*, *m* is not *per se** ψ.

The familiar bronze statue, for example, is a compound of bronze, *m*, and the form

At the same time, a further purpose of the passage is surely to emphasize the difference between what Aristotle says about what answers to the notion of a primary subject here and what is true of what he calls a primary subject earlier in the *Categories*. There is an extraordinary irony in the view Aristotle takes in Z3 of what a primary subject will be like. In the *Categories*, Socrates (say) satisfies the primary-subject criterion, and hence is a primary subject. But in the *Categories*, one way in which Socrates is a subject is that he is a member of various *kinds:* he Is (a) man, an animal, and so on. In the account of a primary subject in Z3, by contrast, the theory of Izzing is dropped, and the primary subject must Have all its predicables accidentally and is not a member of any kind. But if the primary subject, that is, (prime) matter, is not *per se* any predicable from any of the categories, then in particular it is not a substance, and hence hardly a candidate for primary substance. At best, matter is *potentially* – that is, it potentially constitutes – something that belongs to a substance kind. This gives Aristotle the coup de grace in his *reductio*. Both form and the compound material substance are, in their different ways, separate, and each is also a this. Matter, however, at best *potentially* is, that is, potentially constitutes, an item that is separate and a this.[51] And what goes here for matter in general holds even more for *prime* matter at the bottom of Aristotle's ontological ladder. So matter in general, and least of all prime matter, cannot be the only substance.

of a statue, ψ. We know that m itself is a form–matter compound, $m^1 + \psi^1$ (see Chapter 6, Section 4). Now the form of a statue, ψ, supervenes on m: by (ii), however, this is not a source of *per se** predicables for m. At the same time, however, the form ψ^1 is constitutive of m: by (i), therefore, m is *per se* ψ^1. The notion of constitutive form, then, allows us to generate predicables that are *per se** to matter. Among the various levels of matter, prime matter alone has no *per se** predicables in this way. By definition, as we have seen (Chapter 6, Section 4), no form is constitutive of prime matter. Accordingly, by (i), there is no form, ψ, such that prime matter is *per se** ψ. That is, prime matter has no *per se** predicables in this new sense of '*per se**' that is independent of the theory of categories. We know that prime matter exists only if there exists some form, ψ, that supervenes on it: but (ii) assures us that this fact will not generate *per se** predicables of prime matter.

Although Aristotle does not clearly separate out this new kind of *per se** predicables, it seems that, like prime matter, the primary subject too, if it exists, will lack *per se** predicables. But while these further details fall in line with the identification between prime matter and the primary subject Aristotle is arguing for, they do require some cautions about his pronouncements regarding matter at a20–6. On the usual account, a20–6 is offered as a truth about matter in general (Bonitz [1870], 785a25–7; cf. Schofield [1972], p. 100), and it is false that matter in general has no *per se** predicables. On the usual reading, then, the lines cannot tell us what we need to know about *prime* matter in particular to justify identifying prime matter and the primary subject (if one exists) in the way required. Perhaps the best conclusion is that the topic of *per se** predicables is not explicitly on Aristotle's mind in the passage.

51 "Potentially a this": *Metaphysics* H1, 1042a27–8; cf. *De Anima* B1, 412a7–8.

4   The Primary-Subject Criterion and Form

Aristotle argues in *Metaphysics* Z3 that (prime) matter is not separate and not a this, and hence cannot be the only substance. Instead, matter is one of three candidates for substance, and of these – matter, form, and the compound material substance – *form* is his choice for *primary* substance. The forms of natural substances are not separate without qualification (*chōriston haplōs*), which in the sublunary world is the prerogative of compound substances, but they are at least separate in account (*chōriston logōi*) (H1, 1042a28–31; cf. *Physics* B1, 193b4–5). Further, although the point has sometimes been doubted, form is also a this. One way of understanding this is to suppose that being a this is a mark of *particularity,* so that form is a this because it is an unshared and unshareable *particular.*[52] This is the doctrine of individual form. Other accounts stop short of endorsing individual form, but still share the same view of what it means to call something a this; they must suppose that form can be a this in only some indirect way, "by courtesy," as it were, parasitically on the fact that its constitutive form is what determines the nature of the compound substance and that the latter is a this in the full-blooded sense.[53] In contrast to both of these options, I shall argue later (Chapter 11, Section 4) that form is a this in its own right, without being individual form, and in a way that does not depend on its relation to the compound substance.

It is even less straightforward to say how form fares in the face of the old subject criterion from the *Categories*. According to one half of the criterion, primary substance – that is, in the *Metaphysics, form* – is "not (metaphysically) predicated of anything else": this must be squared with the point that in the new theory of (metaphysical) predication in the *Metaphysics,* form is (metaphysically) predicated of matter. This topic is taken up in Chapter 11. The second half of the subject criterion requires that primary substance, that is, form, be "that of which everything else is predicated." But how can this be made out in the context of the new theory of (metaphysical) predication, in which form is not apparently a subject at all? This difficulty in turn may make it hard to sustain the picture of Aristotle for which I am arguing, as fundamentally conservative, intent on preserving as far as possible the old criteria for primary substance, at worst reworking them where he must but everywhere stopping short of throwing them out entirely.

---

52 See, e.g., Frede (1987 [1985]), pp. 75 ff., esp. 77–8; Frede and Patzig (1988), Vol. 1, p. 14; cf. p. 52. Other accounts of what it means to be a this are quite different and offer no invitation to the hypothesis of individual form in the sense recognized by Frede and Patzig, e.g., Loux (1979), pp. 13–14; Code (1986); and Lear (1987).

53 Cf. Ross (1924), Vol. 1, p. 310, on *Metaphysics* Δ8, 1017b25; Loux (1979), pp. 13–14; Kung (1981), n. 6; and Furth (1988), p. 241.

In fact, however, Aristotle himself directly says that form is a subject not only in Z3, but again in the summary at the beginning of *Eta* (H1, 1042a26–9). So the notion of form as a subject does not so much challenge the view of Aristotle as a conservative in the sense indicated as raise the puzzle of how in fact Aristotle can pull off the trick as he apparently assumes he can, despite the evident difficulties.

Aristotle emphasizes that form, matter, and compound material substance are not all subjects in precisely the same way.[54] With at least the last two, it is clear that they are subjects, although hardly "subjects for everything." The form–matter compound, first, is not subject for everything, since it is not a subject to forms. But it is at least a subject to accidents. Matter, in turn, is not a subject to accidents, but it is a subject to forms.[55]

At first sight, form is the least promising candidate of the three for being in some sense a subject. One reading of Aristotle claims to make the point come relatively easily. If we are prepared to recognize a notion of *individual* form in Aristotle such that the form of a given individual substance is unique to it and not shared by another member of the same kind, and if we suppose that the appropriate privileged relation holds between the individual form of a thing and the thing itself, then apparently the form will be a subject to the same accidents

54 See note 8.
55 It is not quite precise, however, to say that in the composition of a given compound material substance, prime matter at the very bottom is subject to *all* the forms in the sequence of forms that extend above it within the compound substance. m^n at the bottom of Aristotle's scheme is supervened on by ψ^n, and the resulting compound, $m^n + \psi^n (= m^{n-1})$, is supervened on by ψ^{n-1}. But these premises do not support a transitivity argument to the conclusion that m^n is supervened on by ψ^{n-1}; see note 46.

In this connection, it is relevant that there are two different relations, 'x is the matter of y'. One is a relation between a matter, m^i, and the compound, $m^i + \psi^i$, of which it is (in some sense) a part: this relation is transitive. The other matter-of relation holds between m^i and ψ^i by itself, and this relation is clearly not transitive. The temptation to think that contrary to what has been urged here, the relation of (metaphysical) predication is transitive may come from identifying that relation with the converse of the second of these different matter-of relations and then falsely inferring from this that it shares the logical properties of the converse of the first.

The place of prime matter as subject only to the form immediately above it in the hierarchy of matters and forms comprising a given compound material substance reveals an important point about how Aristotle's new theory continues to reflect his opposition to Platonic bare substrate theory. In Aristotle's scheme, admittedly, prime matter is a bare substrate, in the appropriately qualified sense. That is, it has no constitutive form. At the same time, it is not truly bare, for prime matter exists only if some form *supervenes on* it (Chapter 6, Section 4). Again, prime matter is not in any sense a subject for *every* predicable: in Aristotle's scheme, as already suggested, an item is subject only for predicables at the level immediately above that subject. A fortiori, then, as we have seen, his theory in the *Metaphysics* does not leave room for the *monolithic* view of the subject of predication, such that one and the same thing is subject for predicables of *every* level higher than that subject itself.

that the thing is. Whether this argument can be made out will depend in part on the account of the privileged relation in question;[56] the argument also requires, of course, that Aristotle indeed holds a doctrine of individual forms in *Metaphysics Zeta* and *Eta*.[57] Short of suggestions that turn on the hypothesis of individual form, I can see only two possible explanations of the "subjecthood" of form. First, the (constitutive) form of a compound substance is not in any sense a subject for predicables, but possibly it is still a *hupokeimenon* in one important respect. In all cases of substantial change, in which an individual substance comes to be, the appropriate form comes to supervene on the appropriate matter and, Aristotle argues, the form *preexists*. It does so, however, not in the Platonic way, without matter (Aristotle is emphatic that no form of natural substances exists without matter), but in cases of natural coming-to-be as the (constitutive) form of the parent, which is another full-fledged member of the same kind as its offspring. In cases of human craftsmanship, meanwhile, form exists beforehand in the mind of the craftsman. Form is a *hupokei-menon*, then, in the attenuated sense that (in the usual case, at least)[58] it preexists whenever a compound substance comes to be. Aristotle stresses that form preexists in this way in *Metaphysics* Z8, and this is the natural sense in which form is a *hupokeimenon* in Z8 if Ross is right that *to holōs hupokeimenon* at Z8, 1033a31–2 is meant to include form.[59] And it happens that the coming-to-be of a compound substance is very much in Aristotle's mind in the summary in H1, where the list of the three kinds of *hupokeimena* is repeated from Z3.

Second, in *Metaphysics* Δ, Aristotle seems close to allowing that soul, which is the form of the living creature, can be the subject to various psychological properties: "A man is alive in virtue of himself: for the soul is a part of the man, and is the primary recipient of life (*en hōi prōtōi to zēn*)" (Δ18, 1022a29–30).[60] That is, a man is alive "in virtue of

56 On the account put forward in Frede and Patzig (1988), the privileged relation is *either* "identity in a certain respect" *or* the fact that the form is the cause of the being of the thing; it follows, they argue, that the predicables that belong to the thing accrue also to its individual form; see note 45. Since I do not understand the notion of "identity in a certain respect," I do not know how to evaluate the argument on the first of the two options given. The second option gives something along the lines of the second alternative discussed in the paragraphs that follow, and yields only an indirect and "extended" sense in which form is a subject.

57 I am not convinced that individual forms offer the only or even the best argument for the status of forms as subjects in *Metaphysics Zeta* and *Eta;* see note 56. Similarly, I argue in Chapter 11 that individual forms are not required to solve difficulties involving forms and universals that come to the fore in particular in *Metaphysics* Z13.

58 The exceptions involve spontaneity and chance; cf. *Metaphysics* Z7, 1032a28–32, b21–26, Z9.

59 See Ross's commentary, Ross (1924), Vol. 2, p. 187.

60 This passage is cited by Ross on *Metaphysics* Z3, 1029a2; see Ross (1924), Vol. 2, pp. 164–5.

himself" because he is alive in virtue of his soul, which is the "primary recipient" of life. In the *De Anima,* however, Aristotle argues against the shift to soul as the subject for psychological predicates:[61]

To speak of the soul as feeling anger is as if one should say that the soul weaves or builds. Doubtless it would be better not to say that the soul pities or learns or thinks, but that the man does so with the soul: and this, too, not in the sense that the motion occurs in the soul, but in the sense that motion sometimes reaches to, sometimes, starts from, the soul. Thus, sensation originates in particular objects, while recollection, starting from the soul, is directed towards the movements or traces of movements in the sense-organs. (A4, 408b11–18; Hicks's translation)

Again:

Reasoning, love and hatred are not attributes of the thinking faculty but of its individual possessor, in so far as he possesses it. Hence when this possessor perishes, there is neither memory nor love: for these never did belong to the thinking faculty, but to the composite whole which has perished, while the intellect is doubtless a thing more divine and is impassive. (A4, 408b25–9; Hicks's translation)

In the case of living things, form, that is, soul, is the primary recipient of various properties ϕ. But instead of saying

The soul ϕ's,

we do better to say that

The man or woman (whose soul it is) ϕ's.

Soul gives the living creature its ability to behave in such-and-such ways; but ultimately it is the creature, not its soul, that exhibits the behaviour in question.

This, I take it, is not just a feature local to Aristotle's philosophy of mind. His account in general of the relation between the compound material substance and its constitutive form requires that its constitutive form bestow on the compound substance its characteristic nature and place it in its appropriate kind. But it is the compound substance, not the form, that is the member of the kind and that exhibits the behaviour characteristic of members of the kind – that thinks, senses, and so on.

In general, then, form is that in virtue of which the compound substance works out its characteristic style of life. This influence manifests itself in two distinct ways. The fact that form is predicated of matter explains how the creature is a member of its kind in the first

---

61 These passages were first brought to my attention by Henry Newell. They are also discussed in Code (1984).

place: this gives matter as one kind of subject. But the fact that a compound substance is a member of a kind is what makes it a fit subject for accidents. It is thanks to form, then, that the subjects that properly Have accidents can do so.[62] This gives a second class of subjects, namely, compound material substances.

All of this can make it seem that – without too much exaggeration – almost anything *except* form can count as a subject. But it may be possible to manufacture out of these materials a somewhat precarious sense in which form too is a subject. Form has a central role in placing a thing in its kind, so that the thing is a suitable subject for accidents. Indirectly, then, and in a suitably extended sense, form too perhaps is a subject.[63] I do not claim to find this reasoning fully convincing. But, outside of the hypothesis of individual form, it is one of the only two ready alternatives I know of for explaining Aristotle's express assertion that forms are subjects.

5   Conclusion

On the account given in previous sections, Z3 is Aristotle's record of what happens when the chief of the old criteria for primary substance from the *Categories* is transplanted "as is" into the new metaphysical context of matter and form in the *Metaphysics*. The primary-subject criterion as it stands is ditched: Aristotle expressly says that it is not sufficient, on the grounds that not only is it unclear, but also it singles out the wrong thing as (primary) substance, if it singles out anything at all (1029a9–11; 18–19). A key part of the chapter, then, is the rejection of the monolithic view of the subject of predication that was central to the argument of the *Categories*. The chapter also acknowledges different ways in which different kinds of items can be subjects (1029a2–5; cf. H1, 1042a26–31), and even makes the problematic claim that what in the new theory takes on the role of primary substance, namely, form, also counts as a subject. Whatever the ultimate success of Aristotle's project, then, it is as clear as perhaps anything can be in the interpretation of *Metaphysics Zeta* that Aristotle is occupied in Z3 with studying the central criterion for primary substance from the *Categories*, telling us that it no longer works "as is" in the new theory of the *Metaphysics* and claiming that in some way or another, which he does not specify further, it can be made to apply after all to his new candidate for primary substance.[64]

---

62 This point is discussed further in Chapter 11, Section 1.

63 Cf. Graham (1987), pp. 282 ff., and Frede and Patzig (1988), Vol. 1, p. 40; see notes 45 and 56. This style of argument, however, makes form at best a subject *indirectly:* in its own right, it is not a subject at all (*De Anima* B2, 414a4 ff., esp. 12–14).

64 I emphasize these points in view of the scepticism of the recent account in Graham (1987). The primary-subject criterion for (primary) substance under study in *Metaphysics* Z3 is branded by Graham as now "an obsolete or irrelevant criterion of

Appendix. A Matter for Magnitude: What Is Left When Length, Breadth, and Depth Are Stripped Away?

Aristotle suggests in *Metaphysics* Z3 that at the final stage of *aphairesis*, we can strip away the actual length, breadth, and depth from a thing to reveal "what is determined by these," namely, (prime) matter. Does this bring to light a sense in which there can be a matter for size, which in itself lacks any given size? And if so, what could this amount to?

Consider the assertion that a given item, *x*, has a given size or set of dimensions, *s*. This claim might mean either of two things. First, it might mean that the size *s* is *constitutive of x*. That is, there is a matter, *m*, such that $x = m + s$. For example, let *x* be a statue of Aristotle. The second thing that might be meant is that *s supervenes on x*. That is, there is a compound, *c*, such that $c = x + s$. Evidence that this second kind of case may exist, where *x* is now matter, appears in *Physics* Δ2:

> Looked at another way, place seems to be *the extension of* the magnitude (*tou megethous diastēma*), ‹its› *matter: for this is different from the magnitude*, but this is what is contained by the form and determined ‹by it› (*to periechomenon hupo tou eidos kai hōrismenon*), as by surface and limit, and matter and the indefinite (*to aoriston*) is of this sort. For, *whenever the limit and the qualities of the sphere are removed* (*aphairethēi*), *nothing is left besides the matter*. (Δ2, 102b6–11; my emphasis)

Here Aristotle contrasts, on the one side, a given physical magnitude and, on the other, the extension of that magnitude, alternatively, its matter, or what is contained and determined by form (or by surface and limit), or what is left when the limit and the qualities of the sphere are removed, or finally, matter or the indefinite.

Suppose now that some size is *constitutive of* a given item, *x*. Then by an obvious *antiduplication* principle, no size also supervenes on *x*. By

substancehood" (p. 231). In line with this, the "incommensurability" hypothesis for which Graham argues greets the developments of Z3 with disparaging incomprehension: "It is curious that he [= Aristotle] should naively invoke a concept of substance so intimately connected with the atomic entities of S1 in trying to explicate the ontology of S2. . . . The fact is that Aristotle is preoccupied with his own housekeeping, and the source of his worries is the agreement of S2 with the principles of S1" (p. 222). Ultimately, Graham comes round to saying that the old criteria from the *Categories* do get changed in the *Metaphysics*: "None of the criteria is really the same," "none of the criteria for substance is really the same"; and even that the meaning of the term 'substance' itself will have shifted, given the Incommensurability thesis (p. 238). But he does not seem to consider the possibility that such shifts are part of the project of "saving the phenomena" and finding some place for the received views about substance, suitably modified, within the new theory of substance. On Graham's account, Aristotle is damned if he does and damned if he does not: if he simply restates material from the *Categories*, he is *inadvertent* and fails to comprehend the difference between his earlier and later theories, but if he tries to reformulate various points from his earlier work, then he is *misguided* and trying for a resolution that according to Graham is logically out of court; see the Introduction to this part.

the same token, if some size *supervenes on x,* then no size is also constitutive of *x.* At the same time, however, by some obvious principles of compounding, we can be sure that if some size, *s,* supervenes on an item, *x,* then there is a compound, *c,* such that $c = x + s$, that is, such that *s* is constitutive of *c.* And if some size *s,* is constitutive of *c,* then there is a matter, *m,* such that $c = m + s$, that is, such that *s* supervenes on *m.*

Given all this, there is an evident sense in which we can sensibly say that a given matter, *m,* "lacks magnitude." For, there can be a matter, *m,* such that while some size supervenes on *m,* still *no size is constitutive of m.* That is, there is no size, *s,* or matter, *n,* such that $n + s = m$. It does not follow from this that there is no *s* and no compound, *c,* such that $m + s = c$, that is, that *m* has no size supervenient on it. To say, then, that no size is constitutive of *m* is not, by itself, implausible. Indeed, the "matter for magnitude" discussed previously in the passage from *Physics* Δ2 clearly satisfies this condition.

Can there be a matter *m* such that no size supervenes on *m* and also no size is constitutive of *m?* For this to be the case, it will have to happen that (i) there is no size, *s,* or compound, *c,* such that $m + s = c$ – that is, no size *supervenes on m* – and also (ii) there is no matter, *n,* and no size, *s,* such that $n + s = m$ – that is, no size is *constitutive of m* either. It is, I take it, false for Aristotle that *m* can exist without magnitude or size in this radical way.[65]

There remains the more modest sense in which *m* can lack magnitude, namely, that there is no size that is constitutive of *m.* This point, generalized, yields the characterization of prime matter given in (T1) in Chapter 6, Section 4. A matter, *m,* is *prime* matter if and only if there is no matter, *n,* and no form, ψ, such that $m = n + ψ$. That is, roughly, prime matter has no (first-order) *constitutive* properties. This, however, by no means implies that prime matter has *no* (first-order) properties, for it can (and must) have *supervenient* properties. In particular, there is no size that is constitutive of prime matter, but this is not to say that no size supervenes on prime matter. Since no prime matter exists without actual specific size in this latter sense, we can talk meaningfully of this or that *amount* or *portion* of prime matter.

In light of this, when at the last stage of *aphairesis* we strip away the length, breadth, and depth of a thing, is there a sense in which what remains lacks size? On the account offered in the body of Chapter 10,

---

65 In *GC* A5, for example, discussing the phenomenon of growth, Aristotle rejects the idea touted in the first, dialectical part of the chapter, that "body and magnitude come to be from what is potentially magnitude and body, but is actually incorporeal (*asōmatou*) and without magnitude" (*amegethous,* 320a29–30), on the grounds that this would give separate existence to the void (b25–8). Similarly, "it is impossible that the matter for magnitude should be *separate*" (321a6–7, my emphasis).

aphairesis is *selective inattention:* we strip away – that is, *disregard* – the actual size, *s,* that supervenes on *m* and consider *m* by itself without regard to *s.* Aphairesis in this sense is possible only because there is some other world possible relative to the actual world in which *m* again exists but some size *other than s* supervenes on *m.* We are *not* supposing, then, that as a result of *aphairesis, s* does not supervene on *m* after all. *Aphairesis* is *not* a matter of "supposing false" the properties that in fact belong to *m.* Hence, we cannot say that the end product of *aphairesis* lacks the size it once had – that there is some size that, before *aphairesis,* supervened on *m* but now as a result of *aphairesis* no longer does so.

Given the modal constraint on *aphairesis* just noted, selective inattention can strip away only properties that *supervene on* an underlying subject. But if some size supervenes on *m,* then by the antiduplication principle already noted, no size is also constitutive of *m.* This gives a sense in which, where *aphairesis* strips away a thing's size, the end product does in itself lack size. By this, however, we mean only that where we strip off the size that supervenes on a thing, what remains is something such that all along no size was or is constitutive of it. As before, however, we do not mean to suggest that after the last step of *aphairesis* Aristotle imagines in Z3, we are left with something that not only has no constitutive size but that also, as the result of *aphairesis,* now lacks the size that formerly supervened on it.

11

Three Puzzles Concerning Form

In the preceding chapter, we considered some consequences of a two-part criterion for primary substance that Aristotle states first in the *Categories* but repeats in the *Metaphysics:* that primary substance is a (metaphysical) subject for everything, while at the same time, it is not itself (metaphysically) predicated of anything else. According to this criterion in the *Categories,* the individual substances, this man or this horse, are primary. Major trouble arises, however, if we allow that *matter* can be a subject for predicables; for on this assumption, Aristotle argues in *Metaphysics* Z3, it follows by the subject criterion that matter alone is primary substance.

In fact, the difficulty is even more radical than Aristotle says. In the new theory of the *Metaphysics,* and in contrast to what Aristotle suggests in Z3, not matter but rather nothing at all fits the subject criterion. In the *Metaphysics,* the monolithic conception of the subject of predication no longer holds good, and in Aristotle's new theory, no one kind of item can be subject for every predicable in the sense intended.

The entry of matter also spells trouble for the second part of the subject criterion, that primary substance is not predicated of anything else. Dual to matter is the notion of form, which is predicated of matter; and form is Aristotle's new choice for primary substance. How, in light of this, can Aristotle continue to hold that primary substance is not itself predicated of a subject and is not a universal?

Again, if form is predicated of matter, even predicated universally of matter, will form be a this or not? If it is a universal, apparently, it cannot be a this; but if it is primary substance, it must be. Must we conclude that form is ill-chosen as primary substance? Or must Aristotle finally bring himself to shake off the old criteria for primary substance from the *Categories?* In fact, I shall argue, Aristotle can find a way of reconciling his choice of form as primary substance with the old criteria for primary substance if these are suitably reworked to fit their new surroundings in the *Metaphysics*. How this can be done is the subject of this chapter.

1 The First Puzzle: Substance, Forms, and Universals

Towards the end of his book of puzzles at *Metaphysics* B6, Aristotle raises the question whether the first principles, or *archai* (whatever these turn out to be), are particular or universal. At 1003a7–9, he gives an argument designed to show that if they are universal, then, absurdly, they will not be substances: "For, none of the things that are common (*ouden tōn koinōn*, b8) signifies a this but a such, but substance ‹signifies› a this." The premises of this argument strike a familiar theme. The argument turns on the idea that there exist two mutually exclusive classes of entities, universals (or suches), on the one hand, and substances (or thises), on the other: if we assume further that the first principles are universals, there follows the troubling conclusion that they cannot be substances. The dichotomy between substances and universals is a continuing feature of Aristotle's metaphysics. It also forms the basis of one of his major criticisms of Plato's theory of ideas, that Platonic forms combine the incompatible characteristics of being both universals and substances.[1]

From the very start, there is work to be done to show why this criticism of Plato cannot be turned against Aristotle's own metaphysical theories. In his earliest theory of predication in the *Categories*, Aristotle holds that a species or secondary substance, man, for example, is predicated of various primary substances, Socrates, Callias, and the rest.[2] In light of Aristotle's own criticism of Plato, his characterization of a species as (in some sense) both a substance and universal to its various members is a troubling combination. In the *Categories*, Aristotle attempts to remove the difficulty by insisting that a species is, after all, a *secondary* substance and, unlike a primary substance, a such and not a this.[3] "Substance most of all," then, is what is never predicated of a subject, but at the same time there exist substances of a lesser grade, which are after all predicable of a subject.[4]

---

1 Plato emerges as an explicit target on these grounds briefly in *Metaphysics* Z13 at 1039a2–3; his views on the same topics are the object of more sustained criticism in Z14 and briefly again at Z16, 1040b27 ff.; see also, e.g., B6, 1003a9–12. M9, 1086a32–b5; *SE*, 22, 178b36–179a10.

2 Predication here is (again) *metaphysical* predication; see the Introduction to Part IV, note 4.

3 *Categories* 5, 3b13–21. Contra Furth (1988), pp. 31–2, Aristotle is unequivocal here that man and animal are *not* thises; cf. *SE*, 22, 178b36–9; *Metaphysics* Z13, 1038b34–1039a3. See also Chapter 1, Section 4.

4 *Categories* 5, 2b15–22.

Later in the *Metaphysics,* however, different measures are called for. Aristotle argues in B6 and elsewhere, most notably in Z13, that an entity cannot be both a universal and a substance, and he taxes Plato with getting this point wrong.[5] The same charge, however, can also apparently be levelled at Aristotle's own theory of forms in the *Metaphysics,* where he suggests at various points that (Aristotelian) forms are substances – in fact, they are *primary* substances – and at other places that they are universals. In the *Metaphysics,* then, Aristotle holds that,

(1) No universal is a substance.

Yet at the same time,

(2) Forms are primary substances

and

(3) Forms are universals.[6]

Together (1), (2), and (3) form an inconsistent set. Aristotle himself does not draw attention to the difficulty, much less say how it should be removed, and some have concluded that his position is beyond repair.[7] On the surface, the difficulty is the same applied to forms as the one that threatened Aristotle's notion of a species in the *Categories,*

---

5 See note 1.

6 No universal is a substance: *Metaphysics* B6, 1003a7–12, Z13, 1038b8–1039a3; cf. Z16, 1040b23, 1041a3–5, H1, 1042a21, I2, 1053b16–18, K2, 1060b21, M10, 1087a22. Aristotelian forms are (primary) substances: *Metaphysics* Z7, 1032b1–2, Z8, 1033b17–18, Z10, 1035b14 ff., Z11, 1037a22 ff., esp. 29 ff., Z17, 1041b7–9 (text as in Ross [1924]). They are universals: *Metaphysics* Z11, 1036a29, M8, 1084b5. (For the notion of *universal* at work here, see *De Interpretatione* 7, 17a39–40, "I mean by universal what is such by nature as to be predicated of many"; cf. Z13, 1038b11–12, and e.g., *An. Pr.* A1, 24a18, *Metaphysics* B3, 999a20–21, Δ26, 1023b29–32.) The point that forms are universals also follows from the fact that form is predicated of matter (see the references in note 11) – that is, universally predicated of different parcels of matter. For forms as universals, see also the discussion in Chapter 6, Section 2. Note, however, that the sense in which forms are universals is contested in Driscoll (1981) and Code (1986); see Section 4.

7 Lesher (1971), pp. 169–78; Sykes (1975), pp. 326–8. Graham (1987) is also among the sceptics. Graham regards Aristotle as either *inadvertent* or, if not inadvertent, *confused* about the changes in his views between the *Categories* and the *Metaphysics* (see the Introduction to this part). It seems to me unlikely that Aristotle is inadvertent with respect to the puzzles which the claim in (1), that no universal is a substance, creates for the new account of forms as primary substances, given his criticism of Plato for trying to make the same things both substances and universals and if, as I have suggested, his notion of *secondary* substance in the *Categories* is designed to shield his own theory there from similar objections. Again, Aristotle's preoccupation with the question 'Are the *archai,* or principles, universal or particular?' in the book of problems at B6, 1003a5–17, taken up again in M10, where he expressly confesses that the difficulties arise whether one's ontology is Platonic or not (1086b14–15), makes it hard to think that he is entirely oblivious to or even disingenuous about the difficulties under discussion. But if he is not inadvertent, can Aristotle properly make adjustments in the prohibition governing substances and universals, which

with the added twist that Aristotle is not willing here to say that forms are not substances in the primary sense, contrary to (2); for this reason, he can gain no advantage from weakening (1) to allow that substances that are not primary can after all be universals. In fact, however, there are grounds for thinking that both Aristotle's own position and his complaint against Plato are now considerably more complicated. In place of the contrast between universals and substances, Aristotle's interest is now in two different *relations*, 'x is universally predicated of y' and 'x is the substance of y'. One and the same thing can, after all – with the appropriate qualifications – be both a substance and a universal. What this amounts to, however, is subtly changed once the needed qualifications are in place. One and the same thing both can be universally predicated of something and can be the substance of something. But one thing is universally predicated of another only if it is *not* the substance of *that very same thing*. More generally,

(1′) If an entity is universal to many things, then it is not the substance of any of them.[8]

dates back to his earlier metaphysical theory, in the hope that again some truth can be salvaged from his earlier account of substance and incorporated into the later theory? As with the account of Z3 (Chapter 10, note 64), Graham is again unsympathetic. On a principle similar to our (1), 'No universal is a substance,' he comments that it is "just a reiteration of S1 principles, which are not now vital elements of his current system, but adventitious dogmas inherited from an earlier stage of thought. They provide gratuitous assumptions which do not further but rather obfuscate the argument of Book vii" (1987, p. 256). And there is no hope in sight of any reinterpretation of (1) that Aristotle may use to save his theory. On the contrary, Aristotle's "stubborn insistence in Chapter 13 on the unmitigated S1 criteria of substance . . . brings his investigation into inner conflict, and his continued dependence on S1 principles in Chapter 17 shows that he has not learned his lesson" (p. 261). The scolding Graham delivers here seems to me out of place. I shall argue that the first puzzle can be resolved if (1) can be rewritten as (1′) (ahead in the main text), where (1′) is well embedded in the theoretical apparatus of Aristotle's later metaphysical theory, as the discussion of (T10) in the Appendix to this chapter is designed to show.

8 The resolutions to the first and second puzzles given in this chapter were first presented at the Conference on Predication at Pitzer College in the spring of 1981 and later published as F. Lewis (1985a). A similar resolution to the first puzzle was arrived at independently by Loux (1979) and by Code (1986); cf. Code (1978), where the essential form of the argument at Z13, 1038b8–15, is spelled out. The use of (1′) to resolve the puzzle is in some ways a variation on the suggestion by Albritton that Aristotle's claim in (1), that no universal is a substance, should be understood to say that "nothing universal in relation to *species*, . . . is the substance of any of *them*" ([1957], p. 705; his emphasis); Albritton's principle is a special case of the more general (1′).

With (1′), compare (T7) in Section (iii) in the Appendix to this chapter. Aristotle does not explicitly state either (1′) or (T7): the nearest he comes is just (1). My defence of (1′) as a reading of (1) is in part its utility in solving the first puzzle. I shall say more on behalf of (1′) later in this section. Finally, a very different kind of support involves the deductive relations (1′) has to other principles at work in the *Metaphysics*, some of which Aristotle does state in exactly the form in which I consider them; details are given in the presentation of Aristotle's views on substance as a formal theory in the Appendix to this chapter.

I shall call this a principle of the *mutual exclusivity* of the two relations in question. Substances and universals, then, do not after all fall into two, mutually exclusive classes, but the relations 'x is the substance of y' and 'x is universally predicated of y' are mutually exclusive, in the sense specified.[9]

This result clears the way for the characterization of Aristotle's own forms as both universals and (primary) substances; for in the theory of the *Metaphysics*, a form is the substance of itself, or in a suitably reduced sense the *substance of* the compound material substance,[10] but it is universally predicated of neither of these, but rather of matter.[11]

At the same time, Aristotle's new principle of mutual exclusivity also allows him to reformulate his complaint against the Platonic theory of forms. For Aristotle often represents a Platonic form as,

9 The logical point here is an entirely simple one. For example, fathers and children do not fall into mutually exclusive classes (children of parents often become fathers, and all fathers are children of parents); but still, if x is the father of y, then x is not a child of y.

10 In the *Metaphysics*, the three notions of essence, definition, and substance are (materially) equivalent: one thing is signified by the definiens in a definition of another just in case the first is the essence of the second (*Topics* A4, 101b21–2, A5, 101b38, A8, 103b9–10, H3, 153a12–22, H5, 154a31–2; *An. Po.* B3, 91a1, B10, 93b29, 94a11; *Metaphysics* Δ6, 1016a33, 1017a6, Δ8, 1017b21–2, Z5, 1031a12, H1, 1042a17; Bonitz [1870], 764b45–57), and again, one thing is the essence of another just in case it is also its substance (*Metaphysics* Z6, 1031b2–3, 31–2). In the case of the essence-of and definition-of relations, Aristotle explicitly separates the *primary* cases, in which only entities that are themselves suitably primary have an essence or a definition, from various *lesser-grade* cases (see the discussions in *Metaphysics* Z4 and Z5; see also Z7, 1033a1–5, with Ross [1924], Vol. 2, pp. 185–6, and Z11, 1037a24–9, 33-b7); his practice seems to indicate a similar distinction in the case of the substance-of relation as well. In the primary cases, a thing is essentially the same as its essence or substance, or as the item signified by its definiens. For example, a form is the same as its substance (Z6, 1031a17–18), and hence it is the substance of itself. A compound material substance, however, has a substance in only a reduced sense: its substance is its form, and the form is *not* the same as the compound substance itself (Z11, 1037a33–b7). The various primary and secondary cases of the three relations involving the notions of substance, essence, and definition are featured in a very general version of mutual exclusivity, which I will discuss briefly later in this section:

  x is the substance or the essence or the definition of y, in either the primary or in any secondary sense of these notions, only if x is not (metaphysically) predicated of y.

There is further discussion in the Postscript to Part III and in greater detail in F. Lewis (1984). The more general formulation of mutual exclusivity brings out a peculiarity in Aristotle's theory of essence in the *Metaphysics* already noted in Chapter 7. We must reject any account of Aristotle's later essentialism that requires that an Aristotelian essence be "essential to every individual having it which is a genuine subject for that attribute" (Cohen [1978], p. 395). On the broader formulation of mutual exclusivity, not only is an essence or form *not* predicated of that of which it is the essence or (constitutive) form, but it is predicated of something *other than* that of which it is the essence or form; see Chapter 7, note 10.

11 *Metaphysics* Z3, 1029a23–4, Z13, 1038b4–6, Θ7, 1049a27 ff.; cf. B1, 995b35, B4, 999a33–4, H2, 1043a5–6; see also Part III, esp. Chapter 6, Sections 2 and 4.

contrary to the mutual exclusivity principle, not only universal to, but also *the substance of,*[12] its various participants.

The most immediate defence of (1') as the appropriate expansion of (1) is that (1') rather than (1) is what Aristotle actually proves in the body of Z13. I argue in the Appendix to this chapter that the formal counterpart of (1') can be proved as a theorem in Aristotle's theory of substance;[13] the general shape of Aristotle's proof can be indicated informally here. Aristotle writes:

(b8) It appears to be impossible that any of the things said universally is a substance. (b9) For first of all, the substance of each thing is the one peculiar to each (*hē idios hekastōi*), which does not belong to another, while the universal ‹is› common; (b11) for that is said to be universal which by nature belongs to many. (b12) Of what, then, will this be the substance? For ‹it must› either ‹be the substance› of all, or of none, but it cannot be ‹the substance› of all; (b13) but if it will be ‹the substance› of one, that one will actually be ‹identical with› the rest; (b14) for those things of which the substance is one and the essence is one, themselves too are one. (Z13, 1038b8–15)

Aristotle's official conclusion, stated at the very beginning at b8–9, like (1), deals with a *non*relational notion of substance *tout court*. But the relational notion of the substance *of* a thing enters immediately in the first lines of the proof itself at b10 and reappears repeatedly throughout. Once the details of Aristotle's argument are spelled out, it will be evident that what he has actually proved is not (1), but (1'). The argument proceeds indirectly. Suppose that x is universal to y and z, where $y \neq z$, and that x is the substance of y ("but if it will be ‹the substance› of one," b13). Now

that is said to be universal which by nature belongs to many. *Of what, then, will this be the substance? For* ‹it must› either ‹be the substance› of all, or of none. (b11–13; my emphasis)

That is, where x is universal to y and z, x is the substance of y just in case it is the substance of z. On the assumption, then, that x is the substance of y, it follows that x is the substance of z. But

those things *of which the substance is one* and the essence is one, themselves too are one. (b14–15; my emphasis)

12 *Metaphysics* M5, 1080a1; cf. A6, 988a8–11, A7, 988b4–5. A similar idea, I believe, is also involved in the anti-Platonic arguments of Z14: see the remarks at the end of note 17. With this view, Aristotle goes against the most natural interpretation of Plato (which he seems to concede elsewhere, e.g., Z4, 1030a13–14), which makes participation an *accidental* relation between a form and its participants (cf. Chapter 1, notes 67 and 68). Strikingly, others of Aristotle's criticisms of Plato depend on precisely this view of participation: this is the main thrust of Aristotle's use of the notion of Izzing in the *Categories*, by way of modifying the Platonic view that sensibles invariably *Have* their various predicables.

13 Cf. the proof of (T10) in Section (iv) of the Appendix. For discussion of the argument, see also Code (1978) and Frede and Patzig (1988) Vol. 2, pp. 248 ff.

That is, where x is the substance of both y and z, $y = z$. Accordingly, $y = z$, contrary to our initial assumption. By *reductio*, then, where x is universal to y and z, it cannot be the case that x is the substance of y. More generally, either by the biconditional extracted from b11–13, or by a repetition of the entire argument,

x is universal to y and z, only if x is not the substance either of y or of z,

which is the formal counterpart of (1′).

It is worth emphasizing that the move from (1) to (1′) as the correct form of his conclusion at 1038b8–15 for Aristotle barely requires comment, given his view in the *Metaphysics* that a primary substance must be the substance *of* something. A second unannounced shift in Aristotle's discussion in Z13 and the following chapters involves not so much the nature as the *number* of the conclusions he means to be arguing for there. In the four chapters that begin with Z13, Aristotle is defending *two* theses: not only that no universal is a substance, as in (1), but also that

(4) No substance is composed of substances.

Not only are the two theses closely interweaved in the argument of Z13, but also each bears with equal effect on the anti-Platonic conclusions of Z14.[14] Finally, they are stated side by side in the summary in the last lines of Z16: "It is clear that both none of the things said universally is a substance, and that no substance is ‹composed› out of substances" (1041a3–5). What accounts for this casual intermingling of these two conclusions? It is not hard to show that the two theses come to the same thing applied to entities that are both substances and also analysed in terms of genus and differentia – to take an easy example that is also the topic of Z14, the Platonic form Man with its genus and differentia, Animal and Two-footed.[15] As a preliminary,

14 For the connection with *Metaphysics* Z14, see 1039a24 and note 17.

15 The *scope* of Aristotle's two conclusions requires some comment. Without question, they are supposed to apply to the relations among the Platonic forms Man, Animal, and Two-footed (Aristotle's stock choice for differentia), which are the subject of Z14. It is almost as certain that his conclusions will also apply to the *Categories*-style genera and species if these are taken as substances of some kind, as they are in the *Categories* (but not in the *Metaphysics;* cf. Section 6, and Chapter 7, Section 5). For these two choices, see Frede and Patzig (1988), Vol. 2. p. 241. Perhaps less easy to decide is the application of the conclusions to the analysis of bona fide Aristotelian forms. Primary substances, that is, forms, are primary definables, and so when Aristotle worries about the question of the Unity of Definition in Z12, for example, and has in mind the notion of definition by *diairesis*, or division, it looks as though forms too must have the structure of a species, and can be resolved into genus and differentia; see Ross (1924), Vol. 2, p. 277, and *Metaphysics* Δ24, 1023a35–b2, 25, 1023b22–5. If so, then Aristotle's conclusions entail that the generic component of an Aristotelian form is a universal but not a substance, so that the form itself is not composed of two substances, each existing in actuality. (Meanwhile, perhaps, the differentia but *not*

we assume that Man is composed of Animal and Two-footed and that Man is a substance; at the same time, Animal is the generic component of Man, and hence a universal. Then if Animal is a universal but not a substance in accordance with (1), it follows that Man is a substance and composed (in part) of Animal, which is not a substance, as (4) requires.[16] Similarly, moving in the opposite direction, if we suppose that Man is a substance and composed (in part) of Animal, which is not a substance, in line with (4), it follows that Animal is a universal but not a substance, as required by (1). This equivalence is important, since it is the basis for Aristotle's claim at the beginning of Z14 that *the very same considerations* at work in Z13 – that is, I take it, (1) and (4) alike – have evident consequences for Platonic views about genus and species forms.[17] I take it as a further virtue in (1') that the relation between the two conclusions also holds in the relevant cases if (1) is expanded to

the genus is the substance of the form.) Notice that the assumption that Aristotelian forms are constructed out of genus and differentia is virtually automatic for those who hold, contrary to what is argued here (Chapter 7, Section 5), that forms in the *Metaphysics* just are the kinds or species (the secondary substances) from the *Categories*.

Last but by no means least, I go on to argue in the main text that Aristotle's conclusions, (1') and (4), apply also at the level of individual Aristotelian substances, for example, a (= $m + \psi$), and to the form ψ that is the substance of a in a suitably reduced sense.

16 This is the weaker form of Aristotle's conclusion (4) to the effect that where a is composed of b and c, it cannot be the case that *both* b and c are substances existing in actuality (Z13, 1039a3 ff.); on this reading, I take it, if a substance is analysed in terms of genus and differentia, the genus will not be a substance, but the differentia can be (cf. Z12, 1038a18 ff.). The weaker form is also required if we apply (4) to individual substances, as two paragraphs below in the main text.

17 *phaneron d' ek autōn toutōn to sumbainon*, Z14, 1039a24: either (1) or (4), both at work in Z13, will apply with equal effectiveness against the Platonic supposition that "ideas are substances existing separately, and the form consists of the genus and the differentiae" (1039a25–6) under attack in Z14. Thus, suppose, for example, that

(a) the genus-form, Animal, and various species-forms, Man, Tiger and so on, are all *substances* (cf. 1039b30–4),

while

(b) Man and the rest are *composed of* Animal together with the suitable differentia, so that Animal is *universal to* each of Man and the others.

If the Platonist is committed to (b), then on the Aristotelian principles of Z13, he must be prepared to give up (a). Thus, supposing that Animal is universal to Man and the other species forms, then by (1), Animal cannot be a substance. Similarly, if Animal is a constituent of Man, Tiger, and the rest, each of which is a substance (and, perhaps, if we agree that the differentia is a substance), then again, by (4), Animal itself cannot be a substance.

Notice that Aristotle also seems inclined to attribute to the Platonist the view that

(a') Animal is the substance *of* Man, Tiger, and the rest

(Z14, 1039b8–9; cf. 9–11, 12–13); if the Platonist still holds to (b) as well, then he is in conflict with the revised principle (1').

(1′) as I suggest. First, I argue that if we deny (4), we must also deny (1), now understanding (1) as (1′). We assume that Animal is universal to the different species Man and Horse, while Man and Horse are each composed of Animal together with the relevant differentia. Suppose also that the Platonic theory agrees with Aristotle's own conclusion in Z12 that the final differentia is a substance (it is the substance *of* the relevant species, so that Two-footed is the substance of Man, etc.).[18] If Animal too is a substance, each of the species Man and Tiger will be composed of substances, contrary to (4). Now if Animal is a substance, presumably it will also be the substance *of* something[19] – that is, perhaps, it will be the substance of Man and Horse. If so, then since Animal is also universal to Man and Horse, it turns out that Animal is both universal to and also the substance of one and the same thing, contrary to (1′).

Similarly, for the same set of cases, if we deny (1′), we must also deny (4). Suppose that Man and Tiger are both substances and also, contrary to (1′), that Animal is both universal to Man and Tiger and also the substance of each – that is, Animal itself is a substance. On the assumption that the respective differentiae are also substances, it follows that Man and Tiger are themselves substances and also composed of substances, contrary to (4). For certain cases, then, the two major theses Aristotle means to defend in Z13–16 are equivalent, and the equivalence survives even if we expand the first thesis, (1), to become (1′).

Our discussion so far has dealt with the application of Aristotle's conclusions (1′) and (4) to the alien entities of Platonic metaphysics. This is in keeping with what I take to be in many ways the *programmatic* or perhaps *abstract* character of Aristotle's working-out of the relations between such notions as substance (or substance-of), predication, and universal, which in important respects proceeds *independently* of the details of any one particular metaphysical theory. His conclusions apply as well to the analysis of the *Categories*-style species and of bona fide Aristotelian forms (see note 15), and in Z13, (4) is applied even to Democritean atoms and to numbers. It is worth emphasizing, then, that (4) and (1′) apply also at the level of individual Aristotelian substances:

No *individual substance* is composed of two items, namely, matter and form, both of them substances in actuality;

and

Nothing is both the substance of *a given individual substance* (here we assume

---

18 Z12, 1038a18–35.
19 For this move, cf. Z14, 1039b9–10, with b12–13.

the appropriately reduced sense of 'substance of') and also predicated of, much less universal to, *that same individual substance*.[20]

Both results are grounded in fundamental facts about the nature of form—matter compounds. An individual substance is composed of a sequence of matters bounded (in the traditional story) by prime matter at the lower end and by proximate matter of the thing and its substantial "last" form at the top (*Metaphysics* α2, 994a3−5, 19−b9). Since there is an upper bound to the sequence of matters involved in the composition of any individual substance (994a19−b6), we know that an individual substance itself has matter, *but is not itself the matter of anything further*. This result leads quickly to the appropriate instance of (4). A given individual substance a is composed of proximate matter m and substantial "last" form ψ, where, standardly, ψ is the substance of a and hence itself a substance. We now know that no (actual) substance is the matter of another substance. It follows that m is not an actual substance, and in general, no individual substance is composed out of two items, a matter and a form, both of them substances in actuality.

There is some intuitive appeal to the idea that the matter of an individual substance cannot be competing with the substance itself for the claim to substance: one material substance in one place at one time is quite enough (see, e.g., Z16, 1040b5−16). Strikingly, instances of Aristotle's strictures about substances and universals in (1'), appropriate at the level of individual substances, can be derived from (4) with the help of existing principles of form—matter compounds. Suppose that there exists an individual substance a, where $a = m + \psi$, so that ψ is the substance of a in a suitably reduced sense of 'substance of'. Suppose also that, contrary to (1'), ψ supervenes on a, so that ψ is predicated of, even universal to, a.[21] If ψ supervenes on a, then by a standard principle of compounding (= [A5], Chapter 6, Section 4), there is some b, such that $b = a + \psi$. Since ψ is the substantial form of a and a is a substance, plausibly, ψ has the same effect in b, that is, b too is a substance. It follows that a substance b is composed out of actual substances a and ψ, contrary to (4). This gives the appropriate instance of (1'): where ψ is the substance (even in some reduced sense) of a, ψ is not predicated of, much less universal to, a.

20 This is in contrast to the view expressed most recently by Furth (1988), pp. 247−8, that one key to understanding Z13 is to restrict the notion of *universal* at work there to items universal to "more than one substance *in the sense of substantial specific kind*" (his emphasis); this restrictive attitude is perhaps a descendant of the suggestion in Albritton 1957), p. 705, quoted in note 8 above.

21 "universal to": see note 69. Alternatively, suppose that there is some other substance, a', and other matter, m', such that $a' = m' + \psi$, and that ψ also supervenes on a'; then ψ is universal to a and to a'.

I have argued that Aristotle is formally committed to (1') in *Metaphysics* Z13 and that, on other grounds too, (1') fits well into the formal fabric of Z13–16. Beyond this, however, is the mutual exclusivity principle in (1') *well motivated* for Aristotle? In the Postscript to Part III, I suggested that Aristotle is committed not only to the narrow version of mutual exclusivity represented by (1'), but much more broadly to the view that

> x is the substance or the essence or the definition of y, in either the primary or in any secondary sense of these notions, only if x is not (metaphysically) predicated of y.

This more general formulation is perhaps related to an important condition on (metaphysical) predication. (Metaphysical) predication, both early and late, is constrained by the principle that a *subject* of predication must first be a member of a *kind;* given this principle, a *noncircularity* argument is easily constructed that apparently leads straight to a version of generalized mutual exclusivity. In Aristotle's later theory, the sequence of thought is this. In the usual case, according to Aristotle, to be a fit subject for predication, a thing must first be a member of a kind.[22] But a thing is a member of a given kind only because it has the appropriate substance or constitutive form. Hence, a thing is a fit subject for predication only because it has the appropriate substance or constitutive form. This role of the substance of a thing supplies the premiss in a noncircularity argument. In its baldest form,

> (i) For any x, x is a fit subject for predication in the first place only because for some y, y is the substance of x in either the primary or some suitably reduced sense. We cannot, then, suppose also that (ii) y is the substance of x in the relevant sense only because y is predicated of x – else (this is the circularity part) what makes x a fit subject for *any* case of (metaphysical) predication is just that y is predicated of $x!$

From this, finally, we conclude that one thing is the substance of another, in either the primary sense or in any reduced sense of 'substance of', only if it is not predicated of that same thing.[23]

---

22 The exception involves prime matter, which does not belong to a kind and has no constitutive form: see Chapter 6, Section 4, and Chapter 10, note 55.

23 Strictly, the noncircularity argument shows only that where x is a subject for predicables only because y is the substance of x, it cannot be the case that y is the substance of x *only because* y is predicated of x; but the broadened version of mutual exclusivity requires us to deny that y is the substance of x *only if* y is predicated of x. We can bridge the gap between 'only because' and 'only if' if we suppose that the only reason for holding the material conditional, contrary to mutual exclusivity, would be if y's being predicated of x were part of the *analysis* of y's being the substance of x. On this assumption, 'only if' can be bumped up to 'only because', and any opponent of broadened mutual exclusivity will be liable to the noncircularity argument given.

An instance of the noncircularity argument is used in Woods (1967), pp. 237–8,

A rather different set of ideas, however, is at work in the earlier metaphysics. Plausibly, if the noncircularity argument and the principle of extended mutual exclusivity work for the substance of a thing, then – by way of adaptation to the *Categories,* where the notion of the substance of a thing makes no appearance – there will be counterparts of the argument and of mutual exclusivity that hold instead for *kinds.* As a first approximation, assume that Socrates could not exist as a subject for any predicables whatever if he were not first a member of a kind – that is, if he Were not first a man. With the aid of this assumption, we can use a version of the noncircularity argument to argue that – contrary to what Aristotle in fact supposes – man is not predicated of Socrates at all.

In the *Categories,* Aristotle guards against this result by stipulating that Socrates' kinds *are* (metaphysically) predicated of Socrates, but they are not predicated of him in the way that his accidents are. His kinds, then, make Socrates a fit subject not for any predicable whatever but for accidents alone. (This is the principle of "Izzing before Having" noted in the Introduction to Part I.) As far as the *Categories* goes, therefore, our mutual exclusivity principle must be transformed into a point about the mutual exclusivity of the two varieties of predication:

x is a kind relative to y only if x is not an accident of y. (In the jargon of Izzing and Having, y Is [an] x only if y does not Have x.)

This result can be proved given the reconstruction of Aristotle's theory in Chapter 2, Section 4; the details are left as an exercise for the reader. With a little stretching, the principle can also be supported by a variation on the noncircularity argument, specially adapted to the theory of the *Categories.* Roughly,

(i) For any x, x is a fit subject for Having accidents in the first place only because for some y, x Is y. It cannot be the case, then, that (ii) x Is y only because x Has y – else (the circularity part) what makes x a fit subject for Having any accidents whatever, y included, is just that x Has y!

This argument blocks the claim that x Is y only *because* x Has y; some more work may give us the conclusion that x Is y *only if* x does not Have y, as mutual exclusivity requires.[24] So a version of mutual exclusivity is

to argue that the form man is not a *kata pollōn legomenon* – that is, that it is not predicated of the individual men; see also Woods (1974–5), p. 178. But Woods does not say how he would bridge the logical gap just noted.

24 The new argument for mutual exclusivity is subject to reservations similar to those noted for the comparable argument in note 23. As it stands, the argument does not show that where x Has a given accident only because x Is y, it cannot also be the case that x Is y *only if* x Has y, contrary to the current version of mutual exclusivity. Much as before, we may want to suppose that x's Having y would be necessary for x's Being

in any case true for Aristotle in the *Categories* and may even be a consequence of the principle of "Izzing before Having" in combination with the appropriate noncircularity argument. I conclude that even without its role in resolving the first puzzle, some version of mutual exclusivity is central to Aristotle's thinking, both early and late.

If the different arguments in favour of (1') succeed, we will have a way of resolving the first puzzle that does not require us to deny (3): we are not forced by the sheer weight of (1) and (2) to suppose that forms cannot after all be universals, so that each form of a natural substance is proprietary to exactly one thing, while two things that belong to the same kind must have forms that are qualitatively indistinguishable but numerically distinct.[25]

---

y, only because *x*'s Having *y* were part of the *analysis* of the fact that *x* Is *y*. This allows us to move up from 'only if' to 'only because', thus bringing the opponent of mutual exclusivity within range of the noncircularity argument given.

A version of this application of the noncircularity argument appears in Dancy (1975), pp. 370–1. There is a hint of the same argument in Owen (1965 [1975]), p. 138.

25 Sellars (1957), pp. 691–9, (1967), pp. 107–18; cf. Harter (1975), pp. 11–18, and Hartman (1976), pp. 545–61, (1977), Chap. 2. More recent proponents of the same view include Lloyd (1981), Frede ([1978] 1987), and Frede and Patzig (1988), and Witt (1989). Notice that the "individual form" treatment of (3) can be developed in two very different ways. On one account, the *only* forms of natural objects are individual forms, so that (3) is straightforwardly false. On other accounts, there are general as well as particular forms, so the puzzle rests on the fallacy of equivocation involving not only (3), where by 'form' Aristotle must mean *general* form, but also (2), where the primary substances are *individual* forms.

For other sceptical treatments of (3) that do not involve the hypothesis of individual form but do find an equivocation in the argument, see the discussion of Driscoll (1981) in Section 4. For the record, others have thought that the puzzle rests on equivocation in a quite different place. Woods (1967), p. 229, for example, argues that Aristotle keeps separate the notions of "things spoken universally," which are neither forms nor substances, and universals *simpliciter*, which are both. Notice that most if not all of the accounts that find an equivocation in the argument think that the equivocation is on the part of Aristotle's interpreters, not Aristotle himself; see the remarks in connection with Driscoll (1981) in Section 4.

Finally, the fact that Aristotle argues for (1') will not help hold off the hypothesis of individual forms if, as Frede and Patzig argue, Aristotle uses (1'), that a universal is not the substance of anything to which it belongs, *as part of a proof of (1) itself*, that a universal is not a substance at all (Frede and Patzig [1988], Vol. 2, pp. 250–1). If (1') entails (1), it will be idle to maintain as I have done that Aristotle *drops* (1) and defends (1') in its place. According to Frede and Patzig, (1) in turn belongs within a larger argument in support of the nominalism they hold is distinctive of the *Metaphysics* that denies existence altogether to Platonic universals and to the species and genera that counted as secondary substances in the *Categories*. (This second phase of the argument is an argument by elimination: a universal cannot be a substance, but since it is not properly speaking a quality either, or a member of any other category, and not even *potentially* a member of the categories, it can have no real existence at all; see Frede [1987 (= 1985)], p. 78, and Frede and Patzig [1988], Vol. 2, p. 241, esp. pp. 246–7.) It will also be open to us to argue that since (1) and (2) can now both be true, we must deny (3), so that forms must be not universals, but individuals, as Frede and Patzig suppose.

The argument from (1') to (1) requires us to assume that if a thing is a universal and also the substance of something, then it belongs to (= is metaphysically predicated of) that very thing:

Finally, the use of the mutual exclusivity principle, (1'), to resolve the first puzzle brings to light an important general feature of Aristotle's enquiry into substance. The puzzle suggests that Aristotle's willingness to retain the earlier condition on substance given in (1) is hopelessly at odds with his new choice of form as primary substance, once we take into account the other properties form takes on in his later theory of predication. Aristotle's response to the difficulty, as I understand it, is not to repudiate outright the condition on substance in (1), or to throw up his hands and suppose that his earlier criteria for substance are irremediably in conflict with the choice of form as primary substance and the role given to form in the new *Metaphysics* theory of predication. Rather, Aristotle chooses to reformulate the condition in (1) so that it is consistent with the selection of form as primary substance and with the properties of forms set out in (3). If a similar policy of reformulation remains in effect in the other puzzles too, then he may succeed in preserving *all* of the received criteria for substancehood (although not necessarily all at face value), even after they have been transplanted to the new context of the *Metaphysics*.

2   The Second Puzzle: Substance, Forms, and Predication

Given the new principle of mutual exclusivity, Aristotle is able to argue again, as we have seen, that Platonic forms are liable to a difficulty from which his own forms are immune. A key ingredient in his

(a) for any x and y, x is a universal and x is the substance of y, only if x belongs to y

(Frede and Patzig, Vol. 2, pp. 250–1). Add to this assumption our (1'), that is (more or less),

(b) for any x and y, x belongs to y only if x is not the substance of y,

together with the further assumption that

(c) a given item a is a universal and a is also the substance of a given particular thing, b.

It is easily shown that these three together form an inconsistent set. (Thus, if a is a universal and also the substance of b, as in (c), then by (a) a does, and by (b) a does not, belong to b.) But why should we blame the contradiction on (c), so that a universal cannot be the substance *of anything*, and hence not a substance, period (for the "hence," see perhaps (A9) in the Appendix), as Frede and Patzig suppose, rather than on assumption (a), which by their own admission is a "missing premiss" (p. 251) and which they do not otherwise defend? Premiss (a) together with (b) forces the denial of (c); if so, we are well on the way to asserting (1), and on this story again, (1) and (2) together argue for the falsity of (3), so that forms must be *individual* forms, as Frede and Patzig want. But for all Frede and Patzig show, it is equally open to us to adopt (b) and (c) and reject (a). To this point, then, the debate over individual forms is a standoff. I do not claim that the hypothesis of individual form is hereby refuted. But the argument so far hardly supports the conclusion that Z13 *forces* ("*erzwingen*") this hypothesis on us, as Frede and Patzig assert (Vol. 2, p. 246).

account of how his own theory satisfactorily obeys the mutual exclusivity principle is the idea that an Aristotelian form is (metaphysically) predicated – in fact, predicated universally – *of matter*. This idea is part of a comprehensive rethinking of some basic metaphysical concepts that Aristotle undertakes after the writing of the *Organon*. By the time of the *Metaphysics*, as we have seen, *forms* rather than individual substances are the primary substances. Individual substances, meanwhile, are analysed as in some sense *compounds* of form and matter in which a given form is *(metaphysically) predicated of* the matter in question.

Yet this idea introduces a second puzzle concerning forms. Aristotle insists in the *Categories* that a substance in the primary sense is what is not predicated of a subject, and in the *Metaphysics*, more generally, that no substance of any kind is predicated of a subject.[26] Both points are clearly directed against Plato's theory of forms, which are (in Aristotle's terms) primary substances and are also participated in by sensibles. The contrast with Plato is no longer so clear in the *Metaphysics*, however. According to the *Metaphysics*, Aristotelian forms are primary substances and also predicable of matter. How, then, can Aristotle repeat his criticism of Plato that no primary substance (or even no substance of any kind) is predicable of a subject? In the *Metaphysics*, Aristotle is apparently committed to these three claims:

(5) No substance is (metaphysically) predicated of a subject.
(2) Forms are primary substances.
(6) Forms are (metaphysically) predicable of matter.

Again, the difficulty is that not all three claims can be true.

The inconsistency is troubling most of all because it again points up a conflict between one of the central criteria for substance, which Aristotle takes for granted both in the *Categories* and later in the *Metaphysics*, and properties of his favoured candidate for (primary) substance in the *Metaphysics*, namely, form. Again, I understand Aristotle's policy in the face of this conflict to be not one of repudiation, so that the old criterion for substance is outright abandoned, but rather one of reformulation. Accordingly, Aristotle modifies his old prohibition in (5) that a substance is not predicated of a subject. As before, he turns his attention away from the notion of being a substance *tout court* to the relation 'x is the substance of y'. Instead of (5), he requires that

(5′) Nothing is both the substance of and (metaphysically) predicated of the very same thing.[27]

---

26 *Categories* 2, 1b3–6, 5, 2a11–14, 3a8–9; *Metaphysics* Δ8, 1017b10–14, 23–4, Z3, 1028b35–1029a2, a7–9, Z13, 1038b15.
27 With (5′), compare (T8) in Section (iv) of the Appendix to this chapter.

So the relations 'x is the substance of y' and 'x is (metaphysically) predicated of y' are also mutually exclusive in the sense of the term already explained in connection with (1') in Section 1 (the relation between (1') and (5') will be discussed shortly). And like (1'), (5') has an obvious relation to the version of generalized mutual exclusivity also discussed in Section 1 (see also the Postscript to Part III).

Once (5) is replaced by (5'), any threat of inconsistency is removed. By (2), we know that a form is a primary substance. We may grant, further, that a form is the substance *of* itself, or (again) in a suitably reduced sense,[28] the *substance of* the compound material substance of which it is the constitutive form. Even so, a form is predicable only of matter, and a form is not in any sense the substance of the matter of which it is predicated. Aristotle's own theory of forms, then, is clearly consistent with (5'). (At the same time, it is not obvious that the rival hypothesis of *individual* form is even relevant to the solution of the puzzle.)[29]

At the same time, again, Aristotle can use (5') to construct a fresh complaint against Plato. For as we have seen, Aristotle sometimes supposes that a Platonic form is the substance of the very sensibles that participate in it. If it is fair to attribute such a view to Plato,[30] then Plato is directly in conflict with (5').

Finally, like the puzzle sketched in Section 1, the present puzzle depends for its resolution on a principle of mutual exclusivity (the two principles are set out in (1') and (5') respectively). This similarity is no accident. There are close connections between the puzzles themselves, as well as between their respective solutions. Assumption (5) in the puzzle just sketched entails (1) in the first puzzle, in an easy way. If a substance is not predicated of even a single subject, then a fortiori it is not predicated universally of more than one subject.[31] Similarly, the new principle (5') entails the new (1'). According to (5'), if a form is predicated of a thing, then it cannot be the substance of that thing. It is a trivial consequence that if a form is universal to, and hence predicated of, *more* than one thing, it cannot be the substance of any of them. This establishes the truth of (1').[32] In this way, the mutual

28 See note 10.
29 It might be suggested that the hypothesis of individual form offers a resolution of the puzzle if in addition to individual forms, there also exist *species* forms, which are universals. Then arguably the second puzzle commits the fallacy of equivocation: by 'forms' in (2), we mean *individual* forms; in (6), *species* forms. But the existence of species forms in addition to individual forms is not acceptable to some advocates of individual form; see, e.g., Frede and Patzig (1988), Vol. 1, Chap. 8.
30 But see note 12.
31 Notice that the two assumptions, (1) and (5), occur within a few lines of one another in Aristotle's discussion of the universal in *Metaphysics* Z13 (1038b8–9 and passim; cf. b15).
32 With this argument, compare the proof that (T8) entails (T10) in the Appendix, Section (iv).

exclusivity of the substance-of and predication relations helps to resolve both of the puzzles sketched.[33]

3 The Third Puzzle: Substance, Forms, Universals, and Thises

Let us return to the passage already quoted from *Metaphysics* B6: if the first principles are universals, then they will not be substances, "for, none of the things that are common (*ouden tōn koinōn*, b8) signifies a this but a such, but substance ‹signifies› a this." In this passage, as we have seen, Aristotle appears to sort universals and substances into two mutually exclusive classes. In the two preceding sections, I have suggested how to reinterpret this move in a way that brings it into line with features of the theories of form and (metaphysical) predication in the central books of the *Metaphysics*. But a puzzle still remains. In the passage from B6, Aristotle's argument turns on the point that universals are suches, but substances are thises, and this idea by itself continues to cause trouble.

In the *Metaphysics,* forms are predicated of and hence universal to matter, as we have seen.[34] But as B6 seems to show, no universal is a this, but rather a such,[35] hence, forms too must be not thises, but suches. At the same time, if forms are Aristotle's choice for primary substances, then by B6 again, forms are thises after all.[36] To all appearances, then, Aristotle is committed to all four members of an inconsistent quartet:

(7) Substances are thises.[37]

(2) Forms are primary substances.

33 Modrak (1979), p. 373, suggests a different resolution of the second puzzle: by (5), Aristotle means only that nothing that is said of *a subject of accidents* is a substance. A similar move is made by Woods (1967), p. 230, and by Driscoll (1981), p. 152, n. 76. But twice when Aristotle asserts (5), he explicitly mentions the idea of matter as a substrate only a few lines away (Z3, 1029a8; cf. a 2–3, 23–4; Z13, 1038b15; cf. b5–6), and it is difficult to suppose that he would so soon forget or forgo the necessary qualification to (5). By contrast, (5') in the text has the virtue not only that it entails (1'), so that the solutions to the two puzzles hang together in a natural way, but also that it is in any case *true* for Aristotle. I discuss both points further in the Appendix to this chapter.

34 See note 6.

35 See also *Categories* 5, 3b10 ff.; *SE* 22, 178b36 ff.; *Metaphysics* Z13, 1038b34–1039a3.

36 Primary substance is a this: the history of this idea begins at *Categories* 5, 3b11 ff. (cf. *SE* 8, 169a35–6) and is reflected in the *Metaphysics* at, e.g., Z3, 1029a28, Z4, 1030a5–6; cf. b12, Z13, 1038b24, Z14, 1039a32, as well as in B6. Now in the *Metaphysics*, we know that *form* is primary substance: it follows that form is a this. Aristotle explicitly makes this last claim at *GC* A3, 318b32; *Metaphysics* Δ8, 1017b23–6, H1, 1042a28–9, Θ7, 1049a35, Λ3, 1070a11, 13.

37 In the *Categories*, Aristotle's principle about thises and substances takes the form

  Primary substances are thises;

later in the *Metaphysics*, as we shall see later in this section, the 'primary' can be dropped, as in (7), so that any actual substance – form or the compound material substance, but *not* matter, which is only potentially a substance – will be a this.

(8) No universal is a this.
(3) Forms are universals.

The quartet is inconsistent because (7) and (2) together imply that a form is a this, while (8) and (3) together imply that it is not.

Of the four claims involved in this puzzle, the idea that forms are universals in (3) is a holdover from the first puzzle, while (2), which identifies form as primary substance, is common to all three puzzles. We saw in discussing the first puzzle that a form can be both a universal and a substance, *but not with respect to one and the same thing*. This appeal to the relational conception of substances and universals renders (2) and (3) harmless in the first puzzle, but it is not clear that a comparable move is available here. Aristotle holds, apparently, that being a universal entails being a such, whereas being a substance entails being a this. But while various relational moves brought us clear of the first puzzle, neither being a this nor being a such is a relational notion. So the fact that a form can (with the appropriate qualifications) be both a universal and a substance, as required by (2) and (3), does not obviously show how we can avoid the absurd conclusion that a form is both a this and *not* a this, but a such.[38]

There remain the two new assumptions, (7) and (8), that make every substance a this and withhold the title from universals, which Aristotle characterizes instead as suches. The two assumptions deserve special scrutiny, for it is far from certain that Aristotle's initial views on these topics survive totally without change in the *Metaphysics*.

The idea in (7) that substances are thises begins life in the *Categories*, where all *and only* individual substances are thises;[39] since individual substances are the primary substances, it follows that all and only *primary* substances are thises. What counts as a this, however, may well change in the new metaphysical context of the *Metaphysics*. I shall argue that Aristotle keeps the idea that all individual substances are

38 In fact, however, as we shall see, the fact that a universal is universal *to something* does figure again in the solution to this puzzle too, but in a slightly different way; cf. (8) with (8′) in Section 4.

39 In the *Categories*, thises are items that are indivisible and one in number (*atoma kai hen arithmōi*, 2, 1b3–9) in the category of substance – that is, they are the lowest members of the category of substance – while indivisibles in general are the lowest members of their respective category. Hence, we have this rule governing all indivisibles:

x is indivisible only if there is no y ($y \neq x$??) such that y Is x.

(This is a slightly weaker version of a principle formulated by Code: different versions of the principle appear in Code [1980] and [1986].) The rule is obeyed in Aristotle's metaphysics both early and late. In the *Categories*, as we have seen, the lowest member of a category is not SAID OF anything else. In the *Metaphysics*, forms are indivisible (Z8, 1034a8) and again obey the rule given: a form is predicable only of *matter* of a compound material substance, and it is false that the matter Is the form in question. Rather, the form is Had by its matter.

thises *but drops the 'and only'*. In the *Metaphysics*, he has a new choice for primary substance, but the connection between being a this and primary substance is sufficiently strong to survive the change in what counts as primary substance: so the new items that qualify as primary substances, namely (Aristotelian) forms, *are also thises*. In the *Metaphysics*, then, all actual substances, forms and individual substances alike, are thises.

If Aristotle is firm in the *Categories* that all and only individual substances are thises, the idea in (8) that no universal is a this follows almost immediately. According to the *Categories*, individual substances are not SAID OF anything else or IN any subject; hence, they are not predicated of anything else; a fortiori, then, they are not universals. Accordingly, no universal is a this, as (8) requires.

It is worth emphasizing, however, that the connection the *Categories* establishes between being a this and not being a universal is far from definitional. The fact that a this is not a universal follows from Aristotle's view in the *Categories* of what counts as a this, namely, individual substances, together with the role that individual substances have in the *Categories* account of (metaphysical) predication. If in some other context something other than an individual substance were a this, we would have to look at the prevailing theory of (metaphysical) predication before we could say whether or not a thing could be not only a this but also a universal. Certainly, the idea that a universal might also be a this is not ruled out by definition.

Predictably, then, the reasoning that makes (8) true in the *Categories* can all too easily unravel in the *Metaphysics*. Although none of the three remaining components of the puzzle commands anything like universal assent, *if* forms are now thises, by (7) and (2), and *if* forms are universals, as (3) alleges, then contrary to (8), some universals are thises after all. And if such a change does take place in the *Metaphysics*, it should not be a total surprise, given the other changes afoot there – the introduction of form in place of the individual substance as primary substance and the role of form in the new scheme of (metaphysical) predication.

At the same time, an important conceptual motivation for the original account of thises in the *Categories* lies in Aristotle's countermoves against the Third Man Argument (TMA), and any changes he may be tempted to make in (8) must not strip him of his protection against the TMA. In the *Categories*, Aristotle can use the *this–such* distinction together with the appropriate constraints on the relation of OM-generation to argue that there can be no chains of OM-generation with more than two members, and so fend off the TMA.[40] But the idea that universals as well as the items they are universal to are thises abandons

40 The argument attached to these claims is given in Chapter 1, Section 4; and Chapter 2, Section 1.

the relevant constraints on OM-generation. So if Aristotle envisions any qualifications in (8), he must be able to say how his new views on thises can continue to give him the protection he needs against the TMA. We will return to this point in Section 6.

4   A Solution to the Third Puzzle: How Forms Can Be Both Universals and Thises

In the *Categories,* as we have seen, Aristotle is firmly committed both to (8), that no universal is a this, and to the claim that all primary substances are thises, which is the ancestor of (7), according to which all actual substances whatever are thises. In the different context of the *Metaphysics,* however, it is hard to see how he can consistently hold both (8) and (7), given that he also holds (2) and (3). The immediate cause of the trouble is that Aristotle now denies himself a move that he took advantage of in the *Categories.* According to the *Categories,* as we have seen, universals like man are *secondary* substances, and secondary substances are suches, not thises, so that there is no harm in asserting in (8) that no universal is a this. In the *Metaphysics,* forms are Aristotle's new choice for primary substances, and forms are thises *because* they are primary substances; so Aristotle could deny that forms are thises only if he were willing either to drop the idea that forms are primary substances or to abandon the connection between thisness and primary substance. Neither move, however, appears likely. Accordingly, if forms are the primary substances, then they must be governed by the claim, common to both the *Categories* and the *Metaphysics,* that all primary substances are thises. They will also be thises on the strength of the more general claim in (7).[41]

But is Aristotle really committed to this result? One way to deal with the difficulty is to challenge the sense in which forms are thises on the grounds that a form is a this in only a deflationary sense.[42] At *De Anima* B1, 412a7–9, Aristotle notes that form is that "in virtue of which a thing is right away called a this." This remark seems to suggest that a form is a this only derivatively or "by courtesy" as a consequence of its relation to what is properly called a this. By itself, and without reference to its function vis-à-vis the compound material substance, however, a form is a such and not a this at all.

41 It is also unlikely that Aristotle would be willing to give up (7). As suggested in Section 3, his argument for (7) is that individual substances are thises because of their standing as primary substances in the *Categories;* forms are thises because they are primary substances in the *Metaphysics;* accordingly, all (actual) substances are thises. So rejecting the argument for (7) again requires dropping either the view that forms are primary substances or the connection between thisness and primary substance.

42 For the deflationary account, see the references in Chapter 10, note 53.

The argument given allows a form to have certain of its properties solely by riding on the coattails of the compound substance of which it is the constitutive form. But is this style of argument appropriate here? A form is what gives a compound material substance its determinate nature, and it may seem odd to find form picking up its character as a this derivatively from the fact that the compound substance is a this, rather than the other way around. We have some motivation, then, for asking whether forms can be thises in some sense that is *not* derivative from the thisness of the compound material substance.[43]

If a form is a this in a full-blown, nonderivative sense, and (7) and (2) can have straightforward readings that make both true, we must turn instead to (8) or (3) for a solution to the puzzle. One response calls (3) into question. We are to agree that substances are thises, by (7), and that no universal is a this, by (8); given that forms are primary substances, by (2), it follows that they cannot be universals. So (3) is flat-out false. This is a familiar argument in favour of *individual form*, in the sense that Socrates and Callias (say), both members of the same lowest kind, man, have forms that are qualitatively indistinguishable but numerically distinct.[44]

An alternative way of handling Aristotle's puzzle again focuses on (3), but without the appeal to individual form. By (8), we seem to know that nothing can be both a universal and a this; in particular, then,

> it is impossible that a form (*eidos*) should be *both* a universal *and* also a this.

The difficulty, of course, is that the first of the troublesome conjuncts is identical with (3), while the second follows directly from (2) and (7). Driscoll suggests that *two* kinds of item are picked out by the overworked word '*eidos*', each of which satisfies *just one half* of the problematic conjunction. Unexpectedly, the claim in the first conjunct, that an *eidos* is a universal, is concerned not with form but with the species or universal compound. The species man, for example, is universal to Socrates, Callias, and the rest, but it is not a this. Meanwhile, the form of a man, namely, the relevant kind of soul, is a this, but it is not a

---

43 At *Metaphysics* B5, 1001b29–32, Aristotle remarks that affections, changes, relatives, positions, and ratios seem to signify the substance of nothing (for they are all said of some subject, and none is a this). It follows from this that a predicable is a this *if it is the substance of something*. But this is a far cry from saying that being the substance of something *makes* a predicable a this or that a predicable is a this *because* it is the substance of something, in contrast to the deflationary account that it is a this (merely) because it is the substance of what is a this in the proper sense.

The "deflationary" account is criticized by Cherniss (1944), p. 351, n. 261. Woods (1974–5) also adopts a nondeflationary reading of the thisness of forms, although his account is very different from that given here.

44 See, e.g., Frede (1987 [= 1985]), pp. 75–80.

universal in the relevant sense. As required, then, no single item satisfies both halves of the problematic conjunction.

On Driscoll's account, *nothing* can be both a universal and a this, and the attempt to show otherwise exploits the different uses of the word '*eidos*', as noted. But Driscoll does not suggest that Aristotle himself was tempted by the ambiguity, so the puzzle is not so much Aristotle's as an artefact of his interpreters, who have failed to spot the ambiguity. Although the distinction between the *Metaphysics* notion of form and a *Categories*-style *eidos* or kind is of the first importance, then, the puzzle is not a true symptom of any strain in Aristotle's own handling of the transition from the theories of the *Categories* to the very different metaphysical context of the *Metaphysics*. But – beyond the desire to see drama in the way Aristotle's own story evolves – it is possible to worry that Driscoll is forced to downplay the idea that real Aristotelian forms, and not just the kinds handed down from the *Categories*, are universals.[45] In particular, he acknowledges that forms are predicated of matter but insists that they are not predicated of countable particulars and hence are not properly universals; but although others have argued the same point, it seems to rest on a questionable view about what is required to pick out or refer to matter.[46]

I shall suppose that forms are universal to matter in a sense of 'universal' that, contra Driscoll, *is* constrained by the claim in (8) that no universal is a this. So we should let (3) stand and move our attention instead to (8). If form is a this and a universal, how can Aristotle also say that all universals are not thises but suches, as (8) requires? I suggest that (8) should be understood to say not that all universals are suches, but rather (mobilizing the relational strategy from before) that everything that is universal *to a this* is itself a such. This gives us this modification of (8):

(8′) If an entity is universal to many things, each of which is a this, then that entity is not itself a this (in fact, it is a such).

Some universals, forms, for example, are not suches but thises.[47] This claim is consistent with (8′), however, for a form is universal to *matter*, and matter is not a this.[48] Unlike our four original assumptions, then, (2), (3), (7), and (8′) do not form an inconsistent set.

45 In fact, Driscoll (1981), p. 151, acknowledges a "weak" sense in which Aristotelian forms proper are universals. For doubts about the distinction between an entity that is "common" and a universal in the strict sense, see Frede and Patzig (1988), Vol. 1, pp. 50–1.
46 See the discussion in Chapter 6, Section 2, and also Code (1986), p. 436.
47 For universals that most likely *are* suches, see the discussion of "universal compounds" in Section 6.
48 A contrast between matter and being a this is implied at *Physics* A7, 191a11–12, and in different ways at *Metaphysics* Δ8, 1017b23–6, Z13, 1038b5–6, Λ3, 1070a9–11 (on

5   Universals and Thises: A Defence of (8′)

Like its predecessors, the third puzzle is worrisome most of all because it indicates a conflict between the criteria for primary substance – here the requirement that a primary substance be a this – and other facts about Aristotle's favoured candidate for primary substance, form. If we suppose that forms are thises, following the rule in (7) that all substances are thises, we run directly into conflict with another property of forms, namely, that they are universal to matter, and hence by (8) not thises after all. Aristotle's response, as I understand it, is once more to preserve the criterion for substance, in this case by replacing the crucial ancillary claim (8) by the more restrictive (8′).

But are there grounds *outside* the puzzle for finding (8′) plausible? Not the least advantage of (8′) is that it is in any case *true* for Aristotle, both early and late. The original (8) was born of controversy with Plato,[49] and (8′) too carries the marks of its anti-Platonic origins. As Aristotle pictures him, Plato holds that a (Platonic) form is universal to sensible particulars and that contrary to (8′) both the form and the sensibles alike are thises. By disdaining the *this–such* distinction, Aristotle suggests, Plato cuts himself off from Aristotle's defence against the TMA. On Aristotle's own account, by contrast, where one item OM-generates another, the first is a this, but the second must be not a this but a such: this by itself prevents the formation of chains of OM-generation with more than two members, so that the TMA is stopped dead in its tracks with the introduction of the first universal, man, "over" the various sensibles that are men.[50] In the *Categories*, accordingly, where man (a secondary substance) is (metaphysically) predicated of different primary substances that are men, the subjects are all thises, but what is predicated is itself a such, exactly as (8′) requires. There is also a second case, not in Aristotle's view liable to a regress argument but for which the same account applies. Suppose that Socrates is pale. This is a case of *cross*-categorial predication, in which the subject is again an individual substance, and hence a this, but what is predicated is drawn from a nonsubstance category and is IN but not SAID OF its subject. But the predicable is again a such, as (8′) requires.

The theory of (metaphysical) predication in the *Categories* also leaves room for cases in which a subject is not apparently an individual substance, and hence is not a this. For example, animal is predicated

---

the last, see Bonitz [1848–9], Vol. 2, pp. 476–7). Aristotle is more explicit elsewhere: *De Anima* B1, 412a7–8; *Metaphysics* Z3, 1029a27–30, H1, 1042a27–28, and esp. Θ7, 1049a27 ff. Apparent evidence to the contrary at *Metaphysics* Z8, 1033b19–24, is discussed in note 55.

49 See the references in note 35.

50 See Chapter 1, Section 4, and Chapter 2, Section 1.

of man, or colour is predicated of pallor, or finally, grammar is predicated of man. In each case, both the predicable and its subject are suches. All three predications, however, are anchored in predications in which the subject is after all a primary substance and a this. Aristotle insists that every predicable is predicated of an individual substance – that is, I have argued, an entity is predicated of something *other than* an individual substance only because there exists an individual substance of which they both are predicated.[51] Animal, for example, is predicated of man only because it is predicated of an individual substance of which man is predicated, Socrates (say), where Socrates is a this; and similarly in the remaining cases.[52]

We can place conditions on (metaphysical) predication in the *Categories* in a way that accommodates these added complexities. We stipulate that

> x is (metaphysically) predicated of y, only if x is a such and *either* (i) y is a this *or* (ii) for some z, z is a this and both x and y are predicated of z.[53]

Condition (i) captures the straightforward case, in which x is a such and y is a this. For example, man is predicated of Socrates, and pallor is predicated of Socrates: here Socrates is a this, and both man and pallor are suches. Condition (ii) makes room for the remaining cases, in which both a predicable and its subject are suches. Here, as we have seen, an entity is predicable of a such only because there is some primary substance or this of which it is predicable. On this account, in the *Categories* in the final analysis *every* universal is universal to a this. In the *Categories*, then, the difference between (8) and (8′) is a difference without a difference, and both assumptions are satisfied equally well.

In all the cases envisioned in the condition given in the preceding paragraph, what is predicated is always a such and never a this. Aristotle's later view differs on this point. By the time of the *Metaphysics*, Aristotle has come to think that (metaphysical) predication is a relation either between an accident and a substance or between a form and a portion of matter.[54] In the first case, what an accident is predicated of is itself a this; what is predicated is again a such. But where a form is predicated of some matter, what the form is predicated of is not a this. And this leaves Aristotle free to say that an Aristotelian form *is* after all a this.[55] The new conditions on predication, then, run as follows:

51 *Categories* 5, 2a34–b6c; cf. b15 ff., b37 ff.
52 For further discussion of the points made in this paragraph, see the discussion in Chapter 2, Section 3.
53 Cf. thesis (a) in Chapter 2, Section 3. I have been helped in thinking about this condition on predication by discussion with Alan Code.
54 See note 11.
55 At *Metaphysics* Z8, 1033b19–24, Aristotle responds to the Platonic suggestion that (Platonic) forms exist "over and above" individual particulars by remarking that

x is (metaphysically) predicated of *y*, only if *either* (i) *y* is a this and *x* is a such *or* (ii) *y* is matter (not a this) and *x* is a this.[56]

Here what is predicated *can* be a this. The new view, however, has this much in common with the earlier one: no more than one term of the predication relation is ever a this. The fact that a form, like the compound substance, is a this is quite consistent with the idea that a this cannot be predicated of a second this, since a form is predicated not of the compound substance, but of matter.

On option (i) permitted in Aristotle's later theory, an entity can be universal to many things, each of which is a this, but that entity is itself not a this but a such.[57] This is exactly as (8′) requires. But Aristotle also allows the possibility that an entity should be both a this and universal to many things: in this case, however, none of the subjects of which it is predicated is a this. This suggests the principle

(8″) If an entity is universal to many things and is itself a this, then none of the things it is universal to is itself a this.

In fact, however, (8″) offers nothing new. Principles (8″) and (8′) are equivalent given the assumption that if an entity is universal to many things, then all of those things are suitably alike; that is, either they are all thises or none is.[58] Accordingly, (8′) by itself is adequate as an underpinning for both halves of Aristotle's later theory, and the place of (8′) is assured in Aristotle's theory, both early and late.

6   Aristotelian Form, Kinds, and the TMA

I have argued that in his earlier works, with an eye to the TMA, Aristotle stipulates that what is in common to a number of thises is itself a such. In the context of his later metaphysical theory in the *Metaphysics*, he suggests, somewhat differently, that a form is a universal and also a this but is predicated universally *of matter,* which is not a this.

"form signifies a such, and is not a this and a definite thing: but ‹a craftsman› makes or ‹a father› begets a such from a this, and whenever it has come to be, it is a this such" (b21–4). Aristotle is sometimes read here as saying that (Aristotelian) form is a such (so apparently Ross [1924], Vol. 2, p. 188, on 1033b19), so that what comes to be is a this such because it is a combination of matter (a this) and form (a such) (cf. Bonitz [1848–9], Vol. 2, pp. 326–7). In fact, however, Aristotle is saying that *Platonic* form is a such, not a this. And what comes to be is a this such because, first, it is an individual substance, and hence a this (see *to de hapan tode, Kallias ē Sōkratēs,* b24) and, second, because it is a member of a *kind,* which is a such (e.g., a man; see b25). Aristotle later analyses the notion of a kind in terms of form and matter in *Metaphysics* Z10 and 11; see Section 6, and the discussion in Chapter 7. I have been helped in thinking about *Metaphysics* Z8 by discussion with Alan Code; see Code (1986), p. 437, n. 73, and, for a contrary account, Loux (1979), pp. 11–12.

56 Cf. (D1) and (A1) through (A6) in Section (i) of the Appendix to this chapter.
57 See the discussion of universal compounds in Section 6.
58 Cf. (T3) in Section (i) of the Appendix.

There is a difficulty, however. If in the context of the new ontology of form and matter, Aristotle allows that a form is both a universal and a this, how is it that in *Metaphysics* Z13 he repeats his criticism of Plato in its earliest form, that the Third Man results from taking a common predicable to be not a such, but a this (1038b35–1039a3)? This account of the conditions that give rise to the TMA is somewhat "hand-me-down": as we already know (Chapter 1), there is more to the TMA than Aristotle's quick formula suggests. There may be other grounds, then, for doubting that Aristotelian form is vulnerable to the TMA. In fact, however, the view that form is predicated universally of matter and is also a this does not run counter even to Aristotle's "hand-me-down" analysis.[59] As I understand that analysis, Plato's forms are vulnerable to the TMA because they break the rule not (simply) that no universal is a this, but rather that nothing universal *to a number of thises* is itself a this. That is, the TMA results (at least in part) from violating not (8), but rather (8'). And Aristotle's own forms *obey* (8'): an Aristotelian form is a this, but it is universal to matter, and matter is *not* a this.

Aristotle's repetition of his earlier, anti-Platonic point in Z13, then, does not undermine his characterization of form as a this. Rather, it sets out a fallback strategy, a necessary caution addressed to philosophers willing to admit entities predicated universally *of compound material substances.*[60] So Aristotle continues to have a convincing rebuttal to the Platonic theory, which takes participation to be a relation between a sensible particular, Socrates, for example, and a Platonic form. His own theory of forms, however, is not vulnerable to objections of this sort.

59 For this reason among others, I do not agree with Owen (1965) that Aristotle has at different stages in his career two different defences against the TMA. The *Categories* bears clear signs of measures meant to head off the TMA; but (as I argue in more detail later in this section) the TMA poses no threat to the ontology of form and matter in the *Metaphysics*, and Aristotle has no need to develop any new response to it there. The fact that Aristotle repeats his earlier response to the TMA in the passage cited from Z13 does not of itself show that Aristotle has no new answer to the TMA in mind, as Dybikowski (1972) supposes, for as we shall see Aristotle's strictures at 1038b35–1039a3 apply only to entities that are predicated universally of *compound material substances* and have no relevance to Aristotelian form, which is predicated of matter. For all we know so far, then, Aristotle may think that the *Metaphysics* ontology of matter and form does require protection against the TMA – but protection of a different sort from that which the remarks at 1038b35–1039a3 are able to provide. This criticism of Dybikowski is due to Driscoll (1981), pp. 154–5. I do not agree with Driscoll's conclusion, however, that Aristotle does in fact contrive a new response to the TMA in the context of the *Metaphysics* ontology of matter and form. Driscoll follows Owen in supposing that by arguing in Z6 that each thing is (essentially) the same as its essence, Aristotle means to deny the nonidentity assumption from the TMA; against this, however, see Code (1985), and Chapter 1, Section 5. The connection between Z6 and the TMA is discussed further in note 66.
60 For this reading of Z13, 1038b35–1039a3, see also Driscoll (1981), pp. 149–51, 153.

At the same time, the basically anti-Platonic strategy sketched in previous paragraphs also exerts a continuing influence on Aristotle's own thinking. For Aristotle, the TMA draws attention in particular to the question of membership by an individual in a kind. Membership in a kind is a distinctively Aristotelian concern. The Platonic theory of Having sees no distinction between an item's belonging to a kind and its (merely) having accidents, so that there is no special problem to membership in a kind beyond the general question of how a sensible can participate in any form. Suppose, however, with Aristotle, that in addition to his accidents, Socrates (say) is also a member of a certain kind. In Aristotle's earlier, *Categories* account of individuals and kinds,[61] the notions of *belonging* and of a *kind* are not open to further analysis. As in Plato's account, the fact that Socrates Is (a) man involves an unanalysed relation (even if it is not Plato's relation) between a sensible and a universal. But Aristotle distances himself from the Platonic account, and at the same time keeps clear of the TMA, by insisting that the kind man, for example, is a secondary substance and, unlike Socrates and the other individuals that belong to the kind, a such and not a this.

Later in the *Metaphysics,* the kinds or secondary substances of the *Categories* reappear, but they are no longer philosophically primitive in Aristotle's theory. Instead, he analyses them as "compounds of this form and this matter taken universally" ("universal compounds," for short).[62] Universal compounds – for example, man, animal, and all those entities "that apply similarly to individuals, but universally" (*ta houtos epi tōn kath' hekasta, katholou d';* Z10, 1035b28) – are universal to compound material substances. By contrast with the secondary substances of the *Categories,* universal compounds in the *Metaphysics* are not substances at all (1035b27–30). But it is reasonable to suppose that Aristotle would say again that they are not thises but suches in line with the anti-Platonic point of Z13 recorded in (8').

By offering an analysis of individuals and kinds in the *Metaphysics,* Aristotle shows us how we can, if we wish, drop the reference to kinds and talk instead of form and matter and of the relation of supervention. According to the *Metaphysics* analysis, Socrates Is (a) man if and only if the form of a man supervenes on the appropriate matter.[63] This analysis assumes that a form can be both a this and also universal to matter. The anti-Platonic point, that an entity that is universal to thises cannot itself be a this, does not invalidate these assumptions, as we have seen, for matter is not a this. Like the theory of universal

---

61 For the two phases in Aristotle's theory of kinds, see Chapter 7, Section 5.
62 Z10, 1035b27–30, Z11, 1037a6–7, and perhaps Z8, 1033b25–6 (but see Ross [1924] on 1033b16).
63 Cf. Chapter 7.

compounds, then, the *Metaphysics* theory of forms conforms to (8'). In both cases, the distinction between thises and suches is sufficient to block the TMA.

In addition to violating the rule about thises and suches, however, more is needed if a theory of universals is to be vulnerable to the TMA. The TMA endeavours to construct an infinite sequence of pluralities of things that are men, where each new plurality demands a new form of man by the One-over-Many and Nonidentity assumptions. As we have seen, a *homogeneity* assumption applies to each of the pluralities in the argument: roughly,

(a) For any plurality, Π, of sensibles that are men, each member of Π *is* a man in the same sense of 'is'.

(b) For any plurality, Π, of men (of any level) and the universal X, where X is "over" Π and is itself a man, each member of the further plurality, Π *with* X, *is* a man in the same sense of 'is'.[64]

There is no reason to think that in the *Metaphysics* theory of forms-as-universals, both parts of the homogeneity condition can be satisfied. In the theory of the *Metaphysics*, the form of a man is universal not to particular men, but to different portions of matter. Plausibly, the form applies to all the portions of matter in the same way, so that there exists a plurality whose members are all portions of matter. Even so, there is no reason to think that the different portions of matter on which the form supervenes and the form itself are all men in the same sense of 'is'. At best, it seems, each portion of matter *constitutes* a man, but it can hardly be said that the form of a man is a man in this same sense of 'is'.[65] There is no temptation, then, to think that the form can be grouped together with the different portions of matter on which it supervenes to produce a higher-level plurality of entities, each of which is a man. Much less is there any reason to postulate the existence of yet another form, which supervenes on the original form and on the original portions of matter alike, and so on to infinity. I conclude that the TMA is quite irrelevant to the theory of forms-as-universals in the *Metaphysics*.[66]

64 For simplicity, this homogeneity condition combines the definition of homogeneity with the condition Homogeneity both given in Chapter 1.

65 At best, the form of a man satisfies a definition that is also in a reduced sense the *definition of* each of the individual men. For the *definition of* relation, see note 10, and F. Lewis (1984).

66 The attempt to connect the theory of Aristotelian forms in the *Metaphysics* with the TMA is often supported by an appeal to the argument of *Metaphysics* Z6. In this chapter, Aristotle is arguing for the thesis that each thing is (essentially) the same as its essence. Part of the argument evidently is conducted within the context of what is for Aristotle an alien, Platonic ontology; for "this result would be sufficiently established, even if ‹Platonic› forms do not exist, and even more so, perhaps, if they do" (1031b14–15). (Here I part company with Ross's translation; a translation along

The view that the (Aristotelian) form of a man and the entities to which it is universal are after all men in the same sense of 'is', contrary to what is argued here, perhaps comes from the assumption that an Aristotelian form is universal *to compound material substances* (so that, oversimplifying, both it and they Are men). But there is no such theory of universals in Aristotle.[67] To suppose otherwise, I suspect, is to confuse two kinds of universals and to import features from the theory of universal compounds or kinds into the theory of (Aristotelian) forms.

By treating kinds in the *Metaphysics* as universal compounds of this form and this matter, "taken universally," Aristotle takes a reductive, but not an eliminative, attitude towards kinds. So long as Aristotle is willing to countenance kinds side by side with Aristotelian forms, his anti-Platonic strictures regarding thises and suches at Z13, 1038b35–1039a3, are also needed to govern the relation between a kind or universal compound and the compound substances to which it is universal. Aristotle's theory of forms too is consistent with these stipulations about thises and suches. But this should not obscure the clear differences between universal compounds and (Aristotelian) forms. In particular, the precautionary moves regarding thises and suches Aristotle reminds us of in Z13 provide essential protection against the TMA not only for the original theory of kinds in the *Categories,* but also for the theory of universal compounds in the *Metaphysics.* But while the theory of (Aristotelian) forms obeys these same stipulations about thises and suches, the original motivation for these stipulations is gone in this case. For unlike a theory of kinds, the theory of (Aristotelian) forms is not even remotely threatened by the TMA.

the lines given here appears also in Schwegler [1847], Vol. 2, p. 116.) Towards the end of Z6, Aristotle gives a regress argument in support of his sameness conclusion: the first steps of the regress are given at 1031b28–30, and the regress is continued to infinity at 1032a2–4. This argument is sometimes connected with the Third Man regress and taken to suggest that like Plato's forms, Aristotelian forms or essences too may be vulnerable to the TMA, unless further precautions are taken. The precautions in question are just the sameness result itself, which is taken to be the negation of the nonidentity assumption that appears in most versions of the TMA. But there are reasons for doubting the relevance of Aristotle's sameness result to the TMA (see Chapter 1, Section 5). Above all, I suspect, the view neglects the fact that Aristotelian forms are not universal to compound material substances, but rather to their matter. And in any case, Aristotle gives no indication that he is still talking about a distinctively Platonic ontology at 1031b28–1032a4, rather than generally about any of the items that fall within the scope of his sameness thesis. In fact, I would argue, Plato's theory of forms drops out of Aristotle's discussion in the chapter after 1031b18. The phrase *auto hekaston* at b19 is often taken to evoke Plato's theory, with the *auto* distinctive of Platonic form talk (see, e.g., 1031a31 earlier in the chapter). In fact, however, I take the *auto* to be ontologically neutral and meant only to contrast each thing itself with its essence; see b26. '*Auto*', then, is a variable for any item that is suitably primary, in the sense laid down at 1031b13–14, and is not tied down to an exclusively Platonic ontology.

67 See Chapter 7, Section 3.

Appendix. Substance and Predication: The Formal Theory

The three puzzles we have considered in this chapter all concern crucial ingredients in Aristotle's characterization of form in the *Metaphysics*, in particular the role that form acquires in the new *Metaphysics* theory of (metaphysical) predication. The puzzles also involve Aristotle's notion of substance and the different criteria for substance that he regards as part of the data for his inquiry. As I have understood him, Aristotle's response to the puzzles is to reformulate certain crucial claims rather than repudiate outright any of the standard conditions on substance. This attitude shapes Aristotle's search for substance in a fundamental way. At the beginning of *Metaphysics Zeta*, Aristotle claims that his study of substance will reveal a definition for that notion (Z1, 1028b6−7, Z2, 1028b31−2). In the event, however, he offers us a medley of lists, of various degrees of authenticity, and an assortment of criteria that again appear to fit his own metaphysical scheme with various degrees of closeness. Aristotle's official conclusion in the *Metaphysics* is that *form* is primary substance, and many of his criteria for primary substance pull in favour of form. Equally clearly, as we have seen, some of his criteria for primary substance are holdovers from the earliest period of his metaphysical thinking and, given the new *Metaphysics* theory of predication, seem to tell *against* the choice of form as primary substance. The proper conclusion, I think, is not that the different criteria are in irrevocable disagreement, so that there can, finally, be no single choice for primary substance that satisfies them all. I prefer to suppose that Aristotle *accepts* all of the traditional criteria for substance, although not necessarily all at face value. Then as a constraint on how, in the final analysis, the various criteria should be understood, he requires that, in the end, they should together pick out a *single* kind of item as primary substance (in fact, they will agree in picking out *form* as primary substance). In this way, Aristotle will be able to save the philosophical appearances, but only by virtue of adapting and reshaping the criteria (or, as in the third puzzle, by modifying a closely related claim), so that conflict no longer exists.

On this account, Aristotle's programme in the *Metaphysics* has a distinctly conservative bent, for it aims to preserve as far as possible the criteria for primary substance from the *Categories* and other earlier works so that they will fit the new ontology of matter and form. I have used the three puzzles to indicate the lines along which the necessary reshapings and adaptations must go. Inevitably, there is the temptation to regard the various rewritings offered as merely ad hoc responses to the puzzles. In fact, however, there is far more to be said on their behalf. In each case, the rewritings express principles that are true for Aristotle, whether or not he chooses to use them in resolving the puzzles. Those principles are each part of the wider metaphysical theory that Aristotle is developing in the *Metaphysics*. In particular, they are part of a deductive network of principles that lies only a small way beneath the surface of the text. "Beneath the surface," because Aristotle does not himself arrange his metaphysics as a formal deductive theory. The very fact that some of the central theses in the *Metaphysics* (as I formulate them) *can* be so arranged, however, is sufficiently impressive testimony to the power and systematic character of Aristotle's thought.

It will be remembered that Accidental Compound Theory set out in Part II was later absorbed into the general theory of compounds presented in Chapter 6, Section 4, of Part III. The general theory of compounds, in turn, can be seen as a part of the larger theory of substance and predication that reaches its fullest development in the central books of the *Metaphysics*. This final body of theory is the subject of this appendix.[68]

(i)   Universals, Thises, and Suches

Aristotle's theory in the *Metaphysics* is both powerful and wide ranging. Of the parts of the theory that are relevant to the three puzzles, perhaps the simplest involves the solution to the third puzzle, sketched in Chapter 11, Section 3. So we will start here.

As noted in Part III, the two relations 'x is an accident of y' and 'x supervenes on y' are undefined. By way of informal explanation, pallor, for example, is an accident of Socrates just in case Socrates is pale, and the form of a table supervenes on a given collection of lumber just in case that lumber constitutes a table. As these explanations suggest, different conditions govern our two undefined relations:

(A1) x is an accident of y, only if x is an accident and y is a compound material substance.

(A2) x supervenes on y, only if x is a form and y is (a portion of) matter.

Further conditions govern the notions of accident, compound substance, and the like that appear in (A1) and (A2):

(A3) x is an accident only if x is a such.

(A4) x is a compound material substance only if x is a this.

(A5) x is a form only if x is a this.

(A6) x is (a portion of) matter only if x is not a this.

(A7) x is a this only if x is not a such.

68 As before, the various elements of the theory are numbered consecutively within this part; where a formula in the theory appears also in some earlier part, it is assigned a fresh number for its appearance in this part.

(A7) requires that *being a this* and *being a such* are mutually exclusive, but they are otherwise undefined.

The relation of (metaphysical) predication can be defined in terms of our two undefined relations:

(D1) x is (*metaphysically*) *predicated of* y if and only if either x is an accident of y or x supervenes on y.

For this definition, see the references in note 11 of this chapter. Finally, we say that

(D2) x is *universal to* y *and* z if and only if x is (metaphysically) predicated of both y and z, and $y \neq z$.[69]

These materials by themselves allow us to derive three theorems:

(T1) x is universal to y and z, and y and z are both thises, only if x is a such.

(T2) x is universal to y and z, and x is a this, only if neither y nor z is a this.

(T3) x is universal to y and z, only if either both y and z are thises or neither is.

(T1) is identical with (8′) in this chapter; it is tailored to the case in which an accident (which is a such) is universal to different compound substances (which are thises), but it will also govern the relation of the universal compound or kind to different compound substances. Theorem (T2) is the same as (8″) at the end of Section 5, this chapter, and is suited most immediately to the case in which a form is universal to different portions of matter. A counterpart of (T3) is mentioned at the end of Section 5.

To prove (T1), (T2), and (T3), suppose that x is universal to y and z. Then by (D1) and (D2), either x is an accident of y and z, or x supervenes on y and z. That is, by (A1) through (A7), either x is a such and y and z are both thises, or x is a this and neither y nor z is a this. The three theorems now follow by elementary logic alone. Finally, notice that given (T3) and the assumption that nothing is both a this and a such in (A7), (T1) and (T2) can each be derived from the other (cf. the discussion at the end of Section 5).

The fact that (T1) can be obtained as a theorem in Aristotle's theory lends at least some measure of support to our use of (8′) in solving the third puzzle sketched in Section 3, this chapter. The use of (8′), that is, (T1), in place of (8) will be discussed further in Section (v).

69 For simplicity, I deal only with the case in which an entity is universal to exactly two things. I do not mean to deny that an item may be universal to just one thing or to more than two, and a definition that is fully adequate for Aristotle's usage will need to leave room for these further cases. Notice that in the case where a universal is universal to exactly one thing, (T8) can be replaced by (T10): the two mutual exclusivity principles collapse into one, as do the first two puzzles.

(ii) The Theory of Substance and Predication: Two Key Principles,
(P1) and (P2)

In this section, I begin the sketch of the part of Aristotle's theory relevant to the first and second puzzles. For simplicity, I begin the story in the middle, with two key principles involving the notions of substance and predication, respectively. More accurately, they involve contrasting properties of the relations 'x is the substance of y' and 'x is predicated of y'.

This choice of starting point should be no surprise. In the *Categories,* Aristotle makes room only for the one-place notion of being a substance *simpliciter.* The notion of the substance *of* a thing emerges elsewhere in the *Organon,* and by the time of the *Metaphysics,* Aristotle holds that any primary substance is the substance *of* something (cf. (A9) in Section (v)). The relation 'x is the substance of y' is one of the key ingredients in the mature theory of substance. I emphasize that we are concerned in this section with Aristotle's *primary* substance-of relation; there are also various secondary cases of the relation, which are not immediately relevant here.[70] To select the primary case of the relation we need, we make this stipulation:

(A8) x is the substance of y only if y is a primary substance

(see note 10). The relation is otherwise undefined.

A second crucial component of the theory of substance is the further relation 'x is (metaphysically) predicated of y' already defined in (D1) in Section (i). Its importance in Aristotle's theory is again entirely predictable. In the very first discussion of substance in the *Categories,* the class of primary substances is marked off in terms of the prevailing theory of predication (2, 1b3–6), and some of the crucial criteria for primary substance in the *Categories* are formulated in terms of predication.[71] By seeming to uphold these criteria in the *Metaphysics,* Aristotle's theory immediately runs afoul of the difficulties discussed in the first three sections of this chapter. Properly understood, however, the notion of (metaphysical) predication continues to play a major role in Aristotle's theory of substance, as we shall see.

In *Metaphysics* Z6, Aristotle suggests that "each thing seems to be not other than its substance" (1031a17–18); at least part of what he means is that they are *identical.* He devotes the body of that same chapter to proving a closely related principle for the essence-of relation (1031a28–1032b11).[72] This gives our first principle, which governs the substance-of relation:

70 See note 10.
71 *Categories* 5, 2b37–3a1; cf. 2a34 ff., b15–17.
72 At Z6, Aristotle argues that each thing is essentially the same as its essence: although essential sameness is not our identity, I take it that it *follows* from the essential

(P1) *x* is the substance of *y* only if *y* = *x*.

At the same time, Aristotle is committed to the view that the predication relation has the contrary property. According to Aristotle's later theory, either an accident is predicated of the compound material substance or a form is predicated of matter (see (D1), (A1), and (A2)). In all cases, what is predicated (a form or an accident) is *distinct from* the subject of which it is predicated (a portion of matter or a substance, respectively). This gives our second principle:

(P2) *x* is predicated of *y* only if *y* ≠ *x*.

(P1) and (P2) are both theorems rather than axioms, for each rests on other, more nearly basic principles in Aristotle's metaphysics. Here, however, I shall concentrate more on their consequences than on how they themselves are to be established.[73] Both singly and taken together, the two principles are rich sources of further theorems. I shall begin with (P1).

(iii) Some Consequences of (P1) by Itself

(P1) asserts the *vacuity* of the substance-of relation. It is easily shown that any vacuous relation is symmetric, transitive, and partially functional: the last of these properties is important for our purposes:

> sameness of two things, that they are identical. Hence, Aristotle is committed to the result that each thing is identical with its essence. It is worth cautioning, however, that this identity result holds only for the *primary* essence-of relation that holds between a primary substance and its essence (for a similar principle governing the primary substance-of relation, see (A8) in Section (ii)); this same result does *not* hold for other, lesser-grade cases, for example, the *essence-of* relation between Socrates (in the *Metaphysics*, *not* a primary substance) and his essence; cf. F. Lewis (1984), pp. 117–18.
>
> 73 (P1) is derived in F. Lewis (1984), p. 96, where it is cited as theorem '(T3)'. The main ingredient of the proof involves the relation '*x* is signified by the definiens in a definition of *y*', '*x* is the definition of *y*' for short. The relevant principle is stated in the *Topics*:
>
> > *x* is the definition of *y* only if *x* is numerically the same as *y*
>
> (A5, 102a7–9, 11–14, 16–17, A7, 103a25–7; cf. Code [1985], Section (IV)(A)). That is, since numerical sameness of the relevant kind implies identity (note 72),
>
> > *x* is the definition of *y* only if *x* = *y*.
>
> Next, recall that the substance-of and definition-of relations are equivalent (note 10); (P1) follows immediately. Despite these antecedents in principles from the *Organon*, (P1) is part of a nest of related principles put to work in *Metaphysics* Z6 to prove the sameness of a thing with its essence (notes 72 and 74; cf. F. Lewis [1985b], pp. 159–66); on this view, (P1) is an essential component of the general *Metaphysics* theory of essence, definition, and substance. (For a similar point about the related principle (T4) at the beginning of Section (iii), see note 74.) (P2), meanwhile, is an easy consequence of (D1), (A1), and (A2) in Section (i), together with the natural assumption that no accident is identical with any compound material substance, and no form is identical with any portion of matter.

(T4) *x* is the substance of *y* and *x* is the substance of *z*, only if
y = *z*.   [*Partial functionality*]

Less formally, things that have the same substance are themselves the
same. This principle is alluded to or asserted by Aristotle at a number
of places in the *Metaphysics*, for example, B4, 999b20, Δ6, 1016b8–9,
cf. a32–b6; Z13, 1038b14–15, cf. 9–10; and Z16, 1040b17. It is also
used in a proof in Z6.[74] (T4) is important also since Aristotle uses it in
combination with (T9) (later in this appendix) to obtain an important
result in *Metaphysics* Z13; this result is given as (T10) (ahead) and also
appears as (1′) in Section 1 of this chapter.

It also follows from (P1) that the converse of the substance-of relation is partially functional:

(T5) *x* is the substance of *y* and *z* is the substance of *y*, only if *x* = *z*.

That is, a thing has at most one substance. Aristotle asserts (T5) side by
side with (T4) at Z16, 1040b17: "The substance of what is one ‹is› one
[= (T5)], and those things whose substance is one in number ‹are themselves› one in number [= (T4)]." He also states a principle closely related to (T5) for the notion of essence at *Topics* Z4, 141a35 (there is a
single [i.e., at most one] *to einai hoper estin* for each thing that is) and for
the notion of definition at *Topics* Z5, 142b35; cf. Z14, 151a33–4,
b16–17 (there cannot be more than one definition for the same thing).

A further consequence of (P1) is this:

(T6) *y* is the substance of *x*, only if *y* is the substance of *y*.   [*Reverse
secondary reflexivity*]

Aristotle states (T6) at *Metaphysics* Z16, 1040b23–4: "The substance
belongs to nothing but to itself and to what has it, of which it is the
substance." Aristotle uses (T6) in a proof in Z6.[75]

---

74 *Metaphysics* Z6, 1031b28–1032a2; cf. F. Lewis (1985b), Section 5(b), and Afterword.
Graham (1987), p. 252, claims that the thesis that "substance is what is unique to an
individual" at Z13, 1038b10, which I transcribe as (T4), "expresses the thesis of
substantial atomism," that is, the view that "the indivisible particular is substance in
the primary sense." He concludes that the thesis is local to Aristotle's earlier theory,
S1, and out of place in the *Metaphysics*. But (T4) is a part of the same network of
principles at work in Z6 that I argue is quite integral to the mature theory of the
Metaphysics; see note 73. In any case, Graham himself concedes that on his reading
"the principle is stated oddly, because according to SA [Substantial Atomism] we
would not even speak of *a* substance that is peculiar to an individual, because the
individual just *is* the substance" (his emphasis). But for "odd" here, read
"impossible": there is no way that Aristotle's statements of (T4) can be converted
into an assertion that individuals are the primary substances or that they are meant
to assert the primacy of individual substances in a jargon acceptable within Aristotle's later theory, S2, as Graham seems to suggest.

75 This is the regress argument to show that each thing, that is, each primary substance, is essentially the same as its essence, at Z6, 1031b28–1032a2; cf. F. Lewis
(1985b), pp. 159–62, where the present (T6) is labelled as '(T3)'.

Finally, (P1) gives a result very close to one of the conclusions of *Metaphysics* Z13:

(T7) x is universal to y and z, only if x is not the substance of both y and z.

That is, what is universal to two distinct things is *not* the substance of *both*. What Aristotle actually concludes in Z13, however, is somewhat stronger: it appears as (T10) later in this appendix. We can prove (T7) given (P1) with only the help of (D2). For suppose that x is universal to y and z, and suppose also, contrary to what is to be proved, that x is the substance both of y and of z. Then by (P1), $x = y$ and $y = z$, so that $y = z$; but by (D2), $y \neq z$. So x is not the substance of both y and z after all.

Theorems (T4) through (T6) may all be derived by the use of (P1) alone; (T7) follows from (P1) with the added help of only (D2). It is worth noticing in passing that (P1) is itself a consequence of (T4) in conjunction with (T6). For suppose that x is the substance of y. Then by (T6), x is the substance of x, and by (T4), $y = x$. That is, if x is the substance of y, then $y = x$, which gives (P1). This result suggests that it is possible to restructure the theory just sketched in a way that makes (T4) and (T6) relatively more basic and (P1) a consequence of them, rather than the other way about. Such a restructuring would be desirable if Aristotle had found (T4) and (T6) in some sense simpler and more immediate than (P1), but I see no evidence that this is in fact his view.

(iv) Some Consequences of Adding (P2)

Let us now add the second principle (P2):

(P2) x is predicated of y, only if $y \neq x$.

It follows immediately from (P2) together with (P1) that the two relations 'x is the substance of y' and 'x is predicated of y' are mutually exclusive:

(T8) x is the substance of y, only if x is not predicated of y.   [*Mutual exclusivity*]

With (T8), compare principle (5′) used in the resolution of the second puzzle in Section 2, this chapter. Principle (5′) itself is a reworking of claim (5) that no substance is predicated of a subject, which appears, for example, in the argument at Z13, 1038b15–16.[76] I argue at the end of this section that the use Aristotle makes of (5) in this argument can be reproduced if we substitute the new (T8) for the old (5).

76 For other appearances of (5), see the references in note 26.

It should come as no surprise that the relations 'x is the substance of y' and 'x is predicated of y' are mutually exclusive, as asserted in (T8) (cf. the discussion in Sections 1 and 2). The proof of (T8) relies on contrasting properties of the two relations, as set out in (P1) and (P2).

One consequence of (T8) that may be surprising is a principle that plays an important role in the argument of *Metaphysics* Z13:

(T9) x is universal to y and z, only if x is the substance of y just in case x is the substance of z.

According to (T9), if something is universal to two distinct things, then it is the substance of the one *if and only if* it is the substance of the other. To prove (T9), suppose that x is universal to y and z. By (D1), x is predicated of y, so that by (T8), x is *not* the substance of y. It follows by the paradoxes of material implication that if x is the substance of y, then x is the substance of z. By similar reasoning, since x is predicated of z by (D1) again, then by (T8), x is not the substance of z, so that if x is the substance of z, then x is the substance of y. Accordingly, x is the substance of y if and only if x is the substance of z.

(T9) is stated somewhat elliptically by Aristotle at Z13, 1038b11–13:[77] " ... for that is said to be universal which is by nature such as to belong to many. Of what, then, will this be the substance? For ⟨it must⟩ either ⟨be the substance⟩ of all, or of none, ... "

Another theorem is one of the main conclusions of *Metaphysics* Z13–16:

(T10) x is universal to y and z, only if x is not the substance either of y or of z.

That is, if something is universal to two (distinct) things, then it is *not* the substance of *either* of them. (T10) is a close variant of (1′) used in solving the first puzzle in this chapter. In Z13, Aristotle proves (T10) using (T4) and (T9) (1038b9–15). The proof is indirect.[78] Suppose that x is universal to y and z, so that by (D2), $y \neq z$. Now let x be the substance of y (see 1038b13, *henos d' ei estai*).[79] Then by (T9), x is the substance of z, and by (T4), $y = z$. But we have seen that $y \neq z$. Hence, x is not the substance of y, and by (T9) again, x is not the substance of z.

It is worth noticing that there are at least three other ways of deriving (T10) given the apparatus we have developed so far. (T10) is a consequence of (T9) and (P1), or of (T9) together with (T7), or

77 Cf. Code (1978), p. 70.
78 The proof is given in greater detail and with the relevant textual support in Section 1.
79 For this move, see Code (1978), p. 70. Code also recognizes the role of (T9) in the argument in Z13 (see his p. 71 and n. 24), but he does not see that (T9) is in fact a theorem for Aristotle, given the truth of (P1).

finally, of (T8) by itself. The proof of (T10) from (T8) alone (eked out by the use of definition (D2)) is perhaps the most instructive, since it offers possibly the best way of seeing *why* (T10) must be true for Aristotle.[80] The proof is again indirect. Suppose that, as before, x is universal to y and to z. Further, let x be the substance of y. Then by (T8), x is not predicated of y. But by (D2), x is predicated of y. Hence, x is not the substance of y. Suppose now that x is the substance of z. Then by a similar use of (T8) and (D2), x both is and is not predicated of z. So x is the substance neither of y nor of z.

This proof shows that (T10) rests at bottom not so much on facts about universals as such as on the fact that the two relations 'x is the substance of y' and 'x is predicated of y' are mutually exclusive, as stated in (T8). Even if a form were predicated of exactly one thing, so that it were not a universal by the lights of (D2), it would still follow that it could not be the substance of that very same thing. It is a trivial consequence that if a form is universal to, and hence predicated of, two distinct things, it cannot be the substance of either of them. As we have seen, we can use (T8) in solving the puzzle sketched in Section 2, this chapter; the success of (T8) there helps explain the utility of (T10) in solving the related puzzle described in Section 1. Both (T8) and (T10) owe their plausibility to the different natures of the substance-of and predicated-of relations.

I have argued that (T10) can be derived from (T8) with the help of definition (D2). (T8) is the formal representation of (5'), itself a reworking of the claim that

(5) No substance is (metaphysically) predicated of a subject,

which formed part of the second puzzle from Section 2. (T10), meanwhile, transcribes (1'), which replaces the original

(1) No universal is a substance

in the first puzzle from Section 1. It is noteworthy that the use of (T8) together with (D2) to get (T10) is matched exactly by an argument that derives the unreconstructed principle (1) from the unreconstructed (5), again with help from (D2). Thus, at Z13, 1038b15–16, Aristotle argues that

(5) No substance is (metaphysically) predicated of a subject,

while

A universal is predicated of a subject

by (D2), so that

---

80 With this proof, compare the informal argument that (5') entails (1') given at the end of Section 2.

(1) No universal is a substance.

The fact that the logical relations Aristotle argues for in the case of his original claims, (1) and (5), can be reproduced for their transformations, (T10) and (T8), in the final form of the theory I am attributing to him provides additional reason for supposing that those transformations fairly represent Aristotle's own thinking.

(v) How to Derive (T10) from (7) and (T1)

The project of getting the logical relations within the new version of Aristotle's theory to match the relations among the claims distinctive of the earlier theory arises again in connection with (T10) and (T1).[81] As we have seen, (T10) is for all practical purposes a representation of (1') in Section 1, this chapter; (1') in turn is a transformation of (1), which was part of the first puzzle also sketched there. Despite the difficulties with (1) that the puzzle brings to light, there is one logical feature of (1) that it would be desirable to have reproduced in (T10). In *Metaphysics* B6, 1003a7–9, and in Z13, 1038b34–1039a2, Aristotle gives us this argument for (1):

(8) No universal is a this.
(7) Substances are thises.[82]

Hence,

(1) No universal is a substance.

The logic of this argument is straightforward. In the theory just sketched, however, (1) is replaced by (T10). Meanwhile, in Section 5, this chapter, (8) has been transformed into (8'), which is given as (T1) in Section (i). Consider now the argument that results from replacing (8) and (1) by their new counterparts:

(T1) x is universal to y and z, and y and z are both thises, only if x is a such.
(7) Substances are thises.

Hence,

(T10) x is universal to y and z only if x is not the substance either of y or of z.

If we can show that the conclusion of this new argument too follows from its premises, then we will have additional support for claiming

81 This section was written in response to a challenge by Charles Young.
82 This claim is not expressly made a premiss of the argument in Z13 (although it appears earlier in the chapter at b24), but it is supplied in B6.

that (8) is fairly rewritten first as (8′) and finally as (T1), and for representing (1) in turn by (1′) and by (T10).

The defence of this argument for (T10) requires us to add one new principle. The principle is fundamental to the new theory of substance in the *Metaphysics;* it is sufficiently basic that it is, I suspect, an axiom rather than a theorem:

> (A9) x is a primary substance if and only if for some y, x is the substance of y.

(A9) formalizes the attitude towards the notion of (primary) substance that typifies the new ontology of the *Metaphysics* (cf. Section (ii)). Given (A9) together with (P1), we can show that

> (T11) x is a primary substance if and only if x is the substance of x.

And as the right–left direction of (A9), we have it that

> (T12) There is a y such that x is the substance of y only if x is a primary substance.

Meanwhile, we can also show that

> (T13) There is a y such that y is the substance of x only if x is a primary substance.

((T13) is equivalent to (A8); alternatively, it can also be derived from (T11).) According to (T12), something is a primary substance if it is the substance *of* something; according to (T13), something is a primary substance if it *has* something as its substance.

With the help of these last two theorems, together with some supplementary principles, we can show how to derive (T10) from (T1) and (7). We assume that x is universal to y and z. The argument now breaks into two halves. (i) Assume further that y and z are both thises. Then by (T1) helped out by (A7), x is not a this, so that by (7), x is not a substance, and a fortiori not a primary substance. By (T12), then, x is not the substance *of* anything. In particular, x is not the substance of y or of z. (ii) Assume further that x is a this. Then by (T1) and (A7) again, y and z are not both thises; in fact by (T3), neither y nor z is a this. (Here, recall that (T1) and (T3) together entail (T2); see Section (i).) By (7), then, neither y nor z is a substance; a fortiori, then, neither y nor z is a primary substance, so that by (T13), nothing is the substance of y or of z. In particular, x is not the substance either of y or of z.

We have now obtained these two results:

> x is universal to y and z, and y and z are both thises, only if x is not the substance either of y or of z.

> x is universal to y and z, and x is a this, only if x is not the substance either of y or of z.

It remains to show that these two together give (T10). We begin by noticing that definition (D2) defines the relation 'x is universal to y and z' in terms of the relation of (metaphysical) predication. We know that there are only two cases of (metaphysical) predication: either x is an accident of y (here x is an accident, and hence a such, while y is a compound material substance, and hence a this), or x supervenes on y (x is a form and a this, and y is matter and not a this). (For these results, we rely on (D1) together with (A1) through (A6).) Accordingly, if x is universal to y and z, then either y and z are both thises or x is a this. Given this conclusion, by elementary logic our two results together are equivalent to (T10):

(T10) x is universal to y and z only if x is not the substance either of y or of z.

Again, facts about the substance-of and predication relations are central to obtaining this result.

Bibliography

This bibliography lists only works explicitly referred to and is not intended to be exhaustive. In particular, I have usually cited Aristotle's text in the editions in the Oxford Classical Text (Oxford, various dates and editors), and these in most cases are not listed separately here.

Ackrill, J. L. *Aristotle Categories and De Interpretatione.* Oxford, 1963.
"Aristotle's Definitions of Psychē." *Proceedings of the Aristotelian Society* 73 (1972–3), pp. 119–33. Reprinted in Barnes, Schofield, and Sorabji (1979), Vol. 4, pp. 65–75.
Adam, C., and Tannery, P., eds. *Oeuvres de Descartes.* 13 vols. Paris, 1897–1913 (cited as *AT* in the text).
Albritton, Rogers. "Forms of Particular Substances in Aristotle's *Metaphysics.*" *Journal of Philosophy* 54 (1957), pp. 699–708.
Alexander, see Hayduck (1891) (for *In Met.*) and Wallies (1891) (for *In Topica*).
Allen, R. E. "Participation and Predication in Plato's Middle Dialogues." *Philosophical Review* 69 (1960), pp. 147–64. Reprinted in Allen (1965), pp. 43–60.
Studies in Plato's Metaphysics. New York, 1965.
Annas, Julia. *Aristotle's Metaphysics: Books M and N.* Oxford, 1976.
Anscombe, G. E. M. "Under a Description." *Nous* 13 (1979), pp. 219–33.
Bäck, Allan T. *On Reduplication: Logical Theories of Qualification.* Munich, 1988.
Barnes, Jonathan. *Aristotle's "Posterior Analytics".* Oxford, 1975.
Review of Hartman (1977). *Philosophical Books* 20 (1979), pp. 57–61.
Barnes, Jonathan, ed. *The Complete Works of Aristotle,* rev. Oxford trans. 2 vols. Princeton, N.J., 1984.
Barnes, Jonathan; Schofield, Malcolm; and Sorabji, Richard, eds. *Articles on Aristotle.* 4 vols. London, 1975.
Barnes, Kenneth. "Aristotle on Identity and Its Problems." *Phronesis* 22 (1977), pp. 48–62.
Bennett, Jonathan. *Locke, Berkeley, Hume: Central Themes.* Oxford, 1971.
Benson, Hugh H. "Universals as Sortals in the *Categories.*" *Pacific Philosophical Quarterly* 69 (1988), pp. 282–306.

Bogen, James. "Moravcsik on Explanation." *Synthese* 28 (1974), pp. 19–25.
  Review of Nussbaum, *Aristotle's De Motu Animalium*. *Synthese* 55 (1983),
  pp. 373–88.
Bogen, James, and McGuire, J. E., eds. *How Things Are*. Dordrecht, 1985.
Bonitz, Hermann. *Aristotelis Metaphysica*. 2 vols. Bonn, 1848–9.
  Index Aristotelicus. Berlin, 1870.
Bostock, David. "Aristotle on the Principles of Change in *Physics* I." In Nuss-
  baum and Schofield (1982), pp. 179–96.
Brody, Baruch A. "Why Settle for Anything Less Than Good Old-Fashioned
  Aristotelian Essentialism?" *Nous* 7 (1973), pp. 351–65.
Burnyeat, Myles. "Is an Aristotelian Philosophy of Mind Still Credible?" In
  Essays on De Anima, ed. Martha Nussbaum and Amelie Rorty (forthcom-
  ing).
Busse, A., and Kalbfleisch, C. *Simplicii In Categorias Commentarium*. Berlin,
  1887–1907.
Carnap, Rudolph. *Meaning and Necessity*. Chicago, 1947.
Cartwright, Richard. "Identity and Substitutivity." In *Identity and Individua-
  tion*, ed. Milton K. Munitz. New York, 1971, pp. 119–33.
Charles, David. "Aristotle on Hypothetical Necessity and Irreducibility."
  Pacific Philosophical Quarterly 69 (1988), pp. 1–53.
Charlton, W. *Aristotle's "Physics" Books I and II*. Oxford, 1970.
Cherniss, Harold. Review of Jaeger (1923). *American Journal of Philology* 56
  (1935), pp. 261–71.
  Aristotle's Criticism of Plato and the Academy. Baltimore, 1944.
  "The Relation of the *Timaeus* to Plato's Later Dialogues." *American Journal of
  Philology* 78 (1957), pp. 225–66. Reprinted in Allen (1965), pp. 339–78.
Code, Alan. "The Persistence of Aristotelian Matter." *Philosophical Studies* 29
  (1976a), pp. 357–67.
  "Aristotle's Response to Quine's Objections to Modal Logic." *Journal of
  Philosophical Logic* 5 (1976b), pp. 159–86.
  "No Universal Is a Substance: An Interpretation of *Metaphysics* Z13,
  1038b8–15." *Paideia* (1978), pp. 65–74.
  "Aristotle on the Sameness of Each Thing with Its Essence." Paper read
  before the Society for Ancient Greek Philosophy, December 1980.
  "The Aporematic Approach to Primary Being in *Metaphysics* Z." *Canadian
  Journal of Philosophy*, suppl. vol. 10 (1984), pp. 1–20.
  "On the Origins of Some Aristotelian Theses about Predication." In Bogen
  and McGuire (1985), pp. 101–31.
  "Aristotle: Essence and Accident." In *Philosophical Grounds of Rationality:
  Intentions, Categories, Ends*, ed. Richard Grandy and Richard Warner.
  Oxford, 1986, pp. 411–39.
Cohen, S. Marc. "The Logic of the Third Man." *Philosophical Review* 80 (1971),
  pp. 448–75.
  "Essentialism in Aristotle." *Review of Metaphysics* 31 (1978), pp. 387–405.
  "Aristotle on Individuation." *Canadian Journal of Philosophy*, suppl. vol. 10
  (1984), pp. 41–66.
  "The Credibility of Aristotle's Philosophy of Mind." In *Aristotle Today: Essays
  on Aristotle's Ideal of Science*, ed. Mohan Matthen. Edmonton, 1987,
  pp. 103–21.

Copi, Irving M. *The Theory of Logical Types*. London, 1971.

Dancy, R. M. "On Some of Aristotle's First Thoughts about Substance." *Philosophical Review* 84 (1975), pp. 338–73.

"On Some of Aristotle's Second Thoughts about Substance." *Philosophical Review* 87 (1978), pp. 372–413.

Descartes, René, see Adam and Tannery (1897–1913) and Haldane and Ross (1911).

Diels, H. *Simplicii In Aristotelis Physica Commentaria*. 2 vols. Berlin, 1882, 1885.

Drake, Frank R. *Set Theory*. Amsterdam, 1974.

Driscoll, John. "*Eidē* in Aristotle's Earlier and Later Theories of Substance." In O'Meara (1981), pp. 129–59.

Duerlinger, James. "Predication and Inherence in Aristotle's *Categories*." *Phronesis* 15 (1970), pp. 179–202.

Dybikowski, James. "Professor Owen, Aristotle, and the Third Man Argument." *Mind* 81 (1972), pp. 445–7.

Fine, Gail. "Owen, Aristotle, and the Third Man." *Phronesis* 27 (1982), pp. 13–33.

"Separation." *Oxford Studies in Ancient Philosophy* 2 (1984), pp. 31–87.

"Separation: A Reply to Morrison." *Oxford Studies in Ancient Philosophy* 3 (1985), pp. 159–165.

Fine, Kit. "The Problem of *De Re* Modality." In *Themes from Kaplan*, ed. Joseph Almog, John Perry, and Howard Wettstein. Oxford, 1990, pp. 197–272.

"Aristotle on Substance." Unpublished paper; available in the Philosophy Library, Dodd Hall, UCLA.

Frede, Michael. *Praedikation und Existenzaussage*. Goettingen, 1967.

Essays in Ancient Philosophy. Minneapolis, 1987.

"Individuen bei Aristoteles." *Antike und Abendland* 24 (1978), pp. 16–39. Reprinted in English as "Individuals in Aristotle," in Frede (1987), pp. 49–71; references here are to the 1987 version.

"Categories in Aristotle." In O'Meara (1981), pp. 1–24. Reprinted in Frede (1987), pp. 29–48; references here are to the 1987 version.

"Substance in Aristotle's *Metaphysics*." In *Aristotle on Nature and Living Things*, ed. Alan Gotthelf. Pittsburgh, 1985, pp. 17–26. Reprinted in Frede (1987), pp. 72–80; references here are to the 1987 version.

Frede, Michael, and Patzig, Gunther. *Aristoteles "Metaphysik Z,"* 2 vols. Munich, 1988.

Frege, Gottlob. "Function and Concept." In Geach and Black (1980), pp. 21–41.

"What Is a Function?" In Geach and Black (1980), pp. 107–16.

Furth, Montgomery. "Transtemporal Stability in Aristotelian Substances." *Journal of Philosophy* 75 (1978), pp. 624–46.

Aristotle Metaphysics Books Zeta, Eta, Theta, Iota. Indianapolis, 1985.

Substance, Form and Psyche: An Aristotelean Metaphysics. Cambridge, 1988.

Geach, Peter. "The Third Man Again." *Philosophical Review* 65 (1956), pp. 72–82. Reprinted in Allen (1965), pp. 265–78.

Geach, Peter, and Black, Max, eds. *The Philosophical Writings of Gottlob Frege*, 3d ed. Oxford, 1980.

Gibbard, Alan. "Contingent Identity." *Journal of Philosophical Logic* 4 (1975), pp. 187–221.

Gill, Mary Louise. *Aristotle on Substance: The Paradox of Unity*. Princeton, N.J., 1989.

Gotthelf, Allan, and Lennox, James G. eds. *Philosophical Issues in Aristotle's Biology*. Cambridge, 1987.

Graham, Daniel W. *Aristotle's Two Systems*. Oxford, 1987.

Granger, Herbert. "Aristotle on Genus and Differentia." *Journal of the History of Philosophy* 22 (1984), pp. 1–23.

Grice, Paul. "Aristotle on the Multiplicity of Being." *Pacific Philosophical Quarterly* 69 (1988), pp. 175–200.

Haldane, Elizabeth S., and Ross, G. R. T., *The Philosophical Works of Descartes*. Cambridge, 1911.

Harter, Edward D. "Aristotle on Primary *Ousia*." *Archiv für Geschichte der Philosophie* 57 (1975), pp. 1–20.

Hartman, Edwin. "Aristotle on Identity." *Philosophical Review* 85 (1976), pp. 545–61.

———. *Substance, Body, and Soul: Aristotelian Investigations*. Princeton, N.J., 1977.

Hayduck, Michael. *Alexandri Aphrodisiensis in Aristotelis Metaphysica Commentaria*. Berlin, 1891.

Heinaman, Robert. "Non-substantial Individuals in the *Categories*." *Phronesis* 26 (1981), pp. 295–307.

Hicks, R. D. *Aristotle "De Anima"*. Cambridge, 1907.

Irwin, T. H. "Plato's Heracleiteanism." *Philosophical Quarterly* 27 (1977), pp. 1–13.

Jaeger, Werner. *Aristotle: Fundamentals of the History of His Development*, 2d ed., trans. Richard Robinson. Oxford, 1948; 1st German ed., Berlin, 1923.

Jaeger, Werner, ed. *Aristotelis Metaphysica*, Oxford Classical Text. Oxford, 1957.

Jones, Barrington. "Individuals in Aristotle's *Categories*." *Phronesis* 17 (1972), pp. 107–23.

———. "Aristotle's Introduction of Matter." *Philosophical Review* 83 (1974), pp. 474–500.

Kaplan, David. "Quantifying In." In *Words and Objections: Essays on the Work of W. V. Quine*, ed. D. Davidson and J. Hintikka. Dordrecht, 1969, pp. 178–214. Reprinted in *Reference and Modality*, ed. Leonard Linsky. Oxford, 1971, pp. 112–44; references here are to the 1971 version.

Kenny, Anthony. *Descartes: A Study of His Philosophy*. New York, 1968.

Kirwan, Christopher. *Aristotle's Metaphysics Books* Γ, Δ, E. Oxford, 1971.

Kneale, W., and Kneale, M. *The Development of Logic*. Oxford, 1962.

Kosman, L. A. "Animals and Other Beings in Aristotle." In Gotthelf and Lennox (1987), pp. 360–91.

Kripke, Saul. "Identity and Necessity." In *Identity and Individuation*. ed. Milton K. Munitz. New York, 1971, pp. 135–64.

———. "Identity and Necessity." In *Semantics of Natural Language*, ed. G. Harman and D. Davidson. Dordrecht, 1972, pp. 253–355.

———. "Speaker's Reference and Semantic Reference." *Midwest Studies in Philosophy* 2 (1977), pp. 255–76. Reprinted in *Contemporary Perspectives in the Philosophy of Language*, ed. Peter A. French, Theodore E. Uehling, Jr., and Howard K. Wettstein. Minneapolis, 1979; references here are to the 1979 version.

Kuhn, Thomas S. *The Structure of Scientific Revolutions*, 2d ed. Chicago, 1970.

Kung, Joan. "Can Substance Be Predicated of Matter?" *Archiv für Geschichte der Philosophie* 60 (1978), pp. 140–59.

"Aristotle on Thises, Suches, and the Third Man Argument." *Phronesis* 26 (1981), pp. 207–47.

Lear, Jonathan. "Active Episteme." In *Mathematics and Metaphysics in Aristotle*, ed. Andreas Graeser. Bern, 1987, pp. 149–74.

Lee, E. N.; Mourelatos, A. P. D.; and Rorty, R. M., eds. *Exegesis and Argument: Studies in Greek Philosophy Presented to Gregory Vlastos. Phronesis*, suppl. vol. 1. Assen, 1973.

Lesher, James. "Aristotle on Form, Substance, and Universals: A Dilemma." *Phronesis* 16 (1971), pp. 169–78.

Lewis, David. "New Work for a Theory of Universals." *Australasian Journal of Philosophy* 61 (1983), pp. 343–77.

Lewis, Frank A. "Accidental Sameness in Aristotle." *Philosophical Studies* 42 (1982), pp. 1–36.

"What is Aristotle's Theory of Essence?" *Canadian Journal of Philosophy* suppl. vol. 10 (1984), pp. 89–131.

"Form and Predication in Aristotle's *Metaphysics.*" In Bogen and McGuire (1985a), pp. 59–83.

"Plato's Third Man Argument and the 'Platonism' of Aristotle." In Bogen and McGuire (1985b), pp. 133–74.

"Aristotle on the Relation between a Thing and Its Matter." Forthcoming in the Proceedings of the 1989 Oriel Metaphysics Conference, ed. David Charles, Mary Louise Gill, and Theodore Scaltsas.

Lloyd, A. C. "Genus, Species and Ordered Series in Aristotle." *Phronesis* 7 (1962), pp. 67–90.

"The Principle That the Cause Is Greater Than the Effect." *Phronesis* 21 (1976), 146–51.

Form and Universal in Aristotle. Liverpool, 1981.

Loar, Brian. "Reference and Propositional Attitudes." *Philosophical Review* 81 (1972), pp. 43–62.

Long, A. A. "Commentators on Aristotle's *Categories.*" Unpublished paper read at the annual meeting of the West Coast Aristotelian Society, Half Moon Bay, Calif., June 1990.

Loux, Michael J. "Form, Species, and Predication in *Metaphysics* Z, H, and Theta." *Mind* 88 (1979), pp. 1–23.

Lukasiewicz, Jan. "The Principle of Individuation." *Proceedings of the Aristotelian Society* suppl. vol. 27 (1953), pp. 69–82.

Mansion, Suzanne. "Sur la composition ontologique des substances sensibles chez Aristote (*Métaphysique* Z 7–9)." In *Philomathes: Studies and Essays in the Humanities in Memory of Philip Merlan*, ed. R. B. Palmer and R. Hamerton Kelly. The Hague, 1971. Reprinted and translated into English in Barnes, Schofield, and Sorabji (1975), Vol. 3, pp. 80–7; references here are to the English version.

Marcus, Ruth. Comment on "Identity, Necessity, and Physicalism," by David Wiggins. In *Philosophy of Logic*, ed. Stephan Koerner. Berkeley and Los Angeles, 1976, pp. 132–46.

Matthen, Mohan. "Greek Ontology and the 'Is' of Truth." *Phronesis* 28 (1983), pp. 113–35.

Matthews, Gareth B. "Accidental Unities." In Nussbaum and Schofield (1982), pp. 223–40.

Matthews, Gareth B., and Cohen, S. Marc. "The One and the Many." *Review of Metaphysics* 21 (1967–8), pp. 630–55.

McCann, Edwin. "Locke and the Idea of Substance" (forthcoming).

Miller, Fred D., Jr. "Did Aristotle Have the Concept of Identity?" *Philosophical Review* 82 (1973), pp. 483–90.

Minio-Paluello, L. *Aristotelis Categoriae et Liber De Interpretatione*, Oxford Classical Text. Oxford 1949.

Modrak, D. K. "Forms, Types, and Tokens in Aristotle's *Metaphysics.*" *Journal of the History of Philosophy* 17 (1979), pp. 371–81.

"Forms and Compounds." In Bogen and McGuire (1985), pp. 85–100.

Moravcsik, J. M. E. *Aristotle: A Collection of Critical Essays.* New York, 1967a.

"Aristotle on Predication." *Philosophical Review* 76 (1967b), pp. 80–96.

"*Aitia* as Generative Factor in Aristotle's Philosophy." *Dialogue* 14 (1975), pp. 623–38.

Morrison, Donald. "Separation in Aristotle's Metaphysics." *Oxford Studies in Ancient Philosophy* 3 (1985a), pp. 125–57.

"Separation: A Reply to Fine." *Oxford Studies in Ancient Philosophy* 3 (1985b), pp. 167–73.

Mourelatos, Alexander P. D. "Aristotle's 'Powers' and Modern Empiricism." *Ratio* 9 (1967), pp. 97–104.

Nehamas, Alexander. "Self-Predication and Plato's Theory of Forms." *American Philosophical Quarterly* 16 (1979), pp. 93–103.

Nussbaum, Martha, and Schofield, Malcolm, eds. *Language and Logos: Studies in Greek Philosophy Presented to G. E. L. Owen.* Cambridge, 1982.

Nuyens, F. *L'Evolution de la psychologie d'Aristote.* Louvain, 1948.

O'Meara, Dominic J., ed. *Studies in Aristotle.* Washington D.C., 1981.

Owen, G. E. L. "A Proof in the *Peri Ideōn.*" *Journal of Hellenic Studies* 77 (1957), Pt. I, pp. 103–11. Reprinted in Allen (1965), pp. 293–312; references here are to the 1965 version.

"Logic and Metaphysics in Some Earlier Works of Aristotle." In *Aristotle and Plato in the mid-Fourth Century, Studia Graeca et Latina Gothoburgensia,* No. 11, ed. I. Duering and G. E. L. Owen, Goteborg, 1960, pp. 163–190. Reprinted in Barnes, Schofield, and Sorabji (1979), Vol. 3, pp. 13–32.

"Inherence," *Phronesis* 10 (1965), pp. 97–105.

"The Platonism of Aristotle." *Proceedings of the British Academy* 50 (1965), pp. 125–50. Reprinted in Barnes, Schofield, and Sorabji (1975), Vol. 1, pp. 14–34.

"Dialectic and Eristic in the Treatment of the Forms." In *Aristotle on Dialectic: The Topics,* ed. G. E. L. Owen. Oxford, 1968, pp. 103–5.

Pelletier, Francis Jeffrey. "Sameness and Referential Opacity in Aristotle." *Nous* 13 (1979), pp. 283–311.

Peterson, Sandra L. *The Masker Paradox.* Unpublished Ph.D. dissertation. Princeton, N.J., 1969.

"A Reasonable Self-Predication Premise for the Third Man Argument." *Philosophical Review* 82 (1973), pp. 451–70.

"Substitution in Technical Aristotelian Contexts." *Philosophical Studies* 47 (1985), pp. 249–56.

Quine, W. V. O. "Notes on Existence and Necessity." *Journal of Philosophy* 40 (1943), pp. 113–27.

Mathematical Logic. rev. ed. Cambridge, Mass., 1951.

Word and Object. Cambridge, Mass., 1960.

From a Logical Point of View. New York, 1961.

"Comments." In *Boston Studies in the Philosophy of Science*, 1961–2. Dordrecht, 1963, p. 103.

Robinson, H. M. "Prime Matter in Aristotle." *Phronesis* 19 (1974), pp. 168–88.

Rorty, Richard. "Genus as Matter: A Reading of *Metaphysics* Z-H." In Lee, Mourelatos, and Rorty (1973), pp. 393–420.

Ross, W. D. *Aristotle Metaphysics*, 2 vols. Oxford, 1924.

Aristotle Physics. Oxford, 1936.

Aristotle Prior and Posterior Analytics. Oxford, 1949.

The Works of Aristotle, Select Fragments. Oxford, 1952.

Russell, Bertrand. *The Principles of Mathematics.* Cambridge, 1903.

Scaltsas, Theodore. Review of Furth (1988). *Philosophical Books* 30 (1989), pp. 82–5.

Schofield, Malcolm. "*Metaph.* Z3: Some Suggestions." *Phronesis* 17 (1972), pp. 97–101.

Schwegler, Albert. *Die Metaphysik des Aristoteles.* Tubingen, 1847.

Sellars, Wilfred. "Vlastos and the Third Man." *Philosophical Review* 64 (1955), pp. 405–37. Reprinted in Sellars (1967), pp. 55–72.

"Substance and Form in Aristotle." *Journal of Philosophy* 54 (1957), pp. 688–99.

"Aristotle's *Metaphysics:* An Interpretation," in *Philosophical Perspectives*, (1967), pp. 73–124.

Simplicius, see Busse and Kalbfleisch (1887–1907) (for *In Catg.*), Diels (1882, 1885) (for *In Phys.*).

Smart, J. J. C., "Sensations and Brain Processes." *Philosophical Review* 68 (1959), pp. 141–56.

Smith, J. A., and Ross, W. D., eds. *The Works of Aristotle Translated into English* (the "Oxford Translation"). Oxford, 1910–52.

Smith, Robin. *Aristotle Prior Analytics.* Indianapolis, Ind., 1989.

Smullyan, Arthur F. "Modality and Description." *Journal of Symbolic Logic* 13 (1948), pp. 31–7.

Sorabji, Richard. *Necessity, Cause, and Blame: Perspectives on Aristotle's Theory.* Ithaca, N.Y., 1980.

"Analyses of Matter, Ancient and Modern." *Proceedings of the Aristotelian Society* 86 (1985–6), pp. 1–22.

Spellman, Lynne. "Specimens of Natural Kinds and the Apparent Inconsistency of *Metaphysics* Zeta." *Ancient Philosophy* 9 (1989), pp. 49–65.

"Referential Opacity in Aristotle." *History of Philosophy Quarterly* 7 (1990), pp. 17–32.

Stahl, Donald E. "Stripped Away: Some Contemporary Obscurities Surrounding *Metaphysics* Z3 (1029a10–26)." *Phronesis* 26 (1981), pp. 177–80.

Strang, Colin. "Plato and the Third Man." *Proceedings of the Aristotelian Society* suppl. vol. 37 (1963), pp. 147–64. Reprinted in *Plato: A Collection of Critical Essays 1, Epistemology and Metaphysics*, ed. Gregory Vlastos. New York, 1971, pp. 184–200.

Sykes, R. D. "Form in Aristotle: Universal or Particular?" *Philosophy* 50 (1975), pp. 311–31.

Vlastos, Gregory. "The Third Man Argument in the *Parmenides." Philosophical Review* 63 (1954), pp. 319–49.

"Addenda to the TMA: Reply to Professor Sellars." *Philosophical Review* 64 (1955), pp. 438–48.

"Plato's 'Third Man' Argument (*Parm.* 132A1–B2): Text and Logic." *Philosophical Quarterly* 19 (1969), pp. 289–301. Reprinted in Vlastos (1973).

Platonic Studies. Princeton, N.J., 1973.

Waitz, Theodor. *Aristotelis Organon Graece.* Leipzig, 1844–6.

Wallies, M. *Alexandri Aphrodisiensis In Aristotelis Topicorum Libros Octo Commentaria.* Berlin, 1891.

Waterlow, Sarah. *Nature, Change, and Agency in Aristotle's Physics.* Oxford, 1982.

White, Nicholas P. "A Note on *Ekthesis," Phronesis* 16 (1971a), pp. 164–8.

"Aristotle on Sameness and Oneness." *Philosophical Review* 80 (1971b), pp. 177–97.

"Origins of Aristotle's Essentialism." *Review of Metaphysics* 26 (1972), pp. 57–85.

"Identity, Modal Individuation, and Matter." *Midwest Studies in Philosophy* 11 (1986), pp. 475–94.

Williams, Bernard. *Descartes: The Project of Pure Enquiry.* Middlesex, 1978.

Williams, C. J. F. *Aristotle's De Generatione et Corruptione.* Oxford, 1982.

"Aristotle's Theory of Descriptions." *Philosophical Review* 94 (1985), pp. 63–80.

Wisdom, John. *Problems of Mind and Matter.* Cambridge, 1934.

Witt, Charlotte. *Substance and Essence in Aristotle.* Ithaca, N.Y., 1989.

Woods, Michael J. "Problems in *Metaphysics* Z, Chapter 13." In Moravcsik (1967a), pp. 215–38.

"Substance and Essence in Aristotle." *Proceedings of the Aristotelian Society* 75 (1974–5), pp. 167–80.

Index of Passages

General Index